Readings in Cultural Anthropology

Classic and Contemporary Perspectives

Readings in Cultural Anthropology

Classic and Contemporary Perspectives

First Edition

EDITED BY **Robin Conley Riner**

Marshall University

Bassim Hamadeh, CEO and Publisher
Jennifer Codner, Senior Field Acquisitions Editor
Michelle Piehl, Senior Project Editor
Emely Villavicencio, Senior Graphic Designer
Stephanie Kohl, Licensing Coordinator
Natalie Piccotti, Director of Marketing
Kassie Graves, Vice President of Editorial
Jamie Giganti, Director of Academic Publishing

Printed in the United States of America.

Contents

Chapter 1

Introduction

What Is Cultural Anthropology?

Anthropology is a comprehensive field of study that seeks to understand human diversity from our evolutionary past to the present. Working within the four classic "subfields"—cultural anthropology, linguistic anthropology, biological anthropology, and archaeology—anthropologists are interested in everything from the genetic similarities between humans and apes to the creative use of language within hip hop communities.

Cultural anthropology, which is the focus of this book, examines the extensive variation of cultures and cultural practices across the globe. Cultural anthropologists are especially interested in the relationship between the individual and their culture. We understand this relationship as bidirectional: human actions and experiences are shaped by the cultures in which we live, and such actions can also shape and change those very cultures. This bidirectional relationship between culture and the individual describes what anthropologists call agency. *Agency* is an individual's culturally constrained ability to act in the world. Through the readings in this volume, you will encounter multiple perspectives on agency, some in which culture is thought to be highly deterministic, meaning it has a very strong impact on shaping who people are and how we act. You will also come across examples in which people actively resist or subtly challenge cultural norms and frameworks.

Cultural anthropology is indeed very similar to other social scientific and humanistic disciplines, such as sociology, history, and psychology. But there are a few characteristics that make cultural anthropology unique among other attempts to study human beings and their experiences. The first of these is anthropology's primary method—*participant observation*. Anthropologists believe that the best way to understand a community and its people is by living with them and participating in their everyday lives. We accomplish this through *ethnographic fieldwork*, which consists of long-term engagement with a group of people (or multiple groups), including participating in their everyday lives—from their mundane, habitual activities to special events. By personally experiencing a new cultural context, anthropologists strive to understand the ordinary, taken-for-granted practices and experiences that make up the "normal" lives of a group of people.

As the name participant observation suggests, the method involves alternating between two roles. Ethnographers fully immerse themselves in the practices of the people we are studying so that we may experience such practices firsthand. At the same time, we need to take a moment to step back and adopt the analytic researcher role, during which we observe and begin to sort through the experiences we have had. This starts the process of cultural analysis, out of which we will produce our results, often presented in a book or series of academic articles called an ethnography. Contemporary anthropologists are experimenting with ways of disseminating their cultural analyses; some are working with media such as film, theater, and digital platforms to present their analyses in unique and more accessible forms.

Cultural anthropology—perhaps obviously—is also unique in its use of culture as the lens through which to view human diversity. The readings in this collection reveal that anthropologists' definitions of culture have evolved throughout the discipline's history. While in the past anthropologists viewed cultures as bounded entities with identifiable and universally comparable characteristics, contemporary cultural anthropologists continually problematize and retheorize the concept of culture, focusing more on how cultures are constructed than on providing a universally applicable definition. All anthropologists, however, agree that culture is one of the most significant human evolutionary developments, and it is what allows us to create and share meaning and pass on skills, knowledge, and beliefs from one generation to the next.

Another attribute that makes cultural anthropology distinct is its reliance on the holistic approach to studying humans. Holism has two related meanings, the first deriving from the four-field structure of anthropology. In this sense, the holistic approach means that anthropologists seek to understand human beings and their lives from multiple angles: their culture, biology, history, and language. In its second sense, the holistic approach suggests that cultures should be understood as integrated wholes. What this means is that in order to understand religious beliefs and practices in a particular cultural setting, for example, it is not sufficient merely to observe religious practices. All aspects of a culture are interrelated; therefore to explain one cultural phenomenon, it is necessary to get a good handle on all aspects of the culture under study. Change in one cultural phenomenon often leads to change in another. The holistic approach is one of the reasons cultural anthropologists conduct ethnographic fieldwork—so that we may gain a holistic view of a culture, rather than merely focusing on one specific aspect.

An additional feature that distinguishes cultural anthropology from other investigations into human life comes from the very foundation of the field—the comparative approach. Early cultural and social anthropologists in the late 19th and early 20th centuries set out to create a broad comparison of cultures across the globe. They were interested in revealing the range of cultural diversity throughout the world, but also in highlighting commonalities among peoples who may appear to live very different lives. Though current anthropologists might not engage in explicitly comparative work, we are all interested in revealing wide-ranging alternatives to our own practices and beliefs, as well as illuminating the connections human beings, however disparate, commonly share. Anthropology thus provides us with a means through which to reflect on our own cultural ways of being and dislodge the taken-for-granted, question what we consider normal and natural, and make what may seem strange familiar—and what appears familiar strange. We use the method of ethnography both to familiarize ourselves with other ways of living and to look anew at our own practices and ideas as if we were encountering them for the first time.

How Has Cultural Anthropology Changed over the Years?

The current practice of cultural anthropology differs greatly from when the field first began in the late 19th century. One of the major changes has been anthropologists' focus on globalization, or the connections among and movements of people, ideas, and cultural phenomena across the world. This shift in focus does not mean that globalization itself is new. In fact, people have been moving and sharing information across the globe for centuries. But many early anthropologists, as mentioned above, treated cultures—especially those deemed "primitive"—as if they were distinct wholes that did not have much contact with one another. Anthropologists of this time often worked with colonial governments to "discover" and better understand groups of people that were considered exotic and untouched by modern ways of life. What many of these researchers failed to recognize (at least in their publications) was that their engagement with these people was already part of a global network. Cultures were already connected by processes such as colonialism in ways often detrimental to the people being studied.

Now, anthropologists are interested in revealing how local communities and ways of living are affected by such global processes and vice-versa (we even question whether it makes sense to classify communities as "local" at all anymore!). This includes thinking critically about the anthropologist's own position within global networks and their potential position of power in relation to the people being studied. When thinking about globalization, we ask questions such as: How do people adapt and change cultural phenomena imported from elsewhere to make them their own? How are "local" ways of doing things shared and often commodified across global networks? How do relationships of power affect the ways in which cultural practices and ideas are created and move across the globe? How do these relations of power inform the formation and distribution of anthropological knowledge?

Anthropologists' increasing concern with the effect their own positioning has on the work they do and the people they study has led to another development in the practice of anthropology: what many call "engaged" or "applied" anthropology. Though ethnographers have long been vocal about political and ethical issues surrounding the groups they study—going all the way back to Margaret Mead and Franz Boas—engaged anthropology, in which anthropologists work explicitly to contribute to the betterment of the communities and people with whom they work, has developed in the last few decades as a robust subfield in and of itself. Anthropologists recognize that those who participate in our research are giving a great deal of themselves, and therefore, it is necessary for us to give back to them in some way. This giving can take a variety of forms, such as serving as an advocate for a particular issue a community is facing, providing education to or about a community, or collaborating with community members to resolve a particular problem with which they may be dealing (Low & Merry, 2010). An anthropologist, for instance, might work with doctors and local residents to come up with a culturally appropriate response to a health issue affecting a specific area or group of people. Or, an anthropologist may work with rural women to negotiate for their rights with national or international governmental bodies in ways that make cultural sense for them. More and more, anthropologists are recognizing that we are not the sole authorities on cultural issues; we necessarily rely on and thus must recognize the knowledge and voices of community members themselves.

What Is This Book About?

This book is designed to highlight some of the foundational works that helped form the discipline of anthropology. It pairs these classic readings with contemporary works that critique early anthropological perspectives and, thus, contribute to the ongoing evolution of the discipline. Each chapter provides perspectives on a particular topic from multiple viewpoints that are situated differently in time and space. The book is designed so that you may read these differing perspectives in conversation with one another and develop an understanding not only of what anthropology is but also how it has developed into the discipline it is today.

Unit One introduces some of the core concepts and methods used in anthropology, including "culture." The readings in this section highlight some differing and potentially problematic ways of understanding and studying culture. This section also explores the methods of ethnographic fieldwork and participant observation, from Malinowski's classic enumeration to a discussion of how the original design of ethnography can be adopted to study virtual worlds.

Unit Two covers a range of topics, all relating to how peoples and groups have been defined and understood both within and outside anthropology. This includes discussions of language, which serves not just as a system of communication but also as a means for creating, sustaining, and dividing communities. Readings in this section also explore kinship and families, and how their definitions and incarnations have changed since early anthropologists attempted to map out extensive kinship systems among those they studied. Part Two additionally focuses on gender, sexuality, race, and ethnicity, and how anthropologists have had to adjust their conceptualization of these forms of identity as these categories continue to shift and change. These chapters also reveal how initial conceptions of gender and race served to promote sexist and racist ideologies within the field and anthropologists' attempts to challenge such ideologies.

Unit Three includes readings on the institutions and practices that have contributed both to community building and inequality and violence across the world. Many of these, such as economic systems, political organizations, and religious systems, were the foci of very early anthropologists who sought to comparatively analyze how these systems were differently organized in a range of cultural contexts. The more contemporary readings in this section address how these institutions operate on a global scale, often contributing to inequality in specific parts of the world. They also explore how people define themselves in relation to such institutions and potentially create them anew in their own culturally meaningful ways.

The book as a whole will take students through the field of anthropology both topically and historically. Students will hopefully gain insight into new ways of understanding people and their relationships to one another, as well as how their lives are shaped by the sociocultural frameworks in which they live. This book illustrates the multiple and diverse ways of living that people are and have been engaged in across space and time. Contemplating these diverse ways of living allows us to recognize that our way of doing things is not the only way. We can then be more accepting of the wide variety of people and cultural practices that exist across the globe, appreciating the cultural value of this range of diversity. At the same time, studying the cultural practices of people who may seem quite different from us allows us to recognize the commonalities among all humans. We all strive to create meaningful lives within the cultural contexts that we call home.

References

Low, Setha M., & Sally Engle Merry. (2010). Engaged Anthropology: Diversity and Dilemmas, An Introduction to Supplement 2. *Current Anthropology* 51(2).

Unit I

Core Concepts and Methods

Chapter 2

The Culture Concept in Anthropology

DISCUSSION QUESTIONS

1. Tylor applies the theory of evolution to his understanding of culture. He likens the study of culture to the natural sciences, arguing that cultures are subject to universal laws just as natural phenomena are subject to the laws of biology and physics. What do you think of this way of studying culture? Are there problems with it? Why might Tylor want to describe anthropology as similar to the natural sciences?
2. Tylor's definition of culture, as "that complex whole which includes knowledge, belief, art, morals, law, custom, and any other capabilities and habits acquired by man as a member of society," is perhaps one of the most often cited definitions within and outside the field of anthropology. What do you think of this definition? Compare his conception of culture to Abu-Lughod's. How does each treat (or fail to deal with) issues of difference and variety within and among groups?
3. According to Abu-Lughod, what is the relationship between self and other created through anthropology's approach to and definition of culture? Do you see this self-other distinction anywhere in Tylor's writing? How could we think differently about this relationship than anthropologists traditionally have?

KEY TERMS

Culture

Race

Survivals

Halfie

Partiality

Orientalism

Tylor, Edward B. 1871. "The science of culture." In *Primitive Culture*. London: John Murray. [excerpt]

Culture or Civilization—Its phenomena related according to definite Laws—Method of classification and discussion of the evidence—Connexion of successive stages of culture by Permanence, Modification, and Survival—Principal topics examined in the present work.

CULTURE OR CIVILIZATION, TAKEN IN ITS wide ethnographic sense, is that complex whole which includes knowledge, belief, art, morals, law, custom, and any other capabilities and habits acquired by man as a member of society. The condition of culture among the various societies of mankind, in so far as it is capable of being investigated on general principles, is a subject apt for the study of laws of human thought and action. On the one hand, the uniformity which so largely pervades civilization may be ascribed, in great measure, to the uniform action of uniform causes : while on the other hand its various grades may be regarded as stages of development or evolution, each the outcome of previous history, and about to do its proper part in shaping the history of the future. To the investigation of these two great principles in several departments of ethnography, with especial consideration of the civilization of the lower tribes as related to the civilization of the higher nations, the present volumes are devoted.

Our modern investigators in the sciences of inorganic nature are foremost to recognize, both within and without their special fields of work, the unity of nature, the fixity of its laws, the definite sequence of cause and effect through which every fact depends on what has gone before it, and acts upon what is to come after it. They grasp firmly the Pythagorean doctrine of pervading order in the universal Kosmos. They affirm, with Aristotle, that nature is not full of incoherent episodes, like a bad tragedy. They agree with Leibnitz in what he calls 'my axiom, that nature never acts by leaps (la nature n'agit jamais par saut),' as well as in his 'great principle, commonly little employed, that nothing happens without sufficient reason.' Nor again, in studying the structure and habits of plants and animals, or in investigating the lower functions even of man, are these leading ideas unacknowledged. But when we come to talk of the higher processes of human feeling and action, of thought and language, knowledge and art, a change appears in the prevalent tone of opinion. The world at large is scarcely prepared to accept the general study of human life as a branch of natural science, and to carry out, in a large sense, the poet's injunction to 'Account for moral as for natural things.' To many educated minds there seems something presumptuous and repulsive in the view that the history of mankind is part and parcel of the history of nature,

Edward Burnett Tylor, "The Science Of Culture," Primitive Culture: Researches Into the Development of Mythology, Philosophy, Religion Language, Art, and Custom, John Murray Publishers Limited, pp. 1-19, 1920.

that our thoughts, wills, and actions accord with laws as definite as those which govern the motion of waves, the combination of acids and bases, and the growth of plants and animals.

The main reasons of this state of the popular judgment are not far to seek. There are many who would willingly accept a science of history if placed before them with substantial definiteness of principle and evidence, but who not unreasonably reject the systems offered to them, as falling too far short of a scientific standard. Through resistance such as this, real knowledge always sooner or later makes its way, while the habit of opposition to novelty does such excellent service against the invasions of speculative dogmatism, that we may sometimes even wish it were stronger than it is. But other obstacles to the investigation of laws of human nature arise from considerations of metaphysics and theology. The popular notion of free human will involves not only freedom to act in accordance with motive, but also a power of breaking loose from continuity and acting without cause,—a combination which may be roughly illustrated by the simile of a balance sometimes acting in the usual way, but also possessed of the faculty of turning by itself without or against its weights. This view of an anomalous action of the will, which it need hardly be said is incompatible with scientific argument, subsists as an opinion patent or latent in men's minds, and strongly affecting their theoretic views of history, though it is not, as a rule, brought prominently forward in systematic reasoning. Indeed the definition of human will, as strictly according with motive, is the only possible scientific basis in such enquiries. Happily, it is not needful to add here yet another to the list of dissertations on supernatural intervention and natural causation, on liberty, predestination, and accountability. We may hasten to escape from the regions of transcendental philosophy and theology, to start on a more hopeful journey over more practicable ground. None will deny that, as each man knows by the evidence of his own consciousness, definite and natural cause does, to a great extent, determine human action. Then, keeping aside from considerations of extra-natural interference and causeless spontaneity, let us take this admitted existence of natural cause and effect as our standing-ground, and travel on it so far as it will bear us. It is on this same basis that physical science pursues, with ever-increasing success, its quest of laws of nature. Nor need this restriction hamper the scientific study of human life, in which the real difficulties are the practical ones of enormous complexity of evidence, and imperfection of methods of observation.

Now it appears that this view of human will and conduct as subject to definite law, is indeed recognised and acted upon by the very people who oppose it when stated in the abstract as a general principle, and who then complain that it annihilates man's free will, destroys his sense of personal responsibility, and degrades him to a soulless machine. He who will say these things will nevertheless pass much of his own life in studying the motives which lead to human action, seeking to attain his wishes through them, framing in his mind theories of personal character, reckoning what are likely to be the effects of new combinations, and giving to his reasoning the crowning character of true scientific enquiry, by taking it for granted that in so far as his calculation turns out wrong, either his evidence must have been false or incomplete, or his judgment upon it unsound. Such a one will sum up the experience of years spent in complex relations with society, by declaring his persuasion that there is a reason for everything in life, and that where events look unaccountable, the rule is to wait and watch in hope that the key to the problem may some day be found. This man's observation may have been as narrow as his inferences are crude and prejudiced, but nevertheless he has been an inductive philosopher 'more than forty years without knowing it.' He has practically acknowledged definite laws of human thought and action, and has simply thrown out of account in his own studies of life the whole fabric of motiveless will and uncaused spontaneity. It is assumed here that they should be just so thrown out of account in wider studies, and that the true philosophy of history lies in extending and improving the methods of the plain people who form their judgments upon facts, and check them upon new facts. Whether the doctrine be wholly or but partly true, it accepts the very condition under which we search for new knowledge in the lessons of experience, and in a word the whole course of our rational life is based upon it.

'One event is always the son of another, and we must never forget the parentage,' was a remark made by a Bechuana chief to Casalis the African missionary. Thus at all times historians, so far as they have aimed at being more than mere chroniclers, have done their best to show not merely succession, but connexion, among the events upon their record. Moreover, they have striven to elicit general principles of human action, and by these to explain particular events, stating expressly or taking tacitly for granted the existence of a philosophy of history. Should any one deny the possibility of thus establishing historical laws, the answer is ready with which Boswell in such a case turned on Johnson: 'Then, sir, you would reduce all history to no better than an almanack.' That nevertheless the labours of so many eminent thinkers should have as yet brought history only to the threshold of science, need cause no wonder to those who consider the bewildering complexity of the problems which come before the general historian. The evidence from which he is to draw his conclusions is at once so multifarious and so doubtful, that a full and distinct view of its bearing on a particular question is hardly to be attained, and thus the temptation becomes all but irresistible to garble it in support of some rough and ready theory of the course of events. The philosophy of history at large, explaining the past and predicting the future phenomena of man's life in the world by reference to general laws, is in fact a subject with which, in the present state of knowledge, even genius aided by wide research seems but hardly able to cope. Yet there are departments of it which, though difficult enough, seem comparatively accessible. If the field of enquiry be narrowed from History as a whole to that branch of it which is here called Culture, the history, not of tribes or nations, but of the condition of knowledge, religion, art, custom, and the like among them, the task of investigation proves to lie within far more moderate compass. We suffer still from the same kind of difficulties which beset the wider argument, but they are much diminished. The evidence is no longer so wildly heterogeneous, but may be more simply classified and compared, while the power of getting rid of extraneous matter, and treating each issue on its own proper set of facts, makes close reasoning on the whole more available than in general history. This may appear from a brief preliminary examination of the problem, how the phenomena of Culture may be classified and arranged, stage by stage, in a probable order of evolution.

Surveyed in a broad view, the character and habit of mankind at once display that similarity and consistency of phenomena which led the Italian proverb-maker to declare that 'all the world is one country,' 'tutto il mondo è paese.' To general likeness in human nature on the one hand, and to general likeness in the circumstances of life on the other, this similarity and consistency may no doubt be traced, and they may be studied with especial fitness in comparing races near the same grade of civilization. Little respect need be had in such comparisons for date in history or for place on the map; the ancient Swiss lake-dweller may be set beside the mediæval Aztec, and the Ojibwa of North America beside the Zulu of South Africa. As Dr. Johnson contemptuously said when he had read about Patagonians and South Sea Islanders in Hawkesworth's Voyages, 'one set of savages is like another.' How true a generalization this really is, any Ethnological Museum may show. Examine for instance the edged and pointed instruments in such a collection; the inventory includes hatchet, adze, chisel, knife, saw, scraper, awl, needle, spear and arrow-head, and of these most or all belong with only differences of detail to races the most various. So it is with savage occupations; the wood-chopping, fishing with net and line, shooting and spearing game, fire-making, cooking, twisting cord and plaiting baskets, repeat themselves with wonderful uniformity in the museum shelves which illustrate the life of the lower races from Kamchatka to Tierra del Fuego, and from Dahome to Hawaii. Even when it comes to comparing barbarous hordes with civilized nations, the consideration thrusts itself upon our minds, how far item after item of the life of the lower races passes into analogous proceedings of the higher, in forms not too far changed to be recognized, and sometimes hardly changed at all. Look at the modern European peasant using his hatchet and his hoe, see his food boiling or roasting over the log-fire, observe the exact place which beer holds in his calculation of happiness, hear his tale of the ghost in the nearest haunted house, and of the farmer's niece who was bewitched with knots in her inside till she fell into fits and died. If we choose out in this way things which have altered little in a long course of centuries, we may draw a picture where there shall be scarce a hand's breadth difference between an English ploughman and a negro of Central Africa. These pages will be so crowded with evidence of such correspondence among mankind, that there is no need to dwell upon its details here, but it may be used at once to override a problem which would complicate the argument, namely, the question of race. For the present purpose it appears both possible and desirable to eliminate considerations of hereditary varieties or races of man, and to treat mankind as homogeneous in nature, though placed in different grades of civilization. The details of the enquiry will, I think, prove that stages of culture may be compared without taking into account how far tribes who use the same implement, follow the same custom, or believe the same myth, may differ in their bodily configuration and the colour of their skin and hair.

A first step in the study of civilization is to dissect it into details, and to classify these in their proper groups. Thus, in examining weapons, they are to be classed under spear, club, sling, bow and arrow, and so forth; among textile arts are to be ranged matting, netting, and several grades of making and weaving threads; myths are divided under such headings as myths of sunrise and sunset, eclipse-myths, earthquake-myths, local myths which account for the names of places by some fanciful tale, eponymic myths which account for the parentage of a tribe by turning its name into the name of an imaginary ancestor ; under rites and ceremonies occur such practices as the various kinds of sacrifice to the ghosts of the dead and to other spiritual beings, the turning to the east in worship, the purification of ceremonial or moral uncleanness by means of water or fire. Such are a few miscellaneous examples from a list of hundreds, and the ethnographer's business is to classify such details with a view to making out their distribution in geography and history, and the relations which exist among them. What this task is like, may be almost perfectly illustrated by comparing these details of culture with the species of plants and animals as studied by the naturalist. To the ethnographer the bow and arrow is a species, the habit of flattening children's skulls is a species, the practice of reckoning numbers by tens is a species. The geographical distribution of these things, and their transmission from region to region, have to be studied as the naturalist studies the geography of his botanical and zoological species. Just as certain plants and animals are peculiar to certain districts, so it is with such instruments as the Australian boomerang, the Polynesian stick-and-groove for fire-making, the tiny bow and arrow used as a lancet or phleme by tribes about the Isthmus of Panama, and in like manner with many an art, myth, or custom, found isolated in a particular field. Just as the catalogue of all the species of plants and animals of a district represents its Flora and Fauna, so the list of all the items of the general life of a people represents that whole which we call its culture. And just as distant regions so often produce vegetables and animals which are analogous, though by no means identical, so it is with the details of the civilization of their inhabitants. How good a working analogy there really is between the diffusion of plants and animals and the diffusion of civilization, comes well into view when we notice how far the same causes have produced both at once. In district after district, the same causes which have introduced the cultivated plants and domesticated animals of civilization, have brought in with them a corresponding art and knowledge. The course of events which carried horses and wheat to America carried with them the use of the gun and the iron hatchet, while in return the whole world received not only maize, potatoes, and turkeys, but the habit of tobacco-smoking and the sailor's hammock.

It is a matter worthy of consideration, that the accounts of similar phenomena of culture, recurring in different parts of the world, actually supply incidental proof of their own authenticity. Some years since, a question which brings out this point was put to me by a great historian—'How can a statement as to customs, myths, beliefs, &c., of a savage tribe be treated as evidence where it depends on the testimony of some traveller or missionary, who may be a superficial observer, more or less ignorant of the native language, a careless retailer of unsifted talk, a man prejudiced or even wilfully deceitful?' This question is, indeed, one which every ethnographer ought to keep clearly and constantly before his mind. Of course he is bound to use his best judgment as to the trustworthiness of all authors he quotes, and if possible to obtain several accounts to certify each point in each locality. But it is over and above these measures of precaution that the test of recurrence comes in. If two independent visitors to different countries, say a mediæval Mohammedan in Tartary and a modern Englishman in Dahome, or a Jesuit missionary in Brazil and a Wesleyan in the Fiji Islands, agree in describing some analogous art or rite or myth among the people they have visited, it becomes difficult or impossible to set down such correspondence to accident or wilful fraud. A story by a bushranger in Australia may, perhaps, be objected to as a mistake or an invention, but did a Methodist minister in Guinea conspire with him to cheat the public by telling the same story there? The possibility of intentional or unintentional mystification is often barred by such a state of things as that a similar statement is made in two remote lands, by two witnesses, of whom A lived a century before B, and B appears never to have heard of A. How distant are the countries, how wide apart the dates, how different the creeds and characters of the observers, in the catalogue of facts of civilization, needs no farther showing to any one who will even glance at the footnotes of the present work. And the more odd the statement, the less likely that several people in several places should have made it wrongly. This being so, it seems reasonable to judge that the statements are in the main truly given, and that their close and regular coincidence is due to the cropping up of similar facts in various districts of culture. Now the most important facts of ethnography are vouched for in this way. Experience leads the student after a while to expect and find that the phenomena of culture, as resulting from widely-acting similar causes, should recur again and again in the world. He even mistrusts isolated statements to which he knows of no parallel elsewhere, and waits for their genuineness to be shown by corresponding accounts from the other side of the earth, or the other end of history. So strong, indeed, is this means of authentication, that the ethnographer in his library may sometimes presume to decide, not only whether a particular explorer is a shrewd, honest observer, but also whether what he reports is conformable to the general rules of civilization. 'Non quis, sed quid.'

To turn from the distribution of culture in different countries, to its diffusion within these countries. The quality of mankind which tends most to make the systematic study of civilization possible, is that remarkable tacit consensus or agreement which so far induces whole populations to unite in the use of the same language, to follow the same religion and customary law, to settle down to the same general level of art and knowledge. It is this state of things which makes it so far possible to ignore exceptional facts and to describe nations by a sort of general average. It is this state of things which makes it so far possible to represent immense masses of details by a few typical facts, while, these once settled, new cases recorded by new observers simply fall into their places to prove the soundness of the classification. There is found to be such regularity in the composition of societies of men, that we can drop individual differences out of sight, and thus can generalize on the arts and opinions of whole nations, just as, when looking down upon an army from a hill, we forget the individual soldier, whom, in fact, we can scarce distinguish in the mass, while we see each regiment as an organized body, spreading or concentrating, moving in advance or in retreat. In some branches of the study of social laws it is now possible to call in the aid of statistics, and to set apart special actions of large mixed communities of men by means of taxgatherers' schedules, or the tables of the insurance office. Among modern arguments on the laws of human action, none have had a deeper effect than generalizations such as those of M. Quetelet, on the regularity, not only of such matters as average stature and the annual rates of birth and death, but of the recurrence, year after year, of such obscure and seemingly incalculable products of national life as the numbers of murders and suicides, and the proportion of the very weapons of crime. Other striking cases are the annual regularity of persons killed accidentally in the London streets, and of undirected letters dropped into post-office letter-boxes. But in examining the culture of the lower races, far from having at command the measured arithmetical facts of modern statistics, we may have to judge of the condition of tribes from the imperfect accounts supplied by travellers or missionaries, or even to reason upon relics of prehistoric races of whose very names and languages we are hopelessly ignorant. Now these may seem at the first glance sadly indefinite and unpromising materials for scientific enquiry. But in fact they are neither indefinite nor unpromising, but give evidence that is good and definite so far as it goes. They are data which, for the distinct way in which they severally denote the condition of the tribe they belong to, will actually bear comparison with the statistician's returns. The fact is that a stone arrow-head, a carved club, an idol, a grave-mound where slaves and property have been buried for the use of the dead, an account of a sorcerer's rites in making rain, a table of numerals, the conjugation of a verb, are things which each express the state of a people as to one particular point of culture, as truly as the tabulated numbers of deaths by poison, and of chests of tea imported, express in a different way other partial results of the general life of a whole community.

That a whole nation should have a special dress, special tools and weapons, special laws of marriage and property, special moral and religious doctrines, is a remarkable fact, which we notice so little because we have lived all our lives in the midst of it. It is with such general qualities of organized bodies of men that ethnography has especially to deal. Yet, while generalizing on the culture of a tribe or nation, and setting aside the peculiarities of the individuals composing it as unimportant to the main result, we must be careful not to forget what makes up this main result. There are people so intent on the separate life of individuals that they cannot grasp a notion of the action of a community as a whole—such an observer, incapable of a wide view of society, is aptly described in the saying that he 'cannot see the forest for the trees.' But, on the other hand, the philosopher may be so intent upon his general laws of society as to neglect the individual actors of whom that society is made up, and of him it may be said that he cannot see the trees for the forest. We know how arts, customs, and ideas are shaped among ourselves by the combined actions of many individuals, of which actions both motive and effect often come quite distinctly within our view. The history of an invention, an opinion, a ceremony, is a history of suggestion and modification, encouragement and opposition, personal gain and party prejudice, and the individuals concerned act each according to his own motives, as determined by his character and circumstances. Thus sometimes we watch individuals acting for their own ends with little thought of their effect on society at large, and sometimes we have to study movements of national life as a whole, where the individuals co-operating in them are utterly beyond our observation. But seeing that collective social action is the mere resultant of many individual actions, it is clear that these two methods of enquiry, if rightly followed, must be absolutely consistent.

In studying both the recurrence of special habits or ideas in several districts, and their prevalence within each district, there come before us ever-reiterated proofs of regular causation producing the phenomena of human life, and of laws of maintenance and diffusion according to which these phenomena settle into permanent standard conditions of society, at definite stages of culture. But, while giving full importance to the evidence bearing on these standard conditions of society, let us be careful to avoid a pitfall which may entrap the unwary student. Of course the opinions and habits belonging in common to masses of mankind are to a great extent the results of sound judgment and practical wisdom. But to a great extent it is not so. That many numerous societies of men should have believed in the influence of the evil eye and the existence of a firmament, should have sacrificed slaves and goods to the ghosts of the departed, should have handed down traditions of giants slaying monsters and men turning into beasts—all this is ground for holding that such ideas were indeed produced in men's minds by efficient causes, but it is not ground for holding that the rites in question are profitable, the beliefs sound, and the history authentic. This may seem at the first glance a truism, but, in fact, it is the denial of a fallacy which deeply affects the minds of all but a small critical minority of mankind. Popularly, what everybody says must be true, what everybody does must be right—'Quod ubique, quod semper, quod ab omnibus creditum est, hoc est vere proprieque Catholicum'—and so forth. There are various topics, especially in history, law, philosophy, and theology, where even the educated people we live among can hardly be brought to see that the cause why men do hold an opinion, or practise a custom, is by no means necessarily a reason why they ought to do so. Now collections of ethnographic evidence bringing so prominently into view the agreement of immense multitudes of men as to certain traditions, beliefs, and usages, are peculiarly liable to be thus improperly used in direct defence of these institutions themselves, even old barbaric nations being polled to maintain their opinions against what are called modern ideas. As it has more than once happened to myself to find my collections of traditions and beliefs thus set up to prove their own objective truth, without proper examination of the grounds on which they were actually received, I take this occasion of remarking that the same line of argument will serve equally well to demonstrate, by the strong and wide consent of nations, that the earth is flat, and nightmare the visit of a demon.

It being shown that the details of Culture are capable of being classified in a great number of ethnographic groups of arts, beliefs, customs, and the rest, the consideration comes next how far the facts arranged in these groups are produced by evolution from one another. It need hardly be pointed out that the groups in question, though held together each by a common character, are by no means accurately defined. To take up again the natural history illustration, it may be said that they are species which tend to run widely into varieties. And when it comes to the question what relations some of these groups bear to others, it is plain that the student of the habits of mankind has a great advantage over the student of the species of plants and animals. Among naturalists it is an open question whether a theory of development from species to species is a record of transitions which actually took place, or a mere ideal scheme serviceable in the classification of species whose origin was really independent. But among ethnographers there is no such question as to the possibility of species of implements or habits or beliefs being developed one out of another, for development in Culture is recognized by our most familiar knowledge. Mechanical invention supplies apt examples of the kind of development which affects civilization at large. In the history of fire-arms, the clumsy wheel-lock, in which a notched steel wheel revolved by means of a spring against a piece of pyrites till a spark caught the priming, led to the invention of the more serviceable flint-lock, of which a few still hang in the kitchens of our farm-houses for the boys to shoot small birds with at Christmas; the flint-lock in time passed by modification into the percussion-lock, which is just now changing its old-fashioned arrangement to be adapted from muzzle-loading to breech-loading. The mediæval astrolabe passed into the quadrant, now discarded in its turn by the seaman, who uses the more delicate sextant, and so it is through the history of one art and instrument after another. Such examples of progression are known to us as direct history, but so thoroughly is this notion of development at home in our minds, that by means of it we reconstruct lost history without scruple, trusting to general knowledge of the principles of human thought and action as a guide in putting the facts in their proper order. Whether chronicle speaks or is silent on the point, no one comparing a long-bow and a cross-bow would doubt that the cross-bow was a development arising from the simpler instrument. So among the fire-drills for igniting by friction, it seems clear on the face of the matter that the drill worked by a cord or bow is a later improvement on the clumsier primitive instrument twirled between the hands. That instructive class of specimens which antiquaries sometimes discover, bronze celts modelled on the heavy type of the stone hatchet, are scarcely explicable except as first steps in the transition from the Stone Age to the Bronze Age, to be followed soon by the next stage of progress, in which it is discovered that the new material is suited to a handier and less wasteful pattern. And thus, in the other branches of our history, there will come again and again into view series of facts which may be consistently arranged as having followed one another in a particular order of development, but which will hardly bear being turned round and made to follow in reversed order. Such for instance are the facts I have here brought forward in a chapter on the Art of Counting, which tend to prove that as to this point of culture at least, savage tribes reached their position by learning and not by unlearning, by elevation from a lower rather than by degradation from a higher state.

Among evidence aiding us to trace the course which the civilization of the world has actually followed, is that great class of facts to denote which I have found it convenient to introduce the term 'survivals.' These are processes, customs, opinions, and so forth, which have been carried on by force of habit into a new state of society different from that in which they had their original home, and they thus remain as proofs and examples of an older condition of culture out of which a newer has been evolved. Thus, I know an old Somersetshire woman whose hand-loom dates from the time before the introduction of the 'flying shuttle,' which new-fangled appliance she has never even learnt to use, and I have seen her throw her shuttle from hand to hand in true classic fashion; this old woman is not a century behind her times, but she is a case of survival. Such examples often lead us back to the habits of hundreds and even thousands of years ago. The ordeal of the Key and Bible, still in use, is a survival; the Midsummer bonfire is a survival; the Breton peasants' All Souls' supper for the spirits of the dead is a survival. The simple keeping up of ancient habits is only one part of the transition from old into new and changing times. The serious business of ancient society may be seen to sink into the sport of later generations, and its serious belief to linger on in nursery folk-lore, while superseded habits of old-world life may be modified into new-world forms still powerful for good and evil. Sometimes old thoughts and practices will burst out afresh, to the amazement of a world that thought them long since dead or dying; here survival passes into revival, as has lately happened in so remarkable a way in the history of modern spiritualism, a subject full of instruction from the ethnographer's point of view. The study of the principles of survival has, indeed, no small practical importance, for most of what we call superstition is included within survival, and in this way lies open to the attack of its deadliest enemy, a reasonable explanation. Insignificant, moreover, as multitudes of the facts of survival are in themselves, their study is so effective for tracing the course of the historical development through which alone it is possible to understand their meaning, that it becomes a vital point of ethnographic research to gain the clearest possible insight into their nature. This importance must justify the detail here devoted to an examination of survival, on the evidence of such games, popular sayings, customs, superstitions, and the like, as may serve well to bring into view the manner of its operation.

Progress, degradation, survival, revival, modification, are all modes of the connexion that binds together the complex network of civilization. It needs but a glance into the trivial details of our own daily life to set us thinking how far we are really its originators, and how far but the transmitters and modifiers of the results of long past ages. Looking round the rooms we live in, we may try here how far he who only knows his own time can be capable of rightly comprehending even that. Here is the 'honeysuckle' of Assyria, there the fleur-de-lis of Anjou, a cornice with a Greek border runs round the ceiling, the style of Louis XIV, and its parent the Renaissance share the looking-glass between them. Transformed, shifted, or mutilated, such elements of art still carry their history plainly stamped upon them; and if the history yet farther behind is less easy to read, we are not to say that because we cannot clearly discern it there is therefore no history there. It is thus even with the fashion of the clothes men wear. The ridiculous little tails of the German postilion's coat show of themselves how they came to dwindle to such absurd rudiments; but the English clergyman's bands no longer so convey their history to the eye, and look unaccountable enough till one has seen the intermediate stages through which they came down from the more serviceable wide collars, such as Milton wears in his portrait, and which gave their name to the 'bandbox' they used to be kept in. In fact, the books of costume, showing how one garment grew or shrank by gradual stages and passed into another, illustrate with much force and clearness the nature of the change and growth, revival and decay, which go on from year to year in more important matters of life. In books, again, we see each writer not for and by himself, but occupying his proper place in history; we look through each philosopher, mathematician, chemist, poet, into the background of his education,—through Leibnitz into Descartes, through Dalton into Priestley, through Milton into Homer. The study of language has, perhaps, done more than any other in removing from our view of human thought and action the ideas of chance and arbitrary invention, and in substituting for them a theory of development by the co-operation of individual men, through processes ever reasonable and intelligible where the facts are fully known. Rudimentary as the science of culture still is, the symptoms are becoming very strong that even what seem its most spontaneous and motiveless phenomena will, nevertheless, be shown to come within the range of distinct cause and effect as certainly as the facts of mechanics. What would be popularly thought more indefinite and uncontrolled than the products of the imagination in myths and fables? Yet any systematic investigation of mythology, on the basis of a wide collection of evidence, will show plainly enough in such efforts of fancy at once a development from stage to stage, and a production of uniformity of result from uniformity of cause. Here, as elsewhere, causeless spontaneity is seen to recede farther and farther into shelter within the dark precincts of ignorance; like chance, that still holds its place among the vulgar as a real cause of events otherwise unaccountable, while to educated men it has long consciously meant nothing but this ignorance itself. It is only when men fail to see the line of connexion in events, that they are prone to fall upon the notions of arbitrary impulses, causeless freaks, chance and nonsense and indefinite unaccountability. If childish games, purposeless customs, absurd superstitions, are set down as spontaneous because no one can say exactly how they came to be, the assertion may remind us of the like effect that the eccentric habits of the wild rice-plant had on the philosophy of a Red Indian tribe, otherwise disposed to see in the harmony of nature the effects of one controlling personal will. The Great Spirit, said these Sioux theologians, made all things except the wild rice; but the wild rice came by chance.

Abu-Lughod, Lila. 1991. "Writing Against Culture." In R. Fox, ed., *Recapturing Anthropology: Working in the Present.* Santa Fe: School of American Research Press.

WRITING *CULTURE* (CLIFFORD AND MARCUS 1986), the collection that marked a major new form of critique of cultural anthropology's premises, more or less excluded two critical groups whose situations neatly expose and challenge the most basic of those premises: feminists and "halfies"—people whose national or cultural identity is mixed by virtue of migration, overseas education, or parentage.[1] In his introduction, Clifford (1986a) apologizes for the feminist absence; no one mentions halfies or the indigenous anthropologists to whom they are related. Perhaps they are not yet numerous enough or sufficiently self-defined as a group.[2] The importance of these two groups lies not in any superior moral claim or advantage they might have in doing anthropology, but in the special dilemmas they face, dilemmas that reveal starkly the problems with cultural anthropology's assumption of a fundamental distinction between self and other.

In this essay I explore how feminists and halfies, by the way their anthropological practice unsettles the boundary between self and other, enable us to reflect on the conventional nature and political effects of this distinction and ultimately to reconsider the value of the concept of culture on which it depends. I will argue that "culture" operates in anthropological discourse to enforce separations that inevitably carry a sense of hierarchy. Therefore, anthropologists should now pursue, without exaggerated hopes for the power of their texts to change the world, a variety of strategies for writing *against* culture. For those interested in textual strategies, I explore the advantages of what I call "ethnographies of the particular" as instruments of a tactical humanism.

Selves and Others

The notion of culture (especially as it functions to distinguish "cultures"), despite a long usefulness, may now have become something anthropologists would want to work against in their theories, their ethnographic practice, and their ethnographic writing. A helpful way to begin to grasp why is to consider what the shared elements of feminist and halfie anthropology clarify about the self/other distinction central to the paradigm of anthropology. Marilyn Strathern (1985, 1987a) raises some of the issues regarding feminism in essays that both Clifford and Rabinow cited in *Writing Culture.* Her thesis is that the relationship between anthropology and feminism is awkward. This thesis leads her to try to understand why feminist scholarship, in spite of its rhetoric of radicalism, has failed to fundamentally alter anthropology, and why feminism has gained even less from anthropology than vice versa.

The awkwardness, she argues, arises from the fact that despite a common interest in differences, the scholarly practices of feminists and anthropologists are "differently structured in the way they organize knowledge and draw boundaries" (Strathern 1987a: 289) and especially in "the nature of the investigators' *relationship to* their subject matter" (1987a: 284). Feminist scholars, united by their common opposition to men or to patriarchy, produce a discourse composed of many voices; they "discover the self by becoming conscious of oppression from the Other" (1987a: 289). Anthropologists, whose goal is "to make sense of differences" (1987a: 286), also constitute their "selves" in relation to an other, but do not view this other as "under attack" (1987a: 289).

In highlighting the self/other relationship, Strathern takes us to the heart of the problem. Yet she retreats from the problematic of power (granted as formative in feminism) in her strangely uncritical depiction of anthropology. When she defines anthropology as a discipline that "continues to know itself as the study of social behavior or society in terms of systems and collective representations" (1987a: 281), she underplays the self/other distinction. In characterizing the relationship between anthropological self and other as nonadversarial, she ignores its most fundamental aspect. Anthropology's avowed goal may be "the study of man [sic]," but it is a discipline built on the historically constructed divide between the West and the non-West. It has been and continues to be primarily the study of the non-Western other by the Western self, even if in its new guise it seeks explicitly to give voice to the Other or to present a dialogue between the self and other, either textually or through an explication of the fieldwork encounter (as in such works as Crapanzano 1980, Dumont 1978, Dwyer 1982, Rabinow 1977, Riesman 1977, Tedlock 1983, and Tyler 1986). And the relationship between the West and the non-West, at least since the birth of anthropology, has been constituted by Western domination. This suggests that the awkwardness Strathern senses in the relationship between feminism and anthropology might better be understood as the result of diametrically opposed processes of self-construction through opposition to others—processes that begin from different sides of a power divide.

The enduring strength of what Morsy (1988:70) has called "the hegemony of the distinctive-other tradition" in anthropology is betrayed by the defensiveness of partial exceptions. Anthropologists (like Ortner, this volume) conducting fieldwork in the United States or Europe wonder whether they have not blurred the disciplinary boundaries between anthropology and other fields such as sociology or history. One way to retain their identities as anthropologists is to make the communities they study seem "other." Studying ethnic communities and the powerless assures this.[3] So does concentrating on "culture" (or on the method of holism based on it, as Appadurai [1988] has argued), for reasons I will discuss later. There are two issues here. One is the conviction that one cannot be objective about one's own society, something that affects indigenous anthropologists (Western or non-Western). The second is a tacit understanding that anthropologists study the non-West; halfies who study their own or related non-Western communities are still more easily recognizable as anthropologists than Americans who study Americans.

If anthropology continues to be practiced as the study by an unproblematic and unmarked Western self of found "others" out there, feminist theory, an academic practice that also traffics in selves and others, has in its relatively short history come to realize the danger of treating selves and others as givens. It is instructive for the development of a critique of anthropology to consider the trajectory that has led, within two decades, to what some might call a crisis in feminist theory, and others, the development of postfeminism.

From Simone de Beauvoir on, it has been accepted that, at least in the modern West, women have been the other to men's self. Feminism has been a movement devoted to helping women become selves and subjects rather than objects and men's others.[4] The crisis in feminist theory (related to a crisis in the women's movement) that followed on the heels of feminist attempts to turn those who had been constituted as other into selves—or, to use the popular metaphor, to let women speak—was the problem of "difference." For whom did feminists speak? Within the women's movement, the objections of lesbians, African-American women, and other "women of color" that their experiences as women were different from those of white, middle-class, heterosexual women problematized the identity of women as selves. Cross-cultural work on women also made it clear that masculine and feminine did not have, as we say, the same meanings in other cultures, nor did Third World women's lives resemble Western women's lives. As Harding (1986:246) puts it, the problem is that "once 'woman' is deconstructed into 'women' and 'gender' is recognized to have no fixed referents, feminism itself dissolves as a theory that can reflect the voice of a naturalized or essentialized speaker."[5]

From its experience with this crisis of selfhood or subjecthood, feminist theory can offer anthropology two useful reminders. First, the self is always a construction, never a natural or found entity, even if it has that appearance. Second, the process of creating a self through opposition to an other always entails the violence of repressing or ignoring other forms of difference. Feminist theorists have been forced to explore the implications for the formation of identity and the possibilities for political action of the ways in which gender as a system of difference is intersected by other systems of difference, including, in the modern capitalist world, race and class.

Where does this leave the feminist anthropologist? Strathern (1987a: 286) characterizes her as experiencing a tension—"caught between structures ... faced with two different ways of relating to her or his subject matter." The more interesting aspect of the feminist's situation, though, is what she shares with the halfie: a blocked ability to comfortably assume the self of anthropology. For both, although in different ways, the self is split, caught at the intersection of systems of difference. I am less concerned with the existential consequences of this split (these have been eloquently explored elsewhere [e.g., Joseph 1988, Kondo 1986, Narayan 1989]) than with the awareness such splits generate about three crucial issues: positionality, audience, and the power inherent in distinctions of self and other. What happens when the "other" that the anthropologist is studying is simultaneously constructed as, at least partially, a self?

Feminists and halfie anthropologists cannot easily avoid the issue of positionality. Standing on shifting ground makes it clear that every view is a view from somewhere and every act of speaking a speaking from somewhere. Cultural anthropologists have never been fully convinced of the ideology of science and have long questioned the value, possibility, and definition of objectivity.[6] But they still seem reluctant to examine the implications of the actual situatedness of their knowledge.[7]

Two common, intertwined objections to the work of feminist or native or semi-native anthropologists, both related to partiality, betray the persistence of ideals of objectivity. The first has to do with the partiality (as bias or position) of the observer. The second has to do with the partial (incomplete) nature of the picture presented. Halfies are more associated with the first problem, feminists the second. The problem with studying one's own society is alleged to be the problem of gaining enough distance. Since for halfies, the Other is in certain ways the self, there is said to be the danger shared with indigenous anthropologists of identification and the easy slide into subjectivity.[8] These worries suggest that the anthropologist is still defined as a being who must stand apart from the Other, even when he or she seeks explicitly to bridge the gap. Even Bourdieu (1977:1–2), who perceptively analyzed the effects this outsider stance has on the anthropologist's (mis)understanding of social life, fails to break with this doxa. The obvious point he misses is that the outsider self never simply stands outside. He or she stands in a definite relation with the Other of the study, not just as a Westerner, but as a Frenchman in Algeria during the war of independence, an American in Morocco during the 1967 Arab-Israeli war, or an Englishwoman in postcolonial India. What we call the outside is a position *within* a larger political-historical complex. No less than the halfie, the "wholie" is in a specific position vis-à-vis the community being studied.

The debates about feminist anthropologists suggest a second source of uneasiness about positionality. Even when they present themselves as studying gender, feminist anthropologists are dismissed as presenting only a partial picture of the societies they study because they are assumed to be studying only women. Anthropologists study society, the unmarked form. The study of women is the marked form, too readily sectioned off, as Strathern (1985) notes.[9] Yet it could easily be argued that most studies of society have been equally partial. As restudies like Weiner's (1976) of Malinowski's Trobriand Islanders or Bell's (1983) of the well-studied Australian aborigines indicate, they have been the study of men.[10] This does not make such studies any less valuable; it merely reminds us that we must constantly attend to the positionality of the anthropological self and its representations of others. James Clifford (1986a: 6), among others, has convincingly argued that ethnographic representations are always "partial truths." What is needed is a recognition that they are also positioned truths.

Split selfhood creates for the two groups being discussed a second problem that is illuminating for anthropology generally: multiple audiences. Although all anthropologists are beginning to feel what might be called the Rushdie effect—the effects of living in a global age when the subjects of their studies begin to read their works and the governments of the countries they work in ban books and deny visas—feminist and halfie anthropologists struggle in poignant ways with multiple accountability. Rather than having one primary audience, that of other anthropologists, feminist anthropologists write for anthropologists and for feminists, two groups whose relationship to their subject matter is at odds and who hold ethnographers accountable in different ways.[11] Furthermore, feminist circles include non-Western feminists, often from the societies feminist anthropologists have studied, who call them to account in new ways.[12]

Halfies' dilemmas are even more extreme. As anthropologists, they write for other anthropologists, mostly Western. Identified also with communities outside the West, or subcultures within it, they are called to account by educated members of those communities. More importantly, not just because they position themselves with reference to two communities but because when they present the Other they are presenting themselves, they speak with a complex awareness of and investment in reception. Both halfie and feminist anthropologists are forced to confront squarely the politics and ethics of their representations. There are no easy solutions to their dilemmas.

The third issue that feminist and halfie anthropologists, unlike anthropologists who work in Western societies (another group for whom self and other are somewhat tangled), force us to confront is the dubiousness of maintaining that relationships between self and other are innocent of power. Because of sexism and racial or ethnic discrimination, they may have experienced—as women, as individuals of mixed parentage, or as foreigners—being other to a dominant self, whether in everyday life in the U.S., Britain, or France, or in the Western academy. This is not simply an experience of difference, but of inequality. My argument, however, is structural, not experiential. Women, blacks, and people of most of the non-West have been historically constituted as others in the major political systems of difference on which the unequal world of modern capitalism has depended. Feminist studies and black studies have made sufficient progress within the academy to have exposed the way that being studied by "white men" (to use a shorthand for a complex and historically constituted subject-position) turns into being spoken for by them. It becomes a sign and instrument of their power.

Within anthropology, despite a long history of self-conscious opposition to racism, a fast-growing, self-critical literature on anthropology's links to colonialism (for example, Asad 1973, Clifford 1983a, Fabian 1983, Hymes 1969, Kuper 1988), and experimentation with techniques of ethnography to relieve a discomfort with the power of anthropologist over anthropological subject, the fundamental issues of domination keep being skirted. Even attempts to refigure informants as consultants and to "let the other speak" in dialogic (Tedlock 1987) or polyvocal texts—decolonizations on the level of the text—leave intact the basic configuration of global power on which anthropology, as linked to other institutions of the world, is based. To see the strangeness of this enterprise, all that is needed is to consider an analogous case. What would our reaction be if male scholars stated their desire to "let women speak" in their texts while they continued to dominate all knowledge about them by controlling writing and other academic practices, supported in their positions by a particular organization of economic, social, and political life?

Because of their split selves, feminist and halfie anthropologists travel uneasily between speaking "for" and speaking "from," Their situation enables us to see more clearly that dividing practices, whether they naturalize differences, as in gender or race, or simply elaborate them, as I will argue the concept of culture does, are fundamental methods of enforcing inequality.

Culture and Difference

The concept of culture is the hidden term in all that has just been said about anthropology. Most American anthropologists believe or act as if "culture," notoriously resistant to definition and ambiguous of referent, is nevertheless the true object of anthropological inquiry. Yet it could also be argued that culture is important to anthropology because the anthropological distinction between self and other rests on it. Culture is the essential tool for making other. As a professional discourse that elaborates on the meaning of culture in order to account for, explain, and understand cultural difference, anthropology also helps construct, produce, and maintain it. Anthropological discourse gives cultural difference (and the separation between groups of people it implies) the air of the self-evident.

In this regard, the concept of culture operates much like its predecessor—race—even though in its twentieth-century form it has some important political advantages. Unlike race, and unlike even the nineteenth-century sense of culture as a synonym for civilization (contrasted to barbarism), the current concept allows for multiple rather than binary differences.

This immediately checks the eay move to hierarchizing; the shift to "culture" ("lower case *c* with the possibility of a final *s*," as Clifford [1988a: 234] puts it) has a relativizing effect. The most important of culture's advantages, however, is that it removes difference from the realm of the natural and the innate. Whether conceived of as a set of behaviors, customs, traditions, rules, plans, recipes, instructions, or programs (to list the range of definitions Geertz [1973a: 44] furnishes), culture is learned and can change.

Despite its anti-essentialist intent, however, the culture concept retains some of the tendencies to freeze difference possessed by concepts like race. This is easier to see if we consider a field in which there has been a shift from one to the other. Orientalism as a scholarly discourse (among other things) is, according to Said (1978:2), "a style of thought based upon an ontological and epistemological distinction made between 'the Orient' and (most of the time) 'the Occident'." What he shows is that in mapping geography, race, and culture onto one another, Orientalism fixes differences between people of "the West" and people of "the East" in ways so rigid that they might as well be considered innate. In the twentieth century, cultural difference, not race, has been the basic subject of Orientalist scholarship devoted now to interpreting the "culture" phenomena (primarily religion and language) to which basic differences in development, economic performance, government, character, and so forth are attributed.

Some anticolonial movements and present-day struggles have worked by what could be labelled reverse Orientalism, where attempts to reverse the power relationship proceed by seeking to valorize for the self what in the former system had been devalued as other. A Gandhian appeal to the greater spirituality of a Hindu India, compared with the materialism and violence of the West, and an Islamicist appeal to a greater faith in God, compared with the immorality and corruption of the West, both accept the essentialist terms of Orientalist constructions. While turning them on their heads, they preserve the rigid sense of difference based on culture.

A parallel can be drawn with feminism. It is a basic tenet of feminism that "women are made, not born." It has been important for most feminists to locate sex differences in culture, not biology or nature. While this has inspired some feminist theorists to attend to the social and personal effects of gender as a system of difference, for many others it has led to explorations of and strategies built on the notion of a women's culture. Cultural feminism (cf. Echols 1984) takes many forms, but it has many of the qualities of reverse Orientalism just discussed. For French feminists like Irigaray (1985a, 1985b), Cixous (1983), and Kristeva (1981), masculine and feminine, if not actually male and female, represent essentially different modes of being. Anglo-American feminists take a different tack. Some attempt to "describe" the cultural differences between men and women—Gilligan (1982) and her followers (e.g., Belenky et al. 1986) who elaborate the notion of "a different voice" are popular examples. Others try to "explain" the differences, whether through a socially informed psychoanalytic theory (e.g., Chodorow 1978), a Marxist-derived theory of the effects of the division of labor and women's role in social reproduction (Hartsock 1985), an analysis of maternal practice (Ruddick 1980), or even a theory of sexual exploitation (MacKinnon 1982). Much feminist theorizing and practice seeks to build or reform social life in line with this "women's culture."[13] There have been proposals for a woman-centered university (Rich 1979), a feminist science (Rose 1983, 1986), a feminist methodology in the sciences and social sciences (Meis 1983; Reinharz 1983; Smith 1987; Stanley and Wise 1983; see Harding 1987 for a sensible critique), and even a feminist spirituality and ecology. These proposals nearly always build on values traditionally associated in the West with women—a sense of care and connectedness, maternal nurturing, immediacy of experience, involvement in the bodily (versus the abstract), and so forth.

This valorization by cultural feminists, like reverse Orientalists, of the previously devalued qualities attributed to them may be provisionally useful in forging a sense of unity and in waging struggles of empowerment. Yet because it leaves in place the divide that structured the experiences of selfhood and oppression on which it builds, it perpetuates some dangerous tendencies. First, cultural feminists overlook the connections between those on each side of the divide, and the ways in which they define each other. Second, they overlook differences within each category constructed by the dividing practices, differences like those of class, race, and sexuality (to repeat the feminist litany of problematically abstract categories), but also ethnic origin, personal experience, age, mode of livelihood, health, living situation (rural or urban), and historical experience. Third, and perhaps most important, they ignore the ways in which experiences have been constructed historically and have changed over time. Both cultural feminism and revivalist movements tend to rely on notions of authenticity and the return to positive values not represented by the dominant other. As becomes obvious in the most extreme cases, these moves erase history. Invocations of Cretan goddesses in some cultural-feminist circles and, in a more complex and serious way, the powerful invocation of the seventh-century community of the Prophet in some Islamic movements are good examples.

The point is that the notion of culture which both types of movements use does not seem to guarantee an escape from the tendency toward essentialism. It could be argued that anthropologists use "culture" in more sophisticated and consistent ways and that their commitment to it as an analytical tool is firmer. Yet even many of them are now concerned about the ways it tends to freeze differences. Appadurai (1988), for example, in his compelling argument that "natives" are a figment of the anthropological imagination, shows the complicity of the anthropological concept of culture in a continuing "incarceration" of non-Western peoples in time and place. Denied the same capacity for movement, travel, and geographical interaction that Westerners take for granted, the cultures studied by anthropologists have tended to be denied history as well.

Others, including myself (1990b), have argued that cultural theories also tend to overemphasize coherence. Clifford notes both that "the discipline of fieldwork-based anthropology, in constituting its authority, constructs and reconstructs coherent cultural others and interpreting selves" (Clifford 1988b: 112) and that ethnography is a form of culture collecting (like art collecting) in which "diverse experiences and facts are selected, gathered, detached from their original temporal occasions, and given enduring value in a new arrangement" (Clifford 1988a: 231). Organic metaphors of wholeness and the methodology of holism that characterizes anthropology both favor coherence, which in turn contributes to the perception of communities as bounded and discrete.

Certainly discreteness does not have to imply value; the hallmark of twentieth-century anthropology has been its promotion of cultural relativism over evaluation and judgment. If anthropology has always to some extent been a form of cultural (self-) critique (Marcus and Fischer, 1986), that too was an aspect of a refusal to hierarchize difference. Yet neither position would be possible without difference. It would be worth thinking about the implications of the high stakes anthropology has in sustaining and perpetuating a belief in the existence of cultures that are identifiable as discrete, different, and separate from our own.[14] Does difference always smuggle in hierarchy?

In *Orientalism,* Said (1978:28) argues for the elimination of "the Orient" and "the Occident" altogether. By this he means not the erasure of all differences but the recognition of more of them and of the complex ways in which they crosscut. More important, his analysis of one field seeks to show how and when certain differences, in this case of places and the people attached to them, become implicated in the domination of one by the other. Should anthropologists treat with similar suspicion "culture" and "cultures" as the key terms in a discourse in which otherness and difference have come to have, as Said (1989:213) points out, "talismanic qualities"?

Notes

None of the many people to whom I am indebted for conversations on which I have built over the years should be held liable for what I made of them. As a Mellon Fellow at the University of Pennsylvania, I benefitted from discussions with Arjun Appadurai, Carol Breckenridge, and various participants in the South Asia Program's seminar on "Orientalism and Beyond." I am grateful also to the members of the 1987–88 Gender Seminar at the Institute for Advanced Study (in which I was able to participate through generous support from the National Endowment for the Humanities) for intense and helpful discussions about feminist theory. Dan Rosenberg first started me thinking critically about the parallels between "culture" and "race." Tim Mitchell helped me clarify many aspects of my argument, as did the participants in the enormously stimulating advanced seminar at the School of American Research, where I first presented this paper. Ultimately, however, it has been the generosity of the Awlad ᶜAli families in Egypt with whom I have lived that has made me seek ways to undermine notions of otherness. My most recent extended stay with them, in 1987, was made possible by a Fulbright Islamic Civilization Award.

1. *Halfies* is a term I borrowed from Kirin Narayan (personal communication).
2. Likewise, Marcus and Clifford (1985) and Marcus and Fischer (1986) gesture toward feminists as important sources of cultural and anthropological critique but do not discuss their work. Fischer (1984, 1986, 1988), however, has long been interested in the phenomenon of biculturality.
3. It is still rare for anthropologists in this society or others to do what Laura Nader (1969) advocated many years ago—to "study up."
4. Its various strategies are based on this division and the series of oppositions (culture/nature, public/private, work/home, transcendence/immediacies, abstract/ particular, objectivity/subjectivity, autonomy/connectedness, etc.) associated with it: (a) women should be allowed to join the valued men's world, to become like men or have their privileges, (b) women's values and work, even if different, should be as valued as men's, or (c) women and men should both change and enter each other's spheres so that gender differences are erased.
5. It does not, Harding adds, dissolve feminism as a political identity, but the most pressing issue in feminist circles now is how to develop a politics of solidarity, coalition, or affinity built on the recognition of difference rather than the solidarity of a unitary self defined by its opposition to an other which had formerly defined it as other. The most interesting thinking on this subject has been Haraway's (1985).
6. For a discussion of the convergence of anthropological and feminist critiques of objectivity, see Abu-Lughod (1990a).
7. In his 1988 address to the American Anthropological Association, Edward Said's central point was that anthropologists had to attend not just to "the anthropological site" but to the "cultural situation in which anthropological work is in fact done" (1989:212).
8. Much of the literature on indigenous anthropology is taken up with the advantages and disadvantages of this identification. See Fahim (1982) and Altorki and El-Solh (1988).
9. See also my discussion of the study of gender in Middle East anthropology (L. Abu-Lughod 1989).
10. In parallel fashion, those who study the black experience are thought of as studying a marked form of experience. It could be pointed out, and has been by such figures as Adrienne Rich, that the universal unmarked form of experience from which it differs is itself partial. It is the experience of whiteness.

11. Crapanzano (1977) has written insightfully about the regular process of distancing from the fieldwork experience and building identifications with the anthropological audience that all anthropologists go through when they return from the field.
12. This is happening, for example, in heated debates in the field of Middle East women's studies about who has the right to speak for Middle Eastern women.
13. Some would like to make distinctions between "womanism" and "feminism," but in much of literature they blur together.
14. Arens (1979), for example, has asked the provocative question of why anthropologists cling so tenaciously to the belief that in some cultures cannibalism is an accepted ritual practice, when the evidence (in the form of eye witness accounts) is so meager (if not, as he argues, absent).

Reference

Abu-Lughod, Lila 1989 Zones of theory in the anthropology of the Arab world. *Annual Review of Anthropology* 18:276–306. 1990a Can there be feminist ethnography? *Women and Performance: A Journal of Feminist Theory* 5:7–27. 1990b Shifting politics in Bedouin love poetry. In *Language and the Politics of Emotion*. C. Lutz and L. Abu-Lughod, eds. New York: Cambridge University Press.

Altorki, Soraya, and Camillia El-Solh 1988 *Arab Women in the Field: Studying Your Own Society*. Syracuse, NY: Syracuse University Press.

Appadurai, Arjun 1988 Putting hierarchy in its place. *Cultural Anthropology* 3:36–49.

Arens, William 1979 *The Man-Eating Myth: Anthropology and Anthropophagy*. New York: Oxford University Press.

Asad, Talal 1973 *Anthropology and the Colonial Encounter*. London: Ithaca Press.

Belenky, Mary, Blithe Clinchy, Nancy Goldberger, and Jill Tarule 1986 *Women's Ways of Knowing*. New York: Basic Books.

Bell, Diane 1983 *Daughters of the Dreaming*. Melbourne: McPhee Gribble/N. Sydney: George Allen & Unwin.

Bourdieu, Pierre 1977 *Outline of a Theory of Practice*. Trans. R. Nice. Cambridge: Cambridge University Press.

Chodorow, Nancy 1978 *The Reproduction of Mothering*. Berkeley: University of California Press.

Cixous, Helene 1983 The laugh of the Medusa. In *The Signs Reader*. K. Cohen and P. Cohen, trans., E. Abel and E. Abe, eds., pp. 279–97. Chicago: University of Chicago Press.

Clifford, James 1983a Power in dialogue in ethnography. In *Observers Observed: Essays on Ethnographic Fieldwork*. G. W. Stocking, Jr., ed., pp. 121–56. Madison: University of Wisconsin Press. 1986a Introduction: partial truths. In *Writing Culture: The Poetics and Politics of Ethnography*. J. Clifford and G. Marcus, eds., pp. 1–26. Berkeley: University of California Press. 1988a On collecting art and culture. In *The Predicament of Culture: Twentieth-Century Ethnography, Literature, and Art*.

James Clifford, pp. 215–51. Cambridge, MA: Harvard University Press. 1988b On ethnographic self fashioning. In *The Predicament of Culture: Twentieth-Century Ethnography, Literature, and Art.* James Clifford, pp. 92–113. Cambridge, MA: Harvard University Press.

Clifford, James, and George E. Marcus, eds. 1986 *Writing Culture: The Poetics and Politics of Ethnography.* Berkeley: University of California Press.

Crapanzano, Vincent 1977 On the writing of ethnography. *Dialetical Anthropology* 2: 69–73. 1980 *Tuhami: Portrait of a Moroccan.* Chicago: University of Chicago Press.

Dumont, Jean-Paul 1978 *The Headman and I.* Austin: University of Texas Press.

Dwyer Kevin 1982 *Moroccan Dialogues: Anthropology in Question.* Baltimore: The Johns Hopkins University Press.

Echols, Alice 1984 The taming of the id: feminist sexual politics 1968–83. In *Pleasure and Danger.* C. Vance, ed. Boston: Routledge and Kegan Paul.

Fabian, Johannes 1983 *Time and the Other: How Anthropology Makes Its Object.* New York: Columbia University Press.

Fahim, Hussein, ed. 1982 *Indigenous Anthropology in Non-Western Countries.* Durham, NC: North Carolina Academic Press.

Fischer, Michael M. J. 1984 Towards a third world poetics: seeing through short stories and films in the Iranian culture area. *Knowledge and Society* 5:171–241. 1986 Ethnicity and the post-modern arts of memory. In *Writing Culture: The Poetics and Politics of Ethnography.* J. Clifford and G. Marcus, eds., pp. 194–233. Berkeley: University of California Press. 1988 Aestheticized emotions and critical hermeneutics. *Culture, Medicine and Psychiatry* 12:31–42.

Geertz, Clifford 1973a The impact of the concept of culture on the concept of man. In *The Interpretation of Cultures.* Clifford Geertz, pp. 33–54. New York: Basic Books.

Gilligan, Carol 1982 *In a Different Voice.* Cambridge, MA: Harvard University Press.

Haraway, Donna 1985 A manifesto for cyborgs: science technology and socialist feminism in the 1980s. *Socialist Review* 80:65–107.

Harding, Sandra 1986 *The Science Question in Feminism.* Ithaca: Cornell University Press. 1987 The method question. *Hypatia* 2:19–35.

Hartsock, Nancy 1985 *Money, Sex, and Power: Toward a Feminist Historical Materialism.* Boston: Northeastern University Press.

Hymes, Dell 1969 *Reinventing Anthropology.* New York: Pantheon.

Irigaray, Luce 1985a *Speculum of the Other Woman.* G. C. Gill, trans. Ithaca: Cornell University Press. 1985b *This Sex Which Is Not One.* C. Porter with C. Burks, trans. Ithaca: Cornell University Press.

Joseph, Suad 1988 Feminization, familism, self, and politics: research as a *Mughtaribi.* In *Arab Women in the Field: Studying Your Own Society.* S. Altorki and C. El-Solh, eds., pp. 25–47. Syracuse, NY: Syracuse University Press.

Kondo, Dorinne 1986 Dissolution and reconstitution of self: implications for anthropological epistemology. *Cultural Anthropology* 1:74–88.

Kristeva, Julia 1981 Women's time. A. Jardine and H. Blake, trans. *Signs* 7:13–35.

Kuper, Adam 1988 *The Invention of Primitive Society: Transformation of an Illusion.* Boston and London: Routledge and Kegan Paul.

MacKinnon, Catherine 1982 Feminism, Marxism, method, and the state: an agenda for theory. *Signs* 7:515–44.

Marcus, George E., and James Clifford 1985 The making of ethnographic texts: preliminary report. *Current Anthropology* 26:267–71.

Marcus, George, and Michael M. J. Fischer 1986 *Anthropology as Cultural Critique: An Experimental Moment in the Human Sciences.* Chicago: University of Chicago Press.

Meis, Maria 1983 Towards a methodology for feminist research. In *Theories of Women's Studies.* G. Bowles and R. D. Klein, eds. Boston and London: Routledge and Kegan Paul.

Morsy, Soheir 1988 Fieldwork in my Egyptian homeland: toward the demise of anthropology's distinctive-other hegemonic tradition. In *Arab Women in the Field: Studying Your Own Society.* S. Altorki and C. El-Solh, eds., pp. 69–90. Syracuse: Syracuse University Press.

Nader, Laura 1969 "Up the anthropologist"—perspectives gained from studying up. In *Reinventing Anthropology.* D. Hymes, ed., pp. 284–311. New York: Random House.

Narayan, Kirin 1989 *Saints, Scoundrels, and Storytellers.* Philadelphia: University of Pennsylvania Press.

Rabinow, Paul 1977 *Reflections on Fieldwork in Morocco.* Berkeley: University of California Press. 1986 Representations are social facts: modernity and post-modernity in anthropology. In *Writing Culture: The Poetics and Politics of Ethnography.* J. Clifford and G. Marcus, eds., pp. 234–61. Berkeley: University of California Press.

Reinharz, Shulamit 1983 Experimental analysis: a contribution to feminist research. In *Theories of Women's Studies.* G. Bowles and R. D. Klein, eds., pp. 162–91. London and Boston: Routledge and Kegan Paul.

Rich, Adrienne 1979 Toward a woman-centered university. In *On Lies, Secrets and Silence,* pp. 125–56. New York: W. W. Norton & Co.

Riesman, Paul 1977 *Freedom in Fulani Social Life.* Chicago: University of Chicago Press.

Ruddick, Sara 1980 Maternal thinking. *Feminist Studies* 6(2): 342–67.

Said, Edward 1978 *Orientalism.* New York: Pantheon. 1989 Representing the colonized: anthropology's interlocuters. *Critical Inquiry* 15:205–25.

Smith, Dorothy 1987 *The Everyday World as Problematic.* Boston: Northeastern University Press.

Stanley, Liz, and Sue Wise 1983 *Breaking Out: Feminist Consciousness and Feminist Research.* London: Routledge and Kegan Paul.

Strathern, Marilyn 1985 Dislodging a worldview: challenge and counter-challenge in the relationship between feminism and anthropology. *Australian Feminist Studies* 1:1–25. 1987a An awkward relationship: the case of feminism and anthropology. *Signs* 12:276–92.

Tedlock, Dennis 1983 *The Spoken Word and the Work of Interpretation.* Philadelphia: University of Pennsylvania Press. 1987 Questions concerning dialogical anthropology. *Journal of Anthropolgical Research* 43: 325–37.

Tyler, Stephen 1986 Post-modern ethnography: from document of the occult to occult document. In *Writing Culture: The Poetics and Politics of Ethnography.* J. Clifford and G. Marcus, eds., pp. 122–140. Berkeley: University of California Press.

Weiner, Annette 1976 *Women of Value, Men of Renown.* Austin: University of Texas Press.

Chapter 3

Methods and Perspectives for Studying Culture

DISCUSSION QUESTIONS

1. This excerpt from Malinowski's ethnography includes his now famous description of his arrival to the Trobriand Islands. What do you learn about doing ethnographic fieldwork from this description? How was Boellstorff's experience entering the world of Second Life similar to or different than Malinowski's? How did each of them make entry into the cultural context they were studying and begin learning about the people there?
2. Why do Malinowski and Boellstorff claim it's important to both talk to (interview) ethnographic participants as well as conduct participant observation of their everyday lives? How is this related to each author's discussion about what kinds of knowledge people have about their own cultures and their ability (or not) to articulate them?
3. Both Malinowski and Boellstorff write about the importance of ethnographers learning about the "imponderabilia of actual life" or, in other words, the mundane and ordinary aspects of life. Why is this important to doing ethnography, and how do ethnographers go about accessing these aspects of life?
4. What are some of the ethical considerations ethnographers must contend with, according to Boellstorff? Did Malinowski address any of these issues? Do you find anything ethically problematic with how Malinowski conducted his research?

KEY TERMS

Ethnography
Elicitation methods
Participant observation
Interviews

Malinowski, Bronislaw. 1922. "The Subject, Method and Scope of this Inquiry." In *Argonauts of the Western Pacific*. Prospect Heights: Waveland Press. [excerpt]

I

The coastal populations of the South Sea Islands, with very few exceptions, are, or were before their extinction, expert navigators and traders. Several of them had evolved excellent types of large sea-going canoes, and used to embark in them on distant trade expeditions or raids of war and conquest. The Papuo-Melanesians, who inhabit the coast and the outlying islands of New Guinea, are no exception to this rule. In general they are daring sailors, industrious manufacturers, and keen traders. The manufacturing centres of important articles, such as pottery, stone implements, canoes, fine baskets, valued ornaments, are localised in several places, according to the skill of the inhabitants, their inherited tribal tradition, and special facilities offered by the district; thence they are traded over wide areas, sometimes travelling more than hundreds of miles.

Definite forms of exchange along definite trade routes are to be found established between the various tribes. A most remarkable form of intertribal trade is that obtaining between the Motu of Port Moresby and the tribes of the Papuan Gulf. The Motu sail for hundreds of miles in heavy, unwieldy canoes, called *lakatoi,* which are provided with the characteristic crab-claw sails. They bring pottery and shell ornaments, in olden days, stone blades, to Gulf Papuans, from whom they obtain in exchange sago and the heavy dug-outs, which are used afterwards by the Motu for the construction of their *lakatoi* canoes.[1]

Further East, on the South coast, there lives the industrious, sea-faring population of the Mailu, who link the East End of New Guinea with the central coast tribes by means of annual trading expeditions.[2] Finally, the natives of the islands and archipelagoes, scattered around the East End, are in constant trading relations with one another. We possess in Professor Seligman's book an excellent description of the subject, especially of the nearer trades routes between the various islands inhabited by the Southern Massim.[3] There exists, however, another, a very extensive and highly complex trading system, embracing with its ramifications, not only the islands near the East End, but also the Louisiades, Woodlark Island, the Trobriand Archipelago, and the d'Entrecasteaux group; it penetrates into the mainland of New Guinea, and exerts an indirect influence over several outlying districts, such as Rossel Island, and some parts of the Northern and Southern coast of New Guinea. This trading system, the Kula, is the subject I am setting out to describe in this volume, and it will be seen that it is an economic phenomenon of considerable theoretical importance. It looms paramount in the tribal life of those natives who live within its circuit, and its importance

Bronislaw Malinowski, "The Subject, Method, And Scope Of This Inquiry," Argonauts Of The Western Pacific: An Account of Native Enterprise and Adventure in the Archipelagos of Melanesian New Guinea, Routledge UK, pp. 1-25, 1922.

is fully realised by the tribesmen themselves, whose ideas, ambitions, desires and vanities are very much bound up with the Kula

II

Before proceeding to the account of the Kula, it will be well to give a description of the methods used in the collecting of the ethnographic material. The results of scientific research in any branch of learning ought to be presented in a manner absolutely candid and above board. No one would dream of making an experimental contribution to physical or chemical science, without giving a detailed account of all the arrangements of the experiments; an exact description of the apparatus used; of the manner in which the observations were conducted; of their number; of the length of time devoted to them, and of the degree of approximation with which each measurement was made. In less exact sciences, as in biology or geology, this cannot be done as rigorously, but every student will do his best to bring home to the reader all the conditions in which the experiment or the observations were made. In Ethnography, where a candid account of such data is perhaps even more necessary, it has unfortunately in the past not always been supplied with sufficient generosity, and many writers do not ply the full searchlight of methodic sincerity, as they move among their facts but produce them before us out of complete obscurity.

It would be easy to quote works of high repute, and with a scientific hall-mark on them, in which wholesale generalisations are laid down before us, and we are not informed at all by what actual experiences the writers have reached their conclusion. No special chapter or paragraph is devoted to describing to us the conditions under which observations were made and information collected. I consider that only such ethnographic sources are of unquestionable scientific value, in which we can clearly draw the line between, on the one hand, the results of direct observation and of native statements and interpretations, and on the other, the inferences of the author, based on his common sense and psycholgical insight.[4] Indeed, some such survey, as that contained in the table, given below (Div. VI of this chapter) ought to be forthcoming, so that at a glance the reader could estimate with precision the degree of the writer's personal acquaintance with the facts which he describes, and form an idea under what conditions information had been obtained from the natives.

Again, in historical science, no one could expect to be seriously treated if he made any mystery of his sources and spoke of the past as if he knew it by divination. In Ethnography, the writer is his own chronicler and the historian at the same time, while his sources are no doubt easily accessible, but also supremely elusive and complex; they are not embodied in fixed, material documents, but in the behaviour and in the memory of living men. In Ethnography, the distance is often enormous between the brute material of information—as it is presented to the student in his own observations, in native statement, in the kaleidoscope of tribal life—and the final authoritative presentation of the results. The Ethnographer has to traverse this distance in the laborious years between the moment when he sets foot upon a native beach, and makes his first attempts to get into touch with the natives, and the time when he writes down the final version of his results. A brief outline of an Ethnographer's tribulations, as lived through by myself, may throw more light on the question, than any long abstract discussion could do.

III

Imagine yourself suddenly set down surrounded by all your gear, alone on a tropical beach close to a native village, while the launch or dinghy which has brought you sails away out of sight. Since you take up your abode in the compound of some neighbouring white man, trader or missionary, you have nothing to do, but to start at once on your ethnographic work. Imagine further that you are a beginner, without previous experience, with nothing to guide you and no one to help you. For the white man is temporarily absent, or else unable or unwilling to waste any of his time on you. This exactly describes my first initiation into field work on the south coast of New Guinea. I well remember the long visits I paid to the villages during the first weeks; the feeling of hopelessness and despair after many obstinate but futile attempts had entirely failed to bring me into real touch with the natives, or supply me with any material. I had periods of despondency, when I buried myself in the reading of novels, as a man might take to drink in a fit of tropical depression and boredom.

Imagine yourself then, making your first entry into the village, alone or in company with your white cicerone. Some natives flock round you, especially if they smell tobacco. Others, the more dignified and elderly, remain seated where they are. Your white companion has his routine way of treating the natives, and he neither understands, nor is very much concerned with the manner in which you, as an ethnographer, will have to approach them. The first visit leaves you with a hopeful feeling that when you return alone, things will be easier. Such was my hope at least.

I came back duly, and soon gathered an audience around me. A few compliments in pidgin-English on both sides, some tobacco changing hands, induced an atmosphere of mutual amiability. I tried then to proceed to business. First, to begin with subjects which might arouse no suspicion, I started to "do" technology. A few natives were engaged in manufacturing some object or other. It was easy to look at it and obtain the names of the tools, and even some technical expressions about the proceedings, but there the matter ended. It must be borne in mind that pidgin-English is a very imperfect instrument for expressing one's ideas, and that before one gets a good training in framing questions and understanding answers one has the uncomfortable feeling that free communication in it with the natives will never be attained; and I was quite unable to enter into any more detailed or explicit conversation with them at first. I knew well that the best remedy for this was to collect concrete data, and accordingly I took a village census, wrote down genealogies, drew up plans and collected the terms of kinship. But all this remained dead material, which led no further into the understanding of real native mentality or behaviour, since I could neither procure a good native interpretation of any of these items, nor get what could be called the hang of tribal life. As to obtaining their ideas about religion, and magic, their beliefs in sorcery and spirits, nothing was forthcoming except a few superficial items of folk-lore, mangled by being forced into pidgin English.

Information which I received from some white residents in the district, valuable as it was in itself, was more discouraging than anything else with regard to my own work. Here were men who had lived for years in the place with constant opportunities of observing the natives and communicating with them, and who yet hardly knew one thing about them really well. How could I therefore in a few months or a year, hope to overtake and go beyond them? Moreover, the manner in which my white informants spoke about the natives and put their views was, naturally, that of untrained minds, unaccustomed to formulate their thoughts with any degree of consistency and precision. And they were for the most part, naturally enough, full of the biassed and pre-judged opinions inevitable in the average practical man, whether administrator, missionary, or trader, yet so strongly repulsive to a mind striving after the objective, scientific view of things. The habit of treating with a self-satisfied frivolity what is really serious to the ethnographer; the cheap rating of what to him is a scientific treasure, that is to say, the native's cultural and mental peculiarities and independence—these features, so well known in the inferior amateur's writing, I found in the tone of the majority of white residents.[5]

Indeed, in my first piece of Ethnographic research on the South coast, it was not until I was alone in the district that I began to make some headway; and, at any rate, I found out where lay the secret of effective field-work. What is then this ethnographer's magic, by which he is able to evoke the real spirit of the natives, the true picture of tribal life? As usual, success can only be obtained by a patient and systematic application of a number of rules of common sense and well-known scientific principles, and not by the discovery of any marvellous short-cut leading to the desired results without effort or trouble. The principles of method can be grouped under three main headings; first of all, naturally, the student must possess real scientific aims, and know the values and criteria of modern ethnography. Secondly, he ought to put himself in good conditions of work, that is, in the main, to live without other white men, right among the natives. Finally, he has to apply a number of special methods of collecting, manipulating and fixing his evidence. A few words must be said about these three foundation stones of field work, beginning with the second as the most elementary.

IV

Proper conditions for ethnographic work. These, as said, consist mainly in cutting oneself off from the company of other white men, and remaining in as close contact with the natives as possible, which really can only be achieved by camping right in their villages (see Plates I and II). It is very nice to have a base in a white man's compound for the stores, and to know there is a refuge there in times of sickness and surfeit of native. But it must be far enough away not to become a permanent milieu in which you live and from which you emerge at fixed hours only to "do the village." It should not even be near enough to fly to at any moment for recreation. For the native is not the natural companion for a white man, and after you have been working with him for several hours, seeing how he does his gardens, or letting him tell you items of folk-lore, or discussing his customs, you will naturally hanker after the company of your own kind. But if you are alone in a village beyond reach of this, you go for a solitary walk for an hour or so, return again and then quite naturally seek out the natives' society, this time as a relief from loneliness, just as you would any other companionship. And by means of this natural intercourse, you learn to know him, and you become familiar with his customs and beliefs far better than when he is a paid, and often bored, informant.

There is all the difference between a sporadic plunging into the company of natives, and being really in contact with them. What does this latter mean? On the Ethnographer's side, it means that his life in the village, which at first is a strange, sometimes unpleasant, sometimes intensely interesting adventure, soon adopts quite a natural course very much in harmony with his surroundings.

Soon after I had established myself in Omarakana (Trobriand Islands), I began to take part, in a way, in the village life, to look forward to the important or festive events, to take personal interest in the gossip and the developments of the small village occurrences; to wake up every morning to a day, presenting itself to me more or less as it does to the native. I would get out from under my mosquito net, to find around me the village life beginning to stir, or the people well advanced in their working day according to the hour and also to the season, for they get up and begin their labours early or late, as work presses. As I went on my morning walk through the village, I could see intimate details of family life, of toilet, cooking, taking of meals; I could see the arrangements for the day's work, people starting on their errands, or groups of men and women busy at some manufacturing tasks (see Plate III). Quarrels, jokes, family scenes, events usually trivial, sometimes dramatic but always significant, formed the atmosphere of my daily life, as well as of theirs. It must be remembered that as the natives saw me constantly every day, they ceased to be interested or alarmed, or made self-conscious by my presence, and I ceased to be a disturbing element in the tribal life which I was to study, altering it by my very approach, as always happens with a new-comer to every savage community. In fact, as they knew that I would thrust my nose into everything, even where a well-mannered native would not dream of intruding, they finished by regarding me as part and parcel of their life, a necessary evil or nuisance, mitigated by donations of tobacco.

Later on in the day, whatever happened was within easy reach, and there was no possibility of its escaping my notice. Alarms about the sorcerer's approach in the evening, one or two big, really important quarrels and rifts within the community, cases of illness, attempted cures and deaths, magical rites which had to be performed, all these I had not to pursue, fearful of missing them, but they took place under my very eyes, at my own doorstep, so to speak (see Plate IV). And it must be emphasised whenever anything dramatic or important occurs it is essential to investigate it at the very moment of happening, because the natives cannot but talk about it, are too excited to be reticent, and too interested to be mentally lazy in supplying details. Also, over and over again, I committed breaches of etiquette, which the natives, familiar enough with me, were not slow in pointing out. I had to learn how to behave, and to a certain extent, I acquired "the feeling" for native good and bad manners. With this, and with the capacity of enjoying their company and sharing some of their games and amusements, I began to feel that I was indeed in touch with the natives, and this is certainly the preliminary condition of being able to carry on successful field work.

V

But the Ethnographer has not only to spread his nets in the right place, and wait for what will fall into them. He must be an active huntsman, and drive his quarry into them and follow it up to its most inaccessible lairs. And that leads us to the more active methods of pursuing ethnographic evidence. It has been mentioned at the end of Division III that the Ethnographer has to be inspired by the knowledge of the most modern results of scientific study, by its principles and aims. I shall not enlarge upon this subject, except by way of one remark, to avoid the possibility of misunderstanding. Good training in theory, and acquaintance with its latest results, is not identical with being burdened with "preconceived ideas." If a man sets out on an expedition, determined to prove certain hypotheses, if he is incapable of changing his views constantly and casting them off ungrudgingly under the pressure of evidence, needless to say his work will be worthless. But the more problems he brings with him into the field, the more he is in the habit of moulding his theories according to facts, and of seeing facts in their bearing upon theory, the better he is equipped for the work. Preconceived ideas are pernicious in any scientific work, but foreshadowed problems are the main endowment of a scientific thinker, and these problems are first revealed to the observer by his theoretical studies.

In Ethnology the early efforts of Bastian, Tylor, Morgan, the German Völkerpsychologen have remoulded the older crude information of travellers, missionaries, etc., and have shown us the importance of applying deeper conceptions and discarding crude and misleading ones.[6]

The concept of animism superseded that of "fetichism" or "devil-worship," both meaningless terms. The understanding of the classificatory systems of relationship paved the way for the brilliant, modern researches on native sociology in the field-work of the Cambridge school. The psychological analysis of the German thinkers has brought forth an abundant crop of most valuable information in the results obtained by the recent German expeditions to Africa, South America and the Pacific, while the theoretical works of Frazer, Durkheim and others have already, and will no doubt still for a long time inspire field workers and lead them to new results. The field worker relies entirely upon inspiration from theory. Of course he may be also a theoretical thinker and worker, and there he can draw on himself for stimulus. But the two functions are separate, and in actual research they have to be separated both in time and conditions of work.

As always happens when scientific interest turns towards and begins to labour on a field so far only prospected by the curiosity of amateurs, Ethnology has introduced law and order into what seemed chaotic and freakish. It has transformed for us the sensational, wild and unaccountable world of "savages" into a number of well ordered communities, governed by law, behaving and thinking according to consistent principles. The word "savage," whatever association it might have had originally, connotes ideas of boundless liberty, of irregularity, of something extremely and extraordinarily quaint. In popular thinking, we imagine that the natives live on the bosom of Nature, more or less as they can and like, the prey of irregular, phantasmagoric beliefs and apprehensions. Modern science, on the contrary, shows that their social institutions have a very definite organisation, that they are governed by authority, law and order in their public and personal relations, while the latter are, besides, under the control of extremely complex ties of kinship and clanship. Indeed, we see them entangled in a mesh of duties, functions and privileges which correspond to an elaborate tribal, communal and kinship organisation (see Plate IV). Their beliefs and practices do not by any means lack consistency of a certain type, and their knowledge of the outer world is sufficient to guide them in many of their strenuous enterprises and activities. Their artistic productions again lack neither meaning nor beauty.

It is a very far cry from the famous answer given long ago by a representative authority who, asked, what are the manners and customs of the natives, answered, "Customs none, manners beastly," to the position of the modern Ethnographer! This latter, with his tables of kinship terms, genealogies, maps, plans and diagrams, proves the existence of an extensive and big organisation, shows the constitution of the tribe, of the clan, of the family; and he gives us a picture of the natives subjected to a strict code of behaviour and good manners, to which in comparison the life at the Court of Versailles or Escurial was free and easy.[7]

Thus the first and basic ideal of ethnographic field-work is to give a clear and firm outline of the social constitution, and disentangle the laws and regularities of all cultural phenomena from the irrelevances. The firm skeleton of the tribal life has to be first ascertained. This ideal imposes in the first place the fundamental obligation of giving a complete survey of the phenomena, and not of picking out the sensational, the singular, still less the funny and quaint. The time when we could tolerate accounts presenting us the native as a distorted, childish caricature of a human being are gone. This picture is false, and like many other falsehoods, it has been killed by Science. The field Ethnographer has seriously and soberly to cover the full extent of the phenomena in each aspect of tribal culture studied, making no difference between what is commonplace, or drab, or ordinary, and what strikes him as astonishing and out-of-the-way. At the same time, the whole area of tribal culture *in all its aspects* has to be gone over in research. The consistency, the law and order which obtain within each aspect make also for joining them into one coherent whole.

An Ethnographer who sets out to study only religion, or only technology, or only social organisation cuts out an artificial field for inquiry, and he will be seriously handicapped in his work.

VI

Having settled this very general rule, let us descend to more detailed consideration of method. The Ethnographer has in the field, according to what has just been said, the duty before him of drawing up all the rules and regularities of tribal life; all that is permanent and fixed; of giving an anatomy of their culture, of depicting the constitution of their society. But these things, though crystallised and set, are nowhere *formulated.* There is no written or explicitly expressed code of laws, and their whole tribal tradition, the whole structure of their society, are embodied in the most elusive of all materials; the human being. But not even in human mind or memory are these laws to be found definitely formulated. The natives obey the forces and commands of the tribal code, but they do not comprehend them; exactly as they obey their instincts and their impulses, but could not lay down a single law of psychology. The regularities in native institutions are an automatic result of the interaction of the mental forces of tradition, and of the material conditions of environment. Exactly as a humble member of any modern institution, whether it be the state, or the church, or the army, is *of* it and *in* it, but has no vision of the resulting integral action of the whole, still less could furnish any account of its organisation, so it would be futile to attempt questioning a native in abstract, sociological terms. The difference is that, in our society, every institution has its intelligent members, its historians, and its archives and documents, whereas in a native society there are none of these. After this is realised an expedient has to be found to overcome this difficulty. This expedient for an Ethnographer consists in collecting concrete data of evidence, and drawing the general inferences for himself. This seems obvious on the face of it, but was not found out or at least practised in Ethnography till field work was taken up by men of science. Moreover, in giving it practical effect, it is neither easy to devise the concrete applications of this method, nor to carry them out systematically and consistently.

Though we cannot ask a native about abstract, general rules, we can always enquire how a given case would be treated. Thus for instance, in asking how they would treat crime, or punish it, it would be vain to put to a native a sweeping question such as, "How do you treat and punish a criminal?" for even words could not be found to express it in native, or in pidgin. But an imaginary case, or still better, a real occurrence, will stimulate a native to express his opinion and to supply plentiful information. A real case indeed will start the natives on a wave of discussion, evoke expressions of indignation, show them taking sides—all of which talk will probably contain a wealth of definite views, of moral censures, as well as reveal the social mechanism set in motion by the crime committed. From there, it will be easy to lead them on to speak of other similar cases, to remember other actual occurrences or to discuss them in all their implications and aspects. From this material, which ought to cover the widest possible range of facts, the inference is obtained by simple induction. The *scientific* treatment differs from that of good common sense, first in that a student will extend the completeness and minuteness of survey much further and in a pedantically systematic and methodical manner; and secondly, in that the scientifically trained mind, will push the inquiry along really relevant lines, and towards aims possessing real importance. Indeed, the object of scientific training is to provide the empirical investigator with a *mental chart*, in accordance with which he can take his bearings and lay his course.

To return to our example, a number of definite cases discussed will reveal to the Ethnographer the social machinery for punishment. This is one part, one aspect of tribal authority. Imagine further that by a similar method of inference from definite data, he arrives at understanding leadership in war, in economic enterprise, in tribal festivities—there he has at once all the data necessary to answer the questions about tribal government and social authority. In actual field work, the comparison of such data, the attempt to piece them together, will often reveal rifts and gaps in the information which lead on to further investigations.

From my own experience, I can say that, very often, a problem seemed settled, everything fixed and clear, till I began to write down a short preliminary sketch of my results. And only then, did I see the enormous deficiencies, which would show me where lay new problems, and lead me on to new work. In fact, I spent a few months between my first and second expeditions, and over a year between that and the subsequent one, in going over all my material, and making parts of it almost ready for publication each time, though each time I knew I would have to re-write it. Such cross-fertilisation of constructive work and observation, I found most valuable, and I do not think I could have made real headway without it. I give this bit of my own history merely to show that what has been said so far is not only an empty programme, but the result of personal experience. In this volume, the description is given of a big institution connected with ever so many associated activities, and presenting many aspects. To anyone who reflects on the subject, it will be clear that the information about a phenomenon of such high complexity and of so many ramifications, could not be obtained with any degree of exactitude and completeness, without a constant interplay of constructive attempts and empirical checking. In fact, I have written up an outline of the Kula institution at least half a dozen times while in the field and in the intervals between my expeditions. Each time, new problems and difficulties presented themselves.

The collecting of concrete data over a wide range of facts is thus one of the main points of field method. The obligation is not to enumerate a few examples only, but to exhaust as far as possible all the cases within reach; and, on this search for cases, the investigator will score most whose mental chart is clearest. But, whenever the material of the search allows it, this mental chart ought to be transformed into a real one; it ought to materialise into a diagram, a plan, an exhaustive, synoptic table of cases. Long since, in all tolerably good modern books on natives, we expect to find a full list or table of kinship terms, which includes all the data relative to it, and does not just pick out a few strange and anomalous relationships or expressions. In the investigation of kinship, the following up of one relation after another in concrete cases leads naturally to the construction of genealogical tables. Practised already by the best early writers, such as Munzinger, and, if I remember rightly, Kubary, this method has been developed to its fullest extent in the works of Dr. Rivers. Again, studying the concrete data of economic transactions, in order to trace the history of a valuable object, and to gauge the nature of its circulation, the principle of completeness and thoroughness would lead to construct tables of transactions, such as we find in the work of Professor Seligman.[8] It is in following Professor Seligman's example in this matter that I was able to settle certain of the more difficult and detailed rules of the Kula. The method of reducing information, if possible, into charts or synoptic tables ought to be extended to the study of practically all aspects of native life. All types of economic transactions may be studied by following up connected, actual cases, and putting them into a synoptic chart; again, a table ought to be drawn up of all the gifts and presents customary in a given society, a table including the sociological, ceremonial, and economic definition of every item. Also, systems of magic, connected series of ceremonies, types of legal acts, all could be charted, allowing each entry to be synoptically defined under a number of headings. Besides this, of course, the genealogical census of every community, studied more in detail, extensive maps, plans and diagrams, illustrating ownership in garden land, hunting and fishing privileges, etc., serve as the more fundamental documents of ethnographic research.

A genealogy is nothing else but a synoptic chart of a number of connected relations of kinship. Its value as an instrument of research consists in that it allows the investigator to put questions which he formulates to himself *in abstracto,* but can put concretely to the native informant. As a document, its value consists in that it gives a number of authenticated data, presented in their natural grouping. A synoptic chart of magic fulfils the same function. As an instrument of research, I have used it in order to ascertain, for instance, the ideas about the nature of magical power. With a chart before me, I could easily and conveniently go over one item after the other, and note down the relevant practices and beliefs contained in each of them. The answer to my abstract problem could then be obtained by drawing a general inference from all the cases, and the procedure is illustrated in Chapters XVII and XVIII.[9] I cannot enter further into the discussion of this question, which would need further distinctions, such as between a chart of concrete, actual data, such as is a genealogy, and a chart summarising the outlines of a custom or belief, as a chart of a magical system would be.

Returning once more to the question of methodological candour, discussed previously in Division II I wish to point out here, that the procedure of concrete and tabularised presentation of data ought to be applied first to the Ethnographer's own credentials. That is, an Ethnographer, who wishes to be trusted, must show clearly and concisely, in a tabularised form, which are his own direct observations, and which the indirect information that form the bases of his account. The Table on the next page will serve as an example of this procedure and help the reader of this book to form an idea of the trustworthiness of any statement he is specially anxious to check. With the help of this Table and the many references scattered throughout the text, as to how, under what circumstances, and with what degree of accuracy I arrived at a given item of knowledge, there will, I hope remain no obscurity whatever as to the sources of the book.

CHRONOLOGICAL LIST OF KULA EVENTS WITNESSED BY THE WRITER

First Expedition, August, 1914—March, 1915.

March, 1915. In the village of Dikoyas (Woodlark Island) a few ceremonial offerings seen. Preliminary information obtained.

Second Expedition, May, 1915—May, 1916.

June, 1915. A Kabigidoya visit arrives from Vakuta to Kiriwina. Its anchoring at Kavataria witnessed and the men seen at Omarakana, where information collected.

July, 1915. Several parties from Kitava land on the beach of Kaulukuba. The men examined in Omarakana. Much information collected in that period.

September, 1915. Unsuccessful attempt to sail to Kitava with To'uluwa, the chief of Omarakana.

October-November, 1915. Departure noticed of three expeditions from Kiriwina to Kitava. Each time To'uluwa brings home a haul of *mwali* (armshells).

November, 1915—*March,* 1916. Preparations for a big overseas expedition from Kiriwina to the Marshall Bennett Islands. Construction of a canoe; renovating of another; sail making in Omarakana; launching; *tasasoria* on the beach of Kaulukuba. At the same time, information is being obtained about these and the associated subjects. Some magical texts of canoe building and Kula magic obtained.

Third Expedition, October, 1917—October, 1918.

November, 1917—*December,* 1917. Inland Kula; some data obtained in Tukwaukwa.

December—February, 1918. Parties from Kitava arrive in Wawela. Collection of information about the *yoyova*. Magic and spells of Kaygau obtained.

March, 1918. Preparations in Sanaroa; preparations in the Amphletts; the Dobuan fleet arrives in the Amphletts. The *uvalaku* expedition from Dobu followed to Boyowa.

April, 1918. Their arrival; their reception in Sinaketa; the Kula transactions; the big intertribal gathering. Some magical formulæ obtained.

May, 1918. Party from Kitava seen in Vakuta.

June, July, 1918. Information about Kula magic and customs checked and amplified in Omarakana, especially with regard to its Eastern branches.

August, September, 1918. Magical texts obtained in Sinaketa.

October, 1918. Information obtained from a number of natives in Dobu and Southern Massim district (examined in Samarai).

Plate I

THE ETHNOGRAPHER'S TENT ON THE BEACH OF NU'AGASI
This illustrates the manner of life among the natives, described on p. 6. Note (with reference to Chs. IV and V) the dug-out log of a large canoe beside the tent, and the ***masawa*** canoe, beached under palm leaves to the left

Plate II

THE CHIEF'S LISIGA (PERSONAL HUT) IN OMARAKANA
To'uluwa, the present chief, is standing in front (cf. Ch. II, Div. V); to the left, among the palms, is the Ethnographer's tent (see p. 6), with a group of natives squatting in front of it

PLATE III

STREET OF KASANA'I (INKIRIWINA, TROBRIAND ISLANDS)
An everyday scene, showing groups of people at their ordinary occupations. (See p. 7.)

PLATE IV

SCENE IN YOURAWOTU (TROBRIANDS)
A complex, but well-defined, act of a *sagali* (ceremonial distribution) is going on. There is a definite system of sociological, economic and ceremonial principles at the bottom of the apparently confused proceedings. (See p. 8.)

To summarise the first, cardinal point of method, I may say each phenomenon ought to be studied through the broadest range possible of its concrete manifestations; each studied by an exhaustive survey of detailed examples. If possible, the results ought to be tabulated into some sort of synoptic chart, both to be used as an instrument of study, and to be presented as an ethnological document. With the help of such documents and such study of actualities the clear outline of the framework of the natives' culture in the widest sense of the word, and the constitution of their society, can be presented. This method could be called *the method of statistic documentation by concrete evidence.*

VII

Needless to add, in this respect, the scientific field-work is far above even the best amateur productions. There is, however, one point in which the latter often excel. This is, in the presentation of intimate touches of native life, in bringing home to us these aspects of it with which one is made familiar only through being in close contact with the natives, one way or the other, for a long period of time. In certain results of scientific work—especially that which has been called "survey work"—we are given an excellent skeleton, so to speak, of the tribal constitution, but it lacks flesh and blood. We learn much about the framework of their society, but within it, we cannot perceive or imagine the realities of human life, the even flow of everyday events, the occasional ripples of excitement over a feast, or ceremony, or some singular occurrence. In working out the rules and regularities of native custom, and in obtaining a precise formula for them from the collection of data and native statements, we find that this very precision is foreign to real life, which never adheres rigidly to any rules. It must be supplemented by the observation of the manner in which a given custom is carried out, of the behaviour of the natives in obeying the rules so exactly formulated by the ethnographer, of the very exceptions which in sociological phenomena almost always occur.

If all the conclusions are solely based on the statements of informants, or deduced from objective documents, it is of course impossible to supplement them in actually observed data of real behaviour. And that is the reason why certain works of amateur residents of long standing, such as educated traders and planters, medical men and officials, and last, but not least, the few intelligent and unbiassed missionaries to whom Ethnography owes so much, surpass in plasticity and in vividness most of the purely scientific accounts. But if the specialised field-worker can adopt the conditions of living described above, he is in a far better position to be really in touch with the natives than any other white resident. For none of them lives right in a native village, except for very short periods, and everyone has his own business, which takes up a considerable part of his time. Moreover, if, like a trader or a missionary or an official he enters into active relations with the native, if he has to transform or influence or make use of him, this makes a real, unbiassed, impartial observation impossible, and precludes all-round sincerity, at least in the case of the missionaries and officials.

Living in the village with no other business but to follow native life, one sees the customs, ceremonies and transactions over and over again, one has examples of their beliefs as they are actually lived through, and the full body and blood of actual native life fills out soon the skeleton of abstract constructions. That is the reason why, working under such conditions as previously described, the Ethnographer is enabled to add something essential to the bare outline of tribal constitution, and to supplement it by all the details of behaviour, setting and small incident. He is able in each case to state whether an act is public or private; how a public assembly behaves, and what it looks like; he can judge whether an event is ordinary or an exciting and singular one ; whether natives bring to it a great deal of sincere and earnest spirit, or perform it in fun ; whether they do it in a perfunctory manner, or with zeal and deliberation.

In other words, there is a series of phenomena of great importance which cannot possibly be recorded by questioning or computing documents, but have to be observed in their full actuality. Let us call them *the inponderabilia of actual life.* Here belong such things as the routine of a man's working day, the details of his care of the body, of the manner of taking food and preparing it; the tone of conversational and social life around the village fires, the existence of strong friendships or hostilities, and of passing sympathies and dislikes between people; the subtle yet unmistakable manner in which personal vanities and ambitions are reflected in the behaviour of the individual and in the emotional reactions of those who surround him. All these facts can and ought to be scientifically formulated and recorded, but it is necessary that this be done, not by a superficial registration of details, as is usually done by untrained observers, but with an effort at penetrating the mental attitude expressed in them. And that is the reason why the work of scientifically trained observers, once seriously applied to the study of this aspect, will, I believe, yield results of surpassing value. So far, it has been done only by amateurs, and therefore done, on the whole, indifferently.

Indeed, if we remember that these imponderable yet all important facts of actual life are part of the real substance of the social fabric, that in them are spun the innumerable threads which keep together the family, the clan, the village community, the tribe—their significance becomes clear. The more crystallised bonds of social grouping, such as the definite ritual, the economic and legal duties, the obligations, the ceremonial gifts and formal marks of regard, though equally important for the student, are certainly felt less strongly by the individual who has to fulfil them. Applying this to ourselves, we all know that "family life" means for us, first and foremost, the atmosphere of home, all the innumerable small acts and attentions in which are expressed the affection, the mutual interest, the little preferences, and the little antipathies which constitute intimacy. That we may inherit from this person, that we shall have to walk after the hearse of the other, though sociologically these facts belong to the definition of "family" and "family life," in personal perspective of what family truly is to us, they normally stand very much in the background.

Exactly the same applies to a native community, and if the Ethnographer wants to bring their real life home to his readers, he must on no account neglect this. Neither aspect, the intimate, as little as the legal, ought to be glossed over. Yet as a rule in ethnographic accounts we have not both but either the one or the other—and, so far, the intimate one has hardly ever been properly treated. In all social relations besides the family ties, even those between mere tribesmen and, beyond that, between hostile or friendly members of different tribes, meeting on any sort of social business, there is this intimate side, expressed by the typical details of intercourse, the tone of their behaviour in the presence of one another. This side is different from the definite, crystalised legal frame of the relationship, and it has to be studied and stated in its own right.

In the same way, in studying the conspicuous acts of tribal life, such as ceremonies, rites, festivities, etc., the details and tone of behaviour ought to be given, besides the bare outline of events. The importance of this may be exemplified by one instance. Much has been said and written about survival. Yet the survival character of an act is expressed in nothing so well as in the concomitant behaviour, in the way in which it is carried out. Take any example from our own culture, whether it be the pomp and pageantry of a state ceremony, or a picturesque custom kept up by street urchins, its "outline" will not tell you whether the rite flourishes still with full vigour in the hearts of those who perform it or assist at the performance or whether they regard it as almost a dead thing, kept alive for tradition's sake. But observe and fix the data of their behaviour, and at once the degree of vitality of the act will become clear. There is no doubt, from all points of sociological, or psychological analysis, and in any question of theory, the manner and type of behaviour observed in the performance of an act is of the highest importance. Indeed behaviour is a fact, a relevant fact, and one that can be recorded. And foolish indeed and short-sighted would be the man of science who would pass by a whole class of phenomena, ready to be garnered, and leave them to waste, even though he did not see at the moment to what theoretical use they might be put!

As to the actual method of observing and recording in fieldwork these *imponderabilia of actual life and of typical behaviour*, there is no doubt that the personal equation of the observer comes in here more prominently, than in the collection of crystalised, ethnographic data. But here also the main endeavour must be to let facts speak for themselves. If in making a daily round of the village, certain small incidents, characteristic forms of taking food, of conversing, of doing work (see for instance Plate III) are found occuring over and over again, they should be noted down at once. It is also important that this work of collecting and fixing impressions should begin early in the course of working out a district.

Because certain subtle peculiarities, which make an impression as long as they are novel, cease to be noticed as soon as they become familiar. Others again can only be perceived with a better knowledge of the local conditions. An ethnographic diary, carried on systematically throughout the course of one's work in a district would be the ideal instrument for this sort of study. And if, side by side with the normal and typical, the ethnographer carefully notes the slight, or the more pronounced deviations from it, he will be able to indicate the two extremes within which the normal moves.

In observing ceremonies or other tribal events, such, for instance as the scene depicted in Plate IV, it is necessary, not only to note down those occurrences and details which are prescribed by tradition and custom to be the essential course of the act, but also the Ethnographer ought to record carefully and precisely, one after the other, the actions of the actors and of the spectators. Forgetting for a moment that he knows and understands the structure of this ceremony, the main dogmatic ideas underlying it, he might try to find himself only in the midst of an assembly of human-beings, who behave seriously or jocularly, with earnest concentration or with bored frivolity, who are either in the same mood as he finds them every day, or else are screwed up to a high pitch of excitement, and so on and so on. With his attention constantly directed to this aspect of tribal life, with the constant endeavour to fix it, to express it in terms of actual fact, a good deal of reliable and expressive material finds its way into his notes. He will be able to "set" the act into its proper place in tribal life, that is to show whether it is exceptional or commonplace, one in which the natives behave ordinarily, or one in which their whole behaviour is transformed. And he will also be able to bring all this home to his readers in a clear, convincing manner.

Again, in this type of work, it is good for the Ethnographer sometimes to put aside camera, note book and pencil, and to join in himself in what is going on. He can take part in the natives' games, he can follow them on their visits and walks, sit down and listen and share in their conversations. I am not certain if this is equally easy for everyone—perhaps the Slavonic nature is more plastic and more naturally savage than that of Western Europeans—but though the degree of success varies, the attempt is possible for everyone. Out of such plunges into the life of the natives—and I made them frequently not only for study's sake but because everyone needs human company—I have carried away a distinct feeling that their behaviour, their manner of being, in all sorts of tribal transactions, became more transparent and easily understandable than it had been before. All these methodological remarks, the reader will find again illustrated in the following chapters.

VIII

Finally, let us pass to the third and last aim of scientific field-work, to the last type of phenomenon which ought to be recorded in order to give a full and adequate picture of native culture. Besides the firm outline of tribal constitution and crystallised cultural items which form the skeleton, besides the data of daily life and ordinary behaviour, which are, so to speak, its flesh and blood, there is still to be recorded the spirit—the natives' views and opinions and utterances. For, in every act of tribal life, there is, first, the routine prescribed by custom and tradition, then there is the manner in which it is carried out, and lastly there is the commentary to it, contained in the natives' mind. A man who submits to various customary obligations, who follows a traditional course of action, does it impelled by certain motives, to the accompaniment of certain feelings, guided by certain ideas. These ideas, feelings, and impulses are moulded and conditioned by the culture in which we find them, and are therefore an ethnic peculiarity of the given society. An attempt must be made therefore, to study and record them.

But is this possible? Are these subjective states not too elusive and shapeless? And, even granted that people usually do feel or think or experience certain psychological states in association with the performance of customary acts, the majority of them surely are not able to formulate these states, to put them into words. This latter point must certainly be granted, and it is perhaps the real Gordian knot in the study of the facts of social psychology. Without trying to cut or untie this knot, that is to solve the problem theoretically, or to enter further into the field of general methodology, I shall make directly for the question of practical means to overcome some of the difficulties involved.

First of all, it has to be laid down that we have to study here stereotyped manners of thinking and feeling. As sociologists, we are not interested in what A or B may feel *qua* individuals, in the accidental course of their own personal experiences—we are interested only in what they feel and think *qua* members of a given community. Now in this capacity, their mental states receive a certain stamp, become stereotyped by the institutions in which they live, by the influence of tradition and folk-lore, by the very vehicle of thought, that is by language. The social and cultural environment in which they move forces them to think and feel in a definite manner. Thus, a man who lives in a polyandrous community cannot experience the same feelings of jealousy, as a strict monogynist, though he might have the elements of them. A man who lives within the sphere of the Kula cannot become permanently and sentimentally attached to certain of his possessions, in spite of the fact that he values them most of all. These examples are crude, but better ones will be found in the text of this book.

So, the third commandment of field-work runs: Find out the typical ways of thinking and feeling, corresponding to the institutions and culture of a given community, and formulate the results in the most convincing manner. What will be the method of procedure? The best ethnographical writers—here again the Cambridge school with Haddon, Rivers, and Seligman rank first among English Ethnographers—have always tried to quote *verbatim* statements of crucial importance. They also adduce terms of native classification; sociological, psychological and industrial *termini technici*, and have rendered the verbal contour of native thought as precisely as possible. One step further in this line can be made by the Ethnographer, who acquires a knowledge of the native language and can use it as an instrument of inquiry. In working in the Kiriwinian language, I found still some difficulty in writing down the statement directly in translation which at first I used to do in the act of taking notes. The translation often robbed the text of all its significant characteristics—rubbed off all its points—so that gradually I was led to note down certain important phrases just as they were spoken, in the native tongue. As my knowledge of the language progressed, I put down more and more in Kiriwinian, till at last I found myself writing exclusively in that language, rapidly taking notes, word for word, of each statement. No sooner had I arrived at this point, than I recognised that I was thus acquiring at the same time an abundant linguistic material, and a series of ethnographic documents which ought to be reproduced as I had fixed them, besides being utilised in the writing up of my account.[10] This *corpus inscriptionum Kiriwiniensium* can be utilised, not only by myself, but by all those who, through their better penetration and ability of interpreting them, may find points which escape my attention, very much as the other *corpora* form the basis for the various interpretations of ancient and prehistoric cultures ; only, these ethnographic inscriptions are all decipherable and clear, have been almost all translated fully and unambiguously, and have been provided with native cross-commentaries or *scholia* obtained from living sources.

No more need be said on this subject here, as later on a whole chapter (Chapter XVIII) is devoted to it, and to its exemplification by several native texts. The *Corpus* will of course be published separately at a later date.

IX

Our considerations thus indicate that the goal of ethnographic field-work must be approached through three avenues:

1. *The organisation of the tribe, and the anatomy of its culture* must be recorded in firm, clear outline. The method of *concrete, statistical documentation* is the means through which such an outline has to be given.
2. Within this frame, the *imponderabilia of actual life,* and the *type of behaviour* have to be filled in. They have to be collected through minute, detailed observations, in the form of some sort of ethnographic diary, made possible by close contact with native life.
3. A collection of ethnographic statements, characteristic narratives, typical utterances, items of folk-lore and magical formulæ has to be given as a *corpus inscriptionum,* as documents of native mentality.

These three lines of approach lead to the final goal, of which an Ethnographer should never lose sight. This goal is, briefly, to grasp the native's point of view, his relation to life, to realise *his* vision of *his* world. We have to study man, and we must study what concerns him most intimately, that is, the hold which life has on him. In each culture, the values are slightly different; people aspire after different aims, follow different impulses, yearn after a different form of happiness. In each culture, we find different institutions in which man pursues his life-interest, different customs by which he satisfies his aspirations, different codes of law and morality which reward his virtues or punish his defections. To study the institutions, customs, and codes or to study the behaviour and mentality without the subjective desire of feeling by what these people live, of realising the substance of their happiness—is, in my opinion, to miss the greatest reward which we can hope to obtain from the study of man.

These generalities the reader will find illustrated in the following chapters. We shall see there the savage striving to satisfy certain aspirations, to attain his type of value, to follow his line of social ambition. We shall see him led on to perilous and difficult enterprises by a tradition of magical and heroical exploits, shall see him following the lure of his own romance. Perhaps as we read the account of these remote customs there may emerge a feeling of solidarity with the endeavours and ambitions of these natives. Perhaps man's mentality will be revealed to us, and brought near, along some lines which we never have followed before. Perhaps through realising human nature in a shape very distant and foreign to us, we shall have some light shed on our own. In this, and in this case only, we shall be justified in feeling that it has been worth our while to understand these natives, their institutions and customs, and that we have gathered some profit from the Kula.

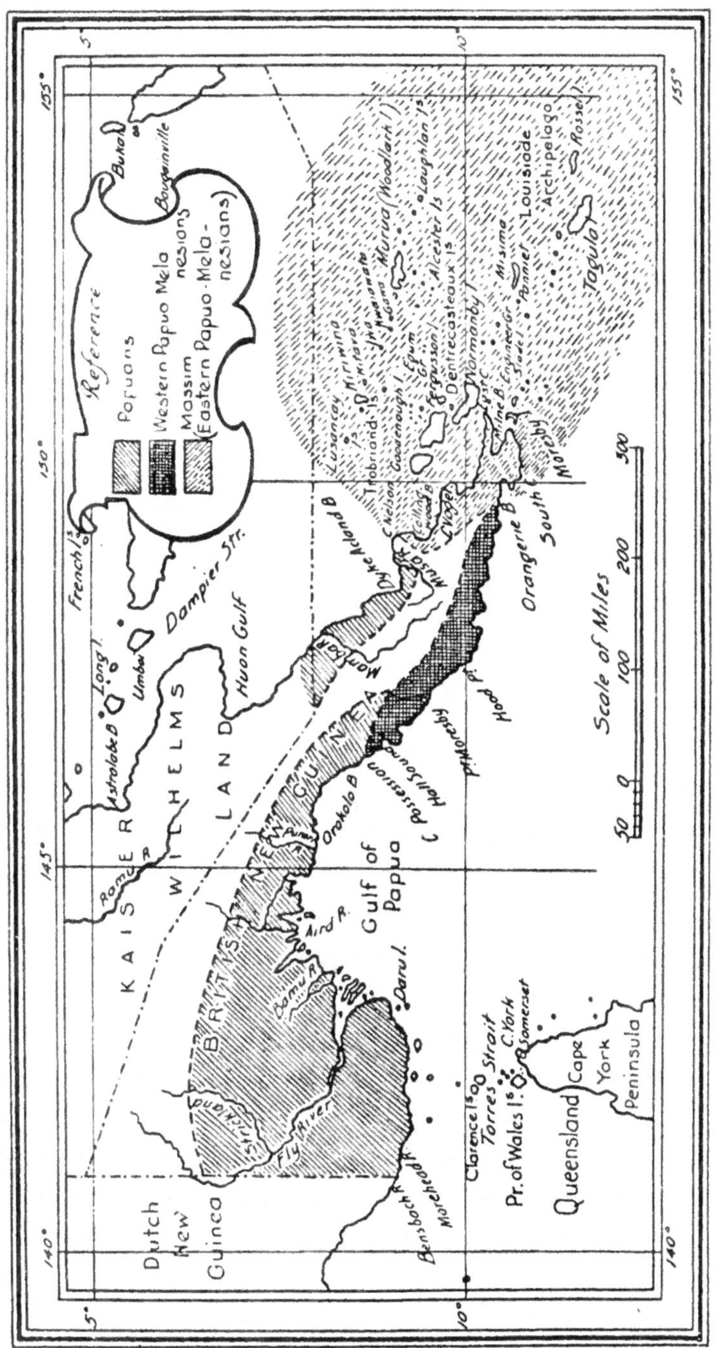

Map II—Diagram showing the geographical area of the Massim and its relation to the districts inhabited by W. Papuo-Melanesians and by Papuans. Reproduced from the "Melanesians of British New Guinea" by kind permission of Professor C. G. Seligman.

Notes

1. The *hiri*, as these expeditions are called in Motuan, have been described with a great wealth of detail and clearness of outline by Captain F. Barton, in C. G. Seligman's "The Melanesians of British New Guinea," Cambridge, 1910, Chapter viii.
2. Cf. "The Mailu," by B. Malinowski, in Transactions of the R. Society of S. Australia, 1915; Chapter iv. 4, pp. 612 to 629.
3. Op. cit. Chapter xl.
4. On this point of method again, we are indebted to the Cambridge School of Anthropology for having introduced the really scientific way of dealing with the question. More especially in the writings of Haddon, Rivers and Seligman, the distinction between inference and observation is always clearly drawn, and we can visualise with perfect precision the conditions under which the work was done.
5. I may note at once that there were a few delightful exceptions to that, to mention only my friends Billy Hancock in the Trobriands; M. Raffael Brudo, another pearl trader; and the missionary, Mr. M. K. Gilmour.
6. According to a useful habit of the terminology of science, I use the word Ethnography for the empirical and descriptive results of the science of Man, and the word Ethnology for speculative and comparative theories.
7. The legendary "early authority" who found the natives only beastly and without customs is left behind by a modern writer, who, speaking about the Southern Massim with whom he lived and worked "in close contact" for many years, says:—" ... We teach lawless men to become obedient, inhuman men to love, and savage men to change." And again:—"Guided in his conduct by nothing but his instincts and propensities, and governed by his unchecked passions. ..." "Lawless, inhuman and savage!" A grosser misstatement of the real state of things could not be invented by anyone wishing to parody the Missionary point of view. Quoted from the Rev. C. W. Abel, of the London Missionary Society, "Savage Life in New Guinea," no date.
8. For instance, the tables of circulation of the valuable axe blades, op. cit., pp. 531, 532.
9. In this book, besides the adjoining Table, which does not strictly belong to the class of document of which I speak here, the reader will find only a few samples of synoptic tables, such as the list of Kula partners mentioned and analysed in Chapter XIII, Division II, the list of gifts and presents in Chapter VI, Division VI, not tabularised, only described; the synoptic data of a Kula expedition in Chapter XVI, and the table of Kula magic given in Chapter XVII. Here, I have not wanted to overload the account with charts, etc., preferring to reserve them till the full publication of my material.

10. It was soon after I had adopted this course that I received a letter from Dr. A. H. Gardiner, the well-known Egyptologist, urging me to do this very thing. From his point of view as archæologist, he naturally saw the enormous possibilities for an Ethnographer of obtaining a similar body of written sources as have been preserved to us from ancient cultures, plus the possibility of illuminating them by personal knowledge of the full life of that culture.

Boellstorff, Tom. 2008. "Method." In *Coming of Age in Second Life: An Anthropologist Explores the Virtually Human.* Princeton: Princeton University Press.

Virtual worlds in their own terms—Anthropology and ethnography—Participant observation—Interviews, focus groups, and beyond the platform—Ethics—Claims and reflexivity.

Virtual Worlds in Their Own Terms.

On August 31, 1925, Margaret Mead arrived on the shores of Samoa "to investigate the particular problem" of whether youth always experience growing into adulthood in terms of stress and conflict (Mead 1928:9).[1] Opening by describing a Samoan dawn that "begins to fall among the soft brown roofs" while "the slender palm trees stand out against a colorless, gleaming sea" (Mead 1928:14), *Coming of Age in Samoa*—the book that resulted from her research—was an immediate international sensation. Translated into fifteen languages, it launched Mead's lifelong career as the foremost popularizer of cultural anthropology.

Five years after her death in 1978, the anthropologist Derek Freeman published *Margaret Mead and Samoa: The Making and Unmaking of an Anthropological Myth* (Freeman 1983). Despite having never produced a book on his own research in Samoa, Freeman "generated unprecedented controversy over Margaret Mead's fieldwork" (Brady 1983:908). His primary claim was that Mead had allowed herself to be misled by her young Samoan interlocutors, taking at face value their tales of adolescent sexual freedom. These charges have not weathered the test of time. Many anthropologists who conducted subsequent fieldwork in Samoa concluded that despite shortcomings in her work, Mead accurately captured many aspects of Samoan culture (e.g., Holmes 1987; Mageo 1998; Orans 1996). Others noted how Freeman omitted scholarship supporting Mead's conclusions (Holmes 1987; Shankman 1996; see also Feinberg 1988; Nardi 1984; Weiner 1983).

In titling this book *Coming of Age in Second Life,* I evoke both the path-breaking spirit of Mead's first book and the late twentieth-century debate it engendered over methods. After all, Freeman's accusation against Mead was that she made things up, and what are virtual worlds if not made up? When I decided to conduct research in Second Life, I did not begin with any specific topic in mind—economics, for instance, or sexuality, or governance. Instead, my founding question was methodological: What can ethnography tell us about virtual worlds?

It may seem preposterous to contend one can study virtual worlds "in their own terms," but condensed in this key phrase is my foundational methodological conceit, which like all such conceits is also a theoretical claim. For the research upon which this book is based I conducted my research entirely *within* Second Life, as the avatar Tom Bukowski. I made no attempt to visit the offices of Linden Lab, the San Francisco-based company that owns and manages Second Life, or to meet Linden Lab staff, though I would sometimes interact with them at conferences, or within Second Life. I also made no attempt to meet Second Life residents in the actual world or learn their actual-world identities, though both happened on occasion. I took their activities and words as legitimate data about culture in a virtual world. For instance, if during my research I was talking to a woman, I was not concerned to determine if she was "really" a man in the actual world, or even if two different people were taking turns controlling "her." Most Second Life residents meeting this woman would not know the answers to such questions, so for my ethnographic purposes it was important that I not know either. Research on online communities that includes meeting residents in the actual world is perfectly legitimate, but addresses a different set of questions (e.g., Orgad 2005; Ruhleder 2000; Wakeford 1999).

To demand that ethnographic research always incorporate meeting residents in the actual world for "context" presumes that virtual worlds are not themselves contexts; it renders ethnographically inaccessible the fact that most residents of virtual worlds do not meet their fellow residents offline. If one wants to study collective meaning and virtual worlds as collectivities exist purely online, then studying them in their own terms is the appropriate methodology, one that goes against the grain of many assumptions concerning how virtual worlds work. Why is the punchline of so many studies of online culture the identification of continuity with the offline? Why does it feel like a discovery that the online bleeds through to the offline, and vice versa?

My decision to conduct research wholly within Second Life had enormous implications, putting into practice my assertion that virtual worlds are legitimate sites of culture. Many writings on virtual worlds emphasize the permeability between the virtual and actual—for instance, by highlighting the actual-world consequences of virtual commerce. In his study of gay male identity, John Campbell claimed that "online and offline experiences blend into a single, albeit multifaceted, narrative of life" (Campbell 2004:100). Yet Campbell's own ethnographic data suggest many ways in which online and offline personas do not match up; for instance, an older gay man might claim to be younger, or "gay men" might not be gay (or even men) in the actual world. In *The Internet: An Ethnographic Approach*, Daniel Miller and Don Slater contended that their "ethnography of the Internet in Trinidad, or of Trinidad on the Internet" demonstrates "how Internet technologies are being understood and assimilated somewhere in particular (though a very complex 'somewhere,' because Trinidad stretches diasporically over much of the world)" (Miller and Slater 2000:1). This assumes that online cultures are ultimately predicated upon actual-world cultures, an assumption sometimes methodologically operationalized by efforts to meet residents of virtual worlds in the actual world, although researchers have long noted the difficulty of ascertaining actual-world identities (Curtis 1992:125). Some researchers have gone so far as to criticize treating any virtual world as "a completely separate, isolated social world" (Kendall 2002:9; see also Wittel 2001:62), or to claim that "one current limitation of the study of [virtual worlds] is that we know little about how online behaviors affect users' behavior offline" (Schroeder 2002:10). Such assumptions are often linked to the belief that "the number-one challenge is generalizability to the real world" (Giles 2007:20). This view presumes that research on virtual worlds must have the ultimate goal of addressing the actual world, which is taken to be the only "real" social world. It is a view predicated on skepticism toward the idea of conducting ethnography in virtual worlds in their own terms: Is there enough detail in them? What about the fact that you can't know who the people are offline?

One risk I run in saying that it is possible to study virtual worlds in their own terms is that like classical ethnographers, I could be seen to be leaving to one side the cross-cutting histories that condition the lives of these worlds and those who participate in them. My response is that since people find virtual worlds meaningful sites for social action, cultures in virtual worlds exist whether we like it or not; our task as ethnographers is to study them. To take virtual worlds in their own terms is not to claim, as some Artificial Life researchers have done, that their computational worlds are totally self-contained (see Helmreich 2004:285). Assuming that the significance of virtual worlds hinges on continuity with the actual world oversimplifies the referential relationships between actual and virtual, obscuring many of their most crucial consequences for culture and the human. It is a commonplace of technology studies that "technologies are developed and used within a particular social, economic, and political context" (Chee 2006:226; see also Franklin 1992:15–17). But with the emergence of virtual worlds, the virtual world itself becomes a particular social, economic, and political context.

Perspectives doubting the possibility of studying virtual worlds in their own terms miss how as virtual worlds grow in size, ethnographic research in them becomes more partial and situated, much like ethnographic research in the actual world. For instance, when Lynn Cherny conducted ethnographic research in ElseMOO in 1994, there were about 100 persons participating in the world, with around 20 online at any one time (Cherny 1999:39–40). In contrast, by the time I submitted the final manuscript for this book in November 2007, there were over ten million registered Second Life accounts, with over 1.5 million people logging on per month and sometimes over 50,000 persons inworld at once. While a few of these residents had met in the actual world before entering Second Life, or met in Second Life and then sought each other out in the actual world, it was no longer possible for the vast majority to do so, or even verify the identities of those they met online.

Because virtual worlds are quite new, it is to be expected that as persons have built and entered them they have imported and reconfigured everyday aspects of the actual world, from gravity and sunlight to embodiment and language. As Auden noted even for the case of literature, "a secondary world must draw its building materials from the primary world, but it can only take such material as its creator is capable of imaginatively recombining and transforming" (Auden 1968:94). Yet despite the fact that "discussions of these technologies [tend to treat] them as enhancements for already formed individuals to deploy to their advantage or disadvantage" (Poster 1996:184), virtual worlds are not just recreations or simulations of actual-world selfhoods and communities. Selfhood, community, even notions of human nature are being remade in them.

Actual-world sociality cannot explain virtual-world sociality. The sociality of virtual worlds develops on its own terms; it references the actual world but is not simply derivative of it. Events and identities in such worlds may reference ideas from the actual world (from landscape to gender) and may index actual-world issues (from economics to political campaigns), but this referencing and indexing takes place within the virtual world. The way persons from Korea participate in Second Life might differ from the way persons from Sweden do. But if Koreans and Swedes really do participate in Second Life differently, that difference will show up within Second Life itself; it will be amenable to ethnographic investigation inworld. This is a crucial difference between ethnography and methodologies that seek an outsider perspective on culture. A political rally for John Edwards in Second Life in 2007 may have referenced an actual-world campaign, but even if video from an actual-world meeting was streamed into the rally, the rally itself took place in the virtual world.

Studying a virtual world in its own terms does not mean ignoring the myriad ways that ideas from the actual world impinge upon it; it means examining those interchanges as they manifest in the virtual world, for that is how residents experience them when they are inworld. Exploring these connections does not entail that every research project on virtual worlds must have an actual-world component. Second Life has trees, which reference trees in the actual world, but if I were to study trees in Second Life it would not always be necessary that I take bark samples from actual-world trees. When the American Cancer Society held a fundraiser in Second Life, I studied how that showed up in Second Life, without any methodological need to go to the headquarters of the American Cancer Society in Atlanta, Georgia (just as very few Second Life residents who participated in that fundraiser traveled to Atlanta).

I am fortunate that this book represented a second project alongside my research in Indonesia: this helped me see how many of the issues raised about ethnography in virtual worlds are common to ethnographic research anywhere. As a result, I will sometimes draw out parallels between my ethnographic work in Second Life and in Indonesia. I do this to illustrate as clearly as possible that not every challenge of researching online culture is unique to that online context. For instance, much of my research in Indonesia concerns gay Indonesians. Both I and these Indonesians are quite clear that the term "gay" comes from outside Indonesia, but when conducting ethnography in Indonesia I do not spend time in San Francisco; I study the term "gay" as it shows up in Indonesia itself. It is not true that every study of, say, Puerto Ricans in New York City is flawed if the researcher does not conduct research in Puerto Rico as well. Treating Second Life as a culture need not imply that it is mistakenly set apart; all ethnographic research has a limited scope, and speaking of the inhabitants of "Indonesia" or "New York City" does not mean one is failing to take forms of interconnection into account.

The goal of *Coming of Age in Second Life* is to demonstrate the existence of a relatively enduring cultural logic shared in some way by those who participate in Second Life, though their stances toward this cultural logic differ. There are many fascinating and distinct subcultures in Second Life, some of which I address in this book and others that I hope to address in future publications. But Second Life is more than the sum of its subcultures, and in this book my primary goal is to explore overarching cultural norms. The idea that culture is like a language has led many astray in the history of social thought.[2] However, one way in which the metaphor (or exemplification) is illuminating is that members of a culture share many things—assumptions, practices, forms of social relations—as speakers of a language share grammar and vocabulary, even when they use that language to disagree. It is these shared elements that make it possible to speak of "English" or "Indonesian," even as we recognize dialects, multilingualism, and fuzzy boundaries between languages. Similarly persons participate in Second Life in many ways, and there are fundamental disagreements over what Second Life is and should be, but these variations and disagreements are only intelligible because articulated against a set of grounding assumptions.

As an anthropologist I examine mundane social interaction in order to identify as many of these grounding assumptions as possible, assumptions whose taken-for-grantedness means they are not always the topic of explicit commentary. I work to show how these assumptions articulate with each other, the histories from which they draw their coherence, and the differing ways those in Second Life follow, transform, and resist them. I do not claim to know how everyone in Second Life thinks and feels (just as I do not claim to know how every Indonesian thinks and feels), only to provide some partial insight into Second Life culture. The ethnography of virtual worlds should not take the methodological form of "culture at a distance"—as when Ruth Benedict, in *The Chrysanthemum and the Sword,* studied Japanese culture during World War II without setting foot in Japan (Benedict 1946). The social sciences and humanities have only begun to acknowledge the speed with which virtual worlds are becoming taken for granted among all age groups and actual-world geographies. What promise do "traditional" anthropological methods hold for studying virtual worlds, which might appear so radically new as to render such methods irrelevant?

Anthropology and Ethnography

The task of this chapter is to explain how I gathered my data, and along the way to raise general points about methodologies for virtual anthropology (or "the ethnography of virtual worlds"). I prefer "virtual anthropology" to "virtual ethnography" because "to qualify the term *ethnography* with the term *virtual* is to suggest that online research remains less real (and ultimately less valuable) than research conducted offline" (Campbell 2004:52). Anthropologists typically do not speak of "legal ethnography," "medical ethnography," and so on: they speak of "legal *anthropology*," "medical *anthropology*," and now virtual *anthropology* as subdisciplines for which an unqualified "ethnography" is the modality.

"Ethnography" is the method anthropologists and others use to study "culture," one of the discipline's originary concepts. In his famous 1871 definition Edward B. Tylor, a founding figure in anthropology, termed culture "that complex whole which includes knowledge, belief, art, morals, law, custom, and any other capabilities and habits acquired by man as a member of society" (Tylor 1871:1). More compelling definitions of culture have appeared since that time, but this early characterization provides a helpful starting point. Tylor refers to a "complex whole"—and what is a virtual world if not a complex whole, however networked?—defined in terms of "capabilities and habits" rather than knowledge and belief; that is, by techne rather than episteme. Since approximately the 1980s, many in anthropology and elsewhere have critiqued the culture concept for eliding issues of difference, inequality, and materiality. Such critiques extend back to the early decades of anthropology, for instance, in British social anthropology, which tended to see "culture" as a German, romantic concept that obfuscated social dynamics (Radcliffe-Brown 1952 [1940]). Most contemporary ethnographers now use the concept in a more refined manner, harking back to Geertz's formulation that as humans we are "incomplete or unfinished animals who complete or finish ourselves through culture—and not through culture in general but through highly particular forms of it" (Geertz 1973a:49). I speak of "culture in virtual worlds" rather than "virtual culture" to underscore how cultures in virtual worlds are simply new, "highly particular" forms of culture.

How to conduct research in virtual worlds has long been a source of consternation. Some of the most significant analyses of virtual worlds have been produced by writers of fiction, and also by persons whose blogs and websites insightfully explore various aspects of cybersociality. Scholars and practitioners from a range of fields including media studies, computer science, informatics, psychology, sociology, literary studies, and cultural studies have also made significant contributions. Yet since the emergence of a scholarly literature on virtual worlds in the early 1990s, many have wondered about the role of a "postorganic anthropology" in understanding them (Tomas 1991:33). Where are the anthropologists? Anthropologists have shed their discipline's Malinowskian associations with the study of "primitive" and "isolated" societies. However, despite the growing enthusiasm for ethnography in virtual worlds, anthropologists—supposedly the experts in ethnographic methods—have been latecomers to the conversation. While a few anthropologists have been involved in online research, in general the discipline has been slow to recognize the foundationally cultural character of virtual worlds, and thus the promise of ethnographic methods for studying them.

Although now commonly identified as useful (e.g., Fornäs et al. 2002:4), some online researchers employ the term "ethnography" in unclear ways. Judith Donath, for instance, identifies it as "an interpretation of closely examined social discourse," but in equating ethnography with interpretation she is silent on what methods are to be used, as well as what constitutes close examination (Donath 1999:31). Most research published before my own investigated text-based formats, including IRC and MUDs, or graphical virtual worlds with a combat emphasis, like Everquest or World of Warcraft. It is possible to research these important virtual worlds ethnographically (e.g., Nardi and Harris 2006), but in terms of methodological experimentation they have limitations. Frank Schaap noted with reference to his research in the role-playing Cybersphere MOO that "I felt I couldn't play an anthropologist as a character, because I didn't know how to fit an Anthropologist or a Researcher into the theme of the world" (2002:29). Researchers in text-based virtual worlds often made assumptions about visuality and embodiment that are simply not applicable to graphical contexts where three-dimensional visualization is fundamental to sociality. Only in the context of text-based virtual worlds could one claim that "by definition online ethnography describes places that are not spaces. Disembodied persons people these places" (Rutter and Smith 2005:84). The idea that online observation and interviewing "might be as legitimate for ethnography as is face-to-face-interaction" (Fornäs et al. 2002:38) assumes that what takes place via the Internet is not "face-to-face." While language is certainly important to the ethnography of virtual worlds, such ethnography is not "language-centered," as in the case of research on online archives (Fabian 2002).

Many analyses of online culture have used symbolic or semiotic frameworks that define culture in terms of knowledge of schemas, cognitive maps, and meaning (e.g., Salen and Zimmerman 2004). Such definitions reflect the mid-twentieth-century "cognitive" anthropological belief that "a society's culture consists of whatever it is one has to know or believe in order to operate in a manner acceptable to its members" (Goodenough 1964:36). Such a view of culture in terms of episteme rather than techne may be attractive to some with backgrounds in game studies because it is congruent with an understanding of social relations in terms of rules. Rules are often identified as the foundational characteristic of anything to be termed a game (De Koven 1978:45; von Neumann and Morgenstern 1944:49); game design, programming, and even playing a game can be seen as crafting, coding, or implementing rules. This has led some researchers to speculate on the possibility that virtual worlds could be manipulated by researchers, providing "the opportunity to see large-scale social outcomes from a truly probabilistic, experimental perspective as in a petri dish" (Castronova 2006:183). Nonetheless viewing culture in terms of rules—rather than in terms of Tylor's more prescient emphasis on capability and habit—has serious limitations. Geertz observed how viewing culture in terms of rules confuses a derived representation with lived social experience; it is like confusing the score of a Beethoven quartet "with the skills and knowledge needed to play it, with the understanding of it possessed by its performers and auditors" (Geertz 1983:11). As Malinowski noted at the outset of the anthropological enterprise, "the Ethnographer has in the field... the duty before him of drawing up all the rules and regularities.... But these things, though crystallized and set, are nowhere explicitly *formulated*" (Malinowski 1922:11).

This impoverished model of culture in terms of knowing rules has methodological implications. It implies that learning a culture is like learning the rules of a game. Since players cannot play a game unless they know they are playing a game and know the rules of that game, it further suggests that people can describe their culture when asked, implying one can learn how a culture works through elicitation methods. By "elicitation methods" I mean methods like interviews or surveys that involve asking questions and receiving answers. In contrast, participant observation is the central methodology for ethnography because it does not require that aspects of culture be available for conscious reflection. It allows the researcher to become involved in crafting events as they occur; participant observation is itself a form of techne. Elicitation methods assume people are able to articulate the various aspects of the cultures that shape their thinking. Yet even a simple example from language shows how this assumption limits our methodological reach. To try to understand virtual worlds based on elicitation methods is like trying to construct a grammar of English by asking speakers to describe how English works. Few English speakers would be able to explain, for instance, that the first "n" in "inconceivable" becomes "m" in words like "impossible" because the following sound ("p," in this case) is a bilabial plosive (that is, made with the lips) and as a result the "n" sound shifts to a bilabial articulation as well. Yet any English speaker "knows" this phonological rule even if they cannot describe it. Like language, many aspects of culture are only imperfectly available for conscious reflection. They take the form of "common sense": in culture "what is essential goes without saying because it comes without saying" (Bourdieu 1977:167). Research on virtual worlds can make effective use of elicitation methods, but must also move beyond them to develop methods based upon techne, not just episteme.

Some aspects of Malinowski's legacy help explain why anthropologists and nonanthropologists alike have been slow to acknowledge the usefulness of ethnography for studying virtual worlds. Matti Bunzl has argued that Franz Boas (1858–1942), a founding figure in United States anthropology, might prove a better historical model. Bunzl notes that "in a Malinowskian framework, the production of anthropological knowledge was a function of mere observation, as long as it occurred across—and, thereby, reproduced—a cultural chasm between ethnographic Self and native Other" (Bunzl 2004:438). This supposed cultural chasm has led many to mistakenly conclude that ethnography will not be objective if researchers are similar to (or personally involved with) those they study, with the result that persons conducting ethnographic research in communities to which they somehow belong may see themselves as "virtual anthropologists" (Weston 1997). In contrast, "in Boas's fieldwork, a constitutive epistemological separation between ethnographer and native was absent" (Bunzl 2004:438). Thus, "Boasian anthropology did not produce 'native' anthropology as the *virtual* Other of 'real' anthropology" (Bunzl 2004:439, emphasis added). Franz Boas was Margaret Mead's teacher at Columbia and wrote the foreword to *Coming of Age in Samoa*. Like Mead, in this book I draw upon a Boasian framework that seeks equality and complicity rather than hierarchy and distance. To some, ethnographic research (including this book) may seem "anecdotal," but such an interpretation fails to recognize how ethnographic research connects seemingly isolated incidents of cultural interchange (Malaby 2006c). This is what Boas identified as a "cosmological" approach to knowledge, which "considers every phenomenon as worthy of being studied for its own sake. Its mere existence entitles it to a full share of our attention; and the knowledge of its existence and evolution in space and time fully satisfies the student" (Boas 1887:642). By holding at bay the scientistic rush to comparison and generalization (often before the phenomena at hand are properly identified and understood), ethnographic analysis "can be crucial ... for imagining the kinds of communities that human groups can create with the help of emerging technologies" (Escobar 1994; see also Jacobson 1996).

As discussed further below, the open-endedness of Second Life meant that I was able to subordinate interviews and surveys to participant observation, the centerpiece of any truly ethnographic approach. Not only did I create the avatar Tom Bukowski; I shopped for clothes for my avatar in the same stores as any Second Life resident. I bought land with the help of a real estate agent and learned how to use Second Life's building tools.[3] I then created a home and office for my research named "Ethnographia," purchasing items like textures, furniture, and artwork. I learned games created and played inside Second Life, like "Tringo" (a combination of Tetris and Bingo) and "primtionary" (a variant of Pictionary).

I wandered across the Second Life landscape, flying, teleporting, or floating along in my hot air balloon, stopping to investigate events, buildings, or people I happened to encounter. I also used the "events" list and notices in Second Life publications to learn of interesting places to visit. In turn, many people stumbled upon my house, either during leisurely explorations of their own or to attend an event I was hosting. I joined many Second Life groups and participated in a range of activities, from impromptu relationship counseling to larger-scale events like a community fair. While I did not seek notoriety, on one occasion my activities garnered brief actual-world press—namely, my experiment of having a friend who was running for city council in my actual-world hometown of Long Beach, California acquire an avatar and hold a campaign event, the first case of an actual-world political candidate appearing in Second Life.

All this experience did not give me a totalizing understanding of Second Life. Ethnographic knowledge is situated and partial; just as most Indonesians have spent more time in Indonesia than I and know many things about Indonesia that I do not know, so many Second Life residents spent more time inworld than I, and every resident had some kind of knowledge about the virtual world that I lacked. One of the many things I did gain from my research was a network of acquaintances and friends, all of whom knew of my research, since my "profile" mentioned that I was an anthropologist. I was struck by how the idea of someone conducting ethnography made sense to residents. My interest tended to be slotted into the kind of reflexivity and curiosity that was common in Second Life, showing up in everything from blogs to the large number of journalists and educators active inworld. Residents often commented upon my seeming comfort with Second Life, particularly my skills at building (an unexpected benefit of my growing up as a video gamer). One resident noted "you seem so comfy in here—like you study it yet still live it." I also encountered residents already familiar with anthropology, as in the following exchange:

> Urma: Do you conduct field research ... participant observation?
> Me: Yeah, participant observation, but also interviews and focus groups
> Urma: Its an interesting topic, Virtual Lives. And its not like you have to go some exotic land. I mean ... it's a far-off place, but it's not like you're studying the culture of the River Valley Dani [in Papua New Guinea, an Indonesian province] or anything lol

I found remarkable the degree to which the challenges and joys of my research in Second Life resembled the challenges and joys of my research in Indonesia. Claims of a methodological chasm between virtual and actual are overstated. For example, Jennifer Sundén's question "How then to start writing a culture that is already written?" is provocative (Sundén 2003:18), but the phrasing elides how actual-world cultures are also "written" in that they are the product of human artifice. I thus disagree with any claim that with regard to virtual worlds "there is no incontrovertible basis on which to decide whether an approach is or is not ethnographic" (Hine 2005:8). I would turn to Marilyn Strathern's thesis that "the nature of ethnography entailed in anthropology's version of fieldwork" involves "the deliberate attempt to generate more data than the investigator is aware of at the time of collection ... Rather than devising research protocols that will purify the data in advance of analysis, the anthropologist embarks on a participatory exercise which yields materials for which analytical protocols are often devised after the fact" (Strathern 2004:5–6). Mead herself summed up this vision of the ethnographic project as an "open-mindedness with which one must look and listen, record in astonishment and wonder, that which one would not have been able to guess" (Mead 1950:xxvi).

Participant Observation

In line with its status as ethnography's signature method, this book is built around an analysis of social interaction gathered through participant observation. Some disciplines focus on the conscious products of culture: texts, dances, codes of law. Anthropologists examine these too, but prioritize the everyday contexts in which people live. A Second Life resident once commented on my participant observation methodology by noting that: "you're mixing up two agendas in Second Life. The research and presumably, just fun and games too. Don't you find that one affects your perceptions of the other?" My chat log reveals that I answered by saying "it's what anthropologists call 'participant observation,' and it does shatter the illusion, but anthropologists tend to believe that methods like surveys give the illusion of objectivity" I also noted that when conducting participant observation research in Indonesia, I also have "fun and games," spending time with friends or going to a movie.

There is no illusion of detached objectivity to shatter in participant observation because it is not a methodology that views the researcher as a contaminant. It constantly confronts the differing forms of power and hierarchy produced through fieldwork, not all of which privilege the researcher. The term "participant observation" is intentionally oxymoronic; you cannot fully participate and fully observe at the same time, but it is in this paradox that ethnographers conduct their best work. Unlike elicitation methods, participant observation implies a form of ethical yet critical engagement between researcher and researched, even when the researcher is clearly not a member of the community being studied. It is "a method of being at risk in the face of the practices and discourses into which one inquires ... [a] serious nonidentity that challenges previous stabilities, convictions, or ways of being ... a mode of practical and theoretical attention, a way of remaining mindful and accountable" (Haraway 1997:190–91). It has long been identified as a method based on vulnerability, even failure, on learning from mistakes: "over and over again, I committed breaches of etiquette, which the natives, familiar enough with me, were not slow in pointing out" (Malinowski 1922:8).

A common tactic in writing on virtual worlds is to emphasize the sensational: men participating as women; nonnormative sex practices like sadomasochism; persons earning large sums of actual-world money through online enterprises. Looking to the unusual to tell us about culture, however, is of limited use. If in the actual world we were to do nothing but read the headlines of our newspapers, magazines, and television reports, we would not have an accurate understanding of everyday life. Similarly extraordinary events in Second Life are fascinating, but paint a misleading picture of its culture. Ethnographers are not oblivious to the newsworthy or the extraordinary, but find that culture is lived out in the mundane and the ordinary. The goal is to find methods attuned to the banal dimensions of human life, what Pierre Bourdieu termed the "habitus": "a subjective but not individual system of internalized structures, schemes of perception, conception, and action" (Bourdieu 1977:86).

To illustrate how participant observation works to discover culture through nonelicited, everyday interaction, consider the following scene, taken with only minor modifications directly from my fieldnotes. On the day in question it was 9:16 p.m. local time when, having logged onto Second Life a few minutes earlier, I took up my friend Kimmy's invitation to come see her new house. I teleported to her location and found myself in the kitchen of a standard-looking two-story house standing on a small island; similar islands dotted the landscape nearby, fitted out with other homes. Kimmy was hanging out with her friend BettyAnne, and the three of us moved to Kimmy's new living room to talk, watching palm trees sway outside the window. Fifteen minutes later, my chat log recorded that we were discussing going to play a game of golf when an unknown person, "Laura," teleported into the kitchen:

> ME: Hello Laura!
> KIMMY: Hi Laura ... can I help you?
> LAURA: Hi, I'm new. Just arrived.
> KIMMY: Ahh, she's a noob [newbie]
> LAURA: Is it possible to change my clothes now?
> ME: Yes, right click on yourself and choose "appearance"
> KIMMY: Here are some clothes. If you go to inventory at the bottom right, they should be in your clothing folder
> LAURA: ty [thank you]
> KIMMY: If you right click the clothing and pick "wear," you should be able to wear it
> LAURA: How about my hair? It's a mess.
> KIMMY: Hmm. I wish I had some prim hair to give you, but I can't transfer any of it. You'll have to go into "appearance" and play with the sliders.

KIMMY: I can give you some landmarks for some great clothing stores though

KIMMY: I got my hair at that place I just gave you a landmark for

LAURA: I'd love some

KIMMY: Check the upper right hand corner. How much money do you have?

LAURA: Zero so far. how can I earn some?

KIMMY: Ah. do you have a freebie account?

LAURA: Yeah, I didn't know which one to choose

ME: The easiest way to "earn" money is to convert dollars into linden dollars using a credit card

KIMMY: Alright, if you had a pay account they would give you money every Tuesday

LAURA: Ty. I will look into it

ME: You can also earn money in a zillion ways but they aren't always easy lol—selling things, stuff like that

KIMMY: The only way you can earn money other than that is dancing at a club, being a stripper or an escort lol ... or find some other job that has a boss that pays you to do a service of some sort.

LAURA: I might go for a look around. Nice talking to you.

KIMMY: Nice to meet you, Laura, keep in touch

LAURA: Alright Kimmy and BettyAnne and Tom, bye:)

[Laura's avatar disappears]

BETTYANNE: Aww, she looks just like I did

KIMMY: lol

KIMMY: We're all born like that

This innocuous scene began when Laura teleported into Kimmy s house as Kimmy, BettyAnne, and myself were talking. Laura probably saw green dots on the world map indicating that three persons were at this location, and came to investigate. We saw her wandering around in the kitchen, looking lost, but she could have been someone bent on "griefing" (harassing or mistreating others, see chapter 7) so we were cautious. Kimmy, BettyAnne, and I clicked on "Laura" to obtain her profile, which informed us that the avatar had been created that very day, meaning she could be an additional avatar (or "alt") of a longtime resident, or the primary avatar of someone entering Second Life for the first time.

It quickly became clear that the latter was the case; Laura was, as Kimmy put it, a "noob" or "newbie" (or doing a convincing job of appearing to be a newbie). When Laura asked how to change her clothes, Kimmy, who had some free-to-copy women's clothes in her inventory, gave some to Laura and explained how to access them. Such generosity was common in Second Life during my fieldwork. Laura's appearance changed as she put on the clothes Kimmy had given her: a pair of faded jeans, a tank top showing off her virtual shoulders. Laura then asked about hair and Kimmy said she wished she had "prim hair" to give her, but "can't transfer" it. "Prim hair" was hair constructed from prims, the objects used to make everything from vehicles to buildings, and was typically better-looking than the default hair that came with one's avatar. However, all of the prim hair Kimmy had was "no transfer"—copies of it could not be given away. This was because prim hair was a relatively valuable commodity and those who sold it usually made their creations "no transfer." Although Kimmy could not give Laura any of the prim hair she had previously purchased, she could give Laura "landmarks" that contained information about the location of stores that sold prim hair.

It was through this commodity that the conversation turned to economic matters. Kimmy told Laura to check the upper-right hand corner of her screen and see how much money she had. Laura replied "zero," which refers to Linden dollars (one U.S. dollar was trading for about 280 Linden dollars at the time). Laura asked "how can I earn some [money]." Kimmy did not answer directly but inquired after what kind of account Laura had. At this point in Second Life's existence there were three levels of membership: a free account with no verification of payment method (like the successful use of a credit card), a free account where a payment method had been verified, which implied the person's actual-world identity was known to Linden Lab; and a "premium" account that cost $9.95 a month (six dollars a month if paid yearly). This premium account, which Kimmy termed a "pay account," paid back about $1.50 in Linden dollars each week at the time, and also allowed one to own land. I mentioned to Laura that she could sell things in Second Life and Kimmy added that she could also make money for service work, including being a stripper or escort. Having received advice and free clothing, Laura thanked Kimmy, BettyAnne, and myself for our help and teleported away to explore some other part of Second Life. After Laura left, BettyAnne said "aww, she looks just like I did," referring to the unadorned and generic look of Laura's brand-new avatar. "We're all born like that," Kimmy replied.

This unassuming excerpt from my thousands of pages of fieldnotes reveals how ethnographic methods draw upon participant observation to find social meanings as they are implicitly forged and sustained in everyday interaction. From this excerpt we gain insight into a range of cultural domains, from gender (discussions about clothing, hair, and work as a stripper involved female-gendered avatars, though the persons involved might be male or transgendered in the actual world), to economics, to ideas about an avatar life course (in which people are "born" as "newbies" and then mature), to language (such as the use of "lol" for "laugh out loud," or the use of emoticons like ":)" for a smiley face). Crucially through such participant observation data we can see links between these cultural domains: rather than an interview or survey that asks about gender, then about economics, and so on, through participant observation we can see which cultural domains crop up together and how they are interconnected. Participant observation demonstrates the historically specific character of "common sense," revealing it to be not "human nature" but culture, one valid yet particular way of living a human life.

When conducting ethnography in virtual worlds, the ability to do things like save chat logs and record audio or video is a great boon in comparison to actual-world environments where audio recording can be disruptive and one is often forced to rely on memory or hastily handwritten notes. However, the ease of obtaining data in virtual worlds can also be a curse, because those very processes of memory and handwriting force ethnographers to focus on what seem to be the most consequential incidents encountered during participant observation. Ethnographers of virtual worlds often face the challenge of filtering through large amounts of data. My own data set constituted over ten thousand pages of fieldnotes from participant observation, interviewing, and focus groups, plus approximately ten thousand additional pages of blogs, newsletters, and other websites.

Interviews, Focus Groups, and Beyond the Platform.

Research is most effective when each component method is keyed to a specific set of questions. Participant observation is useful for gaining a conceptual handle on cultural assumptions that may not be overtly discussed. In comparison to the more isolated contexts of surveys and interviews, it is useful for seeing what kinds of practices and beliefs emerge as members of a particular culture interact with each other. Participant observation can illuminate debates and issues of which the researcher was unaware prior to the research, and so could not have thought to include on a list of interview questions or a survey form. For these reasons, participant observation must be the fundamental method of any full-fledged ethnography. However, anthropologists have always used many methods in addition to participant observation (Ortner 2006:81). In my earlier fieldwork in Indonesia I complemented participant observation with interviews, archival research, the analysis of texts, and focus groups. I found all of these ancillary methods helpful for my research in Second Life as well.

I conducted about thirty formal interviews and thirty informal interviews during my fieldwork. By "formal interview" I mean an interview where I explicitly asked a resident "may I interview you about your experiences in Second Life" and the resident consented. I used a consent form for these interviews, as I did in Indonesia (see figure 3.1). The form was reviewed and approved by the Institutional Review Board at my university (as was my research overall); it would be signed by the resident typing "I agree to participate in your study." As in most ethnographic projects I selected interviewees through a procedure where those already interviewed would recommend acquaintances, or I would discover such persons through my own participant observation. Such a "snowball sampling" method is inappropriate for statistical research, but is a desirable approach for ethnographers, who typically acknowledge their partiality and seek to trace social networks rather than artificially isolate members of a culture through randomization.

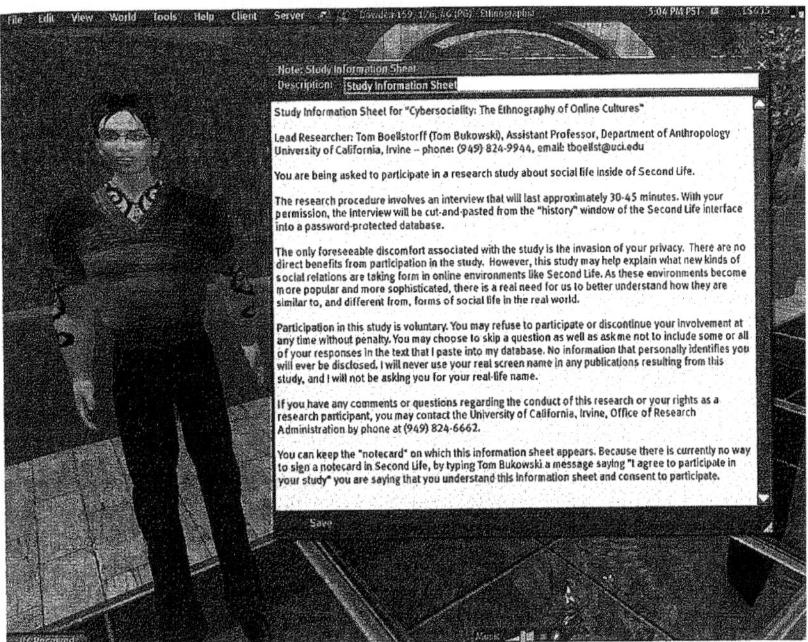

FIGURE 3.1. The consent form used for interviews inside of Second Life.

Interviews can be highly effective when placed in the context of participant observation. Culture can be implicit and even subconscious, but much of it is part of everyday awareness; members of a culture can sometimes be its most eloquent interpreters. In the case of my research, interviews allowed residents to reflect upon their virtual lives and discuss what they saw as significant or interesting aspects of Second Life. Their insights then fed back into my participant observation, in that I learned about new topics or social groups to investigate. While there is a clear hierarchy in any interview context, Second Life residents typically found being interviewed to be a rewarding experience. They appreciated the chance to talk though issues they had often been pondering for some time; interviews were often two-way affairs, with the "interviewee" asking questions to which I would respond. I did not have any problem getting people to agree to an interview. I faced having a list of people wishing to be interviewed; after being interviewed, many residents asked to be interviewed again, or became friends with whom I would socialize on a regular basis. I purposely worked to interview a spectrum of residents, including residents I met in shopping malls, clubs, and other informal contexts, even persons who randomly happened to fly past my house. On a few occasions I conducted group interviews with up to four residents at once. Sometimes this was because a friend of a resident dropped in while the resident was being interviewed and wished to join in. In other cases I interviewed couples in an intimate relationship, or even three people in a polyamorous relationship, as well as persons who were kin in the actual world (a husband and wife, or siblings, or a parent and child).

In addition to these formal interviews, I conducted about the same number of informal interviews that grew out of participant observation. For instance, it often happened that I would be participating in some activity with three or four residents and fall into a conversation about our experiences in Second Life. Then over a period of time, all of the residents would log off save one, and my conversation with that one remaining resident would began to feel like an interview. In such cases it was usually not appropriate to stop the conversation and ask the resident to sign a consent form; instead, I simply followed the normal ethical procedures I would follow when conducing participant observation in Indonesia (see below).

During my research in Indonesia I held a series of focus groups, but found them unhelpful given the amount of work it took to organize them. In Second Life the logistical barriers to convening a group of people were less significant, but despite this fact focus groups were not a core methodology. I created my own group, "Digital Cultures," and held about forty meetings of the group at my home or the homes of other group members throughout my research. These focus groups were organized around a "blurb," or topic that I wrote based on issues of current interest identified through my participant observation work and suggestions by Second Life residents (figure 3.2). The meetings lasted an hour and drew up to forty residents (the maximum number of avatars that most sims could contain during my fieldwork). Unlike interviews, focus groups allowed residents to collectively discuss issues about Second Life. Side conversations and digressions provided their own data, revealing connections residents were drawing between different domains of Second Life culture. Because focus groups were advertised on the Second Life "events" database, they tended to draw residents with an interest in intellectual debate. This makes the over 1,000 pages of chat text I gathered from focus groups more specific than that I gathered from participant observation or even interviews, but "specific" does not mean "biased." The persons who participated in focus groups participated in a wide range of activities and were far from homogenous in their understandings of Second Life culture.

FIGURE 3.2. A focus group at my home in Second Life, Ethnographia (image by author).

While there were residents whose experience was limited to the virtual world itself, often known as "the grid,"[4] for many residents websites, blogs, and even full-fledged periodicals (with staff and advertising) were important, and so I drew upon these as well. Through these media residents offered analysis and commentary on many aspects of the virtual world. As an individual researcher, I could not familiarize myself with every subculture or region of Second Life (just I have not been to many parts of Indonesia). Resident-produced media provided valuable information about parts of Second Life I did not personally research on an intensive basis.[5]

Ethics

Any form of inquiry raises the question of power relationships between the researcher and those studied. The details vary depending upon the personal history of the investigator, the status of the communities examined, and the methodology used, but concerns regarding ethics persist. For some time, anthropologists have examined the implications of the fact that their discipline, like all social scientific and humanistic disciplines, was first formalized in nineteenth-century contexts of colonial encounter (Asad 1973). Questions of power, complicity, and accountability remain part of any ethnographic project—not uncomfortable realities to be broached then set aside, but important sources of insight and collaboration. Such issues are widely seen as pressing with regard to virtual worlds: "online research is marked as a special category in which the institutionalized understandings of the ethics of research must be re-examined" (Hine 2005:5; see also Kendall 2002:241–43). My research was thus not just an experiment in methodology, but an experiment in the ethics of virtual anthropology.

During my research I worked to avoid being identified with any particular subset of residents, although I could only join a limited number of groups and spent more time with some residents than others. My avatar took on different fashions, genders, and even species during my research, but my default embodiment was both white and male, in line with my actual-world embodiment, and I was also openly gay. When debates or conflict broke out in my presence, I did not feign neutrality (I would, for instance, file an "Abuse Report" if I saw someone mistreating another resident), and gave my own opinions in informal conversations, interviews, and focus groups. However, I did work to interact with residents whose political and personal views might not reflect my own.

There is often a misunderstanding of "cultural relativism" that portrays anthropologists as believing there is no way to judge cultures or decide between right and wrong: as if in culture X they believe in killing every third-born child, then we would have no right to say that should not happen. In fact, anthropologists make prescriptive judgments all the time and even work to change cultures, as in the case of my HIV prevention work in Indonesia. Anthropologists know that claims like "in culture X they believe in killing every third-born child" mistakenly assume that cultures are homogenous, without dissent or debate, and do not change over time. The point is not to avoid prescription but to keep description and prescription distinct. For instance, if there were a culture in which some members believed in killing every third-born child, there would be utility in working to understand the cultural logics by which this made sense, without thereby condoning the practice.

In addition to a primary account (like my Tom Bukowski avatar), many Second Life residents also had one or more alternative avatars or "alts"—entirely different avatars with different screen names. The two accounts were indistinguishable from avatars held by two separate persons. I briefly tried experimenting with an alt, but soon decided it was ethically and methodologically inadequate for ethnographic research. I never hid the fact that I was conducting research, going so far as to include this information in my profile. Any resident could read this profile and see that Tom Bukowski was an anthropologist. With an alt, such information would not be available unless I listed it on the alt's profile as well, negating the purpose of an alt in the first place. It might seem that alts could allow an anthropologist to observe an undisturbed culture in action, where people spoke freely without realizing there was a researcher in their midst. What this perspective misses is that ethnography is predicated on *participant* observation, not abstracted observation. Conducting research with an alt would not allow the tension between participating and observing to produce the kinds of complicity and failure that are necessary for ethnographic knowledge.[6]

Aside from the issue of alts, ethical questions can arise due to the possibility that persons could be sitting with the researcher in the actual world. Seeing only the researcher's avatar, residents of the virtual world would not know that additional people were watching the computer screen. I became aware of this issue when, on a handful of occasions, I had such actual-world onlookers. In one case, a colleague sat with me in my actual-world office while I was online with Kiancha, a Second Life acquaintance:

> ME: Hey Kiancha, can't talk long but I have a friend here in my office interested in sl, say hello!
> KIANCHA: I'd love to meet your friend.
> ME: My friend is really impressed—hasn't been in a virtual world before
> KIANCHA: Hello, friend of Tom. Where are you?
> ME: She's here with me in California, lol
> KIANCHA: Ha, she doesn't have an avatar yet, eh?
> ME: No, not yet, but who knows?
> KIANCHA: Tom is really super at adding content to this game, friend.

Note how in this exchange, Kiancha tried to reach beyond the screen and address my friend, asking "where are you?" Since my friend did not have an avatar, I was forced to respond on her behalf. The friend could have typed a response on my computer's keyboard, but the response would have come from my avatar, only adding to the confusion. Despite these barriers, Kiancha still moved between addressing me ("she doesn't have an avatar yet, eh?") and the virtually absent friend ("Tom is really super at adding content," a reference to my discussion groups).

On three occasions I gave conference presentations where I had twenty or thirty people looking over my virtual shoulder in this way. These experiences were even more disconcerting; unlike the example with Kiancha above, there was no way for a Second Life resident to respond to a multitude of virtually disembodied persons. Since they did not have avatars, participants in these conferences also found it hard to relate to me as an avatarized self (Tom Bukowski), and in two instances asked me to exit Second Life in order to address them in the actual world. After these experiences I decided to forbid actual-world persons to observe me online without having avatars of their own, so that they could participate in the virtual world like any other resident.

It is ethically preferable to use a consent form for interviews or any elicitation method; this is because unlike participant observation, elicitation methods create a social situation that would not exist otherwise. For my Second Life research, I had residents sign this consent form using only their screen names. I did this because another aspect to my ethical and methodological practice was that I did not try to verify any aspect of residents' actual-world lives. Residents did not typically offer such information or find it relevant. On those occasions where a resident would provide such information (for instance, that they were disabled, living in Germany, or a forty-eight-year-old housewife with two children), I did not try to confirm these statements. What was important were the contexts in which such information came up and what such information was supposed to accomplish: for instance, did other residents interpret it as a sign of trust or intimacy?

This question of the actual-world lives of residents of virtual worlds extends to the most fundamental questions of selfhood, with important methodological consequences. One could imagine a situation where an actual-world person "Sam" had two avatars, "Jenny" and "Rick," and invested the time so that each avatar had its own social network. One could then imagine an ethnographer like myself interviewing Jenny and Rick on different days without realizing that I was interviewing "Sam" twice. I do not think such a thing happened during my research, but the methodological and theoretical point is that in an important sense it would not matter: Jenny and Rick would be distinct social actors in Second Life, and this would be sufficient warrant to interview each of them. The reverse situation could also take place, for example where "George" and "Donna," a married couple in the actual world, take turns controlling the single avatar "Jenny" in Second Life. I might then interact with Jenny on two different days without realizing that on the first day I was "actually" talking to George, and on the second day "actually" talking to Donna. Since Jenny would be a single social actor and other residents might well know nothing of George and Donna, it would be appropriate to treat my ethnographic data about "Jenny" as coming from a single person.

In my research (as in any ethnographic project), questions of ethics extend from research to writing: it is in its published form that my research has the greatest potential to have positive or negative effects upon Second Life's residents.[7] The most fundamental ethical decision—one I made with regard to my Indonesia research as well—was to maintain confidentiality with regard to resident identities, to protect privacy with regard to their virtual and actual lives. Even when residents said I could name them, I have employed pseudonyms so as not to inadvertently identify their friends. This devotion to confidentiality may seem quaint, since in the context of the Internet there appears to be little remaining expectation of privacy. Typically residents knew that anything they said could be recorded by Linden Lab, by residents nearby, or by a scripted object hidden on a piece of land, and that such recorded information could then be disseminated via a blog or other form of website. Nonetheless attempts to respect privacy were common in Second Life during the time of my research; for instance, residents normally asked permission to quote other residents if writing something for public consumption.

A twist to this principle is that I have also used pseudonyms for the virtual-world identities or "screen names" of Second Life residents.[8] As discussed later, the screen name is the one unchangeable aspect of a Second Life account (as in many virtual worlds), and significant meaning is attached to it. I have also changed details about residents' virtual-world lives that could be used to identify them. I have paraphrased quotations from my residents to make them difficult to identify using a search engine. In some cases I combine quotations from more than one person, or change details of a location or incident, so that the original event cannot be discerned from the narrative. Some may think they can determine the identities of those I discuss in this book, but it will be impossible to know for sure.

The importance of using confidentiality to protect privacy was illustrated by a controversy that broke out in Second Life in October 2004. A professor was teaching a freshman English course focusing on how technology affects communication. Students in the course were given an assignment to spend time in Second Life and write about their experiences. Unfortunately some of these students began posting derisive online commentaries, complete with chat excerpts that included the screen names of Second Life residents. Several discussions were held in Second Life to defuse the controversy, which could have been avoided had the students been trained in ethnographic methods. There are also theoretical reasons for maintaining confidentiality. Confidentiality deemphasizes individual personalities, allowing for a focus on broader cultural logics. In virtual worlds there is often a tendency to emphasize controversies and celebrities; ethnography's real promise lies in showing how banal, unassuming aspects of everyday life have profound consequences for how we think and act.

Claims and Reflexivity

Like all ethnographies, this book is a form of situated knowledge (Haraway 1988), one story of Second Life during a particular period of time. As one person in Second Life put it in a note to those new to the virtual world, "the fundamental rule of Second Life is that everything changes constantly": a different person emphasized "leave Second Life for a week and it's like you've left the country for a decade." I began conducting fieldwork in Indonesia in 1992; since that time Indonesia has witnessed many social and political changes and its population grew from 190 million to about 225 million. In comparison, by the time I completed the manuscript for this book the number of registered accounts grew from 5,000 to over ten million, a 2,000-fold increase.

The purpose of any method is that it allows one to make claims. Statistical methods make claims based on the premise that the community studied has been sampled at random: a researcher might claim that one-third of Californians wish they ate more fruit, with a particular margin of error. Leaving aside all the ways we could debate the meaningfulness of such a claim, and acknowledging the power of quantitative methods to answer certain kinds of questions (e.g., Ducheneaut et al. 2006), it is clear that ethnographic claims work differently. For instance, during my Indonesia research I interviewed and conducted participant observation research with approximately as many persons as I did during my research in Second Life, but Indonesia is a populous nation spread over more than three thousand inhabited islands. In my book *The Gay Archipelago,* which focused on gay and lesbian Indonesians, I emphasized that by saying gay men and lesbian women were found *throughout* Indonesia I was not saying they were found *everywhere* in Indonesia (Boellstorff 2005:23); I also emphasized that I was not claiming I knew how every gay and lesbian Indonesian thought, only some insight into cultural assumptions shared by many such Indonesians. After spending a year with a group of ten or twenty Spaniards, most researchers would gain some fluency in the Spanish language. The language skills acquired could be used to converse with hundreds of millions of people worldwide, though one would not learn every vocabulary item or regional dialect. In an analogous manner, ethnography provides insight beyond the sample of persons with whom the ethnographer directly interacts. The mode of explication in ethnography is rarely the categorical claim or positivist law: "Everyone does X." Instead, ethnographers look for tendencies, habits, assumptions, things that are usually true: "In X society, women are usually ranked over children"; "In Y society, persons typically marry before they are thirty)" In other words, ethnography seeks to know what is *virtually* true. Once again, ethnography comes to the virtual with the "virtual" already in hand.

While quantitative researchers use devices like margins of error and sample size to vouch for their claims, ethnographers rely on what James Clifford identified as "ethnographic authority" (Clifford 1983)—a researcher's claim that "I was there" and so can represent, even partially, the culture in question. In ethnographic writing, vignettes, italicized foreign terms, and long quotations often serve the problematic function of attempting to render the researcher transparent, so that the "real voices" of those studied can be "heard." In this regard it is instructive to note how some virtual-world researchers provide extensive excepts from chat logs. Typographical errors are often retained to give these excerpts a "naturalistic" feel; some researchers go so far as to place such excerpts in a Courier or Arial font that metaphorically stands in for a computer screen by working to "recall and reproduce the hyperbolic regularity of Machine Age typewriting" (Bukatman 1994:80; see, e.g., Baty 1999; Campbell 2004; Dibbell 2006; Kendall 2002; Kivits 2005; Markham 1998; Rheingold 2000; Schaap 2002). Such excerpts often appear as follows:

> You are logged into ExampleMOO. You are in a small room with Sam and Joe.
> Sam: hello there :)
> Joe: how r u? whats going on?
> You: Im fine!

These graphical and narrative devices lie squarely in the tradition of establishing ethnographic authority by having one's materials take on the appearance of "raw data." Such devices appear egalitarian but in fact create more hierarchy, because they imply that to disagree with a researcher's conclusions is to insinuate that the "voices" of those studied are themselves wrong. Must ethnographic authority depend upon a claim that the reader has access to the unmediated voices of those being studied? Or can ethnography work to illuminate culture through the imbrication of data and analysis, a rhetorical analogue to the paradox of "participant observation?"

Excerpts from fieldnotes are nothing new to anthropology, and I will provide such excerpts throughout this book, but I do not try to give them the appearance of raw data. I use the same fonts that I use elsewhere. Given the speed at which people typed and the large number of residents for whom English was not a first language, there was a high tolerance for typographical errors when chatting in Second Life. I have edited out most typographical errors for the sake of readability; this recalls how I translated excerpts from my Indonesia fieldwork into colloquial English. The only "naturalistic" elements I retain are a few emoticons (like:) for a smiley face) and common slang terms or contractions like "im" for "instant message" (such terms are referenced in the glossary).

An interesting aspect of doing research in virtual worlds is that no one is a true "native." Some residents began participating in Second Life earlier than others, but no one was born there. It has been a commonplace that anthropologists are never truly members of the cultures they study. Even for those who are in some way members of the societies in which they conduct research, the fact of being a researcher alters their relationship to the fieldsite. My self-identification as a researcher was meant to replicate this sense of distinction. Yet given that I entered Second Life when it had only 5,000 registered accounts, by the time my research ended I was approximately in the top 0.1 percent of oldest avatars. We were all members of an emergent cultural location for which not only dated terms like "native," but also their contemporary stand-ins, like "indigenous," were inapplicable.

Notes

1. See Holmes 1987:7; Orans 1996:19.
2. Mid-twentieth-century structuralists, for instance. See Kurzweil 1980; Lévi-Strauss 1963.
3. My "first land" and the first Ethnographia was built in the Kane sim; in February 2005 I moved to the Dowden sim, where I built four different versions of Ethnographia, partially because I learned how to make interior spaces work better for interviews and discussions, but primarily because I enjoyed building.
4. Toward the end of my fieldwork, Linden Lab began distinguishing "the grid" from "the world," "the grid" referring to the platform that could be used, in theory, to create virtual worlds other than Second Life.

5. One aspect of Second Life "beyond the platform" that I do not draw upon in this book are "meetups" residents would occasionally hold in the actual world. Such meetups were rare and only a tiny fraction of Second Life residents ever attended them. The only exception to this was that I attended the 2nd "Second Life Community Convention" in San Francisco in August 2006 (an event sponsored by Linden Lab, composed primarily of expert panels discussing various aspects of Second Life).
6. I did not pay residents for their involvement in interviews or focus groups, and was never asked for such compensation.
7. In a sense, leaving an actual-world fieldsite is like going offline, but since one can always log back into a virtual world, one never has to take permanent leave of one's fieldsite. I found that in order to write this book I had to drastically reduce my presence in Second Life for several months, which frustrated many of my fellow residents.
8. This has become a fairly standard procedure in ethnographic work on virtual worlds; see, for instance, Campbell 2004:48; Kendall 2002:241.

Works Cited

Asad, Talal, ed. 1973. *Anthropology and the Colonial Encounter.* New York: Humanities Press.

Auden, Wystan Hugh. 1968. *Secondary Worlds: Essays by W. H. Auden.* New York: Random House.

Baty, S. Paige. 1999. *Email Trouble: Love and Addiction @ the Matrix.* Austin: University of Texas Press.

Benedict, Ruth. 1946. *The Chrysanthemum and the Sword: Patterns of Japanese Culture.* New York: Houghton Mifflin Co.

Boas, Franz. 1887 [1940 version], "The Study of Geography." In *Race, Language, and Culture,* 639–47. Chicago: University of Chicago Press.

———. 2005. *The Gay Archipelago: Sexuality and Nation in Indonesia.* Princeton: Princeton University Press.

Bourdieu, Pierre. 1977. *Outline of a Theory of Practice.* Cambridge: Cambridge University Press.

Brady, Ivan. 1983. "Speaking in the Name of the Real: Freeman and Mead on the Samoa (Introduction)." *American Anthropologist* 85, 4:908–9.

Bukatman, Scott. 1994. "Gibsons Typewriter." In *Flame Wars: The Discourse of Cyber-culture,* ed. Mark Dery, 71–89. Durham, NC: Duke University Press.

Bunzl, Matti. 2004. "Boas, Foucault, and the 'Native Anthropologist': Notes toward Neo-Boasian Anthropology." *American Anthropologist* 106, 3(September):435–42.

Campbell, John Edward. 2004. *Getting It On Online: Cyberspace, Gay Male Sexuality, and Embodied Identity.* New York: Harrington Park Press.

———. 2006. "On the Research Value of Large Games: Natural Experiments in Norrath and Camelot." *Games and Culture* 1, 2(April):163–86.

Chee, Florence. 2006. "The Games We Play Online and Offline: Making *Wangtta* in Korea." *Popular Communication* 4, 3:225–39.

Campbell, John Edward. 2004. *Getting It On Online: Cyberspace, Gay Male Sexuality, and Embodied Identity.* New York: Harrington Park Press.

Cherny, Lynn. 1999. *Conversation and Community: Chat in a Virtual World.* Stanford: CSLI Publications.

Clifford, James. 1983. "On Ethnographic Authority." *Representations* 1, 2(Spring):118–46.

Curtis, Pavel. 1992 [1997 reprint]. "Mudding: Social Phenomena in Text-Based Virtual Realities." In *Culture of the Internet,* ed. Sara Kiesler, 121–42. Mahwah, NJ: Lawrence Erlbaum Associates.

De Koven, Bernard. 1978. *The Well-Played Game: A Player's Philosophy.* Garden City, NY: Anchor Press.

________. 2006. *Play Money: Or, How I Quit My Day Job and Made Millions Trading Virtual Loot.* New York: Basic Books.

Donath, Judith S. 1999. "Identity and Deception in the Virtual Community." In *Communities in Cyberspace,* ed. Marc A. Smith and Peter Kollock, 29–59. London: Routledge.

Ducheneaut, Nicolas, Nick Yee, Eric Nickell, and Robert J. Moore. 2006. "Building an MMO with Mass Appeal: A Look at Gameplay in World of Warcraft." *Games and Culture* 1, 4(October):281–317.

Escobar, Arturo. 1994. "Welcome to Cyberia: Notes on the Anthropology of Cyber-culture." *Current Anthropology* 35, 3(June):211–23.

Fabian, Johannes. 2002. "Virtual Archives and Ethnographic Writing: 'Commentary' as a New Genre?" *Current Anthropology* 43, 5(December):775–86.

Feinberg, Richard. 1988. "Margaret Mead and Samoa: *Coming of Age* in Fact and Fiction." *American Anthropologist* 90, 3(September):656–63.

Fornäs, Johan, Kajsa Klein, Martina Ladendorf, Jenny Sundén, and Malin Sveningsson. 2002. "Into Digital Borderlands." In *Digital Borderlands: Cultural Studies of Identity and Interactivity on the Internet,* ed. Johan Fornäs, Kajsa Klein, Martina Ladendorf, Jenny Sundén, and Malin Sveningsson, 1–47. New York: Peter Lang.

Franklin, Ursula. 1992. *The Real World of Technology.* Concord, Ontario: Anansi.

Freeman, Derek. 1983. *Margaret Mead and Samoa: The Making and Unmaking of an Anthropological Myth.* Cambridge, MA: Harvard University Press.

Geertz, Clifford. 1973a. "The Impact of the Concept of Culture on the Concept of Man." In his *The Interpretation of Cultures,* 33–54. New York: Basic Books.

________. 1983. "From the Natives Point of View": On the Nature of Anthropological Understanding." In his *Local Knowledge: Further Essays in Interpretive Anthropology,* 55–72. New York: Basic Books.

Giles, Jim. 2007. "Life's a Game." *Nature* 445(January):18–20.

Goodenough, Ward H. 1964. "Cultural Anthropology." In *Language in Culture and Society*, ed. Dell Hymes, 36–39. Bombay, India: Allied Publishers Private.

Haraway, Donna. 1988. "Situated Knowledge: The Science Question in Feminism as a Site of Discourse on the Privilege of Partial Perspective." *Feminist Studies* 14, 3(Fall):575–99.

———. 1997. *Modest_Witness@Second Millennium. FemaleMan_Meets_OncoMouse: Feminism and Technoscience*. New York: Routledge.

———. 2004. "The Word for the World is Computer: Simulating Second Natures in Artificial Life." In *Growing Explanations: Historical Perspectives on the Sciences of Complexity*, ed. Norton Wise, 275–300. Durham, NC: Duke University Press.

Hine, Christine. 2005. "Virtual Methods and the Sociology of Cyber-Social-Scientific Knowledge." In *Virtual Methods: Issues in Social Research on the Internet*, ed. Christine Hine, 1–13. Oxford: Berg.

Holmes, Lowell D. 1987. *Quest for the* Real *Samoa: The Mead/Freeman Controversy and Beyond*. South Hadley, MA: Bergin and Garvey.

Jacobson, David. 1996. "Contexts and Cues in Cyberspace: The Pragmatics of Naming in Text-based Virtual Realities." *Journal of Anthropological Research* 52, 4(Winter): 461–79.

Kendall, Lori. 2002. *Hanging Out in the Virtual Pub: Masculinities and Relationships Online*. Berkeley: University of California Press.

Kivits, Joëlle. 2005. "Online Interviewing and the Research Relationship." In *Virtual Methods: Issues in Social Research on the Internet*, ed. Christine Hine, 35–49. Oxford: Berg.

Kurzweil, Edith. 1980. *The Age of Structuralism: Lévi-Strauss to Foucault*. New York: Columbia University Press.

———. 1963. *Structural Anthropology*. New York: Basic Books.

Mageo, Jeannette Marie. 1998. *Theorizing Self in Samoa: Emotions, Genders, and Sexualities*. Ann Arbor: University of Michigan Press.

Malinowski, Bronislaw. 1922. *Argonauts of the Western Pacific*. New York: E. P. Dutton and Co.

Markham, Annette N. 1998. *Life Online: Researching Real Experience in Virtual Space*. Walnut Creek, CA: Altamira Press.

Malaby, Thomas M. 2006c. "Anti-Anti Anecdotalism." *Terra Nova*, (December 30). Available at: http://terranova.blogs.com/terra_nova/2006/12/antiantianecdot.html (accessed January 3, 2007).

Mead, Margaret. 1928. *Coming of Age in Samoa: A Psychological Study of Primitive Youth for Western Civilization*. New York: William Morrow and Co.

———. 1950 [2001 reprint]. "Preface to the 1950 Edition." In *Sex and Temperament in Three Primitive Societies* [first published in 1935], xxv–xxvii. New York: Perennial.

Miller, Daniel, and Don Slater. 2000. *The Internet: an Ethnographic Approach*. Oxford: Berg.

Nardi, Bonnie, and Justin Harris. 2006. "Strangers and Friends: Collaborative Play in World of Warcraft." Proceedings of Conference on Computer-Supported Collaborative Work. Banff, Canada. New York: ACM Press.

Nardi, Bonnie. 1984. "The Height of Her Powers: Margaret Mead's Samoa." *Feminist Studies* 10, 2(Summer):323–37.

Nardi, Bonnie, and Justin Harris. 2006. "Strangers and Friends: Collaborative Play in World of Warcraft." Proceedings of Conference on Computer-Supported Collaborative Work. Banff, Canada. New York: ACM Press.

Orans, Martin. 1996. *Not Even Wrong: Margaret Mead, Derek Freeman, and the Samoans.* Novato, CA: Chandler and Sharp Publishers, Inc.

Orgad, Shani. 2005. "From Online to Offline and Back: Moving from Online to Offline Relationships with Research Informants." In *Virtual Methods: Issues in Social Research on the Internet,* ed. Christine Hine, 51–65. Oxford: Berg.

________. 2006. *Anthropology and Social Theory: Culture, Power, and the Acting Subject.* Durham, NC: Duke University Press.

________. 1996. "Postmodern Virtualities." In *FutureNatural: Nature, Science, Culture,* ed. George Robertson, Melinda Mash, Lisa Tickner, Jon Bird, Barry Curtis, and Tim Putnam, 183–202. London: Routledge.

Radcliffe-Brown, A. R. 1952. "On Social Structure" (originally published in 1940). In his *Structure and Function in Primitive* Society, 188–204. New York: Free Press.

________. 2000. *The Virtual Community: Homesteading on the Electronic Frontier.* Cambridge, MA: MIT Press.

Ruhleder, Karen. 2000. "The Virtual Ethnographer: Fieldwork in Distributed Electronic Environments." *Field Methods* 12, l(February):3–17.

Salen, Katie, and Eric Zimmerman. 2004. *Rules of Play: Game Design Fundamentals.* Cambridge, MA: MIT Press.

________. 2002. "Social Interaction in Virtual Environments: Key Issues, Common Themes, and a Framework for Research." In *The Social Life of Avatars: Presence and Interaction in Shared Virtual Environments,* ed. Ralph Schroeder, 1–18. London: Springer-Verlag.

Schaap, Frank. 2002. *The Words that Took Us There: Ethnography in a Virtual Reality.* Amersterdam: Aksant Academic Publishers.

Shankman, Paul. 1996. "The History of Samoan Sexual Conduct and the Mead-Freeman Controversy." *American Anthropologist* 98, 3 (September):555–67.

________. 2004. *Commons and Borderlands: Working Papers on Interdisciplinarity, Accountability, and the Flow of Knowledge.* Wantage: Sean Kingston Publishing.

Sundén, Jenny. 2003. *Material Virtualities: Approaching Online Textual Embodiment.* New York: Peter Lang.

Tylor, Edward Burnett. 1871. *Primitive Culture, Volume 1: The Origins of Culture.* New York: Harper and Row.

Tomas, David. 1991. "Old Rituals for New Space: *Rites de Passage* and William Gibson's Cultural Model of Cyberspace." In *Cyberspace: First Steps*, ed. Michael Benedikt, 31–47. Cambridge, MA: MIT Press.

von Neumann, John, and Oskar Morgenstern, 1944. *Theory of Games and Economic Behavior*. Princeton: Princeton University Press.

Wakeford, Nina. 1999. "Gender and the Landscapes of Computing in an Internet Cafe." In *Virtual Geographies: Bodies, Space, and Relations*, ed. Mike Crang, Phil Crang, and Jon May, 178–201. London: Routledge.

Weiner, Annette B. 1983. "Ethnographic Determinism: Samoa and the Margaret Mead Controversy." *American Anthropologist* 85, 4(December):909–18.

Weston, Kath. 1997. "The Virtual Anthropologist." In *Anthropological Locations: Boundaries and Grounds of a Field Science*, ed. Akhil Gupta and James Ferguson, 163–84. Berkeley: University of California Press.

Wittel, Andreas. 2001. "Toward a Network Sociality." *Theory, Culture and Society* 18, 6(December):51–76.

Unit II

Culture, Persons, and Identities

Chapter 4

Language and Communication

DISCUSSION QUESTIONS

1. What is an ethnography of communication? How does it relate to Bailey's method used in his study?
2. Hymes breaks down the various components that make up a communicative "message." How does his model of the message help you understand why miscommunication occurs among the customers and store owners in Bailey's article?
3. Analyze a convenience store interaction between an African-American customer and a Korean store owner using Hymes's model of a communicative event, including the seven components Hymes outlines.
4. Hymes suggests that understanding the function of language is just as important as understanding its form and structure. How do language form and function combine in Bailey's study to cause miscommunication? How does language exacerbate or lessen racial tensions in the interactions Bailey describes?

KEY TERMS

Ethnography of communication
Semiotics
Pragmatics
Communicative event
Communication of respect

Hymes, Dell. 2001. "Toward Ethnographies of Communication." In *Foundations in Sociolinguistics: An Ethnographic Approach*. Philadelphia: University of Pennsylvania Press.

The term "ethnography of communication" is intended to indicate the necessary scope, and to encourage the doing, of studies ethnographic in basis, and communicative in the range and kind of patterned complexity with which they deal.[1] That is, the term implies two characteristics that an adequate approach to language must have.

As to scope: one cannot simply take separate results from linguistics, psychology, sociology, ethnology, as given, and seek to correlate them, however partially useful such work may be, if one is to have a theory of language (not just a theory of grammar). One needs fresh kinds of data, one needs to investigate directly the use of language in contexts of situation, so as to discern patterns proper to speech activity, patterns that escape separate studies of grammar, of personality, of social structure, religion, and the like, each abstracting from the patterning of speech activity into some other frame of reference.

As to basis: one cannot take linguistic form, a given code, or even speech itself, as a limiting frame of reference. One must take as context a community, or network of persons, investigating its communicative activities as a whole, so that any use of channel and code takes its place as part of the resources upon which the members draw.

It is not that linguistics does not have a vital role. Analyzed linguistic materials are indispensable, and the logic of linguistic methodology is an influence in the ethnographic perspective. It is rather that it is not linguistics, but ethnography, not language, but communication, which must provide the frame of reference within which the place of language in culture and society is to be assessed. The boundaries of the community within which communication is possible; the boundaries of the situations within which communication occurs; the means and purposes and patterns of selection, their structure and hierarchy—all elements that constitute the communicative economy of a group, are conditioned, to be sure, by properties of the linguistic codes within the group, but are not controlled by them. The same linguistic means may be made to serve various ends; the same communicative ends may be served, linguistically, by various means. Facets of the cultural values and beliefs, social institutions and forms, roles and personalities, history and ecology of a community may have to be examined in their bearing on communicative events and patterns (just as any aspect of a community's life may come to bear selectively on the study of kinship, sex, or role conflict).

It will be found that much that has impinged upon linguistics as variation and deviation has an organization of its own. What seem variation and deviation from the standpoint of a linguist's analysis may emerge as structure and pattern from the standpoint of the communicative economy of the group among whom the analyzed form of speech exists. The structures and patterns that emerge will force reconsideration, moreover, of the analysis of linguistic codes themselves. Just as elements and relations of phonology appear partly in a new light when viewed from the organization of grammar, and just as elements and relations of the grammar appear in a new light when viewed from the organization of sememics (Lamb 1964), so elements and relations of the linguistic code as a whole will appear partly in a new light, viewed from the organization of the elements and relations of the speech act and speech event, themselves part of a system of communicative acts and events characteristic of a group.

To project the ethnography of communication in such a way is tantamount to the belief that there awaits constitution a second descriptive science comprising language, in addition to, and ultimately comprehending, present linguistics—a science that would approach language neither as abstracted form nor as an abstract correlate of a community, but as situated in the flux and pattern of communicative events. It would study communicative form and function in integral relation to each other. In this it would contrast with long held views of linguistics and of what is within linguistics. Some divorce linguistic form from context and function. An old but apt illustration is found in Bloomfield's often cited remark that, if a beggar says "I'm hungry" to obtain food, and a child says "I'm hungry" to avoid going to bed, then linguistics is concerned just with what is the same in the two acts. It abstracts, in other words, from context. In contrast, an influential book has characterized pragmatics in a way exactly complementary as "all those aspects which serve to distinguish one communication event from any other where the sign types may be the same" (Cherry 1961: 225). It abstracts, in other words, from linguistic form.

Such views are not the only ones to be found, but they have been characteristic of linguistics, on the one hand, and social science, on the other, and most practice has exemplified one or the other. For ethnographies of communication, however, the aim must be not so to divide the communicative act or event, divorcing message-form (Cherry's sign-type) and context of use from one another. The aim must be to keep the multiple hierarchy of relations among messages and contexts in view (cf. Bateson, 1963). Studies of social contexts and functions of communication, if divorced from the means that serve them, are as little to the purpose as are studies of communicative means, if divorced from the contexts and functions they serve. Methodologically, of course, it is not a matter of limiting a structural perspective inspired by linguistics to a particular component of communication, but of extending it to the whole.

The ethnography of communication is indebted to the methodological gains from recent studies of linguistic form for its own sake, and to a climate of opinion created by arguments for the significance of formal linguistics. Its roots, however, are deeper and more pervasive. On the one hand, there is the long-term trend away from the study of sociocultural form and content as product toward their study as process—away from study of abstracted categories, departments of culture, toward study of situations, exchanges, and events (cf. Sapir 1933b). On the other hand, there is the continuing trend in linguistics itself toward study of the full complexity of language in terms of what the Prague Circle as long ago as 1929 (the year of Sapir's "The status of linguistics as a science") called "functional and structural analysis," and which Jakobson now designates as interwar efforts towards a "means-ends model" (Jakobson 1963); there are parallels in the perspectives of J. R. Firth (1935—cf. ch. 4 of this volume) and of Sapir (cf. chs. 3, 10 of this volume) in the same period. These traditions have had their vicissitudes, but it is fair to see in the ethnography of communication a renewal of them.

For many people, the place of the ethnography of communication will appear to be, not in relation to one or more traditions in linguistics, but in relation to some general perspective on human behavior. For many, the name of this perspective will be social anthropology, or sociology, or psychology, or some other disciplinary category. The work required does fall somewhere into place within the purview of each such discipline, and there can be no quarrel with any, except to say that the division of the study of man into departmentalized disciplines seems itself often arbitrary and an obstacle. What is essential, in any case, is that the distinctive focus of concern advanced here be recognized and cultivated, whatever the disciplinary label. One way to state the need is to remark that there are anthropological, sociological, and psychological studies of many kinds, but of ethnographic analyses of communicative conduct, and of comparative studies based upon them, there are still few to find. (Chs. 3 and 4 take up relationships with sociology and social anthropology further.)

These remarks apply as well to the field of interest under which others would subsume the concerns represented here, namely, semiotics. De Saussure had proposed semiology as a field more general than linguistics, and Levi-Strauss has characterized it as the study of the life of signs in the bosom of social life, subsuming both linguistics and social anthropology within it (1960). Despite the broad interpretation given the term, however, semiotics (semiology) has continued to suggest most readily logical analysis, and the study of systems of signs as codes alone. The empirical study of systems of signs within systems of use in actual communities seems secondary, when not lost from sight.

Here a division of semiotics in the tripartite formulation of Morris (1946) might serve. Pragmatics, concerned with the use of signs by an interpreter, might be the bridge between the present area of concern and linguistics proper, and stand as name for the cultivation of theory of the use of language (and other codes), alongside theory of their formal and semantic structure (Morris' syntagmatics and semantics). Such a usage of the term 'pragmatics' indeed seems to be gaining vogue in German-language research. Some characterizations of pragmatics, to be sure, would not be adequate, as has been noted above. A conception of pragmatics as concerned with what varies in import, while message-form remains constant, allows for but one of the two relationships between structures of action and structures of communicative form. The relations between means and ends are multiple in both directions, the same means serving sometimes varied ends, and the ends being served by sometimes varied means.

In terms of the criteria systematized by Lamb (1964), we can indeed see a natural extension of grammar to features of action, a pragmemic level if one wishes to call it that. Lamb distinguishes linguistic strata by the twin criteria of "diversification" and "neutralization" (see further ch. 4). Diversification is illustrated by such facts as that one element of meaning can occur in diverse representations (as in *dog house : kennel, or cat house : whore house*); neutralization is illustrated by such facts as that the same representation may serve diverse elements of meaning (as dog in *dog house, dogfight, dognap,* or *cat* in *cat house, cat fight, catnap*). One might well recognize a stratum involving the "pragmeme" as an element or feature of action, since the same feature of action can occur in diverse semantic representations, and the same semantic representations can serve diverse features of action. To use an example from Susan Ervin-Tripp, the same feature of request may be encoded in "Would you get me my coat?" and "Don't you think it's getting cold?"; and conversely, to complete the example, "Don't you think it's getting cold?" may express (among other things) features of literal question or demand for action ("Get me my coat," "Take me inside").

Invaluable as a structural pragmemics would be, it would not suffice for the whole of the subject. Nor, as ordinarily conceived, would communication theory or cybernetics. What is sometimes specifically meant by each of the latter terms would seem to fit, quite importantly indeed, as parts of a general strategy for ethnographic research into communication.

In general, experience suggests that work contributing to study of communication in an ethnographic spirit is likely not to duplicate work under another aegis. Each of the other general notions seems in practice to lose sight of concrete communication, in the sense of actual communities of persons. Forms of formalization, the abstract possibilities of systems, hoped-for keys to mankind as a whole, seem to overshadow the dogged work of making sense of real communities and lives. I find in this a political as well as a scientific liability. In any case, the long-standing, close ties between ethnography and linguistic description; the ethnographic practice of participant observation; and the values placed on the specifics of cultural life and the viewpoint of the other participants in the communication that is ethnography—such traits tend to ensure two characteristics. First, there is likely to be a more egalitarian distribution of detailed interest among the several components of communicative events. Not only the participants and the contents of messages, but also the structures, degrees of elaboration, distinctiveness, values and genres associated with channels, codes, message-forms and settings attract attention partly in their own right—the linguistic codes, of course, as most explicit, and as indispensable, if not wholly adequate, avenues of access to other codes, and to the meanings of other components—but also specialized subcodes and marginal systems, techniques of speech disguise, languages of concealment, drum-languages, ceremonial speech and oratory; the channels, especially when complexly elaborated as in West Africa, or distinctively specialized, as writing for lovers' messages among the Hanunoo of the Philippines; the forms of poetry, ritual speech, and dramatic enactment; and so forth. Such aspects of communication are less likely to receive full due in studies whose concern with communication is not so much with an activity of people, but with fodder for models, or not so much with realization of the purposes of others, as with a way of achieving purposes of one's own. The ethnographer is likely to have, or come to have, the view that models are for people, not people for models; and that there are no masses, only ways of regarding people as masses; that one man's mass is another's public, or community, and that to speak of mass communications is already to express a separateness from the portion of humanity concerned that prejudices the result (see Williams 1960: 315–58). The ethnographer is likely to look at communication from the standpoint and interests of a community itself, and to see its members as sources of shared knowledge and insight. I believe that the only worthwhile future for the sciences of man lies in the realization of such an approach (cf. Hymes 1972c).

The linguistics that can contribute to the ethnography of communication is now generally known as sociolinguistics, and it is here that my own training and experience lie. Such a sociolinguistics, however, is not identical with everything that currently comes under that name. The sociolinguistics with which we are concerned here contributes to the general study of communication through the study of the organization of verbal means and the ends they serve, while bearing in mind the ultimate integration of these means and ends with communicative means and ends generally. Such an approach within sociolinguistics can be called, in keeping with the general term, ethnography of communication, the study of the "ethnography of speaking." (Cf. Hymes 1962, and ch. 4). For the contribution of the ethnography of speaking to be realized, there must be change with respect to a number of orientations toward language. Seven can be singled out as the Pleiades, pointing to the North Star, of this firmament. Primacy must go to (1) the structure, or system of speech (*la parole*); (2) function as prior to and warranting structure; (3) language as organized in terms of a plurality of functions, the different functions themselves warranting different perspectives and organizations; (4) the appropriateness of linguistic elements and messages; (5) diversity of the functions of diverse languages and other communicative means; (6) the community or other social context as starting point of analysis and understanding; (7) functions themselves to be warranted in context, and in general the place, boundaries, and organization of language and of other communicative means in a community to be taken as problematic. In short, primacy of speech to code, function to structure, context to message, the appropriate to the arbitrary or simply possible; but the interrelations always essential, so that one cannot only generalize the particularities, but also particularize the generalities.

It remains that sociolinguistics, conceived in terms of the ethnography of speaking, is ultimately part of the study of communication as a whole. To further establish this context, I shall sketch a general framework in terms of communication proper. The other chapters of this book should be read with the communicative framework in mind.

There are four aspects to the framework, concerned, respectively, with (1) the components of communicative events; (2) the relations among components; (3) the capacity and state of components; and (4) the activity of the whole so constituted. It is with respect to the third and fourth aspects that two topics prominently associated with the topic of communication, communication theory (in the sense of information theory), and cybernetics, find a place.

The Components of Communicative Events

The starting point is the ethnographic analysis of the communicative conduct of a community. One must determine what can count as a communicative event, and as a component of one, and admit no behavior as communicative that is not framed by some setting and implicit question. The communicative event thus is central. (In terms of language the speech event, and speech act, are correspondingly central; see ch. 2).

Some frame of reference is needed for consideration of the several kinds of components copresent in a communicative event. The logical or other superiority of one classification over another is not at issue. What is at issue is the provision of a useful guide in terms of which relevant features can be discerned—a provisional phonetics, as it were, not an a priori phonemics, of the communicative event.

For what has to be inventoried and related in an ethnographic account, a somewhat elaborated version of factors identified in communications theory, and adapted to linguistics by Roman Jakobson (1953;1960), can serve. Briefly put, (1) the various kinds of *participants* in communicative events—senders and receivers, addressors and addressees, interpreters and spokesmen, and the like; (2) the various available channels, and their modes of use, speaking, writing, printing, drumming, blowing, whistling, singing, face and body motion as visually perceived, smelling, tasting, and tactile sensation; (3) the various *codes* shared by various participants, linguistic, paralinguistic, kinesic, musical, interpretative, interactional, and other; (4) the *settings* (including other communication) in which communication is permitted, enjoined, encouraged, abridged; (5) the *forms of messages*, and their *genres*, ranging verbally from single-morpheme sentences to the patterns and diacritics of sonnets, sermons, salesmen's pitches, and any other organized routines and styles; (6) the *attitudes and contents* that a message may convey and be about; (7) the *events* themselves, their kinds and characters as wholes—all these must be identified in an adequate way.

Ethnography here is conceived in reference to the various efforts of Conklin, Frake, Goodenough, Metzger, Romney, and others to advance the techniques of ethnographic work and to conceptualize its goal, such that the structural analysis of cultural behavior generally is viewed as the development of theories adequate to concrete cases, just as the structural analysis of behavior as manifestation of a linguistic code is so viewed. One way to phrase the underlying outlook is as a question of validity. Just as analysis of phonological capabilities must determine what set of phonological features is to be taken as relevant to identification and distinction of phonological sound on the part of the possessors of those capabilities, so analysis of cultural capabilities generally must determine what sets of features are to be taken as relevant to identification and contrast of cultural behavior on the part of the participants. (Sapir's "Sound Patterns in Language" [1925], seen as implying a general statement about the cultural aspect of behavior, remains classic and crucial to the development of anthropological thought in this regard, although it has taken a generation for its ethnographic import to become salient.) Another way to phrase the underlying outlook is as a question of the common element in the situation of ethnographer and person-in-the-culture. Each must formulate from finite experience theories adequate to predict and judge as appropriate or inappropriate what is, in principle, an infinite amount of cultural behavior. (Judgments of grammaticality are a special case.)

Mere observation, however systematic and repeated, can obviously never suffice to meet such high standards of objectivity and validity. As Sapir once observed regarding a rule of avoidance among the Wishram Chinook:

> Incidentally there is a lesson here for the theoretical ethnologist. If the avoidance of man and woman here were known only objectively it would present a situation resembling that, say, in Melanesia. One might suppose then the explanation to be that women were set apart from the man's social fabric because of the low esteem in which they were held, or that men avoided them because of their periodic impure state. Either guess would be a shot far wide of the mark. The moral is that it is as necessary to discover what the native sentiment is as well as to record the behavior.[2]

The point is essentially the same as that of "Sound Patterns in Language," from which stems the current distinction of "etic" and "emic." An "emic" account is one in terms of features relevant in the behavior in question; an etic account, however useful as a preliminary grid and input to an emic (structural) account, and as a framework for comparing different emic accounts, lacks the emic account's validity. The point is an old one in anthropology, only made more trenchant by the clarity with which the point can be made in terms of the contrast between phonetics and phonemics. (See Pike 1954 for coinage of the terms, and conscious development of the perspective from a linguistic basis beyond linguistics, under inspiration from Sapir.) Ethnographic objectivity is intersubjective objectivity, but in the first instance, the intersubjective objectivity in question is that of the participants in the culture. No amount of acoustic apparatus and sound spectrography can crack the phonemic code of a language, and a phonemic analysis, based on the intersubjective objectivity in the behavior of those who share the code, is the necessary basis for other studies, experimental and otherwise. (Cf. Hockett 1955:210–11; Lisker, Cooper, and Liberman 1962.) The same is true for the shared codes which constitute the mutual intelligibility of the rest of cultural behavior. The advantages of such an approach in providing a criterion against which to appraise participants' own explanations and conceptualizations of their behavior, their "homemade models," should be obvious, as should the advantages in providing a basis for controlled comparison, study of diffusion, and any other generalizing or analyzing approach that depends in the last analysis on the adequacy and precision of ethnographic records of cultural behavior. (Ethnographic records, of course, may be of other things: censuses, for example.)

In a discussion of genealogical method, Conklin (1964:25–26), observing that all kinship data derive from ethnographic contexts, makes explicit his assumptions regarding the nature and purpose of ethnography (citing also Goodenough 1956, and noting Frake 1962b, 1964, and a previous article of his own [1962]). The statement applies to communicative data as well as to kinship data, and can be adopted here:

> An adequate ethnography is here considered to include the culturally significant arrangement of productive statements about the relevant relationships obtaining among locally defined categories and contexts (of objects and events) within a given social matrix. These nonarbitrarily ordered statements should comprise, essentially, a cultural grammar (Goodenough 1957a; Frake 1962a). In such an ethnography, the emphasis is placed on the interpretation, evaluation, and selection of alternative statements about a particular set of cultural activities within a given range of social contexts. This in turn leads to the critical examination of intracultural relations and ethnotheoretical models

> (Conklin 1955; Goodenough ms.). Demonstrable intracultural validity for statements of covert and abstracted relationships should be based on prior analysis of particular and generalized occurrences in the ethnographic record (Lounsbury 1955:163–164, 1956; cf. Morris 1946). Criteria for evaluating the adequacy of ethnographic statements with reference to the cultural phenomena described, include: (1) productivity (in terms of appropriate anticipation if not actual prediction); (2) replicability or testability; and (3) economy. In actual field situations, recording activities, analytic operations, and evaluative procedures (in short, the application of ethnographic technique, method, and theory) can, and I think should, be combined. The improvement and constant adjustment of field recording is, in fact, dependent upon simultaneous analysis and evaluation.

Notice that strict conception of ethnography constrains the conception of communication that is admissible. Just as what counts as phonemic feature or religious act cannot be identified in advance, so with what counts as a communicative event. There are, of course, general criteria for phonemic and for communicative status; it is a question of the phenomena by which they are satisfied in a given case. If one examines the writings of anthropologists and linguists, one finds that general conceptions of communicative status vary, sometimes in ways at variance with the conception of ethnography adopted here.

The concept of message would seem to suffice as starting point for any conception, if one grants two kinds of things. The first is that the concept of message implies the sharing (real or imputed) of (1) a code or codes in terms of which the message is intelligible to (2) participants, minimally an addressor and addressee (who may be the same person), in (3) an event constituted by its transmission and characterized by (4) a channel or channels, (5) a setting or context, (6) a definite form or shape to the message, and (7) a topic and comment, i.e., that it says something about something—in other words, that the concept of message implies the array of components previously given. The second is that what can count as instances of messages, and as instances of the components of the event constituted by the transmission of a message, must be determined in the given case along the lines of the ethnographic approach just discussed and just characterized by Conklin.

If one accepts the latter point, then some anthropological conceptions of communication must be judged to exclude too much, or to include too much, or, occasionally, both. To take first the problem of excluding too much, one cannot a priori define the sound of approaching footsteps (Sapir 1921:3) or the setting of the sun (Hockett 1958:574) as not communicative. Their status is entirely a question of their construal by a receiver. In general, no phenomenon can be defined in advance as never to be counted as constituting a message. Consider a case related by Hallowell:

> An informant told me that many years before he was sitting in a tent one afternoon during a storm, together with an old man and his wife. There was one clap of thunder after another. Suddenly the old man turned to his wife and asked, "Did you hear what was said?" "No," she replied, "I didn't catch it." My informant, an acculturated Indian, told me he did not at first know what the old man and his wife referred to. It was, of course, the thunder. The old man thought that one of the Thunder Birds had said something to him. He was reacting to this sound in the same way as he would respond to a human being, whose words he did not understand. The casualness of the remark and even the trivial character of the anecdote demonstrate the psychological depth of the "social relations" with other-than-human beings that becomes explicit in the behavior of the Ojibwa as a consequence of the cognitive "set" induced by their culture. [1964:64]

There are manifold instances from cultures around the world, e.g., to take a recent report, the drinking, questioning and answering in which Amahuaca men are joined by the class of supernaturals known as *yoshi* associated interestingly enough with a specific form of chant and use of the vocal channel (vocal chords tightly constricted) (Carneiro 1964:8). Hallowell's account of the Ojibwa concept of person shows with particular depth the implications of cultural values and world view for occurrences of communicative behavior. As indication of the contribution a conscious ethnography of communication, focused on occurrences of activity such as speech, might make to such anthropological concerns as world view, let me cite one other Ojibwa instance and Hallowell's interpolated regret: having discussed the fact that stones are classified grammatically as animate in gender, and are conceived as potentially capable of animate behavior, especially in ceremonially-linked circumstances, Hallowell records:

> A white trader, digging in his potato patch, unearthed a large stone similar to the one just referred to. He sent for John Duck, an Indian who was the leader of the *wabano*, a contemporary ceremony that is held in a structure something like that used for the Midewiwin (a major ceremony during which stones occasionally had animate properties such as movement and opening of a mouth). The trader called his attention to the stone, saying that it must belong to his pavilion. John Duck did not seem pleased at this. He bent down and spoke to

> the boulder in a low voice, inquiring whether it had ever been in his pavilion. According to John the stone replied in the negative.
>
> It is obvious that John Duck spontaneously structured the situation in terms that are intelligible within the context of Ojibwa language and culture. ... I regret that my field notes contain no information about the use of direct verbal address in the other cases mentioned (movement of stone, opening of a mouth). But it may well have taken place. In the anecdote describing John Duck's behavior, however, his use of speech as a mode of communication raises the animate status of the boulder to the level of social interaction common to human beings. Simply as a matter of observation we can say that the stone was treated as *if* it were a "person," not a "thing," without inferring that objects of this class are, for the Ojibwa, necessarily conceptualized as persons. [1964:56]

Again, within the aboriginal culture of the Wishram and Wasco Chinook of the Columbia River, one must recognize not one but three communicative networks within a community, defined by distinct shared codes. One consisted of normal adults, and children past infancy; a second comprised babies, dogs, coyotes, and the guardian spirits Dog and Coyote, and, possibly old people possessing those guardian spirits; a third comprised those whose guardian spirit experience had granted them the power of being able to interpret the language of the spirits.[3]

If the strict ethnographic approach requires us to extend the concept of communication to the boundaries granted it by participants of a culture, it also makes it necessary to restrict it to those boundaries. To define communication as the triggering of a response (as Hockett [1958:573] has done, and Kluckhohn [1961: 895] has accepted), is to make the term so nearly equivalent to behavior and interaction in general as to lose its specific value as a scientific and moral conception. There are many illustrations possible of actions that trigger response and are not taken as communicative by one or both participants. As an act clearly based on the triggering of response (in another or oneself), sexual intercourse would be an ideal event to test this point; what part, less than all, of triggering of response is sent or received as communication? Again, it is desirable to treat the transmission or receipt of information as not the same as, but a more general category than, communication, the latter being treated as a more specific sphere, necessarily either participated in or constituted by persons (cf. Cherry 1961:247 n). The sound of footsteps or the setting of the sun may be taken as a source of information without being taken as a message (although in either case a receiver may interpret the event as a message).

From this standpoint, genes may transmit information, but the process is communicative only from the standpoint of, and as reported by, an observer and interpreter. For the human observer to report and treat the process experienced or inferred as a communicative one is of course a right not to be challenged, for, formally, it is the same right that the ethnographer accepts when acted upon by an Ojibwa, Wishram, or other participant in a culture. The formal feature is that the evidence for the communicative event is a report by one who did not participate in it as either addressor or addressee. Such reported events (E^n, or narrated events, in Roman Jakobson's symbolization [1957] for the constituents of speech events) are common in myth, for example, and are of course of considerable importance, as when the origin of the world is so described by the ancient Hebrews, or the origin of death explained by the Wishram in a narrative culminating (as is typical for their myths) in an announcement ordaining how that aspect of cultural life is to be and what people will say in its regard.

We deal here, in short, with the fact that the communicative event is the metaphor, or perspective, basic to rendering experience intelligible. It is likely to be employed at any turn, if with varying modes of imputation of reality (believed, supposed, entertained in jest, etc.). It is this fact that underlies the apparently central role of language in cultural life. Of codes available to human beings, language, as the one more than any other capable at once of being explicitly detailed and transcendent of single contexts, is the chief beneficiary under many circumstances of the primary centrality of communication. Under some circumstances, of course, it is not.

In general, any and all of the components of a communicative event, and the occurrence of a message itself, can be imputed by one who adopts the standpoint of an addressor, addressee, or receiver as observer. One consequence is the point already made, but the ethnographic observer must do more than observe to prevent his own habits of imputation from interfering with recognition of where and what participants in another culture impute. Another consequence, since persons can impute either an addressor and intent or an addressee and attention, is to make heuristically useful for ethnographic purposes a characterization of a communicative event as one in which to the observer one at least of the participants is real.

The identification of communicative events and their components has been dwelt on, because it is seldom treated, except incidentally, in most writing relevant to ethnography. The discussion so far has been concerned with gross identification of events as such and of components individually. In point of fact, adequate determination usually will involve more than inventory of channels, setting, etc. The structures of relations among different events, and their components; the capabilities and states of the components; the activity of the system which is the event; all will be involved. Explication of genres of verbal art, once such have been identified (e.g., Ssukung Tu 1963),[4] commonly involves appeal at least to relations among components, and often to their states and activity. Such questions comprise the other aspects of the frame of reference being sketched, and to these we now turn.

Relations Among Components

In one sense, the focus of the present approach is on communities organized as systems of communicative events. Such an object of study can be regarded as part of, but not identical with, an ethnography as a whole.[5] One way in which to indicate that there is a system, either in the community or in the particular event, is to observe that there is not complete freedom of cooccurrence among components. Not all imaginably possible combinations of participants, channels, codes, topics, etc., can occur.

It is to the structure of relations among components that much of the surge of work in sociolinguistics is directed. (Notice that focus on relations among components more readily invites description and comparative analysis of the variety of such marginal systems than does focus on the code alone. Also, more generally, it leads into description and comparison of whatever may characterize such an event or relationship, e.g., talk to babies, whether or not special features characterize it from the standpoint of the code as such. It is equally important to know the characteristics of talk to babies in societies where "baby talk" is eschewed. With regard to message-form, there is much to be discovered and described in the sequential patterning of speech as routines, specialized to certain relationships.)

Ervin-Tripp (1964) suggests that the structures of relations with respect to language will prove to be specific in some ways, to be more than illustration of more general sociological or psychological or cultural notions. The same is likely to prove true for each of the kinds of codes employed in a community. The heuristic assumption is that their separate maintenance implies some specific role for each which is not wholly duplicated by any other (including language). On the other hand, studies focused on the relations among components of communicative events are likely to discern patterns general to them, but partly independent of, and cutting across, the other departments of study into which the events might be cast ethnographically. Once looked for, areal styles, in the use of specific codes, and areal communicative styles generally, are likely to be found. Lomax (1959) has suggested such for musical performance, and Melville Jacobs (1958) has suggested such may be the case for the dramatic performances that enact myths.

It is especially important to notice that delineations of communities in these respects are crucial to understanding of the place of language in culture, and to understanding of the particular place of language in culture signalled by what is commonly called the Sapir-Whorf hypothesis. To assume that differences in language shape or interact with differences in world view is to assume that the functional role of language in relation to world view is everywhere the same. Indeed, anthropological thought quite generally has tended to assume identity, or equivalence of function for language throughout the world (see discussion in Hymes 1961: 1962; 1966b).

When a particular code is considered but one component of communicative events, the studies of the structure of communicative events in a society will provide detailed evidence on the differential ways in which the code enters into communicative purposes and cultural life. The different ways and stages in which a language enters into enculturation, transmission of adult roles and skills, interaction with the supernatural, personal satisfactions, and the like will appear. Languages, like other cultural traits, will be found to vary in the degree and nature of their integration into the societies and cultures in which they occur. It will be possible to focus on the consequences of such differences for acculturation and adaptation of both languages and peoples. Such information has been brought to attention in studies of acculturation, bilingualism, and standard languages. What is necessary is to realize that the functional relativity of languages is general, applying to monolingual situations too.

With particular regard to the Sapir-Whorf hypothesis, it is essential to notice that Whorf's sort of linguistic relativity is secondary, and dependent upon a primary sociolinguistic relativity, that of differential engagement of languages in social life. For example, description of a language may show that it expresses a certain cognitive style, perhaps implicit metaphysical assumptions, but what chance the language has to make an impress upon individuals and behavior will depend upon the degree and pattern of its admission into communicative events. The case is clear in bilingualism; we do not expect a Bengali using English as a fourth language for certain purposes of commerce to be influenced deeply in world view by its syntax. What is necessary is to realize that the monolingual situation is problematic as well. Peoples do not all everywhere use language to the same degree, in the same situations, or for the same things; some peoples focus upon language more than others. Such differences in the place of a language in the communicative system of a people cannot be assumed to be without influence on the depth of a language's influence on such things as world view.

More particularly, if a language is taken as a device for categorizing experience, it is not such a device in the abstract. There remains the question of what may be the set of events in which categorizing dependent upon the language occurs. (The set includes events in which a single person is using a language excogitatively.) Although anthropologists have sometimes talked of the use of language "merely" as a tool of communication, and of the categorizing of experience as if it were a superior category (cf. Hymes 1967c), the role of a language as a device for categorizing experience and its role as an instrument of communication cannot be so separated, and indeed, the latter includes the former. This is the more true when a language, as is often the case, affords alternative ways of categorizing the same experience, so that the patterns of selection among such alternatives must be determined in actual contexts of use—as must also, indeed, the degree to which a language is being used as a full-fledged semantic instrument (as distinct from its use as an expressive, directive, etc., instrument) at all in a given case.

Such considerations broach the third aspect of our frame of reference.

Capacity and State of Components

So far we have considered the identification of events and components, and the structures of relations among them. Now we must consider their capacities, or capabilities, and states. It is here that "communication theory," in the sense in which the term is equivalent to "information theory," enters, with its concern for the measurement of capacity. Although associated primarily with the capacity of channels and codes, the underlying notion extends equally to all components of a communicative event, and to the events of a system.

Questions of capability can be broached in terms of focus upon some one of the components of an event (or the event itself) in relation to all other components in turn. Some topics of longstanding anthropological interest find a place here. The relation of language to environment, both natural and social, in the sense of elaboration of a code's capacity, especially via vocabulary, to deal with snow, cattle, status, etc., as topics, is one. Another is the relationship between the capability of a code, and the capabilities of its users, in the sense of the Whorfian concern with habitual behavior and fashions of speaking. In both cases there must be reference from the start to the distribution in use of the portion of the code in question, both among communicative events and in relation to their other components. (The necessity of this has been argued for the Whorfian problem above; on cultural focus, elaboration of vocabulary, and folk-taxonomy of semantic domains, cf, the views on dependence on context of situation of Brown [1958:255–58], Frake [1961:121–22], Gluckman [1959], Meillet [1906], and Service [1960].)

With regard to participants, differential competence and performance are salient concerns (cf. Gross 1972 mss. a and b; Hymes 1973b). Often this level and the preceding one are but faces of the same coin, the formal structure of relations being grounded culturally in judgments (and facts) as to capability, and circumstances as to capability being dependent upon the structures of relations.

The ethnography of communication deals in an empirical and comparative way with many notions that underlie linguistic theory proper. This is particularly so when linguistic theory depends upon notions such as those of "speech community," "speech act," and "fluent speaker." How varied the capabilities of speakers can be in even a small and presumably homogeneous tribe is sketched incisively by Bloomfield (1927) in a paper that deserves to be classic for its showing that such variation, including possibilities of grammatical mistake, is universal. The range and kind of abilities speakers and hearers show is an area largely unexplored by ethnographers and linguists, but one of great import both to cultural and linguistic theory. (I have tried to draw some implications of a focus on the concept of speakers' abilities in Hymes 1964a and ch. 3.)[6]

Capacity varies with event, and with the states in which participants, channels, etc., may be in the event, including the values and beliefs of participants, as properties of their states that help constitute events as communicative, and that determine other properties. In part the question is one not of what a language does for and to participants, their personalities, culture, and the like, but of what participants, their personalities, and the like, do for and to a language.

Only by reference to the state of participants, moreover, does it seem possible to introduce in a natural way the various types of functions which communicative events may serve for them.

There has been a bias in American linguistics, and in American extensions of linguistic methodology, favoring a "surface–level" approach that stresses identification and segmentation of overt material, and hesitates to venture far into inner structural relations and ascription of purpose. (The bias perhaps reflects the favoring of visual over acoustic space, the trust of the eye, not the ear, that Carpenter and McLuhan [1960:65–70] find characteristic of our society.) In Kenneth Burke's terms, there has been a tendency to treat language and its use as matters of "motion" (as if of the purely physical world), rather than as matters of "action" (as matters of the human, dramatistic world of symbolic agency and purpose) (cf. ch. 7). With all the difficulties that notions of purpose and function entail, there seems no way for the structural study of language and communication to engage its subject in social life in any adequate, useful way, except by taking this particular bull by the horns. The purposes, conscious and unconscious, the functions, intended and unintended, perceived and unperceived, of communicative events for their participants are here treated as questions of the states in which they engage in them, and of the norms by which they judge them. (Those aspects of purpose and function that have to do with feedback, exchange, response to violations of norms, and the like, are considered with the fourth aspect of the present frame of reference, that of the activity of the system.)

For ethnographic purposes, an initial "etic grid" for delineating and "notating" possible types of functions is needed, and it does seem possible to provide one, by considering the possibilities of focus upon each component in turn in relation to each of the others. The grid so derived has proven adequate to accommodate the various schemes of functions, and of functional types of messages, which have come to my attention. Ethnographic work will of course test and probably enlarge and revise it, just as experience of additional languages has enlarged and revised phonetic charts. Literary, philosophical, and other schemes of functions, and of functional types of messages, are also useful as sources of insight and details. (It may prove desirable to undertake a comparative and historical analysis of such schemes, as "home-made models" from our own culture. Among reviews, note Schaff 1962, Part 2, and Stern 1931, ch. 2.)

It must be kept in mind that functions may prove specific to individuals and cultures, and that they require specific identification and labelling in any case, even when subsumable under broad types. The "etic grid" serves only to help perceive kinds of functions that may be present, and possibly to facilitate comparison.

Focus on the addresser or sender in relation to other components entails such types of function as identification of the source, expression of attitude toward one or another component or toward the event as a whole, excogitation (thinking aloud), etc. Such function may be of course intended, attributed, conscious, unconscious. *Focus on the addressee* or other receiver entails such types of function as identification of the destination, and the ways in which the message and event may be governed by anticipation of the attitude of the destination. Persuasion, appeal, rhetoric, and direction enter here, including as well the sense in which the characteristics of the addressee govern the other aspects of the event as a matter of protocol. Effects on receivers may be of course intended, attributed, conscious, unconscious, achieved, frustrated. Focus on *channels* in relation to other components entails such functions as have to do with maintenance of contact and control of noise, both physical and psychological in both cases. *Focus on codes* in relation to other components entails such functions as are involved in learning, analysis, devising of writing systems, checking on the identity of an element of the code use in conversation, and the like. *Focus on settings* in relation to other components entails all that is considered contextual, apart from the event itself, in that any and all components may be taken as defining the setting of the event, not just its location in time and space. Such context has two aspects, verbal and nonverbal from the standpoint of speech, kinesic and nonkinesic from the standpoint of body motion, and, generally, for any one code or modality, context constituted for a message by other messages within the same code or modality, as distinct from context constituted by all other facets of the event. *Focus on message-form* in relation to other components entails such functions as proofreading, mimicry, aspects of emendation and editing, and poetic and stylistic concerns. *Focus on topic* in relation to other components entails functions having to do with reference (in the sense both of linguistic meaning proper and denotation) and content. *Focus on the event* itself entails whatever is comprised under metacommunicative types of function. If the message is taken as subsuming all, or all the immediately relevant, other components, then focus on the message as surrogate of the whole event may be taken as entailing metacommunicative functions ("the message 'this is play' "; Russell's types, etc.; see Bateson 1963 on the importance of this function).

Common broad types of functions associated with each type of focus can be variously labelled: expressive, directive, contact (phatic), metalinguistic, contextual, poetic (stylistic), referential, and metacommunicative are useful. The etic framework implied here can be handled with pencil and paper for visual purposes (and expanded also) by two devices, one of horizontal placement, one of vertical placement, of components relative to each other. In handling the five broad types of components of action used in his analysis (Scene, Act,

Agent, Agency, Purpose), Burke devises various "ratios"; thus, the relation of Scene to Act is the Scene-Act ratio, and can be represented as if a numerator over a denominator: Scene/Act (Burke 1945). In explicating grammatical categories in terms of the components of speech events, Jakobson (1957) discriminates speech events (E^s) and narrated events (E^n), and participants in each (P^s, P^n), expressing relations with a diagonal; thus, the relation of the narrated event to the speech event (involved in verbal categories) is expressed E^n/E^s. Either device could be used to express all the possible combinations and permutations of focus upon the relation of one component of a communicative event to each of the others. Either device is useful in explicating other logical and empirical schemes of functions and functional types of messages in terms of a common denominator, a problem which is a converse in effect of the usual problem of componential analysis. (There one proceeds from etic grid to discover an emic system, here one is concerned to proceed from a possibly emic system to discover an etic grid.)

Most of the functions and components noted above have been discussed with examples of Jakobson 1960 and Hymes 1962.

Activity of The System

Information theory is one topic notably associated with communication; cybernetics is the other. Having taken information theory in its quantitative sense as pertaining to the third aspect of the present frame of reference, we take cybernetics as pertaining to the fourth. Studies concerned with the information theory aspect of ethnographic systems of communication are almost nonexistent, and the case is the same for studies concerned with the cybernetic aspect. One can think in both respects of unpublished work by John Roberts and of a few celebrated and isolated examples in the work of Levi-Strauss (1953) and Bateson (1949; 1958) where sybernetic notions are applied.[7]

The activity of the system is the most general aspect of the four, and ultimately the one in terms of which it is necessary to view the rest. For particular purposes, of course, any one aspect, or part of one, can be segregated for analysis, and there is much to be done in the ethnographic and comparative study of every aspect and component. To take the channel component as an illustration, there are few if any ethnographic studies to compare with Herzog's multifaceted account of the system of channels elaborated among the Jabo of Liberia, considering, as it does, the structure of the code in each, the relation of code and messages in each to base messages in speech, native categories and conceptions, social correlates, and circumstances of use (Herzog 1945). There is a fair variety of reports of specialized uses of the vocal channel, but the account of Mazateco whistle talk by Cowan (1948) again is almost unique in providing a technical linguistic base and ethnographic context that could support controlled comparison. We have noted that paralinguistic and kinesic investigations have but begun to be extended cross-culturally, and attention to the sociopsychological context of attitude toward use of a channel, or modality, for instance the voice and gesture, such as Devereux (1949, 1951) has shown in work with the Mohave, is far to seek. Two general comparative studies (May 1956, Stern 1957) look toward historical interpretation in terms of distribution and origins, but not toward controlled comparison of structures and functions, perhaps because the available data offers little encouragement. Stern's classification of speech surrogates, derived from notions of communication theory, needs clarification and extension to include writing systems, which are logically comprised by the categories. As for the structural and functional aspects of writing and literacy, empirical studies of the diversity of the patterns that occur are few, and as for contrastive studies of their absence, that of Bloomfield (1927) is the only one known to me. Interpretations of the determinism of particular channels, such as those of McLuhan (1962) and of Goody and Watt (1963), and interpretations of the determinism of media (channels) generally, such as are expressed in the orientation of Carpenter and McLuhan (1960) and McLuhan (1964), interesting as they are, seem oversimplified, where not simply wrong, in the light of what little ethnographic base we have. There is a tendency to take the value of a channel as given across cultures, but here, as with every aspect and component of communication, the value is problematic and requires investigation. (Consider for example the specialization of writing to courtship among young people by the Hanunoo, and to a borrowed religion among the Aleut; and the complex and diverse profiles with regard to the role of writing in society, and in individual communicative events, for traditional Chinese, Korean, and Japanese cultures, with regard both to the Chinese texts shared by all and to the materials specific to each.) To provide a better ethnographic basis for the understanding of the place of alternative channels and modalities in communication is indeed one of the greatest challenges to studies of the sort we seek to encourage. At the same time, such work, whether on channels or some other aspect and component, profits from taking into account the complete context of the activity of the system of communication of the community as a whole.

It is with this aspect that the ethnographic study of communication makes closest contact with the social, political, and moral concerns with communication, conceived as value and a determinant in society and in personal lives.

The frame of reference just sketched can be summed up as asking a series of questions: What are the communicative events, and their components, in a community? What are the relationships among them? What capabilities and states do they have, in general, and in particular cases? How do they work?

Some of the variety of current lines of work that can contribute to, and benefit from, ethnographic study of communication can be briefly mentioned.

Linguistic investigation of the abilities and judgments of appropriateness of speakers, when pursued in a thoroughgoing way, must lead into study of the full range of factors conditioning the exercise of judgment and ability. The potential richness of studies of socialization, enculturation, and child development in this regard is manifest. The situation here is parallel to that with regard to the abilities and judgments of adults. Work focused on the linguistic code needs to be extended into concern with the whole of the child's induction into the communicative economy of its community. (Some notes and queries on this are advanced in Hymes 1961b, 1962, 1964e; cf. ch. 3). The importance of concern with the child is partly that it offers a favorable vantage point for discovering the adult system, and that is poses neatly one way in which the ethnography of communication is a distinctive enterprise, i.e., an enterprise concerned with the abilities the child must acquire, beyond those of producing and interpreting grammatical sentences, in order to be a competent member of its community, knowing not only what may possibly be said, but also what should and should not be said.

These studies bear importantly on work in fundamental education and literacy, which raises problems of particular interest; it can be a source of data and insight, and ethnographic studies of communication can contribute to it. The various purposes of educators, workers in literacy, translators, missionaries, and applied anthropologists may be facilitated by prior ethnographic study of the communicative economy with which they are engaged; the same of course applies to teachers and schools in our own society (cf. ch. 5).

Ethnographic work not concerned primarily with communication may make a contribution through precision of focus and detail. Thus one of the accounts of Metzger and Williams (1963: 218–19, 227–28) permits one to determine something of the place of speech, as one communicative modality among others, in a hierarchy of ritual means.[8] With more such analyses one could begin to have controlled comparisons. The study of folk taxonomies, and of ethnographic semantics generally, needs specification of communicative contexts if it is to achieve the implicit goal of discovering the structures of whole vocabularies (cf. Hymes 1964d, and ch. 4). The methods of ethnographic semantics, in turn, are helpful in discovering kinds and components of communicative events.

There is a somewhat different relation to the interest of analytic philosophers in speech acts and modes of language use. Studies in the ethnography of communication afford a necessary ground for empirical testing of the adequacy beyond our own society, or some portion of it, of logical and intuitive analyses of types of act, such as promising, of conversational assumptions, and the like. In turn, ethnography cannot but benefit from additional precision of concepts for etic and typological purposes.

A similar relationship holds with work in paralinguistics, kinesics, and other aspects of codes circumjacent to language in communication. Ethnographic and comparative studies in the context of communication are needed to extend the etic frameworks, and to ascertain emic relevance amidst the wealth of data that even a few minutes of observation can supply. In turn, these investigations are needed to delimit the place and interrelations of modalities, spoken language being but one, in the communicative hierarchy of a community, and as a basis for interpreting the evolution of communication.

The problems of the study of primate communication are in principle the same as those of the ethnographic study of communication in human communities. The importance of studies of primate and other animal communication to help determine, by comparison and contrast, the specific properties of human language, and to help picture its evolutionary emergence, is well known. Ethnographies of communication here play a complementary role, which has yet to gain recognition, since it tends to be assumed that the functions and uses of human language are constant and already known. Empirical questions, such as the minimum role that language can play in the communicative system of a small hunting and gathering community, and of the adequacy of very minimal derived codes in closeknit communities, are not taken into account. Extrapolations as to the relations between code and communicative context at stages of human evolution need a basis in comparative ethnography as well as in formal comparison of codes. Not codes alone, but whole systems of communication, involving particular needs and alternative modalities, must be considered and compared. In general, to the evolutionary approach to culture, ethnographic studies of communication can contribute a framework within which languages can be treated adaptively in ways which articulate with the study of sociocultural evolution as a whole, and with microevolutionary studies (cf. Hymes 1961a, 1964d, 1971d).

What can be sketched now is but an outline of a future in which, one can hope, ethnographic studies of communication will be commonplace, and an ethnographic perspective on the engagement of language in human life the standard from which more specialized studies of language will depart.

Notes

1. This chapter is based upon "Introduction: Toward Ethnographies of Communication," in *The Ethnography of Communication*, ed. by John J. Gumperz and Dell Hymes (Washington, D.C.: American Anthropological Association, 1964), pp. 1–34, issued as Part 2 of the *American Anthropologist* 66(6) (December). It comprises mainly sections VI and VII of that essay. To Susan Ervin-Tripp, John Gumperz, Michael Halliday, Sydney Lamb, Sheldon Sacks, and Dan Slobin, I am indebted for warm discussions of language and its social study; to Bob Scholte and Erving Goffman for pointed argument about the notion of communication; and to Harold C. Conklin, Charles Frake, Ward Goodenough, Floyd Lounsbury, and William C.

Sturtevant, for discussion through several years of the nature of ethnography. To all much thanks and no blame.

2. Spier and Sapir (1930: 217, n. 97). The point and the language indicate that the comment is due particularly to Sapir. The Wishram avoidance is due to the severe punishment, even death, visited for constructive adultery, which offense may be attributed in some circumstances even for private conversation or physical contact. Cf. the last section of Hymes (1966b).
3. With regard to the first and second networks, babyhood lasted "until they could talk clearly" (Spier and Sapir 1930: 218)—in Wishram, of course. With regard to the second, "Such guardian spirits could understand the language of babies. They maintain that a dog, a coyote, and an infant can understand each other, but the baby loses his language when he grows old enough to speak and understand the tongue of his parents" (*ibid.*: 255). With regard of the third, the group may have been individuated into various dyadic relationships between particular persons and spirits, for the example is given as "For instance, one who had gained the protection of Coyote could tell, on hearing a coyote's howl, what person was going to die" (*ibid.*: 239); but men still living, who make no claim to having had guardian spirit experience, recall having been able to understand the import of howls of coyotes (Mr. Hiram Smith, pers. comm.).
4. The classical Chinese writer Ssukung Tu discriminated 24 modes, translated as Grand, Unemphatic, Ornate, Grave, Lofty, Polished, Refined, Vigorous, Exquisite, Spontaneous, Pregnant, Untrammeled, Evocative, Well-knit Artless, Distinctive, Devious, Natural, Poignant, Vivid, Transcendent, Ethereal, Light-hearted, Flowing (Ssukung Tu, as translated [1963] with accompanying discussion by Wu Tiao-kung, "Ssukung Tu's Poetic Criticism," 78–83). Such modes would entail considering the relevant components of the event constituted by the composing or performance of a poem from the standpoint of what is labelled "key" in ch. 2.
5. Notice Conklin (1962: 199): "An adequate ethnographic description of the culture (Goodenough 1957a) of a particular society presupposes a detailed analysis of the communications system and of the culturally defined situations in which all relevant distinctions in that system occur."
6. The term "capability" is used with conscious reference to Tylor's definition of culture (or civilization) as all those capabilities acquired by man in society (1873: 1). I subscribe to the view that what is distinctively cultural, as an aspect of behavior or of things, is a question of capabilities acquired or elicited in social life, rather than a question of the extent to which the behavior or things themselves are shared. The point is like that made by Sapir (1916: 425) with regard to similarity among cultures due to diffusion, namely, that the difference between similarity due to diffusion and similarity due to independent retention of a common heritage is one of degree, rather than of kind. The currency of a cultural element in a community is already an instance of diffusion that has radiated from an individual.

   Sapir's point converges with the focus of grammatical theory on an individual's ability to produce and interpret novel, yet acceptable, utterances. The frequency and degree of spread of a trait is important, but secondary, so far as concerns the criterion for its being a product of cultural behavior, as having a cultural aspect. A sonnet, for example, is such a product, whether or not it goes beyond a desk drawer, or even survives the moment of completion. In the course of the conduct of much cultural behavior, including verbal behavior, it will not be known, or will be problematic to the participants, whether or not some of what occurs and is accepted as cultural, has in fact ever previously occurred, (cf. Hymes 1964a: 33–41). For many problems, it is essential to single out for study phenomena shared to the limits of a community, or as nearly so as possible. For other problems, a group, family, person, or the ad hoc productivity of adaptation to an event, will be the desired focus. To restrict the concept of the cultural to something shared to the limits of a community is an arbitrary limitation on understanding, of both human beings and the cultural.

The perspective sketched here has the same fulcrum as Sapir's "Why cultural anthropology needs the psychiatrist" (1938) (cf. ch. 3). Sapir's insights do not imply reduction of cultural behavior to psychiatric subject matter; he himself explained ([1939] 1949: 579, n. 1):

As some of my readers have from time to time expressed their difficulty with my non-medical use of the terms 'psychiatry' and 'psychiatric,' I must explain that I use these terms in lieu of a possible use of 'psychology' and 'psychological' with explicit stress on the total personality as the central point of reference in all problems of behavior and in all problems of 'culture' (analysis of socialized behavior). ... 'Personology' and 'personalistic' would be adequate terms but are too uncouth for practical use.

Sapir and Chomsky perhaps agree in considering linguistics to be ultimately a branch of psychology, but clearly the kind of psychology each has in mind is different.

7. Goodenough (1957b) introduces communication theory in the Shannon sense into his critical review of an anthropological book on communication (Keesing and Keesing 1956) that does not itself make use of such theory.
8. Verbal means are more pervasive than tactile means, but a tactile means, pulsing, holds the highest level alone; and where the two types of means are combined, it is the verbal type, prayer, that a master curer may delegate.

Bibliography

———. 1963. Exchange of information about patterns of human behavior. In *Information storage and neural control,* eds. W. Fields and W. Abbott. Springfield: Charles C. Thomas.

Bateson, G. 1949. Bali: the value system of a steady state. In *Social Structure: Studies presented to A. R. Radcliffe-Brown,* ed. Meyer Fortes. New York: Oxford University Press.

———. 1958. Naven. 2nd edition. Stanford: Stanford University Press.

________. 1963. Exchange of information about patterns of human behavior. In *Information storage and neural control*, eds. W. Fields and W. Abbott. Springfield: Charles C. Thomas.

Bloomfield, L. 1927. Literate and illiterate speech. *American Speech* 2: 423–439. (Reprinted in *Language in culture and society*, ed. D. Hymes, pp. 391–396. New York: Harper and Row.)

Brown, R. 1958. *Words and things.* Glencoe: The Free Press.

________. 1945. *A grammar of motives.* New York: Prentice-Hall. (Reissued by University of California Press.)

Carneiro, R. L. 1964. The Amahuaca and the spirit world. *Ethnology* 3: 6–12.

Carpenter, E., and McLuhan, M. 1960. *Explorations in communication. An anthology.* Boston: Beacon Press.

Cherry, E. C. 1961. *On human communication. A review, a survey and a criticism. New* York: Science Editions.

________. 1962. Lexicographical treatment of folk taxonomies. In *Problems of lexicography,* eds. F. W. Householder and S. Saporta, pp. 119–141. (Publication 21 of the Indiana University Research Center in Anthropology, Folklore and Linguistics.)

________. 1964. Ethnogenealogical method. In *Explorations in cultural anthropology,* ed. W. Goodenough, pp. 22–55. New York: McGraw-Hill.

Cowan, G. 1948. Mazateco whistle speech. *Language* 24: 280–286.

Devereux, G. 1949. Mohave voice and speech mannerisms. *Word* 5: 268–272.

________. 1951. Mohave Indian verbal and motor profanity. In *Psychoanalysis and the social sciences.* Vol. 3, ed. Geza Roheim. New York: International Universities Press.

Ervin-Tripp, S. 1964. An analysis of the interaction of language, topic and listener. In *The ethnography of communication,* eds. J. J. Gumperz and D. Hymes, pp. 86–102. Washington, D.C.: American Anthropological Association.

Firth, J. R. 1935. The technique of semantics. *Transactions of the philological society,* pp. 36–72. London.

Frake, C. O. 1961. The diagnosis of disease among the Subanun of Mindanao. *American Anthropologist* 63:113–132.

________. 1962b. The ethnographic study of cognitive systems. In *Anthropology and human behavior,* eds. R. Gladwin and W. C. Sturdevant, pp. 72–85. Washington, D.C.: Anthropological Society of Washington.

________1964. A structural description of Subanun 'religious behavior.' In *Explorations in cultural anthropology,* ed. W. H. Goodenough, pp. 111–129. New York: McGraw-Hill.

Gluckman, M. 1959. The technical vocabulary of Barotse jurisprudence. *American Anthropologist* 61: 743–759.

Goodenough, W. 1956. Residence rules. *Southwestern Journal of Anthropology* 12: 22–37.

———. 1957a. Cultural anthropology and linguistics. *Report of the 7th round table meeting*, ed. P. Garvin, pp. 167–173. Washington, D.C.: Georgetown University Press.

———. 1957b. Review of Keesing and Keesing 1956. *Language* 34: 24–29.

Goody, J., and Watt, I. 1963. The consequences of literacy. *Comparative Studies in Society and History,* 5: 304–345.

Gross, L. P. 1973a. Modes of communication and the acquisition of symbolic competence. In *Communications, technology, and social policy,* eds. G. Gerbner, L. Gross, and W. Melody. New York: Wiley.

———. 1973b. Art as the communication of competence. *Social Science Information.* The Hague: Mouton.

Gumperz, J. J. and Hymes, D., eds. 1964. *The ethnography of communication.* Washington, D.C.: American Anthropological Association. (First issued as *American Anthropologist* 66(6), part 2).

Hallowell, A. I. 1964. Ojibwa ontology, behavior and world view. *Primitive views of the world,* ed. S. Diamond, pp. 49–82. New York: Columbia University Press.

Hockett, C. 1955, *A manual of phonology.* (Indiana University Publications in Anthropology and Linguistics; Memoir 11 of the International Journal of American Linguistics.) Bloomington.

———. 1958. *A course in modern linguistics.* New York: Macmillan.

———. 1961b. Linguistic aspects of cross-cultural personality study. In *Studying personality cross-culturally,* ed. B. Kaplan, pp. 313–359. Evanston: Row, Peterson.

———. 1962. The ethnography of speaking. *Anthropology and human behavior,* eds. T. Gladwin and W. Sturtevant, pp. 15–53. Washington, D.C.: Anthropological Society of Washington.

———. 1964a. Directions in (ethno) linguistic theory. *Transcultural studies of cognition,* eds. A. K. Romney and R. G. D'Andrade, pp. 6–56. (Special publication, *American Anthropologist* 66 (3), part 2.) Washington, D.C.: American Anthropological Association.

Herzog, G. 1945. Drum-signalling in a West African tribe. *Word* 1: 217–238.

———. 1961a. Functions of speech: the evolutionary approach. In *Anthropology and education*, ed. F. C. Gruber, pp. 55–83. Philadelphia: University of Pennsylvania.

———. 1964d. A perspective for linguistic anthropology. In *Horizons of anthropology,* ed. S. Tax, pp.92–107. Chicago: Aldine.

———. 1964e. Formal comment. In *The acquisition of language*, ed. U. Bellugi and R. Brown, pp. 107–112. Lafayette: Child Development Publications.

———. 1966b. Two types of linguistic relativity. In *Sociolnguistics,* ed. W. Bright, pp. 114–158. The Hague: Mouton.

———. 1967c. The anthropology of communication. In *Human communication theory*, ed. F. Dance, pp. 1–39. New York: Holt, Rinehart and Winston.

———. 1971d. Foreword. In *The origin and diversification of languages*, by M. Sawdesh; ed. J. Sherzer, pp. v–x. Chicago: Aldine.

________. 1972c. The use of anthropology: critical, political, personal. In *Reinventing anthropology*, ed. D. Hymes, pp. 3–79. New York: Pantheon Books.

________. 1973b. Speech and language: on the origins and foundations of inequality in speaking. *Daedalus* (Summer): 59–86. (Proceedings of the American Academy of Arts and Sciences 102 (3).)

________. 1958. *The content and style of an oral literature.* Chicago: University of Chicago Press.

Jakobson, R. 1953. Chapter 2. In *Result of the conference of anthropologists and linguists,* C. Lévi-Strauss, R. Jakobson, C. F. Voegelin and T. Sebeok, pp. 11–21. (Memoir 8 of the International Journal of American linguistics, Indiana University Publications in Anthropology and Linguistics.) Bloomington. (Reprinted in his *Selected Writings, 2:* 554–567. The Hague: Mouton.)

________. 1957. *Shifters, verbal categories, and the Russian verb.* Cambridge, Mass.: Harvard University, Russian language project. (Reprinted in his *Selected Writings*, 2: 130–147. The Hague: Mouton.)

________. 1960. Concluding statement: linguistics and poetics. In *Style in Language*, ed. T. Sebeok, pp. 350–373. Cambridge, Mass.: MIT Press.

________. 1963. Efforts towards a means-ends model of language in interwar continental linguistics. In *Trends in modern linguistics,* eds. C. Mohrmann, F. Norman and A. Sommerfelt, pp. 104–108. Utrecht: Spectrum Publishers. (Reprinted in his *Selected Writings*, 2: 522–526. The Hague: Mouton, 1971.)

Keesing, F. M., and Keesing, M. M. 1956. *Elite communication in Samoa: a study in leadership.* Stanford: Stanford University Press.

Kluckholn, C. 1961. Notes on some anthropological aspects of communication. *American Anthropologist* 63: 895–910.

Lamb, S. 1964. The sememic approach to structural semantics. *American Anthropologist* 66 (3): 57–78.

Lévi-Strauss, C. 1953. Social structure. In *Anthropology today,* by A. L. Kroeber et al., 524–553. Chicago: University of Chicago Press.

________. 1960. L'Anthropologie sociale devant l'historie. *Annales* 15 (4): 625–737.

Lisker, L., Cooper, F., and Liberman, A. 1962. The uses of experiment in language description. *Word* 18: 82–106.

Lomax, A. 1959. Folk song style. *American Anthropologist* 61: 927–954.

May, L, C. 1956. A survey of glossolalia and related phenomena in non-Christian religions. *American Anthropologist* 58: 75–96.

Meillet, A. 1906. Comment les mots changent de sens. *L'année sociologique* (1905–1906). (Reprinted in *Linguistique historique et linguistique générale*, Vol. 1: 230–271.) Paris: Klincksieck.

McLuhan, M. 1962. *The Gutenberg Galaxy. The making of typographic man.* Toronto: University of Toronto Press.

________. 1964. *Understanding media. The extensions of man.* New York: McGraw-Hill.

Metzger, D., and Williams, G. 1963. Tenejapa medicine I: the cure. *Southwestern Journal of Anthropology* 19: 216–234.

Morris, C. 1946. *Signs, language and behavior.* Englewood-Cliffs: Prentice Hall.

Pike, K. 1967. *Language in relation to a unified theory of the structure of human behavior.* The Hague: Mouton. [Preliminary edition in three parts, 1954, 1955, 1960 from Santa Ana, California: Summer Institute of linguistics, with essentially same numbering but different pagination; pagination here is to the 1967 edition.)

———. 1916. *Time perspective in aboriginal American culture: a study in method.* (Canada, Dept. of Mines, Geological Survey, Memoir 90; Anthropological Series, No. 13) Ottawa: Government Printing Bureau.) (SWES 389–462.)

———. 1921. *Language.* New York: Harcourt, Brace.

———. 1925. Sound patterns in language. *Language* 1: 37–51. (SWES 33–45.)

———. 1933b. Communication. *Encyclopedia of the Social Sciences* 4: 78–81. (SWES 104–109.)

———. 1938. Why cultural anthropology needs the psychiatrist. *Psychiatry* 1: 7–12. (SWES 569–577.)

———. 1939. Psychiatric and cultural pitfalls in the business of getting a living. *Mental Health, Publication No. 9,* 237–244. (American Association for the Advancement of Science.) (SWES 578–589.)

Schaff, A. 1962. *Introduction to semantics.* London: Pergamon Press.

Service, E. 1960. Kinship terminology and evolution. *American Anthropologist 62:* 747–763.

Spier, L., and Sapir, E. 1930. *Wishram ethnography.* (University of Washington Publications in Anthropology 3 (3): 151–300.) Seattle: Washington University Press.

Ssukung, T. 1963. The twenty four modes of poetry. *Chinese Literature 7:* 65–83. Peking Foreign Languages Press.

Stern, G. 1931. *Meaning and change of meaning.* (Göteborg Högskolas Arsskrift, 1932, 38 (1).) Goteborg. (Reprinted, Bloomington: Indiana University Press, n.d. [1963]).

Stern, T. 1957. Drum and whistle languages: an analysis of speech surrogates. *American Anthropologist* 59: 487–506.

Tylor, E. 1871. *Primitive culture.* London: John Murray.

Bailey, Benjamin. 1997. "Communication of Respect in Interethnic Service Encounters." *Language in Society* 26:327–356.

Abstract

Divergent practices for displaying respect in face-to-face interaction are an ongoing cause of tension in the US between immigrant Korean retailers and their African American customers. Communicative practices in service encounters involving Korean customers contrast sharply with those involving African American customers in 25 liquor store encounters that were videotaped and transcribed for analysis. The relative restraint of immigrant Korean storekeepers in these encounters is perceived by many African Americans as a sign of racism, while the relatively personable involvement of African Americans is perceived by many storekeepers as disrespectful imposition. These contrasting interactional practices reflect differing concepts of the relationship between customer and storekeeper, and different ideas about the speech activities that are appropriate in service encounters. (Intercultural communication, respect, service encounters, African Americans, Koreans)[1]

Conflict in face-to-face interaction between immigrant Korean retail merchants and their African American customers has been widely documented since the early 1980s. Newspapers in New York, Washington, DC, Chicago, and Los Angeles have carried stories on this friction; and the 1989 movie *Do the right thing* depicted angry confrontations of this type. By the time that the events of April 1992—referred to variously as the Los Angeles "riots," "uprising," "civil disturbance" or, by many immigrant Koreans, *sa-i-gu* 'April 29'–cast a media spotlight on such relations, there had already been numerous African American boycotts of immigrant Korean businesses in New York and Los Angeles; politicians had publicly addressed the issue; and academics (e.g. Ella Stewart 1989 and Chang 1990) had begun to write about this type of friction.

There are multiple, intertwined reasons for these interethnic tensions in small businesses. An underlying source is the history of social, racial, and economic inequality in American society. In this broader context, visits to any store can become a charged event for African Americans. Thus, according to Austin (1995:32),

> Any kind of ordinary face-to-face retail transaction can turn into a hassle for a black person. For example, there can hardly be a black in urban America who has not been either denied entry to a store, closely watched, snubbed, questioned about her or his ability to pay for an item, or stopped and detained for shoplifting.

Specific features of small convenience/liquor stores, such as the ones studied here, exacerbate the potential for conflict. Prices in such stores are high, many customers have low incomes, and the storekeepers are seen by many as the latest in a long line of economic exploiters from outside the African American community (Drake & Cayton 1945, Sturdevant 1969, Chang 1990, 1993). Shoplifting is not uncommon, and the late hours and cash basis of the stores make them appealing targets for robbery. Nearly all the retailers interviewed had been robbed at gunpoint; this had led some to do business from behind bulletproof glass, making verbal interaction with customers difficult.

In this socially, racially, and economically charged context, subtle differences in the ways that respect is communicated in face-to-face interaction are of considerable significance, affecting relationships between groups. This article documents how differences in the ways that immigrant Korean storekeepers and African American customers communicate respect in service encounters have contributed to mutual, distinctively intense feelings of disrespect between the two groups, and serve as an ongoing source of tension. These contrasting practices for the display of politeness and respect are empirically evident in the talk and behavior that occur in stores, and the negative perceptions that result are salient in interviews of retailers and customers alike.

Respect

The issue of "respect" in face-to-face encounters has been stressed both in the media and in academic accounts of relations between African Americans and immigrant Korean retailers. Ella Stewart (1991:20) concludes that "respect" is important for both groups in service encounters:

> Both groups declared rudeness as a salient inappropriate behavior. The underlined themes for both groups appear to be respect and courtesy shown toward each other. Each group felt that more respect should be accorded when communicating with each other, and that courtesy should be shown through verbal and nonverbal interaction by being more congenial, polite, considerate, and tactful toward each other.

Such analysis suggests that good intentions are all that is required to ameliorate relationships: each group simply has to show more "respect and courtesy" to the other. However, the data presented in this article suggest that, even when such good intentions seem to be present, respect is not effectively communicated and understood. The problem is that, in a given situation, there are fundamentally different ways of showing respect in different cultures. Because of different conventions for the display of respect, groups may feel respect for each other, and may continuously work at displaying their esteem—yet each group can feel that they are being disrespected. This type of situation, in which participants communicate at cross-purposes, has been analyzed most notably by Gumperz 1982a,b, 1992 regarding intercultural communication, though not regarding respect specifically.

The communication of respect is a fundamental dimension of everyday, face-to-face interaction. As Goffman says (1967:46), "the person in our urban secular world is allotted a kind of sacredness that is displayed and confirmed by symbolic acts." These symbolic acts are achieved, often unconsciously, through the manipulation of a variety of communicative channels including prosody, choice of words and topic, proxemic distance, and timing of utterances. Gumperz 1982a, 1992 has shown how cultural differences in the use of such contextualization cues—at levels ranging from the perception and categorization of sounds to the global framing of activities—can lead to misunderstandings in intercultural communication. The focus of this article is the ways in which constellations of interactional features can communicate (dis)respect in service encounters.

The intercultural (mis)communication of respect between African American customers and immigrant Korean retailers is particularly significant for interethnic relations because behavior that is perceived to be lacking in respect is typically interpreted as actively threatening. Thus, according to Brown & Levinson (1987:33), "non-communication of the polite attitude will be read not merely as the absence of that attitude, but as the inverse, the holding of an aggressive attitude." When conventions for paying respect in service encounters differ between cultures, as they do between immigrant Koreans and African Americans, individuals may read each other's behavior as not simply strange or lacking in social grace, but as aggressively antagonistic.

Brown & Levinson posit a classification system for politeness practices that is useful for conceptualizing the contrasting interactional practices of immigrant Korean retailers and African American customers. Following Durkheim 1915 and Goffman 1971, they suggest two basic dimensions of individuals' desire for respect: NEGATIVE FACE wants and POSITIVE FACE wants. Negative face want is "the want of every 'competent adult member' that his actions be unimpeded by others," while positive face want is "the want of every member that his wants be desirable to at least some others" (Brown & Levinson, 62). Stated more simply, people do not want to be imposed on (negative face want); but they do want expressions of approval, understanding, and solidarity (positive face want). Because the labels "positive" and "negative" have misleading connotations, I use the word *involvement* to refer to positive politeness phenomena, and RESTRAINT to refer to negative politeness phenomena. These terms denote the phenomena to which they refer more mnemonically than the terms POSITIVE and NEGATIVE.

Strategies for paying respect include acts of "involvement politeness" and acts of "restraint politeness." Involvement politeness includes those behaviors which express approval of the self or "personality" of the other. It includes acts which express solidarity between interactors—e.g. compliments, friendly jokes, agreement, demonstrations of personal interest, offers, and the use of in-group identity markers. Data from store interactions show that these acts are relatively more frequent in the service encounter talk of African Americans than of immigrant Koreans.

Restraint politeness includes actions which mark the interactor's unwillingness to impose on others, or which lessen potential imposition. These strategies can include hedging statements, making requests indirect, being apologetic, or simply NOT demanding the other's attention to begin with. Restraint face wants are basically concerned with the desire to be free of imposition from others, where even the distraction of one's attention can be seen as imposition. Behaviors that minimize the communicative demands on another—e.g. NOT asking questions, NOT telling jokes that would call for a response, and NOT introducing personal topics of conversation—can be expressions of restraint politeness or respect. Such acts of restraint are typical of the participation of immigrant Korean store—owners in service encounters.

Methods

Fieldwork for this study took place in Los Angeles between July 1994 and April 1995. Data collection methods included ethnographic observation and interviewing in immigrant Korean stores, interviews with African Americans outside of store contexts, and videotaping of service encounters in stores.

I made repeated visits to six stores in the Culver City area, five in South Central, and two in Koreatown. Visits to stores typically lasted from one-half hour to two hours; with repeated visits, I spent over 10 hours at each of three stores in Culver City and one in South Central, and over five hours in one Koreatown store.

Service encounters in two immigrant Korean stores, one in Culver City and one in Koreatown, were videotaped for a total of four hours in each store. Video cameras were set up in plain view, but drew virtually no attention, perhaps because there were already multiple surveillance cameras in each store. The tapes from the Koreatown store are used for the current study because the Culver City store had no Korean customers and a lower proportion of African American customers. During the four hours of taping in this Koreatown store, there were 12 African American customers and 13 immigrant Korean customers.

The encounters with African American customers were transcribed using the conventions of conversation analysis (Atkinson & Heritage 1984),[2] resulting in over 30 pages of transcripts. The encounters in Korean were transcribed by a Korean American bilingual assistant according to McCune—Reischauer conventions, and then translated into English. Transcription and translation of Korean encounters were accompanied by interpretation and explanation—some of which was audio-recorded—by the bilingual assistant while watching the videotapes. In addition, the storekeeper who appears throughout the four hours of videotape watched segments of the tapes and gave background information on some of the customers appearing in the tapes, e.g. how regularly they came to the store. Transcripts of encounters in Korean comprise over 25 pages.

Service Encounter Interaction

In the following sections, I first consider the general structure of service encounters as an activity, delineating two types: SOCIALLY MINIMAL VS. SOCIALLY EXPANDED service encounters. Second, I consider the characteristics of convenience store service encounters between immigrant Koreans, presenting examples from transcripts that show socially minimal service encounters to be the common form. Third, I consider the characteristics of service encounters between immigrant Korean storekeepers and African American customers, using transcripts of two such encounters to demonstrate the contrasting forms of participation in them.

Merritt (1976:321) defines a service encounter as:

> an instance of face-to-face interaction between a server who is "officially posted" in some service area and a customer who is present in that service area, that interaction being oriented to the satisfaction of the customer's presumed desire for some service and the server's obligation to provide that service. A typical service encounter is one in which a customer buys something at a store ...

Service encounters in stores fall under the broader category of institutional talk, the defining characteristic of which is its goal-orientation (Drew & Heritage 1992a). Levinson (1992:71) sees the organization, or structure, of such activities as flowing directly from their goals: "wherever possible I would like to view these structural elements as rationally and functionally adapted to the point or goal of the activity in question, that is the function or functions that members of the society see the activity as having."

The structural differences between Korean-Korean service encounters and those with African American customers that will be described below suggest that the two groups have different perceptions of the functions of such encounters. Even when goals are seen to overlap, participants in intercultural encounters frequently utilize contrasting means of achieving those goals (Gumperz 1992:246). Although African American customers and immigrant Korean shopkeepers might agree that they are involved in a service encounter, they have different notions of the types of activities that constitute a service encounter and the appropriate means for achieving those activities.

The service encounters involving immigrant Koreans and African Americans that are transcribed in this article took place in a Koreatown liquor store between 3 p.m. and 7 p.m. on a Thursday in April 1995. The store does not use bulletproof glass, and from the cash register one has an unobstructed line of sight throughout the store. The cashier is a 31-year-old male employee with an undergraduate degree from Korea; he attended graduate school briefly, in both Korea and the US, in microbiology. He has been in the US for four years and worked in this store for about three and a half years.

Service encounters in this corpus vary widely both in length and in the types of talk they contain. They range from encounters that involve only a few words, and last just seconds, to interactions that last as long as seven minutes and cover such wide-ranging topics as customers' visits to Chicago, knee operations, and race relations. More common than these two extremes, however, are encounters like the following, in which an immigrant Korean woman of about 40 buys cigarettes:

Cash *Annyŏng haseyo*
'Hello/How are you?' ((Customer has just entered store))
Cust *Annyŏng haseyo*
'Hello/How are you?'
Cust *Tambae!*
'Cigarettes!'
Cash *Tambae tŭryŏyo?*
'You would like cigarettes?' ((Cashier reaches for cigarettes under counter))
Cash *Yŏgi issŭmnida*
'Here you are' ((Cashier takes customer's money and hands her cigarettes, customer turns to leave))
Cash *Annyŏnghi kaseyo*
'Good-bye'

Cust	*Nye* 'Okay'

The basic communicative activities of this encounter are: (a) greetings or openings, (b) negotiation of the business exchange, and (c) closing of the encounter.

Greetings, as "access rituals" (Goffman 1971:79), mark a transition to a period of heightened interpersonal access. In these stores, greetings typically occur as the customer passes through the doorway, unless the storekeeper is already busy serving another customer. Greetings in these circumstances include *Hi, Hello, How's it going, How are you?*—or, in Korean, *Annyŏng haseyo* 'Hello/How are you?'

The second basic activity is the negotiation of the business transaction, which includes such elements as naming the price of the merchandise brought to the counter by the customer, or counting out change as it is handed back to the customer. While explicit verbal greetings and closings do not occur in every recorded encounter, each contains a verbal negotiation of the transaction. The negotiation of the business exchange can be long and full of adjacency pairs (Schegloff & Sacks 1973)—involving, e.g., requests for a product from behind the counter, questions about a price, repairs (Schegloff et al. 1977), and requests or offers of a bag. Merritt calls these adjacency pairs "couplets," and she gives a detailed structural flow chart (1976:345) that shows the length and potential complexity of this phase of a service encounter.

The third and final activity of these encounters, the closing, often includes formulaic exchanges: *See you later, Take care, Have a good day,* or *Annyŏnghi kaseyo* 'Goodbye'. Frequently, however, the words used to close the negotiation of the business exchange also serve to close the entire encounter:

Cash	One two three four five ten twenty ((Counting back change))
Cash	(Thank you/okay)
Cust	Alright

This type of encounter—limited to no more than greetings/openings, negotiation of the exchange, and closings—I call a SOCIALLY MINIMAL service encounter. The talk in it refers almost entirely to aspects of the business transaction, the exchange of goods for money; it does not include discussion of more sociable, interpersonal topics, e.g. experiences outside the store or the customer's unique personal relationship with the storekeeper.

However, many service encounters do NOT match this socially minimal pattern. SOCIALLY EXPANDED service encounters typically include the basic elements described above, but also include activities that highlight the interpersonal relationship between customers and storekeepers. These socially expanded encounters are characterized by practices that increase interpersonal involvement, i.e. involvement politeness strategies such as making jokes or small-talk, discussing personal experiences from outside the store, and explicitly referring to the personal relationship between customer and storekeeper.

The initiation of a social expansion of a service encounter is evident in the following excerpt. The African American customer has exchanged greetings with the Korean owner and cashier of the store; the cashier has retrieved the customer's habitual purchase, and begins to ring it up. The customer, however, then reframes the activity in which they are engaged, initiating (marked in boldface) a new activity—a personable discussion of his recent sojourn in Chicago—which lasts for several minutes.

Cash: That's it?
Cust: Tha:t's it ((Cashier rings up purchases.)) ((1.5))
Cust: **I haven't seen you for a while**
Cash: hehe Where you been
Cust: Chicago. ((Cashier bags purchase.))
Cash: Oh really?

The customer's comment *I haven't seen you for a while* instantiates and initiates a new type of activity and talk. The discussion of the customer's time in Chicago is a fundamentally different type of talk from that of socially minimal service encounters. Specifically, it is characterized by talk that is not directly tied to the execution of the business transaction at hand, but rather focuses on the ongoing relationship between the customer and store-keeper. Discussing the customer's trip to Chicago both indexes this personal relationship and, at the same time, contributes to its maintenance.

Such sharing of information helps constitute social categories and co-membership. To quote Sacks (1975:72),

> Information varies as to whom it may be given to. Some matters may be told to a neighbor, others not; some to a best friend, others, while they may be told to a best friend, may only be told to a best friend after another has been told, e.g., a spouse.

In introducing talk of his trip to Chicago, the customer asserts solidarity with the cashier: they are co-members of a group who can not only exchange greetings and make business exchanges, but who can also talk about personal experiences far removed from the store.

This type of talk, which indexes and reinforces interpersonal relationships, distinguishes socially expanded service encounters from minimal ones. My data contain a wide range of such talk which enhances personal involvement. Specific practices include, among many others, talk about the weather and current events (*Some big hotel down in Hollywood, all the windows blew out*), jokes (*I need whiskey, no soda, I only buy whiskey*), references to commonly known third parties (*Mr. Choi going to have some ice?*), comments on interlocutors' demeanor (*What's the matter with you today?*), and direct assertions of desired intimacy (*I want you to know me.*).[3] Through their talk, customers and retailers create, maintain, or avoid intimacy and involvement with each other. These individual service encounters—an everyday form of contact between many African Americans and immigrant Koreans—are fundamental, discrete social activities that shape the nature and tenor of interethnic relations on a broader scale.

Service Encounters Between Immigrant Koreans

Before examining immigrant Korean interaction with African Americans, I consider service encounters in which the customers as well as the storekeepers are immigrant Koreans. These Korean—Korean interactions provide a basis for comparison with African American encounters with Koreans. If, for example, the taciturnity and restraint of retailers in their interaction with African Americans were due solely to racism, one would expect to find retailers chatting and joking with their Korean customers and engaging in relatively long, intimate conversations.

In fact, the retailers in Korean—Korean encounters display the same taciturn, impersonal patterns of talk and behavior that they display with African American customers, even in the absence of linguistic and cultural barriers. The Korean—Korean interactions are even shorter and show less intimacy than the corresponding interactions with African American customers. Ten of the 13 service encounters with immigrant Korean customers were socially minimal, while only 3 of the 12 encounters with African Americans were socially minimal. Unlike their African American counterparts, immigrant Korean customers generally do not engage in practices through which they could display and develop a more personal relationship during the service encounter, e.g. making small talk or introducing personal topics. The example of a Korean woman buying cigarettes, transcribed above, is typical of encounters between Korean merchants and customers. Racism or disrespect are not necessarily reasons for what African Americans perceive as distant, laconic behavior in service encounters.[4]

I have no recorded data of service encounters involving African American store-owners with which to compare these encounters with immigrant Korean ones. I did, however, observe many interactions between African American customers and African American cashiers who were employed in stores owned by immigrant Koreans. Interactions between customers and such African American cashiers were consistently longer, and included more social expansions and affective involvement, than the corresponding encounters with immigrant Korean cashiers in the same stores.

Of the three socially expanded service encounters among immigrant Koreans, two involve personal friends of the cashier from contexts outside the store, and the third is with a child of about 10 years who is a regular customer at the store. According to Scollon & Scollon (1994:137), the communicative behavior that East Asians display toward those whom they know and with whom they have an ongoing personal relationship ("insiders") differs drastically from the behavior displayed toward those in relatively anonymous service encounters ("outsiders"):

> One sees quite a different pattern [from "inside" encounters] in Asia when one observes "outside" or service relationships. These are the situations in which the participants are and remain strangers to each other, such as in taxis, train ticket sales, and banks. In "outside" (or nonrelational encounters) one sees a pattern which if anything is more directly informational than what one sees in the West. In fact, Westerners often are struck with the contrast they see between the highly polite and deferential Asians they meet in their business, educational, and governmental contacts and the rude, pushy, and aggressive Asians [by Western standards for subway-riding behavior] they meet on the subways of Asia's major cities.

In my data, service encounter communicative behavior among Korean adults could be predicted by the presence or absence of personal friendship from contexts outside the store. Socially expanded encounters with immigrant Korean adults occurred only when those adults were personal friends of the cashier, with whom he had contact outside the store. The cashier did not have a relationship with the child customer outside the store; but criteria for expanding encounters with children, and the nature of the expansions, may be different than for adults. In this case, the social expansion included a lecture to the child on the necessity of working long hours, and the child formally asked to be released from the interaction before turning to go.

Even in socially expanded service encounters among adult Korean friends, interlocutors may at times display a relatively high degree of restraint. For example, in the following segment, the cashier encounters a former roommate whom he has not seen in several years, who has by chance entered the store as a customer. The cashier and this customer had shared an apartment for two months in Los Angeles, more than three years prior to this encounter, and the customer had later moved away from Los Angeles.

When the customer enters the store, he displays no visible surprise or emotion at this chance encounter with his former roommate. He initially gives no reply to the cashier's repeated queries, "Where do you live?", and gazes away from the cashier as if nothing had been said. After being asked five times where he lives, he gives a relatively uninformative answer, "Where else but home?"

Cash Ŏ'
'He y!' ((Recognizing customer who has entered store Cashier reaches out and takes customer's hand Customer pulls away and opens cooler door)) ((3 0))
Cash *Ŏdi sarŏ*
'Where are you living?'
Cash Ŏ?
'Huh?' ((7 0))
Cash *Ŏdi sarŏ*
'Where are you living?' ((5))
Cash *Ŏdi sarŏ*
'Where are you living?' ((Cashier and customer stand at the counter across from each other)) ((2 5))
Cash Ŏ?
'Huh?' ((Customer gazes at display away from cashier Cashier gazes at customer))
Cash *Ŏdi sarŏ*
'C'mon, where are you living?' ((1 0))
Cust ( )
Cash Ŏ?
'Huh?' ((Cashier maintains gaze toward customer, customer continues to gaze at display)) ((7 0))
Cash *Ŏdi sanyanikka?*
'So, where are you living?' ((3 0))
Cust *Ŏdi salgin, chibe salji*
'Where else, but home?' ((1 0))
Cash Ŏ?
'huh?'
Cash *Chibi ŏdi nyago?*
'So where is your house?'

In this opening segment of transcript, the cashier has asked the customer six times where he lives—10 times if the follow-up *Huh?'s* are included. The customer does not reveal to his former roommate where he lives, even as he stands three feet away from him, directly across the counter.

The customer's initial unresponsiveness in this encounter is striking by Western standards of conversational cooperation (Grice 1975). The cashier, however, does not seem to treat the customer's behavior as excessively uncooperative, e.g. by becoming angry or demanding an explanation for his interlocutor's lack of engagement. A Korean American consultant suggested that the customer's restraint was a sign not of disrespect, but of embarrassment (perhaps regarding his lack of career progress), which could explain the cashier's relative patience with uninformative responses.

This apparent resistance to engagement, however, is precisely the type of behavior cited by African Americans as insulting, and as evidence of racism on the part of immigrant Korean storekeepers:

> When I went in they wouldn't acknowledge me. Like if I'm at your counter and I'm looking at your merchandise, where someone would say "Hi, how are you today, is there anything I..." they completely ignored me. It was like they didn't care one way or the other.
>
> They wouldn't look at you at all. They wouldn't acknowledge you in any way. Nothing. You were nobody ... They'd look over you or around you. (46-year-old African American woman)
>
> ... to me, many, not all, many of them perceive Blacks as a non-entity. We are treated as if we do not exist. (50-year-old African American male gift shop owner)

The customer's reluctance to acknowledge the cashier verbally or to respond to his questions—and the cashier's lack of anger at this—indicate that, at least in some situations, relatively dispassionate and impassive behavior is not interpreted by Koreans as insulting or disrespectful.

The taciturnity of the customer in this interaction, and of immigrant Korean storekeepers and customers more generally, is consistent with descriptions of the importance of *nunch'i* among Koreans—roughly 'perceptiveness', 'studying one's face', or 'sensitivity with eyes' (M. Park 1979, Yum 1987). It is a Korean interactional ideal to be able to understand an interlocutor with minimal talk, to be able to read the other's face and the situation without verbal reference. Speaking, and forcing the interlocutor to react, can be seen as an imposition: "to provide someone with something before being asked is regarded as true service since once having asked, the requester has put the other person in a predicament of answering 'yes' or 'no' " (Yum 1987:80).

This ideal, of communicating and understanding without talk, is present in the two most important religio-philosophical traditions of Korea—Confucianism and Buddhism. Confucian education stresses reading and writing, rather than speaking. Talk cannot be entirely trusted and is held in relatively low regard:

> To read was the profession of scholars, to speak that of menials. People were warned that "A crooked gem can be straightened even by rubbing; but a single mistake in your speech cannot be corrected. There is no one who can chain your tongue. As one is liable to make a mistake in speech, fasten your tongue at all times. This is truly a profound and urgent lesson ..." (Yum 1987:79)

In Buddhism, communication through words is generally devalued: "there is a general distrust of communication, written or spoken, since it is incomplete, limited, and ill-equipped to bring out true meaning" (Yum 1987:83). Enlightenment and understanding in Korean Buddhism is achieved internally, unmediated by explicit utterances: "The quest for wordless truth—this has been the spirit of Korean Buddhism, and it still remains its raison d'être" (Keel 1993:19).

The data from service encounters presented here suggest that this cultural ideal, of understanding without recourse to words, exists not only in religio-philosophical traditions, but may extend in certain situations to ideals of behavior in everyday face-to-face interaction.

Service Encounters Between Immigrant Koreans and African Americans

As noted above, the service encounters with African American customers are characterized by more personal, sociable involvement and talk than the Korean—Korean encounters. While social expansions with Korean adult customers occurred only with personal friends of the cashier from contexts outside the store, only one of the nine African American customers in socially expanded encounters was friends with the cashier outside the store context.

Although the encounters with African Americans are longer and in many ways more intimate than the corresponding ones with Korean customers, close examination reveals consistently contrasting forms of participation in the service encounters. Overwhelmingly, it is the African American customers who make the conversational moves that make the encounters more than terse encounters focusing solely on the business transaction. Repeatedly, African American customers, unlike the immigrant Korean storekeepers and customers, treat the interaction not just as a business exchange, but as a sociable, interpersonal activity—by introducing topics for small-talk, making jokes, displaying affect in making assessments, and explicitly referring to the interpersonal relationship between cashier and customer.

Immigrant Korean retailers in these encounters are interactionally reactive, rather than proactive, in co-constructing conversation. Videotaped records reveal, for example, repeated instances where African American customers finish turns when discussing issues not related to the business transaction, and then re-initiate talk when no reply is forthcoming from the storekeepers. African American customers carry the burden of creating and maintaining the interpersonal involvement.

When immigrant Korean store keepers do respond to talk, many responses display an understanding of referential content of utterances—but no alignment with the emotional stance, of the customer's talk, e.g. humor or indignation. Consider the reaction to ASSESSMENTS, i.e. evaluative statements that show one's personal alignment toward a phenomenon (Goodwin & Goodwin 1992). These are not met by storekeepers with second-assessments of agreement. When they do respond to assessments with affect, e.g. smiling at a customer's joke and subsequent laughter, their displayed levels of affect and interpersonal involvement are typically not commensurate with those of the customers.

The relative restraint of storekeepers in interaction with African American customers is not only a function of cultural preference for socially minimal service encounters and situated, interactional restraint; it also reflects limited English proficiency. It is more difficult to make small-talk, to joke, or to get to know the details of a customer's life if communication is difficult. Restraint politeness can be expressed by NOT using the verbal channel, i.e. silence; but involvement politeness requires more complex verbal activities—e.g. using in-group identity markers, showing interest in the other's interests, and joking.

The phonological, morphological, and syntactic differences between Korean, an Altaic language, and English, an Indo-European one, make it difficult to achieve fluency, and store-owners have limited opportunities for study. Even among those who have been in America for 20 years, many cannot understand English spoken at native speed, and many express embarrassment about speaking it because of limited proficiency.[5]

Videotaped records of interaction do NOT reveal constant hostility and confrontations between immigrant Korean retailers and African American customers; this finding is consistent with many hours of observation in stores. Some relationships, particularly those between retailers and regular customers, are overtly friendly: customers and storekeepers greet each other, engage in some small talk, and part amicably. Observation and videotape do not reveal the stereotype of the inscrutably silent, non-greeting, gaze-avoiding, and non-smiling Korean storekeepers which were cited by African Americans in media accounts and in interviews with me. However, videotaped records do reveal subtle but consistent differences between African Americans and immigrant Koreans in the forms of talk and behavior in service encounters. These differences, when interpreted through culture-specific frameworks, can contribute to and reinforce pejorative stereotypes of store-owners as unfriendly and racist, and of customers as selfish and poorly bred.

In the following section I detail these differences in interactional patterns in transcripts of two socially expanded service encounters. The first interaction is with a middle-aged African American man who is a regular at the store. The cashier was able to identify him immediately on videotape in a follow-up interview; he said that the customer had been coming to the store two or three times a week for at least three and a half years. This encounter shows notably good and comfortable relations, typical of encounters with regular customers, but at the same time it displays the asymmetrical pattern of involvement described above. The second interaction is a much longer one that occurs with a 54-year-old customer who is new to the area and the store, and who may be under the influence of alcohol at the time. Contrasting forms of participation are particularly evident in this second interaction.

Encounter 1

In this interaction, a neatly dressed African American man in his 40s, carrying a cellular phone, comes into the store to buy a soda and some liquor. He is a regular at the store, but at the time of videotaping he had been away in Chicago for a month. The cashier is behind the counter, and the store-owner is standing amid displays in the middle of the store. The store-owner, about 40, has been in America for 20 years. He received his undergraduate degree from the University of California, Los Angeles; he studied math and computer science, he told me, because his English was not good enough for other subjects He is more outgoing and talkative with customers than most of the storekeepers of his age, or older, who were observed

Following greetings, the customer begins to treat the activity not just as a business transaction, but as an opportunity to be sociable, e g by introducing personal narratives about his long absence from Los Angeles and his experiences in Chicago

((Customer enters store and goes to soda cooler))
Cust [Hi]
Own [How ar]e you?
((Customer takes soda toward cash register and motions toward displays)) ((7 5))
Cust Wow you guys moved a lot of things around
Cash Hello, ((Cashier stands up from where he was hidden behind the counter))
Cash Heh heh
Cash How are you? ((Cashier retrieves customer's liquor and moves toward register))
Cust What's going on man? ((Cashier gets cup for customer's liquor)) ((8))

Cust How've you been?
Cash Sleeping
Cust eh heh heh ((1 8))
Cash That s it?
Cust Tha t's it ((Cashier rings up purchases)) ((1 5))
Cust I haven't seen you for a while
Cash hehe Where you been
Cust Chicago ((Cashier bags purchase))
Cash Oh really?
Cust [yeah]
Cash [How] long?
Cust For about a month ((1 2))
Cash How's there
Cust Co l'!
Cash [Co ld?]
Cust [heh] heh heh heh
Own Is Chicago cold?
Cust u h! ((lateral headshakes)) ((1 4)) man I got off the plane and walked out the airport I said "Oh shit "
Cust heh heh heh
Own I thought it's gonna be nice spring season over there
Cust Well not now this is about a month—I been there—I was there for about a month but you know () damn ((lateral headshakes))
((Customer moves away from cash register toward owner)) ((1 4))
Cust Too co ?'
Cust I mean this was really cold
Own (They have snowy) season there
Cust I've known it to snow on Easter Sunday (())
Cust Alright this Sunday it'll be Easter (())
Cust I've seen it snow Easter Sunday
((15-second discussion, not clearly audible, in which the owner asks if there are mountains in Chicago, and the customer explains that there are not))
Cust See th-this-California weather almost never changes
Cust ((Spoken slowly and clearly as for non-native speaker)) back there it's a seasonal change, you got fall, winter, spring
Own mm hm
Cust You know

Cust But back there the weather sshhh ((lateral headshake))
Cust: It's cold up until June
Cust: I mean these guys like they—they wearing lon:g john:s from September until June
Own: (It's hot season, June)
Cust: He—here it's hot, but there it's ((lateral headshake))
Cust: (Really) ((Customer moves toward exit.))
Own: Kay [see you later]
Cust: [see you later]
Cust: Nice talking to you

Although this customer has come into the store to buy a soda and liquor, he also displays interest in chatting, particularly about his sojourn in Chicago and the climate there. After the initial greetings, he comments on how much the store displays have changed: *Wow you guys moved a lot of things around*. This comment is consistent with the fact that he's been away; it provides an opening for a reply such as *We moved those a long time ago*, or another such comment that would display acknowledgment that the customer hasn't been in the store for some time. But neither cashier nor owner responds to his comment. The customer's use of the present perfect tense (*How've you been?*)—as opposed to present tense (*How are you?* or *How ya doing?*)—draws attention to the fact that he hasn't had contact with these storekeepers for a period of time beginning in the past and ending as he speaks; again this invites discussion of the fact that he hasn't been to the store for an unusually long time. The cashier answers the question *How've you been?* with *Sleeping*, treating it as referring to the present. The English present perfect tense is expressed with a past tense form in Korean, and may have led the cashier to interpret the question as a form of present tense.

The cashier places the customer's habitually preferred liquor on the counter without the customer's requesting the item. In doing so, the cashier, without talk, shows that he knows the customer, at least his business exchange habits. As the cashier rings up the purchase, the customer again uses the present perfect tense, indexing his relatively long absence from the store, commenting: *I haven't seen you for a while*. This comment not only indexes his long absence from the store, but draws the cashier into conversation. The comment is typically made by a person who has remained in one place while another has left and come back. In this case there is no indication that the cashier has been away. In fact, as an immigrant Korean working in a liquor store, he probably spends 80 or more hours a week in the store, up to 52 weeks each year.

The customer's seeming reversal of roles—speaking as if the cashier, rather than he, had been away—has the function, however, of drawing the cashier into conversation. The customer does not simply introduce the topic he wants to discuss; he compels the cashier to ask him about the topic. If the customer had simply stated, *I've been in Chicago for a month and it was cold,* his audience could simply have nodded and acknowledged it. Instead the speaker chooses an interactional strategy that compels a question from his interlocutors, increasing interpersonal involvement.

The customer's delivery displays a relatively high level of affective personal involvement: he uses profanity (*Oh shit*), falsetto voice, hyperbole (*they wearing long johns from September until June*), elements of African American English syntax (*they wearing*) and phonology (*col'*), and relatively high-volume laughter. The cashier and owner, however, do not display such a high level of affective personal involvement in the interaction, even through channels which are not dependent on linguistic proficiency. They do not laugh during the encounter, for example, and the owner is looking down unsmiling when the customer recounts his reaction (*Oh shit*) when getting off the plane in Chicago.

This disparity in levels of personal involvement is particularly apparent as the customer makes repeated assessments that display his alignment toward the weather in Chicago. According to Goodwin & Goodwin (1992:166),

> this alignment can be of some moment in revealing such significant attributes of the actor as his or her taste and the way in which he or she evaluates the phenomena he or she perceives. It is therefore not surprising that displaying congruent understanding can be an issue of some importance to the participants.

Assessments provide a locus for interlocutors to show a common understanding and orientation through verbal and/or non-verbal markers of agreement with the assessment. Even when an individual has little knowledge of the referent of an assessment, positive response to the assessment will show emotional understanding and alignment with the assessor.

Explicit practices for displaying this alignment are highly developed among African Americans in the interactional pattern of "call-and-response," in which one actor's words or actions receive an immediate, often overlapping, response and confirmation from others (Smitherman 1977). Call-and-response marks involvement and congruent understanding with explicit vocal and non-verbal acts. Responses that overlap the caller's action are not seen as disrespectful interruptions, but rather as a means of displaying approval and of bringing caller and responder closer together.

While most often studied in formal performances—e.g. concerts, speeches, or sermons—relatively animated back-channel responses also characterize everyday talk of (and particularly among) many African Americans. Smitherman (1977:118) points out that differing expectations and practices of back-channel responses can lead to the breakdown of interethnic communication:

> "call-response" can be disconcerting to both parties in black-white communication ... When the black person is speaking, the white person ... does not obviously engage in the response process, remaining relatively passive, perhaps voicing an occasional subdued "Mmmmmmhhm." Judging from the white individual's seeming lack of involvement, the black communicator gets the feeling that the white isn't listening... the white person gets the feeling that the black person isn't listening, because he "keeps interrupting and turning his back on me."

In the encounter under consideration, the storekeepers display little reaction to the customer's assessments—much less animated, overlapping responses. The customer makes repeated assessments of the extreme cold of Chicago, e.g. *Co:l'!; Oh shit; damn; Too col'; this was really cold; back there the weather sshhh; it's cold up until June; they wearing lon:g john:s from September until June;* and *there it's* [lateral headshake]. The cashier smiles at the customer's *Oh shit* and immediately succeeding laughter, but other assessments get no such show of appreciation. The owner's responses to these dramatic assessments tend toward checks of facts: *Is Chicago cold?; I thought it's gonna be nice spring season over there;* and *It's hot season, June.* The Korean storekeepers show little appreciation for the cold of Chicago, thereby failing to align themselves and display solidarity with the customer making these assessments.

Following two of these assessments *(co:l'* and *I got off the plane and walked out the airport I said "Oh shit")*, the customer laughs. According to Jefferson (1979:93),

> Laughter can be managed as a sequence in which speaker of an utterance invites recipient to laugh and recipient accepts that invitation. One technique for inviting laughter is the placement, by speaker, of a laugh just at completion of an utterance, and one technique for accepting that invitation is the placement, by recipient, of a laugh just after onset of speaker's laughter.

The customer's laughter following his utterances matches this pattern precisely, but cashier and owner do not accept the invitation to laugh. Not only do they fail to accept the invitation to laugh, but the owner actively declines the invitation to laugh. He does this not through silence, which would allow the speaker to pursue recipient laughter further, but by responding to the customer's laughter with serious talk of facts, i.e. the temperature in Chicago: *Is Chicago cold?* and *I thought it's gonna be nice spring season over there.* As Jefferson says,

> In order to terminate the relevance of laughter, recipient must actively decline to laugh. One technique for declining a postcompletion invitation to laugh is the placement of speech, by recipient, just after onset of speaker's laughter, that speech providing serious pursuit of topic as a counter to the pursuit of laughter.

The owner's response to the customer's invitation to laugh serves as an effective counter to the invitation.

Finally, the customer's comment upon leaving (*Nice talking to you*) suggests his attitude toward this service encounter: it wasn't just an encounter about doing a business transaction, it was a time to enjoy talking personally and make connections to people. Such an attitude is consistent with observations and videotaped records, which show African American customers consistently engaging in a relatively high degree of sociable, interpersonal interaction in service encounters.

The customer's parting comment, *Nice talking to you,* has no equivalent in Korean. The closest expression might be *sugo haseo,* which has a literal meaning close to 'Keep up the good work," but is used to mean 'Thank you and goodbye'. Reference to work may serve as a more appropriate social currency ('Keep up the good work') than reference to talk ('Nice talking to you'), consistent with cultural ideals of relative taciturnity in service encounters.

This asymmetrical pattern of interaction occurs despite apparent attempts by both parties to accommodate to the perceived style or linguistic proficiency of the other. Both cashier and owner, for example, make repeated inquiries about the customer's trip to Chicago (*How long?; How's there.*) and the weather there (*Is Chicago cold?; They have snowy season there*). Showing interest in one's interlocutor's interests is a basic form of involvement politeness (Brown & Levinson 1987:103), and one that is absent in the encounters between immigrant Koreans that do not involve intimate friends or children. The cashier and owner are adopting a relatively involved style. The customer also appears to adapt his speech behavior to his interlocutors, in this case for non-native speakers. He explains and repeats his assessments after they draw no second-assessment of agreement (*I've known it to snow on Easter Sunday... Alright this Sunday it'll be Easter... I've seen it snow Easter Sunday*); and he shifts to a slow and enunciated register to explain the seasonal weather of Chicago (*back there it's a <u>seasonal</u> change, you got fall, winter, spring*). Thus both parties accommodate to the other, narrowing differences in communication patterns; but the accommodation is not necessarily of the type or degree that can be appreciated by the other, to result in a more synchronous, symmetrical interaction.

Encounter 2

This second encounter of a Korean immigrant shop-owner and cashier with an African American customer is much longer, lasting about 7 minutes, with distinct episodes—including two instances when the customer moves to the exit as if to leave, and then returns to re-initiate conversation. Five excerpts from the encounter are presented and discussed.

The customer's talk and communicative behavior are in sharp contrast to that of immigrant Korean customers. He not only engages in interactional practices that increase interpersonal involvement, e.g. talk of personal topics; he also explicitly states that he wants the storekeepers to know him, and he pledges extreme solidarity with them—e.g. he tells them to call him to their aid if their store is threatened in future "riots." His interaction with the storekeepers suggests that he has different ideas about the relationship between customers and storekeepers than do immigrant Koreans, and different ideas about the corresponding service encounter style.

This customer's explicit expressions of solidarity and intimacy with the storekeepers are matched with an interactional style that includes many of the characteristics—e.g. relatively high volume, volubility, and use of profanity—that immigrant Korean retailers have characterized as disrespectful (Ella Stewart 1989, 1991, Bailey 1996). While this customer's interactional style is "emotionally intense, dynamic, and demonstrative" (Kochman 1981:106), relative to most of the African American customers at this Koreatown store, it shares many features with the style regularly observed in stores in low-income South Central Los Angeles.

The customer, a male in his 50s, has visited the store just once before, the previous night. He is accompanied by his nephew, who does not speak during the encounter. The customer is wearing a warm-up suit and has sunglasses resting on top of his head. His extreme expressions of co-membership with the storekeepers as he talks to them, along with the jerkiness of some of his arm motions, suggest that he may have been drinking. It is not uncommon for customers at mom-and-pop liquor stores to display signs of alcohol use when they are at the store. This customer's speech is not slurred, however, and he does not appear to be unsteady on his feet.

This new customer arrives at the store speaking to his nephew at relatively high volume. The encounter proceeds as a socially minimal service encounter until the African American customer, following the pattern described above, reframes the activity by introducing a personal topic from outside the store context (his recent move to the area) and referring to his personal relationship with the cashier:

((Customer arrives talking to his companion, who is later identified as his nephew))

Cust	( ) thirty-seven years old (in this) ass
Cust	Motherfucker ((1 0))
Cash	Hi ((Customer approaches counter)) ((2))
Cust	How's it going partner? euh ((Cashier nods)) ((1 0))
Cust	You got them little bottles?
Cash	(eh) ((Customer's gaze falls on the little bottles)) ((3 5))
Cust	One seventy-five! ((Customer gazes at display of bottles)) ((2 0))
Cust	You ain't got no bourbon? ((1 2))
Cash	No we don't have bourbon ((1 0))
Cust	I'll get a beer then
Cust	((turns to nephew)) What would you like to drink? what do you want? ((Customer selects beverages and brings them to the cash register)) ((7 5))
Cash	Two fifty ((Cashier rings up purchase and bags beer)) ((4 5))
Cust	I just moved in the area I talked to you the other day You [remember me]?
Cash	[Oh yesterday] last night
Cust	Yeah
Cash	[(O h yeah)] ((Cashier smiles and nods))
Cust	[Goddamn, shit] [then you don't–]
Own	[new neighbor, huh?] ((Customer turns halfway to the side toward the owner))
Cust	Then you don't <u>know</u> me
Cash	[(I know you)] ((Cashier gets change at register))
Cust	[I want you to <u>know</u>] me so when I walk in here you'll know me I smoke Winstons Your son knows me
Cash	[Ye ah]
Cust	[The yo]ung guy
Cash	There you go ((Cashier proffers change))
Cust	[Okay then]
Cash	[Three four] five ten ((Cashier steps back from counter))

The interaction with the storekeepers proceeds as a socially minimal service encounter until the customer volunteers personal information about himself (*I just moved in the area*) and raises the history of his relationship with the cashier (*I talked to you the other day You remember me?*) Although the cashier shows that he remembers the customer (*Oh yesterday, last night*), the customer continues as if the cashier didn't know or remember him The customer's *goddamn, shit then you don't know me* is spoken at high volume, but with a smile, suggesting humor rather than anger

Though the cashier acknowledges having seen the customer before, his turns are oriented toward completing the transaction Except for the words *last night,* his acknowledgments of this customer's history with the store (*Oh yeah, I know you, Yeah*) are spoken in overlap with the customer's words, and only in response to the customer's assertions

The customer does not acknowledge it when the cashier shows that he remembers him Perhaps the recognition does not count when it requires prompting (*Then you don't* <u>*know*</u> me), but rather must be done immediately and spontaneously. The customer then explicitly states that he wants the cashier and the owner to know him (he moves his gaze back and forth between them). *I want you to* <u>*know*</u> *me so when I walk in here you 'll know me I smoke Winstons Your son knows me.* This customer is concerned with the storekeepers "knowing" him he wants them to know him now and on future store visits, and he finds it worth noting that one of the other employees (*your son*), already knows him.

Knowing a customer's habitual purchases and brand preferences (e g Winstons) is one way of "knowing" the customer, and storekeepers frequently ready a customer's cigarettes or liquor without being asked, minimally, this customer wants to be known in this way. Subsequent talk, however, suggests that "knowing" him will involve a more personal, intimate relationship, and one that involves specific types of talk and behavior.

The data presented here suggest that immigrant Korean retailers and African American customers have differing notions of what it means to "know" someone in a convenience store context, and differing ideas about the kinds of speech activities entailed by "knowing" someone in this context. Different ideas about what it means to know someone may apply not just to service encounters, as described above, but to any encounter between relative strangers Thus M Park (1979 82) suggests that, by Western standards, Koreans are restrained and impersonal with those who are not intimate friends or part of a known group.

> The age-old cliché, "Koreans are the most courteous people in the East" is rather rightly applied only to inter-personal interaction among ingroups or hierarchical groups Koreans tend to be [by Western standards] impolite or even rude when they interact with outgroups like outsiders or strangers Everyone outside the ingroup is likely to be treated with curiosity or caution or even a bit of suspicion ...

It may be difficult for these storekeepers to extend what for them is an intimate communicative style to a relative stranger.

In America, many communicative activities—e.g. greetings, smiles, and Smalltalk—occur in interactions both with friends and with relative strangers. The communicative style extended to both strangers and friends relatively emphasizes the expression of casual solidarity and explicit recognition of personal details.

> Personal treatment in American life includes use of the first name, recognition of biographical details and acknowledgements of specific acts, appearances, preferences and choices of the individual. Cultural models are given by salesmen and airline hostesses. Their pleasant smiles, feigned and innocuous invasions of privacy, "kidding" and swapping of personal experiences constitute stereotypes of personal behavior ... Signs of friendship, the glad handshake, the ready smile, the slap on the back... have become part of the normal way of behavior. (Edward Stewart 1972:55, 58)

Everyday speech behavior among strangers in America includes practices that would be reserved for talk among relative intimates in Korea.

Such differing assumptions about appropriate communicative style in service encounters, and about the relationship between customer and server, may underlie the contrasting forms of participation in the encounter under consideration. When the customer states that he wants the storekeepers to know him, the cashier's *Yeah* and subsequent *There you go,* as he hands back change, fail to engage the topic of knowing the customer. The cashier is reframing the activity as a business transaction, specifically the closing of the business negotiation component, and perhaps the entire encounter. The return and counting of change (*There you go; Three four five ten*) is used in many service encounters as a way of closing not only the business negotiation, but also the entire interaction.

The customer, however, does not treat this as the end of the encounter. Instead, he treats this as a time to discuss details of his life outside the store:

Cust	And then I–I've got three months to be out here
Cash	How's [here] ((Cashier steps back from counter and gazes down))
Cust	[I'm going] to school
Cash	How's here
Cust	I'm going to– (2) locksmith school
Cash	Oh really
Cust	Yeah so after that–because I had a () knee operation ((Customer rolls up pant leg to show scars)) ((4 2))
Cust	I had a total knee so my company is retiring my–old black ass at fifty-four ((Customer smiles and gazes at owner)) ((6))
Own	(mmh) ((Owner shakes his head laterally and gazes away from the customer))

Cust	And they give me some money
Cash	Huh ((Cashier bares his teeth briefly in a smile))
Cust	So I'm spending my money at your store on liquor heh heh heh heh hah hah hah hah hah ((Customer laughs animatedly, turning toward the owner who does not smile, but who continues lateral headshakes as he takes a few steps to the side))
Own	You still can work?

The business exchange has been completed, and the customer initiates discussion of a series of personal topics. He volunteers how long he will be in Los Angeles, what he is doing there, details of his medical history, and his current employment status. He goes so far as to roll up his pant-leg to show the scars from his knee replacement operation. He has said that he wants these storekeepers to "know" him, and he's giving them some of the information they need to know him. In doing so he is treating them as co-members of an intimate group, i.e., the circle of people who can see his knee scars, even though by some standards they are virtual strangers. The customer is treating the social distance between himself and the storekeepers as small, his interactional style increases involvement between him and the storekeepers.

The cashier's talk displays some interest in the interaction, e.g., his initial query *How's here* displays understanding of the customer's statement (*I've got three months to be out here*) and invites further comment. The customer, however, does not answer the question. The non-standard form *How's here* (for 'How do you like it here?') may not have been understood by the customer, and comprehension may have been further hindered by the cashier's non-verbal actions. During the first *How's here,* the cashier's arm is in front of his face, and his gaze is not on the customer, during the second, he's shifting his weight to lean on a counter to the side. The even intonation contour of *How's here* may also prevent the customer from realizing that a question is being asked. Even when a storekeeper expresses involvement in an interaction, his or her limited. English proficiency may prevent the customer from understanding the expression of interest.

The customer concludes this introduction with a joke that stresses the humorous nature of his relationship with the liquor store owners he is sharing the proceeds from his disability payments with them. His smile and laughter at this situation are an invitation to his audience to share in his laughter (Jefferson 1979). The store-owner and cashier fail to join in this laughter, the cashier displays a fleeting, stiff smile, and the owner none at all. Not only do cashier and owner fail to accept the invitation to laughter, but as in the previous encounter, the owner, through his subsequent question, ACTIVELY DECLINES the invitation to laughter. His question *You still can wotk?* is a serious pursuit of a topic that effectively counters the customer's pursuit of laughter. The question proves his comprehension of the customer's prior talk, but displays no affective alignment or solidarity with the customer's humor. Even though the store-owner can understand the referential content of the words, he does not participate in the interactional activity of laughing—the preferred response to the customer's laughter.

It is also, of course, possible that the owner is displaying a dispreferred response because he does NOT want to display alignment perhaps he thinks that people take advantage of social programs when they could support themselves through their own work—a sentiment voiced in interviews with immigrant Korean retailers in a variety of forms. This active declination to laugh, however, also occurs in my data during talk about morally less sensitive topics, e.g., the weather, with both African American and Korean customers, this suggests a pattern of declining invitations to laughter that is unrelated to personal opinions about the topic at hand.

In the next two minutes of talk and interaction (not transcribed here), the customer gets change for a five-dollar bill, and then explains to the owner that his former employer doesn't want him to work for fear that they would have to redo his knee operation if he resumed work. The customer takes his bag of purchases from the counter, and moves to the door as if to leave (the owner says *See ya*), but he stops in the doorway, then re-enters the store to resume talking. He discusses the exact amount of money he receives per month for his disability, compares it to the amount of money he made previously, and reiterates that if he goes to work now, his disability benefits will be cut off.

In the next segment, transcribed below, the customer explains that he is being re-trained for a new job. He begins to depart, and then once again returns from the threshold of the exit door to re-initiate talk.

Cust	So I gotta get another trade Just like if you get hurt in the liquor store business, you gotta go get another trade. So I gotta go get another trade For them to pay me the money. So I'm gonna get another trade But then like—after I get another trade they pay me (a sum) a lump sum of money? And I'm gonna do what I wanna do ((8))
Cust	They only gonna give me about sixty or seventy thousand ((1 4))
Cust	Plus– my schooling— ((1 0))
Cust	So—I got to take it easy for a little bit ((Customer moves toward exit))
Cust	That's why I'm gonna buy enough of your liquor (so I can take it)
Own	Alright, take care
Cust	Okay ((Customer pauses in doorway))

This segment is characterized by dramatically asymmetrical contributions to the interaction. Not only does the customer do most of the talking, but there is a noticeable absence of response to his statements. He gives up his turn at talk five times in this short segment, but receives a verbal response only once. The customer only gets verbal collaboration, in this segment, in leaving the store—which suggests that these storekeepers may be more proficient at closing interactions with customers than they are at sociable, personal discussion with them.

The lack of verbal response to the customer's talk is particularly noteworthy because he is making statements that invite easy responses. The fact that he's going to get a lump sum of money and *do what I wanna do* makes relevant such questions as *How much are you going to get?* or *What are you going to do when you get the money?* The amount of money he's going to get (*sixty or seventy thousand*) similarly invites comment, e. g., *That's great,* or *That's a lot of money,* or again, *What are you going to do with it?* The customer's *Plus my schooling* invites questions about the details of the schooling, beyond the fact (stated earlier) that it's locksmith school. The customer's reference to buying *enough of your liquor* also provides an opening for storekeeper recognition of his patronage, e.g., *We appreciate your business.* The silence of the storekeepers displays restraint, but not interest or involvement.

The immigrant Korean storekeepers' lack of overt response to the customer's talk forms a stark contrast with the African American pattern of call-and-response described above. Smitherman (1977:108) emphasizes the importance of responding to a speaker, regardless of the form of the response: "all responses are 'correct'; the only 'incorrect' thing you can do is not respond at all." By this standard, the storekeepers' lack of response is inappropriate.

In the next segment, although the customer has once again moved to the door, and the owner has said goodbye, the customer re-enters the store and more talk follows. After learning the storekeepers' names, the customer invokes the events of April 1992. He tells the store-owners that he will come to their aid if they have problems in the future, and goes on to discuss his philosophy of race relations:

Cust	What's your name? ((Customer re-enters store and approaches the owner))
Own	Han Choi ((6))
Cust	Han? ((Customer shakes hands with the owner)) ((1 2))
Cust	What's your name? ((Customer shakes cashier's hand))
Cash	Shin
Cust	Chin?
Cash	No, [Shin]
Cust	[Okay] () Shin?
Cash	Yeah
Own	What's yours (then)?
Cust	Larry
Own	Larry

Cust	I'm a gangsta from Chicago, Larry Smith Anybody fuck with you, this black—I seen them riots and things and they was fucking up with the Korean stores and the—and the what's his name stores? And I was in Vietnam and everything like that
Own	[(Our) neighbors friendly (here)]
Cust	[Well—() well let me] tell you something—nobody fuck with your store, if I catch 'em making fuck with your store () you just call me down
Own	Alright
Cust	I'll fuck'em up ((Customer reaches out and shakes the owner's hand, the owner's arm is limp and he is pulled off balance by the handshake)) ((8))
Cust	Because I believe in people not Koreans, not Blacks, not Whites, not this, I believe in people ((4))
Cust	Right there ((Customer taps the owner on the chest twice, in rhythm with the two words *right there*))

The customer, who has created and emphasized solidarity with the storekeepers throughout their interaction, continues to reinforce his solidarity and co-membership with them. After learning their names and shaking their hands—an act of physical intimacy—he makes two explicit assertions of solidarity.

His initial assertion of solidarity is dramatic: he promises with high volume and affect that he will respond to their call for help, and "fuck up" anyone who is harming them or their store. He has seen the havoc of Los Angeles in April 1992 on TV; but he is a Vietnam veteran, so he has the capacity to deal with such events. The storekeepers' enemies are his enemies; he and the storekeepers are co-members of an intimate group, a group whose members will risk harm to protect each other.

He reiterates this sentiment of solidarity by explaining his readiness to act on their behalf based on his personal philosophy: *Because I believe in people not Koreans, not Blacks, not Whites.* Social distance between him and these storekeepers is low; race is not a barrier. He emphasizes his intimacy with the store-owner by tapping him on the chest, once more making physical contact, and citing this specific store-owner as an example of the people in whom he has faith.

Following the segment transcribed above, there are two minutes of talk (not transcribed here) during which the customer discusses his beliefs about the basic sameness of people, regardless of race, and his criticisms of those who make society racist. The customer utters more than 10 words for each of the store-owner's words during this period. The service encounter comes to an end with the following turns:

((The customer speaks with high volume and animation, and sounds almost angry during these penultimate two turns. He is gesticulating so strongly that his sunglasses become dislodged from atop his head and he has to reposition them as he talks))

Cust Okay what I'm saying is () if you throw five kids (in the middle of the floor) and don't tell them what they are nothing like that they just grow up to be people (())

Cust They don't even know () that they Black they don't even know they Korean they don't know that they. White they don't know this and that It have to be an old person like you or me, George Washington and all these motherfuckers. Martin Luther King and all these motherfuckers

((The customer has begun moving toward the exit. His vocal register shifts suddenly to one of low volume and affect for his final turn. He gazes first at the owner and then the cashier as he waves goodbye))

Cust Anyway—have a good day

Own Later ((Customer turns and exits))

As this interaction progresses, the storekeepers become more and more reticent while the customer becomes more and more outspoken. Although the customer has dominated the talk throughout the interaction, his volume and affect level get higher as it progresses, and he holds the floor an ever higher proportion of the time. In the final two minutes of talk, the customer is literally following the owner from place to place in the store, leaning over the shorter man, and repeatedly touching him on the chest as he makes his points.

This asymmetry in participation occurs despite apparent efforts at accommodation by both customer and storekeepers. Thus the storekeepers ask more questions that display interest in the customer—*How's here; You still can work?*—than they ask of non-intimate adult Korean customers. The customer adapts his speech for non-natives, e.g., by using an example to explain his job retraining (*Just like if you get hurt in the liquor store business, you gotta go get another trade*); and he introduces a topic that might be of particular interest to them, e.g., Los Angeles civil unrest that could threaten their store. As in the first encounter, however, the mutual accommodation may not be of the degree or type that can be fully appreciated by the other party, or can result in more symmetrical participation in the encounter.

Mismatch in politeness orientations can have a self-reinforcing, spiraling effect that exaggerates differences in politeness style as interaction continues, this can exacerbate misunderstandings and mutual negative evaluations. The more this African American customer cheerfully talks and stresses his camaraderie with the store-owner, the more the retailer withdraws and declines involvement. This may be a more general phenomenon in interethnic communication Borrowing a term from Bateson, 1972 Tannen (1981 138) concludes that speakers from backgrounds with contrasting linguistic practices frequently respond to each other in "complementary schismogenetic fashion", i.e., "the verbal devices used by one group cause speakers of the other group to react by intensifying the opposing behavior, and vice versa "

Since, for many African-Americans the nature of good and respectful service encounter relations involves relatively great personal involvement, this customer may be redoubling his efforts to create solidarity as he encounters the retailers' increasing reticence. For the store-owner, the appropriate response to a customer's increasing intimacy may be the silence or avoidance that demonstrates restraint. In this instance, the pattern does not escalate out of control. The owner maintains a degree of engagement, although he appears uncomfortable at times, and the customer does not react as if he is being ignored, although his increasing affect as the interaction proceeds may well be related to the low level of response he gets from the storekeepers.

However, this self-escalating cycle may contribute to confrontations that have occurred elsewhere. Media and informant accounts of confrontations between retailers and African Americans often stress the seeming suddenness with which storekeepers, perceived to be inscrutably impassive, suddenly explode in anger at customers. As customers persist in behaviors that the retailer perceives as invasive, the storekeeper will remain silent, the customer will not know that he or she is doing something that the storekeeper finds inappropriate, and will increase the intensity of the involvement behaviors in reaction to the restraint of storekeepers. When the weight of the trespass against sensibilities becomes too grave, the store–owner will feel justified in lashing out (Kochman 1981 118, 1984 206). Conversely, the increasingly restrained behavior of store-owners, as customers express ever-greater friendliness, can lead to customer outbursts and accusations of storekeeper racism. Storekeepers report repeated instances in which customers have suddenly (and to the storekeepers, inexplicably) accused them of being racists.

Conclusion

Divergent practices for displaying respect in service encounter interaction are an ongoing cause of tension between immigrant Korean retailers and their African American customers. The two groups have different concepts of the relationship between customer and storekeeper, and different ideas about the speech activities that are appropriate in service encounters. The talk of immigrant Koreans focuses almost exclusively on the business transaction at hand, while the talk of African American customers includes efforts toward more personal, sociable interaction.

The interactional patterns that are apparent in videotaped records are consistent with data that come from dozens of hours of observation in various stores, and from interviews with storeowners, customers, and consultants. The seeming avoidance of involvement on the part of immigrant Koreans is frequently seen by African Americans as the disdain and arrogance of racism. The relative stress on interpersonal involvement among African Americans in service encounters is typically perceived by immigrant Korean retailers as a sign of selfishness, interpersonal imposition, or poor breeding (Bailey 1996).

The focus of this article on miscommunication should not be taken to mean that immigrant Korean merchants and African American customers can never communicate effectively, or never have friendly relationships. The overwhelming majority of African American customers and immigrant Korean retailers that I observed get along, and relationships between retailers and regular customers (40–80% of the clientele at stores I visited) are often very positive. Retailers often know regular customers' family members and other details of their lives; and many retailers engage in friendly small-talk with such customers, even when limited English proficiency makes it difficult. This type of relationship, which often results only after longer contact, can change mutual perceptions, as described by an African American woman in her 50s:

> I find that they shy away from you until you get to know them. Like this lady, the Korean store, I've been in the neighborhood for years and years, and she's friendly with everybody cause she knows everybody but when they don't know you, they're shy, and you think they're prejudice. They might be, but you just have to get to know them. They're nice people once you get to know them.

This article has focused on one source of interethnic tensions: miscommunication due to cultural and linguistic differences. Socio-historical conditions—e.g., social, economic, and racial inequality—are also clearly sources of tensions between African Americans and immigrant Korean storekeepers. Within a social and historical context, however, there are specific linguistic and cultural practices that can ameliorate or exacerbate tensions between groups. The goal of this essay has been to shed light on communicative processes that can lead to tensions between groups in face-to-face interaction, in the hope that understanding linguistic and cultural bases of differences in communication patterns can make these differences less inflammatory.

Notes

1. Initial fieldwork for this research was funded by a Research Institute for Man/Landes Training Grant. Many thanks to Alessandro Duranti for extensive comments on repeated drafts of the UCLA M.A. thesis on which this article is based. Thanks also to Jae Kim, who transcribed and translated the Korean service encounters, and who shared much with me about the language, lives, and perceptions of Korean immigrants in Los Angeles.
2. Transcription conventions are as follows Speakers are identified with an abbreviation in the far left column, e.g., "Cust" for "Customer," "Cash" for "Cashier," and "Own" for "Owner " A question mark in this column indicates that the speaker's identity is not clear to the transcriber Descriptions of non-verbal activities are in double parentheses, e.g., ((Customer enters store)) Note also the following

((4 3))	Numbers in parentheses indicate the length of time in seconds during which there is no talk Single parentheses are used for intra-turn silences, double parentheses for silences between turns
()	A period in parentheses or double parentheses indicates a stretch of time, lasting no more than two-tenths of a second, during which there is no talk
	A colon indicates that the preceding sound was elongated in a marked pronunciation
?	A question mark indicates a marked rising pitch
	A period indicates a marked falling pitch
( )	Parentheses that are empty indicate that something was said at that point, but it is not clear enough to transcribe Parentheses around words indicate doubt about the accuracy of the transcribed material. A slash between words in parentheses indicates alternate possibilities
hhh	*h*'s connected to a word indicate breathiness, usually associated with laughter
[ ]	Brackets enclose those portions of utterances that are spoken in overlap with other talk. The overlapping portions of talk are placed immediately above or below each other on the page
!	An exclamation point indicates an exclamatory tone
,	A comma indicates a marked continuing intonation in the sound(s) preceding the comma
–	Text that is underlined was pronounced with emphasis, i.e., some combination of higher volume, pitch, and greater vowel length
'	A single apostrophe replaces a letter that was not pronounced, e.g., *col'* for *cold,* when the *d* is not pronounced
–	A hyphen or dash indicates that speech was suddenly cut-off during or after the preceding word

Transcriptions of Korean data follow Martin et., al (1967 xv)

3. This category includes practices that might seem to vary significantly in degree of intimacy, however, immigrant Koreans do not treat such distinctions as relevant in most encounters with immigrant Korean customers. As described in the section on encounters between immigrant Koreans, small-talk about the weather (for example) does not occur independently of, or more frequently than, talk of more personal matters
4. This is not meant to deny the role of racism in tensions between African Americans and immigrant Korean retailers Racism permeates American society, and it provides a cogent explanation for a wide variety of historical, social, and economic phenomena, including behavior in face-to-face interaction Quotes from store-owners interviewed in other studies (e.g., Ella Stewart 1989, K Park 1995), attest the blatant racism of some storekeepers. The point here is not that immigrant Korean merchants are or are not racist, but rather that many immigrant Korean interactional practices upon which African American customers base assumptions of racism are not valid indices of racism, because retailers use identical practices with immigrant Korean customers
5. The difficulty of mastering English for adult speakers of Korean is suggested by the grammatical interference evident in the following utterance by a storekeeper who had been in Los Angeles over 20 years When asked where her husband was, she replied *Husband some merchandise buy* (i.e., 'My husband is buying some merchandise '). The subject-object-verb word order of Korean is used, rather than the subject-verb-object word order of English. The present tense form of *buy* is used, rather than present progressive, this parallels Korean usage, in which the present tense form of action verbs can indicate present progressive meaning. The possessive pronoun *my* is elided, since it would be understood from context in Korean (Lee 1989 90).

References

Atkinson, J Maxwell, & Heritage, John (1984), eds *Structures of social action Studies in conversation analysis* Cambridge & New York Cambridge University Press

Austin, Regina (1995) Moving beyond deviance Expanding Black people's rights and reasons to shop and to sell *Penn Law Journal* 30, 30–34

Bailey, Benjamin (1996) *Communication of respect in service encounters between immigrant Korean retailers and African-American customers* M A thesis, University of California, Los Angeles

Bateson, Gregory (1972) *Steps to an ecology of mind* New York Ballantine

Brown, Penelope, & Levinson, Stephen (1987) *Politeness Some universals in language usage* Cambridge & New York Cambridge University Press

Chang, Edward (1990) *New urban crisis Korean—Black conflicts in Los Angeles* Dissertation, University of California, Berkeley

——— (1993) Jewish and Korean merchants in African American neighborhoods. A comparative perspective *Amerasia Journal* 19, 5–21

Drake, St Clair, & Cayton, Horace (1945) *Black metropolis A study of Negro life in a northern city* New York Harper & Row

Drew, Paul, & Heritage, John (1992a) Analyzing talk at work An introduction In Drew & Heritage (eds), 3–65

———, & ——— (1992b), eds *Talk at work Interaction in institutional settings* Cambridge & New York Cambridge University Presss

Duranti, Alessandro, & Goodwin, Charles (1992), eds *Rethinking context Language as an interactive phenomenon* Cambridge & New York Cambridge University Press

Durkheim, Emile (1915) *The elementary forms of the religious life* London Allen & Unwin

Goffman, Erving (1967) The nature of deference and demeanor In his *Interaction ritual Essays on face-to-face behavior,* 47–95 New York Pantheon

——— (1971) *Relations in public Mtcrostudies of the public order* New York Basic Books

Goodwin, Charles, & Goodwin, Marjorie H (1992) Assessments and the construction of context. In Duranti & Goodwin (eds), 147–90

Grice, Paul (1975) Logic and conversation. In Peter Cole & Jerry Morgan (eds), *Syntax and semantics,* 3, 41–58 New York Academic Press

Gumperz, John (1982a) *Discourse strategies* Cambridge & New York Cambridge University Press

——— (1982b), ed *Language and social identity* Cambridge & New York Cambridge University Press

——— (1992) Contextualization and understanding. In Duranti & Goodwin (eds), 229–52

Jefferson, Gail (1979) A technique for inviting laughter and its subsequent acceptance declination. In George Psathas (ed), *Everyday language Studies in ethnomethodology,* 79–96 New York Irvington

Keel, Hee-Sung (1993) Word and wordlessness. The spirit of Korean Buddhism *Korea Journal* 33, 11–19

Kochman, Thomas (1981) *Black and White styles in conflict* Chicago University of Chicago Press

——— (1984) The politics of politeness Social warrants in mainstream American public etiquette *Georgetown University Roundtable on Languages and Linguistics* 1984, 200–209

Lee, Hansol H B (1989) *Korean grammar* Oxford & New York Oxford University Press

Levinson Stephen (1992) Activity types in language. In Drew & Heritage (eds), 66–100

Martin, Samuel, et., al (1967) *A Korean English dictionary* New Haven, CT Yale University Press

Merritt, Marilyn (1976) On questions following questions (in service encounters) *Language in Society* 5, 315–57

Park, Kyeyoung (1995) The re-invention of affirmative action Korean immigrants' changing conceptions of African Americans and Latin Americans *Urban Anthropology* 24, 59–92

Park, Myung-Seok (1979) *Communication styles in two different cultures Korean and American* Seoul Han Shin

Sacks, Harvey (1975) Everyone has to lie. In Mary Sanches & Ben Blount (eds), *Sociocultural dimensions of language use*, 57–79 New York Academic Press

Schegloff, Emanuel, Jefferson, Gail, & Sacks, Harvey (1977). The preference for self-correction in the organization of repair in conversation *Language* 53, 361–82

Schegloff, Emanuel, & Sacks, Harvey (1973) Opening up closings *Semiotica* 7, 289–327

Scollon, Ron, & Scollon, Suzanne Wong (1994) Face parameters in East-West discourse. In Stella Ting-Toomey (ed), *The challenge of facework*, 133–58. Albany State University of New York Press

Smitherman, Geneva (1977) *Talkin' and testifyin'. The language of Black America* Boston Houghton Mifflin

Stewart, Edward (1972) *American cultural patterns* Chicago Intercultural Press

Stewart, Ella (1989) *Ethnic cultural diversity An interpretive study of cultural differences and communication styles between Korean merchants/employees and Black patrons in South Los Angeles* M A thesis, California State University, Los Angeles

________ (1991) Ethnic cultural diversity Perceptions of intercultural communication rules for interaction between Korean merchants/employees and Black patrons in South Los Angeles Paper presented to the 19th Annual Conference of the National Association for Ethnic Studies at California State Polytechnic University, Pomona, CA

Sturdevant, Frederick (1969), ed. *The ghetto marketplace* New York Free Press

Tannen, Deborah (1981) New York Jewish conversational style *International Journal of the Sociology of Language* 30, 133–49

Yum, June-Ock (1987) Korean philosophy and communication. In D Lawrence Kincaid (ed), *Communication theory Eastern and Western perspectives*, 71–86 San Diego Academic Press

Chapter 5

Kinship and Families

DISCUSSION QUESTIONS

1. Goody identifies the transference of property as one of the most important factors influencing marriage norms and practices among the many cases he investigates. What are some other factors that influence marriage discussed by Goody? What are the main influences on marriage practices among the Khevsur people studied by Manning?
2. What do you think of Goody's cross-cultural, comparative method for studying marriage practices and their motivations? How does it compare to Manning's deep ethnographic look into one cultural group? What different lessons do you learn from each?
3. How does Goody provide a holistic perspective on marriage practices? Do you think Manning provides a similarly holistic perspective?
4. In the time Manning did his research, desire became a new factor influencing marriages among the Khevsurs. What led to this shift? How are marriage practices and choices among the Khevsur linked to norms of gender and sexuality?

KEY TERMS

Divergence
Bilateral descent
Unilineal descent
Exogamy

Goody, Jack. 1969. "Inheritance, Property, and Marriage in Africa and Eurasia." *Sociology* 3(1):55–76

Summary This paper tries to utilize the cross-cultural material presented by G. P. Murdock in the Ethnographic Atlas to analyse the concomitants of differences in the system of inheritance, particularly with respect to the contrast between Africa and Eurasia. In the major Eurasian societies property tends to be distributed directly, from parents to children of both sexes (i.e. by diverging devolution); in Africa property largely devolves between persons of the same sex, laterally as well as lineally. An attempt is made to show the distribution of diverging devolution and its association with the payment of dowry, with monogamy, with in-marriage of various sorts, and with kin terms that differentiate the nuclear family from more distant kin. The tight control of property represented by diverging devolution is in turn seen as deriving from the intensive exploitation of resources which is also linked to the growth of complex political institutions. These associations are tested and held to be established.

MANY OF THE DETAILED OBSERVATIONS OF pre-colonial African society come from West Africa, and especially from the Gold Coast. For this region was not only the closest part of Black Africa but also of the greatest economic interest, especially when the Portuguese lost their monopolistic hold on the coast and the way was open for the Protestant business men of the western seaboard, Holland, England, Scandinavia, and north Germany to develop the interlocking trade in gold, slaves, and firearms which stood them in such stead in the early years of capital accumulation that preceded the development of industry in Europe.

During this period, at the end of the seventeenth century, the Dutch factor, William Bosman, was struck by certain features of social organization of the Gold Coast which he saw as fundamentally different from those he had grown up with in Western Europe. Bosman was on the coast for some 14 years and published his observations in 1704 under the title of *A New and Accurate Description of the Coast of Guinea, divided into the Gold, the Slave, and the Ivory Coasts.* In the twelfth letter of his book, the author writes 'Of the Negroes manner of Marrying'. 'Marriage here is not over-loaded with Ceremonies, nor have they any Notion of a Praevious Courtship to bring on a Match: here are no tedious Disputes on account of Marriage Settlements .... The Bride brings no other Fortune than her Body, nor does the Man want much; 'tis sufficient if he has enough to defray the Expence of the Wedding-Day' (1967: 197–98). He further observes the corollary of the absence of dowry, that 'Married people here have no community of Goods; but each hath his or her particular Propriety. ... On the Death of either the Man or the Wife, the respective Relations come and immediately sweep away all, not leaving the Widow or Widower the least part thereof. . .' (202).[1]

Thus Bosman sees that not only is conjugal community of property rare, but that a deceased's estate is not called upon to support the surviving spouse. This fact is linked to the absence of a marriage settlement, to the absence of a woman's portion of the patrimony which she brings with her into marriage as a dowry.[2] If a woman brings nothing at marriage, she gets nothing when the union is dissolved. Bosman also notes a related fact, though he does not perceive its interrelatedness. He observes that except at Accra, inheritance is matrilineal. Even in the matrilineal societies property is sex-linked ... 'the eldest Son of his Mother is Heir to his Mothers Brother or her Son, as the eldest Daughter is Heiress of her Mothers Sister or her Daughter' (203). That is to say, property descends 'homogeneously' e.g. *between* males, even when it goes *through* females.[3]

In earlier publications, I have emphasized the importance of inheritance as a variable (1958, 1959, 1962) and suggested that in the domestic domain one of the major differences between African and Eurasian societies lies in the fact that in Eurasia diverging inheritance (i.e. 'bilateral' inheritance, where property goes to children of both sexes) is common, especially in the major civilizations, whereas in Africa it is virtually unknown. The absence of diverging inheritance is linked to the absence of dowry in Africa,[4] since dowry is essentially a process whereby parental property is distributed to a daughter at her marriage (i.e. *inter vivos*) rather than at the holder's death (*mortis causa*). I therefore include dowry as part of the process of diverging devolution'. The property a woman receives through dowry or 'bilateral' inheritance establishes some variety of a conjugal fund, the nature of which may vary widely. This fund ensures her support (or endowment) in widowhood and eventually goes to provide for her sons and daughters.

I have elsewhere tried to analyse the concomitants of diverging devolution in the Eurasian setting and have discussed some of the implications of this difference for comparative sociological studies.[5] In a paper on 'Adoption in Cross-Cultural Perspective' (1968), I have outlined some of the interlinking variables (unavoidably these are mostly 'qualitative variables' in the statistical sense) that I regard as concomitants of diverging devolution. I should add that I see the system of the transmission of property (i.e. devolution) as being the independent variable in some of these instances and as the intervening or dependent variable in others; for in the main it seems to occur where agriculture is intensive and the means of production are in relatively short supply. In this present paper I try to test certain hypotheses concerning diverging devolution by another means, namely, the recent Ethnographic Atlas. The 1967 version of this sample consists of 80 columns of data on 863 societies from all parts of the globe.[6] This instrument enables us to check some of the statements that sociologists generate about societies, usually on the basis of the one or two in which they have worked and the handful they currently have in memory store. Clearly the number of aspects that one can test is limited. For example, it could be suggested that the extent of ceremonial performed at rites of passage in the individual's life cycle is positively correlated with the amount of work (in terms of the handing over of rights and duties, etc.) that has to be done. Where marriage establishes a conjugal fund (as in dowry systems) the wedding ceremonial will be more elaborate than where it does not; where funerals redistribute the dead man's property, they will be more elaborate than where a holder divests himself of his property during his lifetime.[7] But this information is not coded in the present Ethnographic Atlas and to read through a representative sample of the relevant material would be very time-consuming. In other cases the information exists, though not always in quite the form one optimally needs. When this is so, I have carried out tests of the relevant aspects of the hypothesis.[8] In so doing, I am not seeking to explain all of one 'variable' by another; in the example I gave of the relationship between life-cycle ceremonies and devolution, it is obvious that other factors are at work. The predictions are for a positive association, a significant trend, not a one to one relationship. In many branches of the social sciences a hypothesis is rejected if the probability value is less than .05, while an association of 0.33 on a phi test is understood to be high (the scale runs between — 1 and + 1); to this convention I will adhere in this paper.[9]

There are two kinds of problem involved in trying to make such a test, namely, those to do with the instrument and those to do with the analytic concepts. From the analytic standpoint, it is the transmission of major items of property that is clearly going to be of greater significance, especially the transmission of basic productive resources (usually land); but in the code the distinction between land and movables is made for inheritance but not for dowry. Secondly, there is a potential difficulty in deciding when property diverges. For example, a daughter may inherit her father's property in her own right or as an epiclerate, that is, a residual heir in the absence of brothers. Nevertheless the overall distinction is clear. In the main Eurasian societies, a close female inherits before a more distant male, even where both are members of the same patrilineal descent group. In Africa south of the Sahara, a woman only inherits male property when there are no males left in the wider kingroup, and even then it is a very rare occurrence.

The specific problems to do with the instrument are twofold. Firstly the composers note that the inheritance data has not been easy to code; indeed they describe the code as inadequate (1967: 167). The second point has to do with marriage transactions. Since I define devolution as transmission between holder and heir (see Goody 1962: 312), whether or not it takes place at death, I include dowry in these operations. Indeed I include not only the 'direct dowry' (the property passed from 'parents' to a daughter on her marriage), I also include the 'indirect dowry', that is, property passed by the groom to the bride at marriage.

Such prestations are often spoken of as bridewealth or brideprice, but I would limit these terms to prestations that pass between the kin of the groom and the kin of the bride, and that can therefore be used to provide wives for the girl's brothers; in short, they form part of a system of circulating or on-going exchange. I suspect that most accounts fail to make a distinction between these types of prestation, despite the different social implications that they have. Hence what I would regard as (indirect) dowry may sometimes have been reported as brideprice.

As with most kinds of sociological analysis the measuring rods and the measurements themselves are bound to be less than perfect. But however crude, even such rough comparisons provide some degree of confirmation or contradiction of hypotheses about human social organization. On the one hand this procedure gets us out of the unsystematic comparisons upon which so much comparative sociology is based and on the other hand liberates us from certain of the limitations of the structural-functional method. It is no part of my intention to substitute one approach for another; different methods answer different problems. Indeed it is a sign of the relative immaturity of the social sciences that so many of their practitioners presume that there is a single approach to the sociological verities, an attitude which makes them more akin to philosophers than to other behavioural scientists.

Bearing in mind the limitations of this and other methods, I first looked at the distribution of diverging devolution (or the woman's property complex')[10] in different continents, that is, the distribution of those systems where diverging inheritance or dowry are found. This information was found in the following form in the Ethnographic Atlas:

1. all societies where daughters have a share in either land (column 74: c, d) or movable property (76: c, d);
2. all societies with dowry as the main or alternative method of marriage transaction (12: d; 13: d).

The negative cases consist of all those that remained once the diverging devolution data had been extracted, less those societies with no individual property rights or no rule of transmission (74: o; 76: o)[11] and those societies where there was no information on the relevant columns (74, 76, 12).

The first run was a purely distributional one, in order to confirm or refute the suggested differences between Africa and Eurasia. Table 5.1 shows the distribution according to the continental classification used by the Atlas. The following points emerge from it:

1. In Africa, diverging devolution is rare, i.e. it occurs in 5 per cent of the cases. Bosman's observation thus has general significance.
2. In America, there is a large proportion of societies with no individual property rights or transmission rule. The reason is that in many of the hunting and gathering

societies individuals had little property, except personal equipment, and this was often destroyed at death.[12] On-going productive property was minimal.

3. In America, the relatively large number of societies with diverging inheritance is in part a question of the importation of European norms through imperial conquest. The Mayan-speaking people of Yucatan have the same practice (Redfield 1934: 61ff.), but I do not know whether this is an aspect of early Mayan inheritance or a European import (the people of Chan Kom have long been Christian). Eurasian religious and secular codes (including Islam) promote diverging devolution independently of other factors.
4. In Eurasia and the Pacific, the number of societies with diverging devolution is approximately 40 per cent of the total. However, this figure includes the major civilizations in the area, whose populations are more numerous and whose influence greater. It is suggested that the societies with homogeneous devolution are mostly those outside the major traditions i.e. 'tribal' societies of various kinds, especially those without intensive agriculture.

TABLE 5.1 Diverging Devolution by Continent

		Continent				
		Eurasia and Circum-Mediterranean	**Africa**	**America**	**Pacific**	**Total**
Diverging devolution	Present	84	12	32	32	160
	Absent	72	175	58	41	346
No individual property rights or no rule of transmission		2	3	70	2	77
		158	190	160	75	583
			Total of table			583
			No information (N.I.) on devolution			
						280
						863

In sum, the distributional table shows that systems of devolution in Africa differ from those associated with the major Eurasian civilizations, being of the homogeneous rather than the diverging kind.

What about the correlates of these differences in devolution? It seems probable that where women are receivers of male property considerable attention will be paid to their marriage arrangements. An heiress is often not allowed to marry just anyone; her spouse is more likely to be chosen for her. Other women too are likely to marry (and to want to marry) within rather than without; for unless a woman marries 'well' her standard of living might drop, and this would be a matter of concern to herself as well as her kinsfolk. It seemed plausible to test this assumption by means of the data on pre-marital virginity (col. 78); a stress on virginity at marriage could be held to indicate, *inter alia*, the degree of control exercised on women by society, kin, and self. It also limits the possibility of conflicting claims on the estate in which a woman has rights. Table 5.2 shows a positive association between the diverging devolution of movable property, with a probability value of .001.

TABLE 5.2 Prohibited Premarital Sexual Behaviour and Diverging Devolution

		Prohibition on Premarital Sex		
		Present	**Absent**	**Total**
Diverging devolution	Present	56	30	86
	Absent	70	97	167
No individual property rights or no rule of transmission		12	38	50
1. Top quadrant: phi = 0.22, $x^2 = 12.22$, $p < .001$			Total of table	303
			N.I. on sexual relations	256
			Sexual relations precluded by very early marriage age	24
2. 'No rights' etc. added to 'absent' phi = 0.25, $x^2 = 18.55$, $p < .001$			N.I. on devolution	280
				863

N.B. The prohibition is coded in col. 78: P, *V* = present, *A*, *F*, *T* = absent

A further hypothesis is generated by this suggestion that where women are recipients of male property, there will be a greater tendency to control their marriages. When women are heirs, or even residual heirs, they may be encouraged to marry within a certain range of kin; this was the case with the daughters of Zelophehad in ancient Israel as well as in the epiclerate of classical Athens. The Atlas does not permit us to assess the incidence of these kind of marriages but it does enable us to get an idea of the association of one form of in-marriage, that is, endogamy (in kin, caste, or local group), with diverging devolution. The results are given in Table 5.3. In it I have included all societies shown in column 19 (Community Organization) as having 'a marked tendency toward local endogamy', as well as the societies in column 69 (Caste Stratification) that have either 'complex caste' or 'ethnic' stratification. I predicted that complex caste itself would be positively associated with diverging devolution. Defined 'culturally', in terms of Hindu ideology, caste, is clearly limited to the Indian sub-continent. Defined 'sociologically', as a closed, in-marrying, stratum, caste is still largely confined to the Eurasian continent, or other areas where Eurasian whites have established themselves (e.g. North America, Southern Africa, the Saharan fringes).[13] Racial factors, which because of their visibility provide one of the most universal cards of identity used by man, also enter into the ban on intermarriage. But here again property is heavily involved, for there appears little reluctance for men to engage in sexual unions, as distinct from marriage, with women of the lower orders. It is the sexuality of their own sisters they are concerned to protect, and the notions regarding the purity of women that attach to caste systems and the concern with their honour that marks the Mediterranean world cannot be divorced from the position of women as carriers of property.

The association of complex caste[14] with diverging devolution is weak (phi = 0.076), the probability being $<.10$; this is unacceptably low and represents the only prediction we have to set aside. I do not at present offer any explanation of the low figure, except to point out the limited number of cases involved. Since all these cases are included in the endogamy table, I have not presented them separately. In view of the fact that I later give a summary table of results comparing the predictive value of divergent devolution as compared with 'bilateral kinship' and 'diverging inheritance of land', I should add that the latter comes off second best (phi = 0.04; $p < .5$) and bilateral kinship third (phi = −0.08).

Another kind of in-marriage is the union with cousins. Certain of these are property–conserving as far as women are concerned, especially the father's brother's daughter marriage;[15] in societies with agnatic descent groups, this woman falls within a man's own group. Table 5.4 presents the results for father's brother's daughter marriage; there is clearly a positive association with the preferred form, but if one includes the cases where it is permitted the level of association is somewhat less (phi = 0.31, $p < .001$).

TABLE 5.3 In-Marriage (Endogamy) and Diverging Devolution

		Endogamy		
		Present	Absent	Total
Diverging devolution	Present	36	124	160
	Absent	33	313	346
No individual property rights or no rule of transmission		4	73	77
			Total of table	583
1. Top quadrant: phi = 0.18 $x^2 = 15.61$ $p < .001$			N.I. on devolution	280
				863
2. 'No rights' etc. added to 'absent' phi = 0.19 $x^2 = 20.05$ $p < .001$				

N.B. Endogamy is coded in col. 19: *D* = present: *E, C, T, B, A* = absent; and in col. 69: *C, E* = present: *D, O* = absent

TABLE 5.4 Father's Brother's Daughter Marriage and Diverging Devolution

		Preferred	Permitted	Prohibited	Total
Diverging devolution	Present	13	29	105	147
	Absent	3	17	287	307
No individual property rights or no rule of transmission		0	1	72	73
			Total of table		527
1. Top quadrant: (permitted and preferred together) phi = 0.30 $x^2 = 41.01$ $p < .001$			N.I. FaBrDa marriage		56
			N.I. on devolution		280
					863
2. 'No rights' etc. added to 'absent': phi = 0.32 $x^2 = 53.48$ $p < .001$					

N.B. Col. 25 codes cross-cousin marriage: *D, F, Q* = Father's brother's daughter marriage permitted; col. 26, a = preferred; the remainder are negative.

Control over property can be exercised by the number as well as the kind of marriage and I predicted a connection between diverging devolution and monogamy. Where both males and females require parental property for the maintenance of their status, and where resources are limited, then large polygynous families are likely to have an impoverishing effect. Only the very rich can afford the luxury of many children without dropping in the economic hierarchy. In dowry systems wives may be thought of as augmenting a man's wealth and hence polygyny could be advantageous to him; but every marriage would establish its own conjugal fund and differentiate each spouse according to the marital property she brings. There are obvious difficulties for a man in setting up a plurality of such funds (though less so when the women are sisters). The test shows a positive association between diverging devolution and monogamy (Table 5.5).

Like monogamy, polyandry also limits the number of wives and heirs with whom the property has to be divided and this form of marriage again displays a positive association with diverging devolution. Indeed in Tibet the provision of one legitimate heir-producing wife for a group of brothers is explicitly thought of as a way of keeping the balance between people and land (Carrasco 1959: 36). The Atlas includes only four cases of polyandry, three of which are found in conjunction with diverging inheritance.[16]

The residence of a married couple is a further factor likely to be influenced by property considerations; a rich wife can make a poorer husband move to her natal home and the well-to-do father-in-law may have the same power over (and attraction for) his daughter's husband. Not every woman will display these magnetic powers, which depend essentially upon the differential distribution of wealth; it is only the rich or epicleratic daughter who finds herself in such a position. So that we should not expect a straightforward uxorilocal pattern of post-marital residence but rather an ambilocal one, where a married couple may choose to reside with either the kin of the bride or of the groom depending upon their relative position. There is another possibility: if an independent conjugal fund is established at marriage, bride and groom may also establish an independent (i.e. neolocal) residence.[17]

TABLE 5.5 Monogamy and Diverging Devolution

		Monogamy		
		Present	Absent	Total
Diverging devolution	Present	59	99	158
	Absent	29	315	344
No individual property rights or no rule of transmission		10	66	76

		Monogamy		
		Present	Absent	Total
		Total of table		578
1. Top quadrant: phi = 0.35 x^2 = 62.60 $p < .001$		N.I. on monogamy		5
		N.I. on devolution		280
				863
2. 'No rights' etc added to 'absent' phi = 0.332 x^2 = 64.18 $p < .001$				

Present = *M* in Col. 14 or 15.
Absent = Other entries in cols. 14 and 15.

TABLE 5.6 Residence and Diverging Devolution

		Alternative Residence (i.e. Bilocal, neolocal, and virilocal with alternatives)		
		Present	**Absent**	**Total**
Diverging devolution	Present	53	106	159
	Absent	48	296	344
No individual property rights or no rule of transmission		32	45	77
		Total of table		580
1. Top quadrant: phi 0–22 x^2 = 25.45 $p < .001$		N.I. on residence		3
		N.I. on devolution		280
				863
2. 'No rights' etc. added to 'absent': phi = 0.15 x^2 = 13.41 $p < .001$				

N.B. Alternative residence here includes neolocal residence (see text): it is coded in cols. 16 and 17: present = *Pu, Vu, Pm, Vm, N* (including all alternatives on col. 17). *B*, (including all alternatives on col. 17).
Absent = others.

TABLE 5.6A Residence, Diverging Devolution and Bilateral Kinship Residence

		Residence			
		Bilocal (*B+*)	Neolocal (*N+*)	Virilocal with uxorilocal alter natives (*Pu, Vu, Pm, Vm*)	Other
Diverging devolution	Present	19	20	14	106
	Absent	6	9	33	296
'No rights' etc.		18	0	14	45
Bilateral kinship					
	Present	52	28	75	155
	Absent	11	12	36	487

The results of this test are shown in Table 5.6. However the overall figures conceal part of the problem, and a further breakdown is given in Table 5.6a. From this table it will be seen that, while bilocal and neolocal marriage are definitely correlated with diverging devolution, the correlation is negative where the alternative forms of marriage represent less than one-third of the total (*Pu, Pm, Vu, Vm,* in the code). The latter finding is contrary to my hypothesis. However the determinants of residence are not of course limited to property. Indeed in this instance it seemed possible that the absence of unilineal descent groups (i.e. 'Bilateral descent') would prove to have a close association with the patterns of residence. In Table 5.6a diverging devolution and bilateral kinship are compared in terms of their association with types of residence.

I return to this question later when I compare 'bilaterality' and 'diverging devolution' as variables. Here I want to point out that it is only in respect of residence that kinship is a better predictor than the transmission of property. Part of the answer emerges from a study of the figures for the residence patterns of societies that have 'no individual property rights or no regular rules of transmission'. The interesting point about Table 5.6a is the very large proportion of these societies that include marriages of the 'bilocal' or 'virilocal with alternatives' type—no doubt because there is no immovable property to tie anyone anywhere. There are more societies with 'uxorilocal with virilocal alternative' in this category (13) than in the societies with property (9).

Property considerations, in the shape of diverging devolution, also seemed logically connected with kin terms. Only in exceptional cases (where there are no descendants, male, female or adopted) do brothers (or more usually brother's sons) inherit under such systems. So that the three characteristics of this type of transmission are (i) it is intergenerational, (ii) it is direct and (iii) close females are preferred to distant males. Indeed devolution occurs within the nuclear family, while the establishment of separate conjugal funds differentiates sibling from sibling, parents from children. Though cousins may be possible 'intestate' heirs, they rarely inherit. The emphasis is on direct transmission, even if one has to adopt.

It seemed possible that this 'isolation' of the nuclear family, as manifested in conjugal funds and direct inheritance, would be reflected in a kinship terminology that differentiated siblings from cousins.[18] There are several ways in which brothers (for I confine the discussion to males) may be set apart from other kin. Firstly, under an 'Eskimo' (e.g. English) system they are distinguished from all cousins. Secondly, cousins may be distinguished not only from siblings but among themselves; this is the case with descriptive terminology ('descriptive or derivative'). Table 5.7 shows the positive correlation between terminologies that isolate siblings and diverging devolution.

While I have used inheritance, or rather devolution, as the independent variable, it is independent only in a certain context. For these hypotheses raise a further series of questions concerning the incidence of diverging devolution itself. Why should the African and Eurasian patterns be so different? I suggest that the scarcer productive resources become and the more intensively they are used, then the greater the tendency towards the retention of these resources within the basic productive and reproductive unit, which in the large majority of cases is the nuclear family. There are several reasons for this hypothesis. Intensive agriculture, whether by plough or irrigation, permits a surplus of production over consumption that is sufficient to maintain an elaborate division of labour and a stratification based upon different 'styles of life'. An important means of maintaining one's style of life, and that of one's progeny, is by marriage with persons of the same or higher qualifications.[19] We should therefore expect a greater emphasis upon the direct vertical transmission of property in societies with intensive rather than extensive exploitation of agricultural resources. This system of direct vertical transmission (i.e. from parents to children) tends to make provision for women as well as men. The position of women in the world has to be maintained by means of property, either in dowry or inheritance—otherwise the honour of the family suffers a set-back in the eyes of others. This also means that they are likely to become residual heirs in the restricted sibling groups that monogamy permits, the property going to female descendants before collateral males, even when these are members of the same agnatic clan.

TABLE 5.7 Sibling Kin Terms and Diverging Devolution

		Sibling Kin Terms		
		Present	**Absent**	**Total**
Diverging devolution	Pres-ent	60	83	143
	Absent	42	221	263
No individual property rights or no rule of transmission		6	67	73
1. Top quadrant: phi = 0.29 x^2 = 33.26 *P* < 001		Total of table		479
		N.I. on kin terms		104
		N.I. on devolution		280
				863
2. 'No rights' etc. added to 'absent' phi = 0.30 x^2 = 43.99 *p* < .001				

N.B. The figures are derived from col. 27. Positive includes the Eskimo and descriptive categories. As defined in the code, Sudanese and Iroquois terminologies may also include cases where siblings are differentiated from all other cousins. In Table 5.7 these terminologies have been included in the negative cases but another test will be run showing Iroquois and Sudanese as a mixed category.

The other aspect of intensive agriculture bearing upon the conditions for the emergence of diverging devolution is the expansion of population it allows, another factor making for scarcity of land. Where intensive agriculture is dependent upon the plough, the increase in production is partly a result of the greater area a man can cultivate; once again, land becomes more valuable, especially the kind of land that can sustain permanent cultivation by means of the simpler type of plough.

Intensive exploitation of resources can be variously measured. Table 5.8 shows the firm association that exists between the presence of the plough and diverging devolution. The information on the absence of plough agriculture is not altogether satisfactory since the absence of an entry in column 39 might mean either no information or no plough; however the presence of the plough is such an obvious feature of human societies that the chance of error should be small.

TABLE 5.8 Plough Agriculture and Diverging Devolution

		Plough Agriculture		
		Present	**Absent**	**Total**
Diverging devolution	Present	64	96	160
	Absent	43	303	346
No individual property rights or no rule of transmission		0	77	77
1. Top quadrant: phi = 0.31 $x^2 = 49.88$ $p < .001$		Total of table		583
		N.I. on devolution		280
				863
2. 'No rights* etc. added to 'absent': phi = 0.34 $x^2 = 68.96$ $p < .001$				

N.B. On Col. 39 the absence of an entry might mean no plough or no information.

The Atlas also gives a separate code for intensive agriculture (col. 28 *I*, *J*) and it is possible to retest the hypothesis on this column. Table 5.9 shows that the results support those of Table 5.8, though the association is somewhat less strong.

Intensive agriculture is virtually a condition of the extensive differentiation by styles of life that in turn encourages the concentration of property by inheritance and marriage. The concentration of property is maintained by diverging devolution, which takes the form of direct vertical transmission; hence the importance of 'sonship', real and fictional (which includes daughters), in these areas of social action.[20] We would therefore expect to find diverging devolution associated with complex stratified societies of all types, whether characterized by caste or class. This hypothesis, tested in Table 5.10, is linked with the suggestion that diverging devolution encourages in-marriage, which I tested earlier. Endogamy is clearly one way of limiting the consequences of the transmission of property through women. Other systems of complex stratification may restrict marriage *de facto* if not *de jure*.

TABLE 5.9 Intensive Agriculture and Diverging Devolution

		Intensive Agriculture		
		Present	**Absent**	**Total**
Diverging devolution	Present	87	73	160
	Absent	104	242	346
No individual property rights or no rule of transmission		3	74	77
		Total of table		583
1. Top quadrant: phi = 0.23 x^2 = 27.53 $p < .001$		N.I. on devolution		280
				863
2. 'No rights' etc. added to 'absent' phi = 0.28 x^2 = 44.21 $p < .001$				

N.B. Intensive agriculture is coded in col. 28: present = *I, J*; absent = others.

TABLE 5.10 Stratification (Caste and Class) and Diverging Devolution

		Present	**Absent**	**Total**
Diverging devolution	Present	50	109	159
	Absent	29	315	344
No individual property rights or no rule of transmission		1	76	77
		Total of table		580
1. Top quadrant: phi = 0.29 x^2 = 43.51 $p < .001$		N.I. on devolution		280
		N.I. on stratification		3
				863
2. 'No rights' etc. added to 'absent' phi = 0.31 x^2 = 57.41 $p < .001$				

N.B. Caste here is the category coded *C* in col. 69; class is *C* and *E* in col. 67.

The same hypothesis can be tested in column 33 which provides 'a measure of political complexity'. I have included here only the larger states. In surveying the major Eurasian civilizations, I found all (in differing degrees) to be characterized by diverging devolution: women were usually residual heiresses to their brothers, in addition to which they received a dowry if they married away. These forms of marriage prestation and inheritance are recorded in the Greek, Roman, and Hebrew and Chinese texts and in Babylonian, Hindu, and Buddhist law-books. For such societies were all literate; indeed testamentary inheritance, as Maine pointed out, was sometimes used to divert property from a man's agnates, who were his residual heirs. But more often and more universally the institution of adoption (often of agnates) and the 'appointed daughter' were used to ensure the direct vertical transmission of property. In general, these literate societies fall into the category of 'large states' (or are closely linked to them) and the association with diverging devolution, tested in Table 5.11, is shown to be firm.

TABLE 5.11 Large States and Diverging Devolution

		Large States		
		Present	Absent	Total
Diverging devolution	Present	42	110	152
	Absent	31	307	338
No individual property rights or no rule of transmission		0	77	77
		Total of table		567
		N.I. on devolution		280
1. Top quadrant: phi = 0.24, $x^2 = 28.18$, $p < .001$		N.I. on polity		16
				863
2. 'No rights' etc. added to 'absent' phi = 0.27, $x^2 = 40.32$, $p < .001$				

N.B. Present, 3 and 4 in col. 33; absent, 0, 1, 2, though 1 and 2 represent 'petty and larger paramount chiefdoms or their equivalent'.

Alternative Predictions

To test my hypothesis, I predicted that the presence of different types of descent groups would be less closely associated with the variables examined than would the transmission of property. The runs done for diverging devolution were repeated for the nearest equivalent in kinship terms, i.e. bilateral 'descent' or kinship, that is to say those societies which possessed neither patrilineal nor matrilineal descent groups. The results are compared in Table 5.12. In every case except for residence diverging devolution has a stronger association with the variables than does 'bilateral kinship'. The general point that I would make here is that while anthropologists have given most attention to kinship factors, there are a number of important areas of social life where the mode of distributing property appears to be more significant. This is not a matter of trying to substitute one monolithic form of explanation for another. Nor yet of equating (as some writers have tended to do) kinship and property. The two variables are closely interlocked in pre-industrial societies where the basic means of production are almost universally transmitted between close kin. My interest is in attempting to specify the way in which they are associated, particularly with a view to ascertaining the influence of differences in systems of transmission upon kinship relations. Causal direction is not of course something one can establish by correlational analysis alone; though causal inferences can be made by means of statistical techniques it needs to be supplemented by a study of changing situations.[21]

I suggested therefore that 'bilateral descent' (or rather 'bilateral kinship') would be a worse predictor. On the other hand, the vesting of landed property in women, as distinct from movables alone, was thought likely to produce more significant results, anyhow as far as residence is concerned. The Atlas does not say when a dowry includes land; information on this is provided only for inheritance. The results of this comparison are presented in Table 5.12 and summarized in Table 5.12a. While in every case except residence bilateral kinship (i.e. the absence of unilineal descent groups) is less closely associated with the variables than diverging devolution (as I had suggested), the inheritance of land comes second to diverging devolution and is a worse rather than a better predictor. As I have earlier noted this excludes societies with a landed dowry (and in inheritance of land by women) which may well be a better predictor; but I make no attempt to explain this result.

Conclusions

Tylor long ago pointed out the adaptive functions of exogamy for human societies (1889). Mankind, he remarked, was faced with the alternative of marrying out or being killed out. In-marriage on the other hand is a policy of isolation. One reason (and there are of course others) for such a policy is to preserve property where this is transmitted through both

TABLE 5.12 Relative Accuracy of Prediction Achieved by Three Variables, Diverging Devolution, Bilateral Descent and Diverging Inheritance

	Table No. and Name	2. Pre-marital Sex	3. Endogamy	4. Father's Brother's Daughter Marriage	5. Monogamy	6. Residence	7. Sibling Kin Terms	8. Plough	9. Intensive Agriculture	10. Stratification	11. Large States
Diverging devolution	phi	0.22	0.18	0.30	0.35	0.22	0.29	0.31	0.23	0.29	0.24
	P<	.001	.001	.001	.001	.001	.001	.001	.001	.001	.001
'Bilateral Kinship'	phi	0.10	0.11	0.04	0.13	0.44	0.10 (0.30)*	−0.02	−0.09	0.11	0.02
	P<	.05	.001	N.S.	.001	.001	N.S.	N.S.	N.S.	.001	N.S.
Diverging inheritance of land	phi	0.18	0.19	0.26	0.25	0.33	0.22 (0.21)*	0.18	0.160	0.20	0.17
	P<	.01	.001	.001	.001	.001	.001	.001	.001	.001	.001

* Eskimo terms only.

TABLE 5.12A Rank Ordering of Significance of Correlations Between Pairs of Variables

Table No. and Name	2. Pre-marital Sex	3. Endogamy	4. Father's Brother's Daughter Marriage	5. Monogamy	6. Residence	7. Sibling Kin Terms	8. Plough	9. Intensive Agriculture	10. Stratification	11. Large States
Diverging devolution	1	1	1	1	2	1	1	1	1	1
P	(.001)	(.001)	(.001)	(.001)	(.001)	(.001)	(.001)	(.001)	(.001)	(.001)
'Bilateral kinship'	3	3	3	3	1	3	3 N.S.	3 N.S.	3	3
P	(.05)	(.001)	N.S.	(.001)	(001)	N.S.	(Neg.)	(Neg.)	(.001)	N.S.
Diverging inheritance of land	2	2	2	2	3	2	2	2	2	2
P	(.01)	(.001)	(.001)	(.001)	(.001)	(.001)	(.001)	(.001)	(.001)	(.001)

males and females, to encourage marriages with families 'of one's own kind' and thus to maintain property and prestige. The positive control of marriage arrangements (exogamy is a negative control) is stricter where property is transmitted to women. It is a commentary on their lot that where they are more propertied they are initially less free as far as marital arrangements go, though the unions into which they enter are more likely to be monogamous (or even polyandrous).

In this paper I have tried to test by means of the Ethnographic Atlas a set of hypotheses to do with the concomitants of diverging devolution, derived from a more intensive study of the literature on a number of societies in Eurasia and Africa. Though the information is imperfect and the instrument limited, my basic suggestions are all confirmed (except for caste). Bilateral kinship was a worse predictor except for certain types of residence; on the other hand, the inheritance of land was also worse, which the theory did not anticipate. These results, which are summarized in Table 5.12, are reinforced by the fact that the hypotheses are interlocked and were formulated in advance.

I have shown that Eurasian and African societies differ in their systems of transmitting property; these differences are correlated with differences in the types of marriage prestation, the extent of control over women, both before marriage and in terms of marriage partners (and probably, too, after marriage though this I could not test). Differences in the nature of a man's estate are indicated in the greater prevalence of terms that isolate the sibling group, an indication of the differences in the type of descent corporation found associated with the systems for the devolution of property and with modes of agriculture. Both the means of production and the relationships of production have certain marked differences.

It is a failure to recognize these differences in the type of descent corporation (even when both can be described as 'patrilineal descent groups') that seems to have caused much of the controversy over the application of descent or alliance models to the study of such societies and it is significant that so-called 'descent theorists' have generally worked in societies with homogeneous devolution and the 'alliance theorists' in societies with diverging devolution. It should be apparent that where marriage involves a re-arrangement of property rights of the dowry kind, then conjugal, affinal, sibling, and filial relationships are likely to display qualitative differences from systems of the African kind. It also follows that the organization of descent groups will differ under these two conditions. The ballplay between rival 'theorists' has obscured the basic differences in the material they are dealing with.

I shall pursue this point in another place; meanwhile I conclude by pointing to the association of diverging transmission with intensive (and plough) agriculture, with large states and with complex systems of stratification. In such societies social differentiation, based on productive property, exists even at the village level; to maintain the position of the family, a man endows (and controls) his daughters as well as sons, and these ends are promoted by the tendency towards monogamous marriage.[22] Indeed it is significant that the strongest associations of diverging devolution are with monogamy and plough agriculture.

Notes

Note: The data presented in this paper have subsequently been analysed by a type of multivariate analysis, in fact a combination of pathway and linkage techniques. The results are embodied in a further paper, *Causal inferences concerning diverging devolution*, by Jack Goody, Barrie Irving, and Nicky Tahany, which it is hoped to publish shortly.

1. Bosman was accustomed to the conjugal community of Roman Dutch Law. But the absence of a dowry was apparent even to Englishmen reared under the qualified unity of conjugal property which was a feature of their Common Law. This broad distinction between Africa and Europe still persists. 'Marriage in Ashanti between free persons ... does not lead to community of property between the spouses, still less to the sinking of the wife's legal persona in her husband's' (Allott 1966: 191).
2. The absence of a dowry is enshrined in local usage of English and French. For the Europeans, having no word for prestations that passed from the family of the groom to that of the bride, used the word, they had 'dot' or 'dowry', for a very different set of transactions. These terms are still sometimes used for 'bridewealth' and other prestations.
3. Barton used the term 'homoparental' but this presents difficulties for matrilineal inheritance.
4. Noted for example by Goode 1963: 167.
5. This work is in the course of preparation.
6. This material was punched on cards and tape as it appeared. However when work was about to start, a revised and more restricted version of the data was published (April 1967), and this then had to be punched first in an alphabetic code (as printed) and later in a numeric code since the former created problems for the small store computer (8K) that was available for the data-processing. Since then a version has been made available on cards. The pack used is available at the cost of reproduction to those interested; it has also been stored at the S.S.R.C. Data Bank, Department of Sociology, University of Essex.
7. Goody 1962: v.
8. I have used all the data from the Atlas and have not sampled it in the way suggested by Murdock, 1967: 114. The reasons for this are purely practical and I shall conduct further tests when time allows.
9. The phi coefficient is also known as the Kendall partial rank coefficient (Siegel 1956: 225–26).

10. In speaking of the 'woman's property complex' I refer to her access to property held by males. Under systems of homogeneous inheritance, women have property but it is either inherited from women or self-acquired.
11. This entry has been shown separately on the tables as it could be argued (in some cases) that it is equivalent to the absence of diverging devolution.
12. Property was also destroyed during the life-time of the holder in the well-known case of the potlatch.
13. See Goody, Incorporation and Marriage Policy in Northern Ghana (1969).
14. For definitions of these terms, see Murdock 1957: 166.
15. If preferred father's brother's daughter marriage is run against other preferred cross-cousin marriages, the results are phi = 0.42, $x^2 = 18.16$, p <.001.
16. If monogamy and polyandry are included together as positive cases, the association with diverging devolution gives a phi of 0.37 (p <.001).
17. Logically, neolocal residence is less firmly attached to diverging devolution than are bilocal or the less evenly distributed systems of alternative residence. But the boundaries of 'neolocal' residence are difficult to discriminate (how separate is 'separate'?).
18. Murdock 1967: 158.
19. In my account of the LoWiili of Northern Ghana (1956), I suggested that the increased differentiation of wealth militated against the movement of property outside the co-residential group. The specific feature of this group that inhibits a dispersal of the property is its character as a unit of production. Where self-acquired property (income) begins to play a greater part than inherited wealth (capital), then there will be increasing reluctance to allow property to go outside, as is bound to be the case where the residential pattern is incongruent (or partially so, as in a fully fledged system of double descent) with the mode of inheritance.
20. This point is developed elsewhere (Goody 1968a).
21. I have tried to approach this problem in my comparative work on the LoWiili and the LoDagaba, as well as in a separate essay (Goody 1968b).
22. This paper represents the preliminary results of the comparative research I have undertaken with the help of a grant from the Social Science Research Council. I have hoped for some years to carry out such a survey but it would have been impossible but for the help, by means of this grant, of my assistant in research, Mrs. L. March. I should also like to thank Dr. L. Slater for the programming, and Dr. E. N. Goody, for comments and advice. Little systematic comparison has been carried out in Europe since the work of Hobhouse, Wheeler, and Ginsberg (1915); like all recent writers on the subject I am much indebted to G. P. Murdock for making his collection of data available in the shape of the Ethnographic Atlas.

Bibliography

ALLOTT, ANTHONY N. 1966. The Ashanti law of property. *Zeitschrift für vergleichende Rechtswissenschaft.* 68: 129–215.

BOSMAN, WILLIAM. 1967. *A new and accurate description of the coast of Guinea.* London: Frank Cass (First English ed. 1705).

CARRASCO, PEDRO. 1959. *Land and policy in Tibet.* (Am. Eth. Soc.). Seattle: Univ. of Washington Press.

DRIVER, HAROLD EDSO. 1961. Introduction to statistics for comparative research, *Readings in cross-cultural methodology* (ed. Frank W. Moore). New Haven: H.R.A.F.

GOODE, WILLIAM J. 1963. *World revolution and family pattern.* New York: Free Press.

GOODY, JACK. 1956. *The social organisation of the LoWiili.* London: H.M.S.O. (Second ed. 1967).

GOODY, JACK. 1958. The fission of domestic groups among the LoDagaba, *The developmental cycle in domestic groups* (Cambridge Papers in Social Anthropology, No. 1). Cambridge: University Press.

GOODY, JACK. 1959. The mother's brother and the sister's son in West Africa. *J. R. Anthrop. Inst.* 89: 61–88.

GOODY, JACK. 1962. *Death, property and the ancestors.* Stanford: University Press.

GOODY, JACK. 1968a. Adoption in cross-cultural perspective. *Comparative Studies in Society and History.*

GOODY, JACK. 1968b. Inheritance, social change and the boundary problem, *Lévi-Strauss Festschrift* (ed. J. Pouillon and P. Maranda). The Hague: Mouton.

GOODY, JACK. 1969. Marriage policy and incorporation in northern Ghana, *From tribe to nation in Africa* (ed. R. Cohen and J. Middleton). San Francisco: Chandler.

HOBHOUSE, L. T. WHEELER, G. C. and GINSBERG, M. 1915. *The Material Culture and Social Institutions of the Simpler Peoples.* London.

MURDOCK, GEORGE P. 1960. Cognatic forms of social organization, *Social structure in south-east Asia* (Viking Fund Pubs, in Anthrop. No. 29). Chicago: Quadrangle Books.

MURDOCK, GEORGE P. 1967. Ethnographic atlas: a summary. *Ethnography 6:* 109–236.

REDFIELD, ROBERT. 1934. *Chan Kom: a Maya village.* Washington D.C.: Carnegie Institute of Washington.

SIEGEL, SIDNEY. 1956. *Nonparametric statistics for the behavioral sciences.* New York: McGraw-Hill.

TYLOR, EDWARD B. 1889. On a method of investigating the development of institutions: applied to laws of marriage and descent. *J. Anthrop. Inst.* 18: 245–269.

Manning, Paul. 2015. "Demons, Danger, and Desire: The 'Aragvian' Sexual Revolution." In *Love Stories: Language, Private Love, and Public Romance in Georgia*. University of Toronto Press.

THE KHEVSUR IDEOLOGY OF SEXUALITY REPRESENTED desire as a dangerous, almost magical force that was destructive both for individuals and for collective norms. Such destructive desire was also strongly associated with women. In the first chapter we saw that Khevsurs located desire within a cosmological framework of myth: desire itself was not created by God, but came to be the moment God created both boys and girls, who desired each other but had no way to express this desire; they could only pine for each other, so they perished from desire. God then weakened this strictly (hetero) sexual desire by transferring it from sexual others to other kinds of desire: desire for things such as drinking horns, tobacco, and clothing. He also instituted the practice of *sts'orproba* and its rules to give heterosexual desire a delimited means of expression. The association of destructive desire with femininity also probably referenced this cosmological framework: Khevsur cosmology was sharply dualistic, divided according to gender; all of creation was created either by a masculine God (or children of god) or a feminine Devil (or demons). Since the normative, collective order was overseen by male shrine attendants and meetings of the all-male *jari*, and was instituted by masculine divinities, it is easy to see how anything that was disruptive of this order, for example individual sexual desires, would be associated with feminine demons and spirits.

A good example of this association of desire with femininity comes from another portion of Khevsur cosmology: demonology. It is common in many societies to create imaginary demonic or monstrous others who display equally monstrous sexualities that are somehow an inversion of the normal human condition of sexual desire. Western vampires, for example, display a peculiar sexuality whereby drinking blood takes on an erotic value paralleling sex between humans. In other regions of Georgia there is a female goblin called an *ali*, who seduces and destroys young men; if captured and domesticated by cutting her wild tousled hair and trimming her fingernails, she can become an unwilling wife who always seeks her lost hair and nails like a hidden treasure. If she finds them, she becomes free and exacts a terrible revenge for her marital abduction. This spirit seems to be exploring, on the imaginary plane, anxieties about the dangers inherent in the common practice of marital abduction (Manning, 2014b).

For the Khevsurs, the demonic sexual other *par excellence* was the *dobili* ("sworn sister") (see also Manning 2014a). Every male shrine god (there are only male gods) had a set of female demonic consorts, his "sworn sisters." Male shrine gods did not marry their consorts, since marriage was for humans alone; they instead engaged in something very like *sts'orproba* with these beautiful female demons. These demons, who had their own special shrines, were placated by humans with sacrifices that were in every way the inverse of those used for male divinities: instead of sheep, goats were sacrificed (A. Ochiauri 2005: 81), and instead of silver cups, clay cups were used (A. Ochiauri 2005: 373). These demonic powers could take the form of small children, beautiful or old women, as well as monstrous or animal forms (snakes, pigs, birds, or in one case a "mist-colored horse"). They typically came out to "play" at dawn and dusk (A. Ochiauri 2005:81, 191, 233, 336).

These creatures were said to be particularly dangerous for women and children, perhaps expressing indirectly the rivalry between real human *dzmobilis* and the future spouse of their lover. With men, however, like the *ali* of the plains, they engaged in all manner of licentious sexual behavior that was diametrically opposed to all other sexual practices: they were promiscuous (allowed in *sts'orproba,* but not marriage); they always engaged in sexual intercourse (allowed in marriage, not so much in *sts'orproba);* lying down with a *dobili,* even in a dream, made a man ritually impure (as in marriage but not with *sts'orproba* [Baliauri 1991: 63]); they were completely fecund, every sexual act producing children (children are allowed in marriage, forbidden in *sts'orproba*), but they produced only more beings who were like or worse than themselves, and consequently, they destroyed their own young (Mak'alatia 1984: 236–37).

As in most cultures, Khevsur cultural identity—the cultural sense of self—was defined at its boundaries, by reference to *alterity* or "otherness," that is, to real or imagined *others* who did not share their customs and norms. Khevsurs explored many of their anxieties about desire by reference to cosmological origins in myth and by imagining monstrous feminine others whose insatiable sexualities were the inversions of normative human sexuality. This is a kind of extreme cosmological alterity. But otherness was also explored on the historical, human plane, where some sort of collective norm was violated because of individual desires; these events also produced historical narratives of scandal and drama which, like myths and monsters, indicated the dangers of desire to the collective order.

Even as they told myths that located their norms within a divine cosmology that included demonic others, Khevsurs were also aware that their sexual practices and other norms were not widely shared by nearby human others. The Khevsurs were surrounded by other peoples: the Chechens and Ingush to the north, the Tush and Kisti to the east, the Mokhevians to the west, and the Pshavians who dwelled in the lower parts of the river valleys to the south. Of all these groups, only the Pshavians had anything like the sexual customs of the Khevsurs, and the Pshavians were the only others with whom the Khevsurs were likely to intermarry. Even so, the Khevsurs imagined the Pshavian sexual practices of *ts'ats'loba,* which were for the most part very similar to their own *sts'orproba*, to be in many ways familiar, and yet at the same time strange, inversions of their own practices.

Although the Pshavians were imagined as being "the opposite" of Khevsurs in certain ways, the Khevsur imagination of absolute sexual alterity on the human plane was summed up instead in the figure of the Russian. All local groups that did not share the norms of the Khevsurs could be characterized by the term *kochriani*, which meant, in everyday language, "those who do not have the customs of the Khevsurs"; in the divine language (*jvart ena* "the language of crosses") that was used, for example, by the spirit mediums called *kadagi* ("oracle") in order to give voice to the gods, this same term simply meant "Russian." At the time these sexual practices were still current, Khevsurs were under the rule of the Russian empire or, later, the Soviet Union, in which the dominant population was Russian. As a people living in strongholds high in the mountains, Khevsurs initially experienced Russian rule as an occasional incursion into their traditional life, and in general most customs like marriage were practiced according to traditional law. As Russian rule moved from occasional encounters to a continuous presence in everyday life, however, Russian "law" (*k'anoni*) became an external force opposed to the "rules" (*ts'esi*) that defined the Khevsurs. Russian law included religious and civil regulations of customs pertaining to sexuality, in particular marriage.

In addition to this external set of norms imposed by force, summed up with concepts of "Russian rule" and "Russian law," Khevsurs imagined and encountered individual Russians as beings exemplifying a kind of almost nonhuman sexuality, essentially embodying a sexual shamelessness equivalent to dogs. It is probably significant that the most common word for "prostitute" among the Khevsurs was the Russian borrowing *mat'ushk'a* (literally "little mother, mama" in Russian, where the term had no such negative meanings or connotations). Russian rule would eventually turn Khevsurs into Russians, it was thought, so to talk about Russian rule was to talk about the impending doom of Khevsur rules and Khevsur communal identity, and to compare Khevsurs to Russians was to compare them to whores, dogs, creatures with no sense of honor or shame (*namusi*), who lacked any concern for name or fame (*sakheli*) or shame (*sirtskbvili*). Particularly in the sphere of desire, violations of the rules of the Khevsurs, whatever their source, represented a potential threat to Khevsur identity. By not containing their desires as they should, Khevsurs would lose their identity and become others, "become Russians."

Even within the Khevsur community the Khevsurs were also aware that their own norms showed some internal variation in this area, as in many other things. The Khevsurs were a *very* small group of people, numbering a handful of thousands, living on either side of the main range of the Caucasus mountains, which divided their village communes (*temi:* groups of villages usually occupying a single valley) into two broad groups: those that lived on "this side" (*piraket*) of the Caucasus (the southern flanks, closer to the plains of Georgia adjoining

Pshavi, mostly in tributaries of the Aragvi basin, including Khakhmati), and those that lived on "the other side of the mountains" *(mtis iket)*, further from Pshavi and the plains of Georgia, on the borders of Chechnya (Figure 5.1). According to Baliauri, the Khevsurs who lived beyond the mountains (e.g., the district containing Shat'ili) accepted that the norms of those who lived on "this side" were always correct. If there was a conflict that could not be resolved, or where the rules were unclear, in "far" transalpine Khevsureti, they always sent emissaries to "near" cisalpine Khevsureti to ascertain what the authoritative rules and norms were, whereas the Khevsurs who lived on "this side of the mountains had no interest in anyone elses norms because they believed their own practices were authoritative and that they were the best conservators of tradition (Baliauri 1991:157).

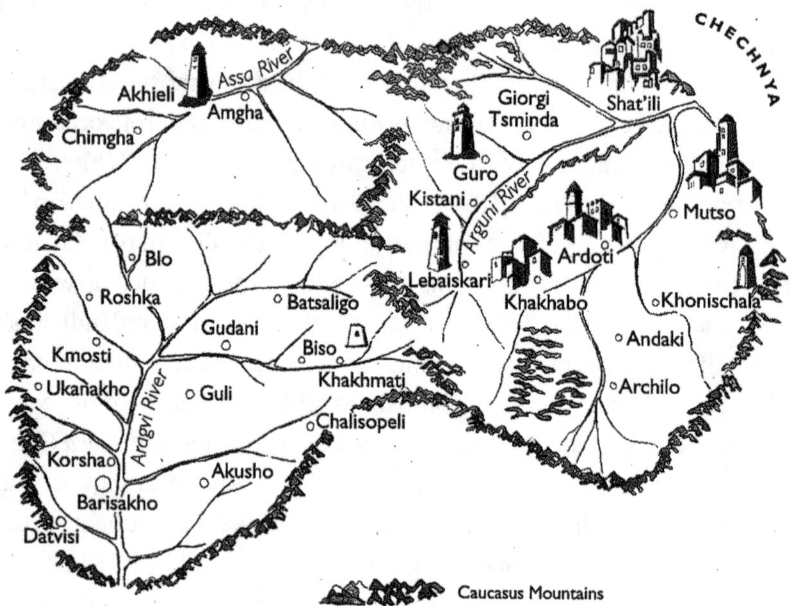

FIGURE 5.1 Detailed map of the villages and districts *(temi)* of Khevsureti. Courtesy of Lisa Gronseth.

As we have seen, individual sporadic violations of the norms of sexuality occurred here and there, and, especially when marriage was also involved, these violations were a source of a particular kind of historical narrative of scandal, producing ephemeral arguments and conversations, gossip, and poetry of censure *(shairi)*. Here I am interested primarily in more concerted challenges to the normative order of sexuality, where whole generations of Khevsur boys, and in particular girls, rose to challenge the normative order of sexuality, advocating both for more permissive practices of *sts'orproba* and also more permissive rules of marriage that would allow sexual partners of *sts'orporba* to marry one another based on mutual desire rather than marriage by compulsion or force to strangers.

Around the time of the beginning of the First World War (in which the Khevsurs participated as soldiers, as subjects of the Russian empire against Germany), right before the Russian Revolution (1917), two major revolutionary challenges emerged to question the traditional order of *sts'orproba* and marriage. From around 1913–15, young people in a small corner of Khevsureti began to experiment with the form of lying down in *sts'orproba,* which led to a scandal across Khevsureti. This was called "Aragvian (*araguli*) *sts'orproba*" because it was innovated by the young people of the Aragvi region, so named because it consists of a set of villages in "near" Khevsureti closest to Pshavi, at the headwaters of the Aragvi river that flows into Pshavi; the residents of which area are called "Aragvians" (*Aragvelebi*) (Baliauri 1991:156–73).

Around the same time (1914–17) in the same general region, young women announced, often by means of poetry, that they had no intention of marrying strangers by compulsion, and would henceforth only marry those they themselves desired, usually their *dzmobilis.* This particular innovation was in part clearly related to the former change in sexual practices, but it was also occasioned by the introduction of Russian law, and specifically marriage law and Orthodox Church marriage, neither of which corresponds to Khevsur customary law or religion. Particularly important was the fact that the Russian marriage law and religious practice combined to make divorce a much more difficult and shameful affair; for Khevsur women in particular, this meant that they would not be able to escape an undesirable husband as they had in the past, simply by returning home or living with their relatives. Marriage to strangers in the face of such a strict marriage law became more ominous and potentially dangerous (Baliauri 1991: 34–40).

It is surely no coincidence that these two events—a revolutionary new form of sexual practice and an equally revolutionary demand to choose marriage partners—occurred around the same historical period. This was also the time when our two main Khevsur ethnographers (Natela Baliauri and Aleksi Ochiauri) themselves violated the rules of marriage and became exiles from their own communities (1914). To understand how a change in the customs of lying down was related to a change in marriage, we first need to understand the external problem of Russian law in relation to Khevsur customs of marriage. We also need to understand the specific changes in *sts'orproba,* and how these related to and affected marriage.

Russian Marriage

Russian colonial administrators and priests considered Khevsurs to be lapsed members of the Orthodox Christian faith, which was the Russian state religion, and hence sought to "restore" them to Orthodoxy. Khevsur marriage ritual did not involve Orthodox church weddings ("writing the cross" before a Orthodox priest), and Khevsurs found the Orthodox ritual to be shameful. The change in ritual during this time meant endless complications: in particular, as discussed above, Khevsurs found that Russian marriage laws made divorce, which had hitherto been relatively easy for either a boy or a girl, much more onerous, shameful, and difficult. Previously, although the boy and the girl who would be married were often virtual strangers, they could also divorce easily; the woman could return to her relatives and live with them (though she would likely not be able to remarry). However, after the change, boys and girls became much more interested in finding out more about their potential marriage partner, because leaving them would become more difficult.

The problem was that the pool of potential marriage partners, according to Khevsur rules, could not include anyone who was already well known to one: excluded were people of the same clan or village, and especially anyone with whom one was acquainted sexually, that is, a *sts'orperi,* or even worse a *dzmobili.* To marry one's erstwhile sexual partner would change how one viewed that person, and how one viewed *sts'orproba* itself: the pair would no longer be classified as virtual siblings, and hence this was regarded as a sign of sexual depravity. After the girls of near Khevsureti announced (presumably through poems as well as face to face) that they would no longer "marry by compulsion" (*dzalit*), this meant that the ideal marriage partner could now be someone one already knew, including people of the same surname, people from the same village or village commune, and especially one's existing lovers (*sts'orperis, dzmobilis*). As we have seen, the fantasy of a marriage to one's existing romantic partner had occurred before, but it was an idle fantasy, or worse, something that could lead to exile or suicide if the partners actually acted on this fantasy and eloped; now it became a central demand occasioned by the changes in Russian marriage law. And boys and girls did, indeed, begin to elope with their lovers (including our main ethnographers of Khevsur romance!), producing immense tensions, exiles, and even the death of one or the other of the lovers. Since marriage relations typically formed connections with people from outside one's own area (exogamy), it was comparatively cost-free to alienate people who were already strangers, but the same move could now create great conflicts within individual communities and villages.

It was actually comparatively easy to dissolve a proposed marriage partnership with a stranger to make way for a marriage partner one actually desired. (*Elchis* often played a key role in this activity, too.) The strategems could be as simple as pretending to have a dreadful illness, or claiming that the shrine divinities themselves opposed the marriage. If this failed to dissuade the potential spouse, a girl might steal off to hide somewhere, in the woods, with a distant relative. Her relatives would search for her, thinking perhaps she had killed herself or had fallen off a cliff into the water and drowned. She would find a way to inform them that she was not dead, but that if they didn't let her have her way, she would indeed kill herself: if her arranged marriage had not proceeded too far, then she was now free to marry someone else (Baliauri 1991:35).

The Aragvian Way of Love

At around the same time, the sexual practices of *sts'orproba* also began to change, beginning in a small area of near Khevsureti, specifically the Aragvi region, which forms the only passage from Khevsureti to Pshavi, and spreading from there. Since *sts'orproba* was a relationship that took place not only within a village, but also between villages and communities while visiting, this new form of sexual practice soon spread, as lovers from different communities encountered the new practice and either adopted it themselves and taught it to their lovers, or rejected it, at the same time rejecting their erstwhile lover. And as the practice spread, word of the practice spread too, through gossip and poetry, producing a general sense of scandal and conflict within and between different communities.

What were the "Aragvian rules" of *sts'orproba?* Some things remained the same, including the fact that the girl went to the boy at night, initially with the mediation of the *elchi.* In addition, as elsewhere in Khevsureti, there was an absolute absence of force or compulsion, particularly of the girl by the boy; the girl remained absolutely free (Baliauri 1991:158). No one would be compelled to adopt these new rules, so if they became familiar with them, they would be seen as having desired to do so.

The differences lay primarily in the rules of what was allowed in "lying down." As we have seen before, the Khevsur "rules" of lying down were very specific about exactly how the bodies were to be arranged with respect to one another, exactly who could touch whom where, and so on. In Aragvian lying down, these rules were relaxed, possibly even dispensed with. The girl allowed the boy to touch her wherever he wished, and she herself would open his shirt and kiss him on the neck and chest. The boy, if the girl allowed, could kiss her on the face and neck, place his head on her chest, open her *paragi* (beaded collar) and embrace her in this way. Absolutely no attention was paid to the placement of the lower body, and they could lie together however they liked, embracing each other with their whole bodies (Baliauri 1991:158). Sometimes the girl would even lie *on top* of the boy, which was sometimes singled out as being particularly scandalous. Other changes were brought in too. In the relationship between *dzmobilis,* for example, the use of affectionate "pet names" for one's lover became common, a practice that for some reason other Khevsurs found to be particularly strange and newsworthy (Baliauri 1991:160).

Of course, one could not lie down with just anyone at any time in this way. Just as there were variations in the rules of how lying down was arranged and what could be done, depending on factors such as kinship distance, relative acquaintance, and whether it was "out of respect" or "out of desire," so Aragvian rules could be used only with certain others. Initially, it would happen only within the community with one's existing lovers, if they were of like mind, and if they were not, even proposing it often ended the relationship entirely. One could not engage in this new style of lying down with real kin, or with potential affines (marital kin, as when one visits one's future spouse and is laid down with his or her relatives). Precisely those people with whom one lay down "without desire," that is, siblings and future in-laws, were banned. Clearly, Aragvian rules emphasized and maximized "lying down" as an expression of erotic desire, and were appropriate only for those relations where such desire was in general felt to be appropriate.

So what was so scandalous about Aragvian *sts'orproba?* Aragvian rules maximized the linkage of lying down with sexual desire. Since the rules of *sts'orporba* were designed to give *limited* expression to desire, this change produced a sense of lack of self-control, and the accusation of depravity became possible. Girls might censure other girls who followed these practices as follows (Baliauri 1991:159):

> "You whore! I am not disgraced and shamed like you, am I? Your and my womanhood are not of the same kind, you who lack name and shame! Men know me, *sts'orperis* do not laugh at me in their heart like they do you!"

To which the girl who follows these practices might reply with irony, defending her autonomy against these voicings of communal norms:

> "Why, you are a good girl, aren't you? No one is asking you about my affairs, little sister. Do you really think it bothers me what you think, you poor thing? Your talk and the barking of a dog are all the same to me."

But the problem went further than simple accusations of depravity, which, as we will see, were easily and often disputed, since the new rules amounted to little more than a relaxation of some of the old rules. More significantly, when one adopted these new rules, one could no longer proceed with the fiction that *sts'orproba* and *dzmobiloba* was really just some sort of sibling relationship. The two practices became more and more an unambiguous expression of eroticism, which was vaguely linked with "depravity" but which moreover directly gave a lie to the idea that the lovers "look on each other like brother and sister." If boys and girls looked on each other with this kind of desire, then the rules of their relations could no longer proceed under the assumption that their meetings were purely siblinglike: desire became potentially consequential (leading to marriage, for example), and the fictional magic circle of sociable sexuality could therefore collapse.

This could have pervasive effects on the rest of social life, particular the freedom and autonomy of girls. Since the general freedom of girls to move about as they wished in Khevsureti was predicated on the imputation of generally siblinglike innocence with respect to her own desires and the desires of others, the existence of a new set of genres of expressing sexual desires more directly meant that not everyone was equally trustworthy or self-controlled. Such a situation, it was felt, would have the negative consequence of disrupting the freedom and autonomy of movement that characterized girls, and boys too. Just as a family would restrict the movement of a girl from the house if she had many suitors who might marry her by abduction—with or without her implied consent, marital abduction could be equivalent to what we would call rape, kidnapping, or simply elopement—so too would they do so for more general reasons. As word of this new practice became widespread, communities often became conflicted on the issue, often split between generations or households, and families would begin to restrict the movements of their girls. To explain these restrictions, they would often invoke the stereotyped figure of the Russians and Russian rule to explain her new loss of autonomy:

> They [parents and brothers] would say to the girl: "Now such a time has come upon Khevsureti that, even boys are not allowed to go out anywhere, let alone girls. The Khesvurs have turned into Russians, who can be trusted? These days boys and girls have become Russians. Those alive today are mingled together like goats and she-goats, they have lost all sense of name [*sakheli*] and shame [*sirtskhvili*]" (Baliauri 1991:159)

If indigenous accounts saw the main negative result of these practices as being a general increase in Russian-style depravity, they also emphasized that the principal consequence of such depravity would be that the girls could lose their freedom and autonomy because of the lack of trust in the self-control of others that would result.

The second negative consequence was that this new form of desire would lead to the desire to marry whomever one wanted, and specifically one's existing lover. As a result, this same period was characterized by a general disruption of proposed marriage partnerships by *dzmobili* relations, as *dzmobilis* became rivals of marriage partners in a new way, namely as potential, if scandalous, marriage partners themselves. This jeopardized the way in which these two relations were kept apart, and romance thus became no longer sociable, something pursued for its own sake, but consequential, a prelude to marriage. When one couple eloped, for example, in the period where these new practices of lying down became connected to new ideas about marriage partners, the older generation again blamed the changes on the advent of Russian law and Russian mores:

> According to others, however, although they [the couple that eloped] were not related, it was all the same: the rules of Khevsureti [*khevsuretis ts'esi*] was being destroyed by [Russian] law [*k'anonit*], which no one approved of. The

> people were outraged anyway. They heard poems composed by women, saying that "we will get married to people even from our own clan [*gvari,* surname] and whoever we ourselves want." The old people blamed this matter on the Russians and even in laments they bewailed the fact that they had fallen into the epoch of the Russians, that Khevsureti was ruined, girls and boys were ruined, Russian ways have come among us, girls sleep with boys shamelessly and then intend to marry them. They lie to the people saying "we are *dzmobilis* and how could we get married?," girls have become sluts, and so on. (Baliauri 1991: 42)

Thus, according to the traditionalist argument, this was all going to lead to a complete collapse of Khevsur identity and norms (virtues of self-control, shame, etc.), so that everyone would become shameless Russians. Emancipating desire, by combining erotic desire with choice of marriage partner, could lead not only to the eradication of *sts'orproba* in general (Baliauri 1991:160), but also to the loss of autonomy and freedom of women in particular. The general freedom and autonomy of men and especially women to come and go and do as they pleased hung in a precarious and paradoxical balance: if the young people did as they pleased (sexual autonomy), then they would lose their more general freedom and autonomy. The virtues of Khevsur women— that they were bold, daring, proud, free, autonomous, and willful—would be lost. Khevsur women would become like Russians ("sluts, whores"), and as a consequence they would end up like Georgian women of the plains, shut into their houses with restricted mobility.

The entire conflict, then, turned on different interpretations of autonomy and freedom. As we will see in the case studies of these scandals, Khevsur girls in particular presented their cases always in terms of these same virtues and ideals of freedom and autonomy, too. Conversations about these new norms therefore resulted in a kind of antinomy, an unresolvable contradiction between two arguments that are both equally rational, because both sides proceeded largely by championing a different interpretation of the same basic Khevsur ideals of autonomy and freedom. Even if some interpretations saw these new rules as being evidence of depravity (lack of shame and self-control) or Russian domination (loss of Khevsur freedom), which amounts to the same thing, the arguments that Baliauri has her nonfictional characters voice typically explore an internal contradiction and a deep ambivalence between desire and self-restraint within the norms and ideals of Khevsur culture and notions of person, rather than external contradictions between Russian and Khevsur norms (an argument, usually easily dismissed, that the Aragvian norms directly represented in themselves a "Russian" form of fornication).

Baliauri presents cases showing the consequences of the spread of this form of relationship across Khevsureti. Each revolves around a conflict between individual desire and communal norms, much like a Greek drama with individual hero and communal chorus. Some of these antiheroes, followers of new practices, were boys and others were girls, some involve hearsay or even imagined conversations linked to events, others involve exchanges of satirical *shairi* poetry, but all are stories built around real historical events with real historical individuals. But these antiheroes are no straw men or straw women, nor are they simply villains. We have no reason to believe they were other than real historical persons, but lest their arguments be dismissed on the basis of moral failings, the characters are idealized: the women are beautiful, proud, free, and hard-working, the men gallant and attractive; they are not in themselves bad people, but they always meet their exclusion by the community with defiant proclamations of their own autonomy, countering the derision and condemnation they receive with real arguments that make sense in the same terms that the arguments mustered against them do.

References

Baliauri, Natela. 1991. *Sts'orproba Khevsuretshi.* Tbilisi: Tbilisi University.

Mak'alatia, Sergi. 1984 (1935). *Khevsureti.* Tbilisi: Nak'aduli.

Manning, Paul. 2014a."Once Upon a Time There Was Sex in Georgia." *Slavic Review* 73 (2): 265–86. http://dx.doi.org/10.5612/slavicreview.73.2.265.

Manning, Paul. 2014b. "When Goblins Come to Town: The Ethnography of Urban Hauntings in Georgia." In *Monster Anthropology in Australasia and Beyond,* ed. Yasmine Musharbash and Geir Presterudstuen, 161–77. New York: Palgrave Macmillan.

Ochiauri, Aleksi. 2005. *K'artuli Xalxuri Dgheobebis K'alendari: Khevsureti. T'omi 2.* Tbilisi: Ena da K'ult'ura.

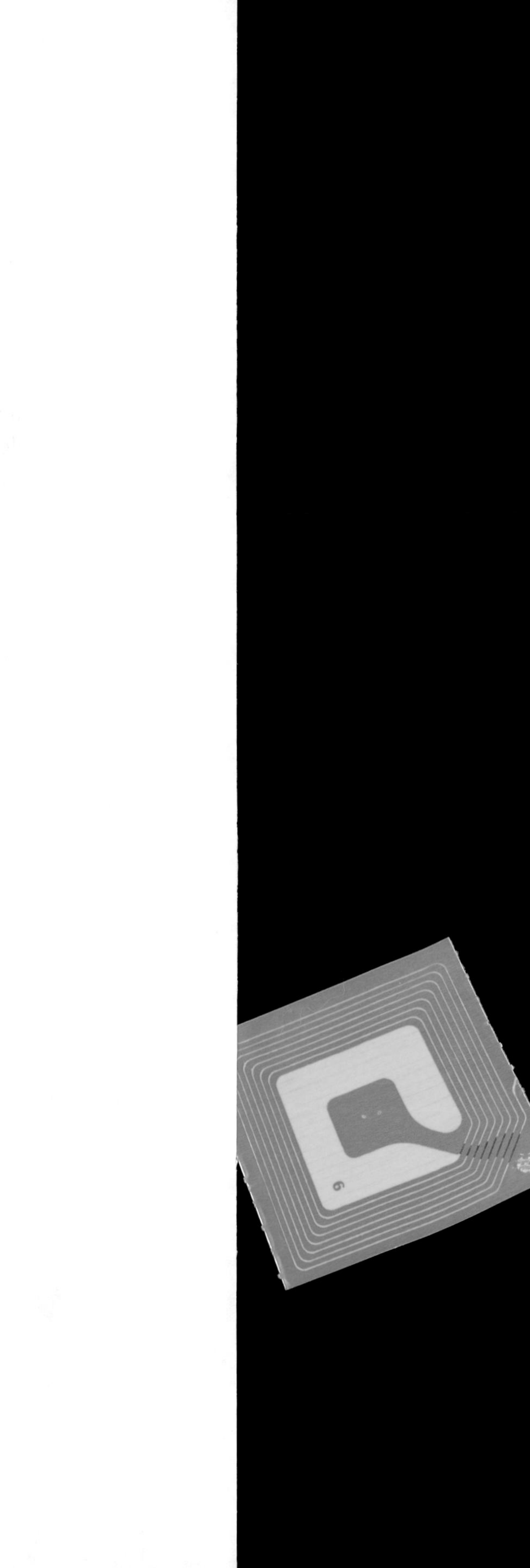

Chapter 6

Gender and Sexuality

DISCUSSION QUESTIONS

1. Rosaldo discusses the use of anthropological findings, especially regarding our evolutionary ancestors, to make claims about women's status in the world today. What does she find problematic about this practice?
2. Rosaldo critiques the view of gender as rooted in biologically-based differences. How, instead, does she suggest we understand gender? How do Samoans view sex and gender, according to Tcherkezoff?
3. Rosaldo argues that "human cultural and social forms have always been male dominated." Do you agree with her argument? Why or why not? How does male domination affect the lives of Samoans, especially those of fa'afafine and tomboys? How do women display power in a variety of ways, both in Rosaldo's account and in Samoa, despite male domination?
4. Tcherkezoff argues that *fa'afafine* and *tomboy* identities are both shaped by the differing ways in which women and men (and other gendered categories of people) are sexualized in Samoan society. Explain this argument. How does this lead to *fa'afafines* being generally more accepted in Samoan society than *tomboys*?

KEY TERMS

Patriarchal

Matriarchal

Heteronormativity

Transgender

Rosaldo, Michelle. 1980. "The Use and Abuse of Anthropology: Reflections on Feminism and Cross-Cultural Understanding." *Signs* 5(3):389–401.

THIS IS AN ARTICLE ABOUT QUESTIONS. Feminists have managed, in recent years, to impress a matter of undeniable importance on both academic and popular audiences alike. Previously blinded by bias, we have begun a "discovery" of women and have reported a good deal of data on women's lives, needs, and interests that earlier scholars ignored. Sexist traditions have, of course, made our records uneven. Now more than ever we see just how little is known about women. And the urgency experienced by current researchers is fueled by a recognition that invaluable records of women's arts, work, and politics are irretrievably lost. Our theories are—the saying goes—only as good as our data. As was suggested in a recent review of anthropological writings on sex roles, "What is clearest in the literature reviewed is the need for further investigation. ... What is most impressive about this literature is the overwhelming number of specific researchable questions it has produced. Hopefully the social force which inspired anthropological interest in women's status will sustain this interest through the long second stage of research fashioned to explore these hypotheses."[1]

But whatever we do or do not know, my sense is that feminist thinking—in anthropology at least—faces yet a more serious problem. Many a fieldworker has spent her months in the hills with predominantly female companions. These women spoke of their homes and children and husbands. They told us about men who fed, loved, or beat them; and they shared with us their experiences both of triumph and disappointment, their sense of their own strengths and powers, and the burden of their workaday chores. Female informants have told us about ties among kin and the politics surrounding marriage; they probably labeled each pot and each knife in their homes with a tale about work, obligation, and structurally significant bonds. Contrary to those anthropologists who have suggested that our problems lie in incomplete reports or, even worse, in inarticulate and "silent" female voices,[2] I would suggest that we hear women speak in almost all anthropological descriptions. We have, in fact, plenty of data "on women"; but when it comes to writing about them, all too few of us know what to say. What is needed, I will suggest, is not so much data as questions. The feminist discovery of women has begun to sensitize us to the ways in which gender pervades social life and experience; but the sociological significance of feminist insight is potentially a good deal deeper than anything realized as yet. What we know is constrained by interpretive frameworks which, of course, limit our thinking; what we *can* know will be determined by the kinds of questions we learn to ask.[3]

The Search for Origins

The significance of these all too general remarks for anthropology becomes clear when we consider the following observation. Few historians, sociologists, or social philosophers writing today feel called upon—as was common practice in the nineteenth century—to begin their tales "at the beginning" and probe the anthropological record for the origins of doctors in shamans or of, say, Catholic ritual in the cannibalism of an imagined past. Where turn-of-the-century thinkers (one thinks here of persons as diverse as Spencer, Maine, Durkheim, Engels, and Freud) considered it necessary to look at evidence from "simple" cultures as a means of understanding both the origins and the significance of contemporary social forms, most modern social scientists have rejected both their methods and their biases. Rather than probe origins, contemporary theorists will use anthropology, if at all, for the comparative insight that it offers; having decided, with good cause, to question evolutionary approaches, most would—I fear—go on to claim that data on premodern and traditional forms of social life have virtually no relevance to the understanding of contemporary society.

Yet it seems to me that quite the opposite is true of the vast majority of recent feminist writing. If anthropology has been too much ignored by most contemporary social thinkers, it has achieved a marked—though problematic—pride of place in classics like *Sexual Politics* and *The Second Sex*. Simone de Beauvoir, Kate Millett, Susan Brownmiller, Adrienne Rich, all introduce their texts with what seems to anthropologists a most old-fashioned evocation of the human record. On the assumption that preparing meals, making demands of sons, enjoying talks with women friends, or celebrating their fertility and sexual vitality will mean the same thing to women independent of their time and place, these writers catalog the customs of the past in order to decide if womankind can claim, through time, to have acquired or lost such rightful "goods" as power, self-esteem, autonomy, and status. Though these writers differ in conclusions, methods, and particulars of theoretical approach, all move from some version of Beauvoir's question, "What is woman?" to a diagnosis of contemporary subordination and from that on to the queries: "Were things always as they are today?" and then, "When did 'it' start?"

Much like the nineteenth-century writers who first argued whether mother-right preceded patriarchal social forms, or whether women's difficult primeval lot has been significantly improved in civilized society, feminists differ in their diagnoses of our prehistoric lives, their sense of suffering, of conflict, and of change. Some, like Rich, romanticize what they imagine was a better past, while others find in history an endless tale of female subjugation and male triumph. But most, I think, would find no cause to question a desire to ferret out our origins and roots. Nor would they challenge Shulamith Firestone, who, in her important book, *The Dialectic of Sex*, cites Engels to assert our need first to "examine the historic succession of events from which the antagonism has sprung in order to discover in the conditions thus created the means of ending the conflict."[4] Firestone suggests, in fact, that we seek out the roots of present suffering in a past which moves from history back to "primitive man" and thence to animal biology. And most recently, Linda Gordon, in her splendid account of birth control as it has related to developments in American political life,[5] attempted in less than thirty pages to summarize the history of birth control throughout the premodern world, providing her readers with a catalog of premodern practices and beliefs that is disappointing both as history and as anthropology. In a book concerned to show how birth control agitation has fit into a history of leftist politics in the modern United States (its meaning bound to changes in the nature and organization of our families and our economy), I was surprised to find that anthropology was used to universalize contemporary political demands and undermine our present sense of singularity. There is something wrong—indeed, morally disturbing—in an argument which claims that the practitioners of infanticide in the past are ultimately our predecessors in an endless and essentially unchanging fight to keep men from making claims to female bodies.

By using anthropology as precedent for modern arguments and claims, the "primitive" emerges in accounts like these as the bearer of primordial human need. Women elsewhere are, it seems, the image of ourselves undressed, and the historical specificity of their lives and of our own becomes obscured. Their strengths prove that we can be strong. But ironically, and at the same time that we fight to see ourselves as cultural beings who lead socially determined lives, the movement back in evolutionary time brings in inevitable appeal to biological givens and the determining impact of such "crude" facts as demography and technology. One gets the feeling that birth control today is available to human *choice*, while in the past women's abilities to shape their reproductive fates were either nonexistent or constrained by such mechanical facts as a nomadic need to move, the need for helpers on the farm, or an imbalance between food supply and demography. We want to claim our sisters' triumphs as a proof of our worth, but at the same time their oppression can be artfully dissociated from our own, because we live with choice, while they are victims of biology.

My point here is not to criticize these texts. Feminists (and I include myself) have with good reason probed the anthropological record for evidence which appears to tell us whether "human nature" is the sexist and constraining thing that many of us were taught. Anthropology is, for most of us, a monument to human possibilities and constraints, a hall of mirrors wherein what Anthony Wallace called the "anecdotal exception" seems to challenge every would-be law; while at the same time, lurking in the oddest shapes and forms, we find a still familiar picture of ourselves, a promise that, by meditating on New Guinea menstrual huts, West African female traders, ritualists, or queens, we can begin to grasp just what—in universal terms—we "really" are.

But I would like to think that anthropology is more than that. Or, rather, I would claim that anthropology asked to answer ideologies and give voice to universal human truth is ultimately an anthropology limited by the assumptions with which it first began and so unable to transcend the biases its questions presuppose. To look for origins is, in the end, to think that what we are today is something other than the product of our history and our present social world, and, more particularly, that our gender systems are primordial, transhistorical, and essentially unchanging in their roots. Quests for origins sustain (since they are predicated upon) a discourse cast in universal terms; and universalism permits us all too quickly to assume—for everyone but ourselves perhaps—the *sociological* significance of what individual people *do* or, even worse, of what, in biological terms, they are.[6]

Stated otherwise, our search for origins reveals a faith in ultimate and essential truths, a faith sustained in part by cross-cultural evidence of widespread sexual inequality. But an analysis which assumes that sexual asymmetry is the first subject we should attempt to question or explain tends almost inevitably to reproduce the biases of the male social science to which it is, quite reasonably, opposed. These biases have their bases in a pervasive, individualistic school of thought that holds that social forms proceed from what particular persons need or do, activities which—where gender is concerned—are seen to follow from the "givens" of our reproductive physiology. And so, for feminists and traditionalists alike, there is a tendency to think of gender as, above all else, the creation of biologically based differences which oppose women and men, instead of as the product of social relationships in concrete (and changeable) societies.

The Problem of Universals

It would be nice to overthrow convention at this point and find myself entitled to proclaim that anthropological fact definitively belies sexist assumptions. Were anthropological evidence available that denied the universal place of gender in the organization of human social life, the association of women with reproduction and care for infant young, or the relevance of women's reproductive role to the construction of women's public status, much of the difficulty in what I have to say could be avoided. More narrowly, could I cite a single instance of a truly matriarchal—or, for that matter, sexually egalitarian—social form, I could go on to claim that all appeals to universal "nature" in explaining women's place are, simply, wrong. But instead, I must begin by making clear that, unlike many anthropologists who argue for the privileged place of women here or there, my reading of the anthropological record leads me to conclude that human cultural and social forms have always been male dominated. By this, I mean not that men rule by right or even that men rule at all and certainly not that women everywhere are passive victims of a world that men define. Rather, I would point to a collection of related facts which seem to argue that in all known human groups— and no matter the prerogatives that women may in fact enjoy—the vast majority of opportunities for public influence and prestige, the ability to forge relationships, determine enmities, speak up in public, use or forswear the use of force are all recognized as men's privilege and right.[7]

But I have moved, intentionally, too fast. In order to evaluate the conclusion just put forth, it seems important first to pause and ask what, substantively, has been claimed. Male dominance, though apparently universal, does not in actual behavioral terms assume a universal content or a universal shape. On the contrary, women typically have power and influence in political and economic life, display autonomy from men in their pursuits, and rarely find themselves confronted or constrained by what might seem the brute fact of male strength. For every case in which we see women confined, by powerful men or by the responsibilities of child care and the home, one can cite others which display female capacities to fight back, speak out in public, perform physically demanding tasks, and even to subordinate the needs of infant children (in their homes or on their backs) to their desires for travel, labor, politics, love, or trade. For every cultural belief in female weakness, irrationality, or polluting menstrual blood, one can discover others which suggest the tenuousness of male claims and celebrate women for their productive roles, their sexuality or purity, their fertility or perhaps maternal strength. Male dominance, in short, does not inhere in any isolated and measurable set of omnipresent facts. Rather, it seems to be an aspect of the organization of collective life, a patterning of expectations and beliefs which gives rise to imbalance in the ways people interpret, evaluate, and respond to particular forms of male and female action. We see it not in physical constraints on things that men or women can or cannot do but, rather, in the ways they think about their lives, the kinds of opportunities they enjoy, and in their ways of making claims.

Male dominance is evidenced, I believe, when we observe that women almost everywhere have daily responsibilities to feed and care for children, spouse, and kin, while men's economic obligations tend to be less regular and more bound up with extrafamilial sorts of ties; certainly, men's work within the home is not likely to be sanctioned by a spouse's use of force. Even in those groups in which the use of physical violence is avoided, a man can say, "She is a good wife, I don't have to beat her," whereas no woman evokes violent threats when speaking of her husband's work. Women will, in many societies, discover lovers and enforce their will to marry as they choose, but, again, we find in almost every case that the formal initiation and arrangement of permanent heterosexual bonds is something organized by men. Women may have ritual powers of considerable significance to themselves as well as men, but women never dominate in rites requiring the participation of the community as a whole. And even though men everywhere are apt to listen to and be influenced by their wives, I know of no case where men are required to serve as an obligatory audience to female ritual or political performance. Finally, women often form organizations of real and recognized political and economic strength; at times they rule as queens, acquire followings of men, beat husbands who prefer strange women to their wives, or perhaps enjoy a sacred status in their role as mothers. But, again, I know of no political system in which women individually or as a group are expected to hold more offices or have more political clout than their male counterparts.

Thus, while women in every human group will have forms of influence and ways of pursuing culturally acknowledged goals, it seems beside the point to argue—as many anthropologists in fact have—that observations such as mine are relatively trivial from the woman's point of view or that male claims are often balanced by some equally important set of female strengths.[8] Some women, certainly, are strong. But at the same time that women often happily and successfully pursue their ends, and manage quite significantly to constrain men in the process, it seems to me quite clear that women's goals themselves are shaped by social systems which deny them ready access to the social privilege, authority, and esteem enjoyed by a majority of men.

Admittedly, we are dealing with a very problematic sort of universal fact. Every social system uses facts of biological sex to organize and explain the roles and opportunities men and women may enjoy, just as all known human social groups appeal to biologically based ties in the construction of "familial" groups and kinship bonds. And much as "marriage," "family," and "kinship" have, for anthropologists, been troubling but, it seems, quite unavoidable universal terms, so I would claim the same thing holds for something like "male dominance." Sexual asymmetry, much like kinship, seems to exist everywhere, yet not without perpetual challenge or almost infinite variation in its contents and its forms. In short, if the universalizing questions are the ones with which we start, the anthropological record seems to feed our fear that sexual asymmetry is (again, like kinship, and the two, of course, are linked) a deep, primordial sort of truth, in some way bound to functional requirements associated with our sexual physiology. Though various, our gender systems *do* appear more basic than our ways of organizing our economies, religious faiths, or courts of law. And so, at much the same time that the evidence of behavioral variation suggests that gender is less a product of our bodies than of social forms and modes of thought, it seems quite difficult to believe that sexual inequalities are not rooted in the dictates of a natural order. Minimally, it would appear that certain biological facts—women's role in reproduction and, perhaps, male strength—have operated in a nonnecessary but universal way to shape and reproduce male dominance.

Domestic/Public as Explanation

A common feminist response to the facts that I have outlined here has been, essentially, to deny their weight and argue that the evidence we have itself reflects male bias. By focusing on women's lives, researchers have begun to reinterpret more conventional accounts and school us to be sensitive to female values, goals, and strengths. If formal authority is not something women enjoy, so, this research claims, we ought to learn to understand informal female powers; if women operate in "domestic" or "familial" spheres, then we must focus our attention on arenas like these, wherein women can make claims.[9] The value of scholarship of this sort is that it shows that when we measure women against men we fail to grasp important structural facts which may, in fact, give rise to female power. But while this point is an important one—to which I will return—the tendency to ignore imbalances in order to permit a grasp of women's lives has led too many scholars to forget that men and women ultimately live together in the world and, so, that we will never understand the lives that women lead without relating them to men. Ignoring sexual asymmetry strikes me as an essentially romantic move, which only blinds us to the sorts of facts we must attempt to understand and change.

An alternative approach,[10] elaborated in a set of essays by Chodorow, Ortner, and myself,[11] has been to argue that even universal facts are not reducible to biology. Our essays tried to show how what appears a "natural" fact must yet be understood in social terms—a by-product, as it were, of nonnecessary institutional arrangements that could be addressed through political struggle and, with effort, undermined. Our argument was, in essence, that in all human societies sexual asymmetry might be seen to correspond to a rough institutional division between domestic and public spheres of activity, the one built around reproduction, affective, and familial bonds, and particularly constraining to women; the other, providing for collectivity, jural order, and social cooperation, organized primarily by men. The domestic/public division as it appeared in any given society was not a necessary, but an "intelligible," product of the mutual accommodation of human history and human biology; although human societies have differed, all reflected in their organization a characteristic accommodation to the fact that women bear children and lactate and, because of this, find themselves readily designated as "mothers," who nurture and care for the young.

From these observations, we argued, one could then trace the roots of a pervasive gender inequality: Given an empirical division between domestic and public spheres of activity, a number of factors would interact to enhance both the cultural evaluations and social power and authority available to men. First, it appeared that the psychological effects of being raised by a woman would produce very different emotional dispositions in adults of both sexes; because of the diverging nature of preoedipal ties with *their* mothers, young girls would grow up to be nurturant "mothers" and boys would achieve an identity that denigrates and rejects women's roles.[12] In cultural terms, a domestic/public division corresponded to Ortner's discussion of "natural" versus "cultural" valuations,[13] wherein such factors as a woman's involvement with young and disorderly children would tend to give her the appearance of less composure, and, therefore, of less "culture" than men. Finally, sociologically, the views prevalent in our analytical tradition (and at least as old as Plato) that public activities are valued, that authority involves group recognition, and that consciousness and personality are apt to develop most fully through a stance of civic responsibility and an orientation to the collective whole—all argued that men's ability to engage in public activities would give them privileged access to such resources, persons, and symbols as would sustain their claims to precedence, grant them power and disproportionate rewards.

Whatever its difficulties, the account, as it stands, seems suggestive. Certainly, one can find in all human societies some sort of hierarchy of mutually embedded units. Although varying in structure, function, and societal significance, "domestic groups" which incorporate women and infant children, aspects of child care, commensality, and the preparation of food can always be identified as segments of a larger, overarching social whole. While we know that men are often centrally involved in domestic life and women will, at times, range far beyond it, one can, I think, assert that women, unlike men, lead lives that they themselves construe with reference to responsibilities of a recognizably domestic kind.

Thus, even such apparently "egalitarian" and communally oriented peoples as the Mbuti Pygmy gatherer-hunters of southern Africa require that women sleep in individual huts with infant children.[14] And women hide with children in these huts while men collectively enjoin the blessings and support of their forest god. Mbuti women do have a role in men's religious rites, but only to observe and then disrupt them. As if defined by their domestic and individual concerns, these women are entitled only to break up the sacred fire which joins all Pygmies to men's god; their power does not permit them to light the fires that soothe the forest and give collective shape to social bonds.

Examples like this are not hard to find, nor would they seem to pose real difficulties of interpretation. The evidence of peasant societies abounds with celebrated public men who are constrained by "honor" to defend their families' claims to "face," while the women seem to lack authority beyond the households where they live. But although denigrated in public "myth," these women "in reality" may use the powers of their "sphere" in order to attain considerable influence and control.[15] Domestic women in such peasant groups have powers which the analyst can hardly minimize or dismiss, and yet they are constrained in spatial range and lack the cultural recognition associated with male activities in the public realm.

In short, domestic/public as a general account seems to fit well with some of what we know of sex-linked action systems and of cultural rationales for male prestige, suggesting how "brute" biological facts have everywhere been shaped by social logics. Reproduction and lactation have provided a functional basis for the definition of a domestic sphere, and sexual asymmetry appears as its intelligible, though nonnecessary, consequence. Much as, in very simple human groups, the constraints of pregnancy and child care seem easily related to women's exclusion from big-game hunting—and thus from the prestige which comes of bringing in a product requiring extrahousehold distribution[16]—so, in more general terms, domestic obligations and demands appear to help us understand why women everywhere are limited in their access to prestigious male pursuits. Finally, our sense of sexual hierarchy as a deep and primary sort of truth appears compatible with a theory that asserts that mother-child bonds have lasting social and psychological ramifications; sociological constraints appear consistent with psychological orientations that arise through female-dominated patterns of child care.[17]

As should be clear by now, I find much that is compelling in this universalist account; but at the same time I am troubled by some of what appear to be its analytical consequences. In probing universal questions, domestic/public is as telling as any explanation yet put forth. Certainly, it seems more than reasonable to assume that marriage and reproduction shape the organization of domestic spheres and link them to more public institutional forms in ways that are particularly consequential for the shape of women's lives. Specifically, if women care for children and child care takes place within the home, and, furthermore, if political life, by definition, extends beyond it, then domestic/public seems to capture in a rough, but telling, set of terms the determinants of women's secondary place in all human societies.

But if this account "makes sense" in universal terms, I would go on to claim that when we turn to concrete cases, a model based upon the opposition of two spheres assumes—where it should rather help illuminate and explain—too much about how gender really works. Just as "kinship systems" vary far too widely to be viewed as mere reflections of established biological constraints (and anthropologists have argued endlessly as to whether kinship should be understood as something built upon the biologically "given" facts of human genealogy), so the alignments of the sexes seem at once too similar to deny a universal common base and yet too various to be understood adequately in terms of any universal cause. Pygmy women do not hide in huts because of the requirements of domestic life; rather, their assignment to small huts appears a consequence of their lack of power. American women may experience child care as something that confines them to the home, but I am quite sure that child care is *not* what many American households are about.[18] By linking gender, and in particular female lives, to the existence of domestic spheres, we have inclined, I fear, to think we know the "core" of what quite different gender systems share, to think of sexual hierarchies primarily in functional and psychological terms, and, thus, to minimize such sociological considerations as inequality and power. We think too readily of sexual identities as primordial acquisitions, bound up with the dynamics of the home, forgetting that the "selves" children become include a sense, not just of gender, but of cultural identity and social class.

What this means ultimately is that we fail to school ourselves in all the different ways that gender figures in the organization of social groups, to learn from the concrete things that men and women do and think and from their socially determined variations. It now appears to me that woman's place in human social life is not in any direct sense a product of the things she does (or even less a function of what, biologically, she is) but of the meaning her activities acquire through concrete social interactions. And the significances women assign to the activities of their lives are things that we can only grasp through an analysis of the relationships that women forge, the social contexts they (along with men) create—and within which they are defined. Gender in all human groups must, then, be understood in political and social terms, with reference not to biological constraints but instead to local and specific forms of social relationship and, in particular, of social inequality. Just as we have no apparent cause to look for physiological facts when we attempt to understand the more familiar inequalities in human social life—such things as leadership, racial prejudice, prestige, or social class—so it seems that we would do well to think of biological sex, like biological race, as an excuse rather than a cause for any sexism we observe.

Stated otherwise, I now believe that gender is not a unitary fact determined everywhere by the same sorts of concerns but, instead, the complex product of a variety of social forces. The most serious objections to my 1974 account have demonstrated—with good cause, I think—that "women's status" is itself not one but many things, that various measures of women's place do not appear to correlate among themselves, and, furthermore, that few of them appear to be consistently related to an isolable "cause."[19] The failure of attempts to rank societies in terms of "women's place" or to explain apparent variations in the amounts of privilege women elsewhere may enjoy (in terms consistent with cross-cultural data) suggests that we have been pursuing something of a ghost—or, rather, that an investigator who asks if women's status here or there ought to be reckoned high or low is probably conceptually misguided.

To talk of women's status is to think about a social world in ultimately dichotomous terms, wherein "woman" is universally opposed to "man" in the same ways in all contexts. Thus, we tend repeatedly to contrast and stress presumably given differences between women and men, instead of asking how such differences are themselves created by gender relations. In so doing, we find ourselves the victims of a conceptual tradition that discovers "essence" in the natural characteristics which distinguish us from men and then declares that women's present lot derives from what, "in essence," women are, portraying social roles and rules as products not of action and relation in a truly human world, but of self-serving individuals who perform by rote.

Notes

This paper, previously known as "Thoughts on Domestic/Public," was first presented to a Rockefeller Conference on Women, Work and Family in September 1977. I am grateful to participants in that conference and, in particular, to Heidi Hartmann and Catharine Stimpson for their insightful comments. Jane Atkinson, Jane Collier, Rose Coser, Karen Mason, Judith Modell, Fred Myers, Bridget O'Laughlin, Leslie Nadelson, Sherry Ortner, Renato Rosaldo, and Sylvia Yanagisako are all thanked for their critical readings of that and later drafts.

1. Naomi Quinn, "Anthropological Studies on Women's Status," *Annual Review of Anthropology* 6 (1977): 181–222, esp. p. 222.
2. Edwin Ardener, "Belief and the Problem of Women," in *The Interpretation of Ritual,* ed. J. LaFontaine (London: Tavistock Publications, 1972); Shirley Ardener, *Perceiving Women* (New York: John Wiley & Sons, 1975).
3. See Annette G. Weiner, "Sexuality among the Anthropologists and Reproduction among the Natives," unpublished manuscript (Austin: University of Texas at Austin, Department of Anthropology, 1978), and "Trobriand Kinship from Another View: The Reproductive Power of Women and Men," *Man* 14, no. 2 (1979): 328–48, for probably the most articulate of anthropologists writing about the need for us to radically reconceptualize traditional perspectives on society and social structure if we are to do more than "add" data on women to what remain, in structural terms, essentially male-biased accounts. At the same time, however, her "reproductive model" strikes me as dangerously close to much of the nonrelational thinking criticized below.
4. Shulamith Firestone, *The Dialectic of Sex: The Case for Feminist Revolution* (New York: Bantam Books, 1975), p. 2.
5. Linda Gordon, *Woman's Body, Woman's Right* (New York: Penguin Books, 1975).
6. N. C. Mathieu, "Homme—Culture, Femme—Nature?" *L'Homme* 13, no. 3 (1973): 101–13.
7. See Louise Lamphere, "Review Essay: Anthropology," *Signs: Journal of Women in Culture and Society* 2, no. 3 (1977): 612–27.
8. See Elsie B. Begler, "Sex, Status and Authority in Egalitarian Society," *American Anthropologist* 80, no. 3 (1978): 571–88; or Ruby Rohrlich-Leavitt, Barbara Sykes, and Elizabeth Weatherford, "Aboriginal Women: Male and Female Anthropological Perspectives," in *Towards an Anthropology of Women,* ed. R. Reiter (New York: Monthly Review Press, 1975), for reasonable attempts to tilt the balance. A juxtaposition of these two articles—which come to radically opposed characterizations of women's lot in Australian aboriginal societies—is informative for what it says about the difficulty of deciding what is, ultimately, an evaluative argument in empirical terms.

9. See, e.g., Susan Carol Rogers, "Female Forms of Power and the Myth of Male Dominance: A Model of Female/Male Interaction in Peasant Society," *American Ethnologist* 2 (1975): 727–56; Yolanda Murphy and Robert Murphy, *Women of the Forest* (New York: Columbia University Press, 1974); and Margery Wolf, *Women and the Family in Rural Taiwan* (Stanford, Calif.: Stanford University Press, 1972).
10. There is a third alternative, which situates itself somewhere between the two extremes cited here, namely, that of stressing variation and trying to characterize the factors that make for more or less "male dominance" or "female status." Karen Sacks ("Engels Revisited," in *Woman, Culture and Society,* ed. M. Rosaldo and L. Lamphere [Stanford, Calif.: Stanford University Press, 1974]) and Peggy Sanday ("Women's Status in the Public Domain," in ibid.) provide examples, though it is interesting to note that while forswearing universalism both in fact make use of an analytical separation between domestic and public in organizing their variables. Martin King Whyte, in *The Status of Women in Preindustrial Societies* (Princeton, N.J.: Princeton University Press, 1978), argues (most cogently, I think) that only by studying variation will we begin to understand any of the processes relevant to the formation or reproduction of sexual inequalities, and therefore that methodological and political wisdom both require us to disaggregate summary characterizations concerning sexual status into their component parts. I agree with him and, further, was pleased to see that his empirical study led toward the recognition that it is virtually impossible to "rank" societies in terms of women's place. His conclusions agree with mine in that he comes to see more promise in a comparative approach that looks for social structural *configurations* than one concerned with summary evaluations. Because he is able to show that particular variables mean different things in different social contexts, his results call into question all attempts to talk, cross culturally, about the components of women's status or their ever-present causes.
11. Nancy Chodorow, "Family Structure and Feminine Personality"; Sherry Ortner, "Is Female to Male as Nature Is to Culture?"; and Michelle Rosaldo, "Woman, Culture and Society: A Theoretical Overview," in Rosaldo and Lamphere.
12. Nancy Chodorow, "Being and Doing," in *Woman in Sexist Society: Studies in Power and Powerlessness,* ed. V. Gornick and B. K. Moran (New York: Basic Books, 1971); and Chodorow, "Family Structure and Feminine Personality."
13. Ortner, "Is Female to Male as Nature Is to Culture?"
14. Colin M. Turnbull, *The Forest People* (New York: Simon & Schuster, 1961).
15. Louise Sweet, ed., "Appearance and Reality: Status and Roles of Women in Mediterranean Societies," *Anthropological Quarterly,* vol. 40 (1967); and Rogers (n. 9).
16. Ernestine Friedl, *Women and Men: An Anthropologist's View* (New York: Holt, Rinehart & Winston, 1975), p. 21.

17. Nancy Chodorow, *The Reproduction of Mothering* (Berkeley: University of California Press, 1978); and Juliet Mitchell, *Psychoanalysis and Feminism* (New York: Random House, 1974).
18. The issue is complex. A number of recent analysts have pointed to the way in which modern American family ideology leads us to think about the roles of women as defined by a necessary association of certain functions (e.g., nurturance, altruism, "diffuse enduring solidarity"; see David M. Schneider, *American Kinship: A Cultural Account* [Englewood Cliffs, N.J.: Prentice-Halt Inc., 1968]) with certain persons (close kin) and in particular with mothers (Sylvia Junko Yanagisako, "Women-centered Kin Networks in Urban Bilateral Kinship," *American Ethnologist* 4, no. 2 [1977]: 207–26). R. Rapp ("Family and Class in Contemporary America: Notes Towards an Understanding of Ideology," *Science and Society* 42, no. 3 [1978]: 278–300) makes it particularly clear, however, that the ways in which this ideology of "familial bonding" maps onto groups of coresidents is problematic and varies with social class. Furthermore, Diane K. Lewis ("A Response to Inequality: Black Women, Racism, and Sexism," *Signs: Journal of Women in Culture and Society* 3, no. 2 [1977]: 339–61) makes the cogent point that our belief in the necessary association of women and domestic functions often blinds us to the fact that, in our society, marginalization ("domestication") is more a consequence than a cause for lack of power.
19. These points are developed with reference to empirical data most fully in recent writings by Quinn (n. 1) and Whyte (n. 10). Whyte's findings make it clear, in particular, that male dominance is not something that lends itself to ranking in cross-culturally significant terms (see n. 10). That this conclusion undermines *all* arguments concerning women's status as analytically problematic—and requires that we look instead for pattern in the social structuring of gender (a conclusion very close to that of this paper)—is, however, something even Whyte has barely realized.

Tcherkézoff, Serge. 2014. "Transgender in Samoa: The Cultural Production of Gender Inequality." In *Gender on the Edge: Transgender, Gay, and Other Pacific Islanders.* University of Hawaii Press.

THIS CHAPTER DEALS WITH THE DIFFICULTIES involved in describing or even evoking the sociocultural paths followed by Samoan *fa'afāfine* and *tomboy*s. Both labels were invented and both social categories are constructed from a heteronormative discourse—mainstream Samoan discourse and some academic literature. From these perspectives, *fa'afāfine* are persons whose families and neighbors characterize them as boys at birth but who, later in life (usually in late childhood or early adolescence), are said to act "in the way of women" (*fa'a-fafine,* the plural of the term being *fa'afāfine*). However, they never introduce themselves as "*fa'afāfine*," but by their own given names. If queried about their gender, they reply that they are "girls."[1]

The chapter broaches another gendered category, which few in main-stream Samoan society are willing to talk about openly—that is, girls or women who are said to be born as girls but who come to be viewed as acting in the way of men at roughly the same stage in life as when boys become *fa'af*āfine. There are two differences between them and *fa'afāfine.* First, they don't claim to be of the other gender: they assert that they are girls, not boys. Second, there is no straightforward Samoan term that designates them as being "in the way of boys or men." When Samoans refer to them, they use various circumlocutions (e.g., "exhibiting the behavior of boys or men") or, more pithily, the English borrowing "*tomboy.*" I italicize this word to indicate the particular meaning it has in Samoa.

This contrast between *fa'afafine* and *tomboy* is not just a matter of terminology but runs deeper, in that Samoans born as boys who act like girls have at their disposal a much broader range of identificational practices than Samoans born as girls who act like boys. The contrast is obvious in everyday public behavior, but it is sharpest in the context of the pursuit of fulfillment of sexual desire. The contrast also colors affective relations between non-heteronormative individuals and their families. Under the superficial symmetry between boys who act like girls and girls who act like boys (or the adult equivalents) lies a profound asymmetry—indeed a sharp social inequality—which has yet to receive any analytic attention in writings about gender and sexuality in Samoa or elsewhere in the Pacific Islands. And this asymmetry works directly to the detriment of *tomboy*s.

Instead of attempting to "define" *fa'afafine* and *tomboy* in the context of Samoan gender configurations, I investigate the claims that *fa'afāfine* and *tomboy*s make about their own identity and how others talk about them and engage with them. Thus I place the term "transgender" in quotation marks, as it is not a self-characterization but a term that only emerges in discourse *about* them, usually of an academic nature. When used in the heteronormative discourse, it runs the risk of focusing attention on how mainstream Samoan and outside observers view the *trans*-formation of *fa'afāfine*'s and *tomboys*' identity at birth and later in life. Such a discourse about transformation in gender is part of the wider difficulty inherent in gender studies, which constantly must guard against presupposing a universal sex-gender binary opposing male to female and men to women, and then evaluating the extent to which gender and sexual manifestations in each specific society "fit" this binary model or, on the contrary, are "trans-," "liminal," and so on.[2]

Talking about *Fa'afāfine* and *Tomboys*

As many other authors have explained, the word *"fa'afafine"* is made up of a very common and polysemic prefix, *fa'a-*, which in this case can be translated as "in the way of," and the noun *fafine* "woman." The latter is to be understood in the restricted sense that it has come to take on in Samoa (at a time that I am unable to identify), namely to refer to a potential or actual female sexual partner. When speaking Samoan, however, *fa'afāfine* assert that they are *teine*, "girls," or *tama'ita'i*, "ladies." In thirty years' worth of fieldwork in Samoa, I have never heard anyone say about her– or himself, "I am a *fa'afafine*" (although the situation may be different for Samoans in the diaspora).[3]

For these reasons, instead of *"fa'afafine,"* I use the term *"fa'ateine"* and the feminine pronoun to refer to them, although this choice is a prescriptive rather than a descriptive one. Ideally, one would also forego the prefix *fa'a-*, because they say that they *are* girls (or ladies) and not just *like* girls. For sake of distinguishing non-heteronormative persons from normative females (*teine*), however, I will stick to the prefixed version of the term.

In the early 1980s, Aiono Dr. Fanaafi Le Tagaloa, a highly respected Samoan scholar and founder of Samoan studies at the University of Samoa, whom I am proud to consider as a mentor throughout the 1980s, told me, "You should not use the word *'fa'afafine,'* it is not really Samoan, it post-dates contact with Europeans; the old Samoan word was *'fa'ateine.'* " There is no evidence of this term in early European narratives, but then there is no evidence either of a word *"fa'afafine,"* and thus this linguistic chronology remains open to discussion. But her remark does suggest the fact that, for a number of *fa'ateine*, the term *"fa'afafine"* carries connotations that they strongly reject. Because of the narrow meaning of the Samoan word *"fafine,"* namely a female person within a potential or actual sexual relationship, *"fa'afafine"* gives the misguided impression that the *fa'ateine*'s life is entirely centered on matters of sex. The fact that some Samoan scholars think that the word *"fa'afafine"* is a neologism is also symptomatic of the feeling that the category is a product of modernity, particularly as it now manifests itself to mainstream society (e.g., through the display of fashion and in dance shows). These feelings are echoed elsewhere in the Pacific (Alexeyeff 2008, 2009; Besnier 2002, 2004, 2011; Grépin 1995, 2001; Good, this volume; Elliston, this volume).

The term *"tomboy,"* in contrast, has a rather different configuration. It is obviously a borrowing from the slightly old-fashioned English word, which itself has a complex linguistic history, and which has come to refer to a girl who behaves in a manner that observers consider "boy-like." Although it is unclear when it entered the Samoan vocabulary, today the term has a precise meaning: a girl or woman who acts like a man in contexts where "strength" (*mālosi*) is particularly central to the definition of manhood. This concept encompasses a wide range of connotations, such as the capacity for hard physical work, in olden days the ability to win wars, to be good at competitive sports, and to be sexually successful. During my fieldwork in the 1980s, the term *"tomboy"* did not necessarily imply sexual attraction to girls, whether "straight" girls or other *tomboys*.[4] Today, however, it does have this connotation. Contemporary mainstream Samoan interlocutors sometime use the borrowed term *"lisipia,"* "lesbian," as their world is increasingly penetrated by global discourses that identify people in terms of the object of their sexual desire.

When I attempted to avoid the borrowed term *"tomboy"* in my conversations with Samoans, I ran into problems: any attempt I made to attach the prefix *fa'a-* ("in the way of") to a variety of words denoting male humans (e.g., *tamaloa,* "adult man," *tama,* "boy, young man," or *tane,* "man as husband, male") either remained unintelligible to Samoan interlocutors or were interpreted literally to refer to someone or something that was somehow "man-like" in a temporally and contextually bounded way. Evidently the word *"fa'afafine"* has no straightforward antonym.

This asymmetry is significant beyond lexical concerns. The fact that *"fafine"* has sexual connotations gives the word *"fa'afafine"* unequivocally sexual connotations. Who can be sexually "like a woman" other than women? Only those born as boys and who later behave "like women" in that they are available for sexual relations with men where they take the insertee role. Theoretically possible terms like *"fa'atamaloa"* to refer to the opposite category do not have any sexual connotations, because the term *"tamaloa"* (and others like it) has no such connotations. This asymmetry touches upon a much wider asymmetry—the fact that in Samoa men can be "men" without being sexual beings, whereas that possibility is far less readily available to women.

The absence of non-borrowed terms for *tomboys* may also be related to their lack of ideological and practical visibility. Some heteronormative Samoans, for example, maintain that *tomboys* "are not part of our custom" (*aganu'u*). Similarly, visitors to Samoa may never see or hear about *tomboys* (there are no shows organized by *tomboys*, for instance), while they will immediately notice the presence of *fa'ateine* in such highly visible contexts as families, shows, and sports.[5]

Western Discourses about *Fa'afāfine*

Since Western or other discourses are silent about Samoan *tomboys*, my discussion of Western representations of non-heteronormative Samoans focuses exclusively on *fa'ateine*. Despite sustained criticism, Western media continue to represent Samoan *fa'ateine* and equivalent categories elsewhere in the Pacific Islands as "homosexuals." If we assume that homosexuals are people who are erotically attracted to one another, then *fa'ateine* cannot be thus characterized because they never express an erotic desire for one another, and in fact are emphatically adverse to it (cf. Schmidt 2001), and this erotic aversion appears to be sustained even in more cosmopolitan regions of the Pacific Islands, such as the Cook Islands (Alexeyeff 2008, 2009). *Fa'ateine* are only sexually interested in those they called, in the 1980s, a *"mata,"* a Pig Latin inversion of the word *"tama"* (boy, young man), which refers to a "straight" man but implies that he could have sexual relations with a *fa'ateine*.

Another very common idea in the Western imagination is that Samoan families that do not have enough girls forcibly bring up one of their boys as a girl. This particular mythology has widespread currency and has been repeated over and over again across media, countries, authors, and times. "*Fa'afafine* play a useful role in the family," asserts a documentary made for television, "their muscular body provides help. ... In the past, when there were not enough girls in the house, parents would raise one boy as a girl" (*National Geographic* 2007). Yet, over decades of fieldwork, I have never seen a case of such a practice, nor have I heard of one, even when I queried people with whom I was very close. In fact, no family in Samoa would impose on a child the enormous difficulties associated with life as a *fa'ateine*, which vastly outweigh whatever any advantage a family would derive from a *fa'ateine*'s labor contribution (cf. Schoeffel, this volume).

In their eagerness to "explain" the presence of *fa'ateine* in Samoan society, Western observers have provided a number of other functionalist accounts. One is based on the assumption that society must provide "counter-models" of normative behavior and selfhood. In a society in which the ideal type of boyhood and young manhood is so sharply defined by "strength," particularly as it is visually inscribed in the body's muscularity, this ideal type is difficult to achieve for most boys, and effeminate boys provide an ideal counter-model against which other boys can define themselves (Shore 1981, 209–210). It is true that Samoan society does set a high standard for the visuality of "strength" in young men's bodies, and that this "strength" *(mālosi)* is an overdetermined concept in Samoan culture. But the exact sociological and cultural operations of the "counter-modeling" that society so desperately would fabricate remain completely obscure, particularly in terms of the material and psychological "costs" to families and individuals.[6]

Another functionalist argument evokes the contradiction between two normative ideals concerning sexuality in traditional Samoa. One demands that girls remain virgins until marriage, while the other prescribes that young men be as sexually active as possible to demonstrate their masculine "strength." *Fa'ateine* would provide a solution to this normative contradiction by offering sexual services to young men "as if" they were girls. But here again, the logic falters. The fact is that *fa'ateine*'s relationships with "straight" men present a power imbalance, for as *fa'ateine* view these relationships as both sexual and affective, straight men approach them in much more utilitarian fashion, at least in their overt representation. Thus, in addition to providing sexual satisfaction, a *fa'ateine* provides material gifts to her straight lover, which inverts the normative representation of heterosexual courting, in which a boy offers gifts to the girl in the hope that in turn she will offer him the ultimate gift of her virginity (an imbalance that Besnier 1997 has documented in some detail for Tonga and that is echoed elsewhere in the world, e.g., Kulick 1998 on Brazil). Negative reciprocity suffuses the relationship between a *fa'ateine* and a straight man, and thus the specter of exploitation looms large in the life of *fa'ateine*. But to posit negative reciprocity as an explanation for the presence of *fa'ateine* in Samoan society is based on a highly uncritical understanding of the constitution of social relations.

The *Fa'ateine*'s Mother

When a young male child displays behaviors that appear to emulate his sisters', however briefly and sporadically, particularly a predilection for women's household work and dancing in the female style (*siva*), it does happen that his mother (or other elder female relatives) encourages these behaviors. This encouragement may be playful (particularly in the presence of others), but in other cases may be sustained. It is important to note that these dynamics do not constitute a matter of upbringing but rather a reaction to a child's actions, and they certainly do not support the tired old myth about parents "bringing up boys to be girls" in order to balance out a gendered division of labor (see Schoeffel, this volume).

What motivates a child to engage in such behavior is very difficult to assess, although it is suggestive to note that certain dynamics in Samoan society may encourage the perception that a boy is "like a girl" in the universal context of the unstable nature of gender assignation in adolescence. This perception may originate with a general discomfort with a male physique perceived as lacking the "strength" that is so central to Samoan male identity. Whether this deficiency is associated with a physical impairment or simply with a spindly physique, or anything in between, it quickly becomes the object of mockery. I have witnessed situations in which a skinny boy engaged in activities that elicited compliments rather than teasing, such as his performing the female solo part of a *siva* dance, whose graceful and delicate choreography showcases femininity, a performance that mother and sisters would applaud vigorously while also finding it humorous.

Such situations engender ambiguity. While the mother and her daughters greet such performances approvingly and may even encourage them, the father and his sons will at best consistently mock them or, at worst, will beat the child up in an effort to instill some sense of gender into him. In either case, the effect will be to encourage the child to seek the company and approval of his mother and sisters—the exact reverse of what male relatives intend. But the opposite scenario can occur with equal ease: the mother's spontaneous reaction of treating the child as a girl can lead the child to reject this gender assignation with increasing assertiveness when he is old enough to do so. Last, all intermediate possibilities are attested: the *"fa'afafine* assignation" may be to the boy's liking for a while or for certain purposes, but then he grows up following a normative path, getting married and having children, none of whom will become a *fa'ateine* if he can help it; or, even worse, in some cases he will join the ranks of fathers who have no interest in trying to understand what can take place in their sons' psychology during adolescence.

The sociological question that emerges from all this concerns the mother: What motivates a Samoan mother to find pleasure in witnessing her son taking on a non-normative gendering and even in some cases encouraging it? Samoan mothers often express regret that, once they reach adolescence, their sons begin to live beyond the realm of both their authority and their affection, and in this respect fathers and mothers have an asymmetrical relationship with their male children, as fathers do not see their relationship with their sons as following such a path. This regret suggests the possibility that some mothers may unconsciously seek to keep their sons close to them by treating them like a girl.

This hypothesis finds some support from an excursus into kinship terminology. Samoan fathers' children are termed *"atali'i"* if male and *"afafine"* if female, terms that remain constant from birth to adulthood. Gender is central to these kinship terms, which are unequivocally distinct, nonreciprocal, and absolute. In other words, they correspond precisely to "son" and "daughter" respectively in European languages. In contrast, a mother's children, called *tama,* are undifferentiated with reference to gender, although it is possible to add an adjective to the term *tama* to specify gender (*tama tama,* "son"; *tama teine,* "daughter"). This gender-neutral basic terminology applies to collateral descent: a man can refer to his sister's child as *"tama sā,"* literally "sacred child" (although this term is now outdated), but the term is gender–neutral. The basic term *"tama"* therefore always refers to a woman's child.

The gender-neutral terms that mothers use to refer to children thus contrast with the obligatorily gendered terms that fathers use, suggesting that children's gender is potentially interchangeable for mothers but not so for fathers. These observations resonate with the fact that mothers easily accept *fa'ateine* sons, while fathers do not accept any gender crossing.

The *Tomboy* Child's Family Relations

Although mothers may indulge their young sons to engage in *fa'ateine* practices while fathers never do, neither mothers nor fathers encourage *tomboy* tendencies in their daughters. Parents never provide any affective compensation for girls' *tomboy* behavior and on the contrary only deplore it. Yet one finds *tomboy* girls in a not unsubstantial number of Samoan families.

As in the case of *fa'ateine,* young girls who fail to live up to the standards against which they are measured, in their case that of the ideal young Samoan girl, may be drawn to self-identify and be identified as a *tomboy.* Parents and siblings encourage this identification, although in this case in negative fashion. These dynamics may be only obliquely related to gender. In one case that I witnessed in the course of my fieldwork, when a baby girl was born, everyone around her marveled at the fairness of her complexion, an iconic sign of beauty in Samoa, as in the rest of the Pacific.[7] As she grew up, however, she displayed a pre-*tomboy* comportment by spending a great deal of time outdoors, thus violating the expectation that girls stay indoors and take responsibility for household chores, which also ensures that their complexion is not affected by the sun. The child in question grew "black," said her relatives, and she became the butt of her parents' and siblings' ceaseless teasing: she was told she was an ugly duckling. Not surprisingly, the girl's behavior increasingly became that of a *tomboy,* behavior she seemed to cultivate, and later in life she became bisexual.

Another case concerns two sisters close in age. One had a light complexion and pleasant features, for which she was complimented from a young age; the other, with a dark complexion and a puffy-looking face, was mocked, and calling her names became a family habit. One became the object of boys' assiduous courting and engaged in exclusively heterosexual practices, while the other became a *tomboy,* with an aggressive demeanor, and eventually exclusively engaged in sexual relations with other women, surreptitiously while she remained in Samoa but more openly once she emigrated overseas.

There is thus a sharp contrast between the affective relationships that *fa'ateine* and *tomboy*s maintain with their families. While the rejection of the *fa'ateine* by her father and brothers certainly provides grounds for a multitude of psychological problems, she finds herself included by her mother and her sisters, sometimes even coddled, but at least never rejected. Nonetheless, this tension between rejection and approval never colors the *tomboy*'s relationships with her close kindred. I have seen a father good-naturedly teaching his daughter to throw a good punch, but these games are not sustained, and the father quickly changed from stating, "All my children, daughter included, must know how to defend themselves," to mocking and then becoming angry at the same daughter for being too openly *tomboy.*

The socialization of a *tomboy* is far from easy. She asserts herself as a girl and others consider her to be one. For her brothers, she remains a girl for the purpose of one of the most fundamental norms of Samoan (and other Western Polynesian) culture—brother–sister avoidance once they reach adolescence. But her relationship with her brothers is fraught: they brush her off and scold her if seniority entitles them do so. With her sisters, there is competition and jealousy, and she is put down by her sisters' ability to perform difficult feminine tasks, such as plaiting fine mats (even if she does it just as well as they do). She gains no prestige, only mockery, for her ability to perform heavy physical tasks. In contrast, the *fa'ateine* asserts that she is a "girl" and thus, exempted from abiding by brother–sister avoidance, is free to socialize with her sisters, who encourage her self-identification as a *fa'ateine* and provide her with a role model to emulate.

The *tomboy*'s inability to find a place and a role model in the family has serious consequences. In cases I have known, she exaggerates her *tomboy* identification and may become the school bully constantly punished for beating her classmates to a pulp. Even if she performs well academically, she remains unconvincing in the eyes of her close kindred, because for them the studious girl is by definition self-effacing, demure, bookish, and obedient. Boys are not expected to be diligent, but the *tomboy* is considered to be worse than the worst of boys. As a result, she receives little support in her studies, as neither her family nor her teachers have any faith in her academic abilities. This socialization to an aggressive, confrontational, and independent self is reminiscent of Nancy Chodorow's (1978) classic feminist psychoanalytic account of the oppositional socialization of boys in Western (middle-class) society, but it is all the more poignant in that it takes place in a society that places so much emphasis on sociality.

Coming of Age as a *Tomboy*

Things come to a head with the awakening of sexual desire. A *tomboy*'s sexuality is subject to less surveillance than those of her heteronormative sisters because her parents believe (erroneously) that she has no interest in boys. Paradoxically, it is the parents who consider her "transgender," failing to see her as a girl and to hear her assertions that she is a girl. As a result, she can find herself embroiled in sexual activity much more easily than her closely supervised and frequently admonished sisters, and may find herself pregnant at a young age.

The result is dramatic. Under normal circumstances, a daughter who becomes pregnant out of wedlock is a source of crushing shame for parents and brothers. This shame and the resulting anger it arouses are even greater in the case of *tomboy*s, as family members see the *tomboy* daughter as having doubly "deceived" them. While parents and brothers are expected to prevent all daughters and sisters from being interested in boys, in *tomboy*s this attraction is an abomination. Was she "feigning" *tomboy* behavior in order to mislead those responsible for her? Not only is her comportment "ugly" (*mātagā*) on a daily basis, but she also brings untold shame onto her close relatives by demonstrating to all and sundry that she has fooled them.

One case narrated to me in detail, while perhaps extreme, illustrates the general ideological landscape that surrounds such situations. When the *tomboy* gave birth to a girl, her mother took the baby away from her and banished her to live with cousins on another island of the Samoan archipelago—the culmination of a sense of rejection and abandonment in the tomboy daughter, who would later talk about her baby girl in tears. Sent overseas, she turned to the bottle and became a butch lesbian; but her violent behavior consistently put off potential lovers or made relationships short-lived.

Another asymmetry between *fa'ateine* and *tomboy*s is the fact that the former cultivate sociality with one another in such contexts as fashion shows and sports, while the latter do not. In fact, they are prevented from doing so because the sight of congregating *tomboy*s immediately evokes in the minds of others the suspicion that they are sexually involved, whereas *fa'ateine* seen together arouse no such suspicion, as sexual attraction between them is unthinkable. This contrast is indeed tragic: one category elaborates a sociality that others (particularly young women) not only approve of but even seek out; the other category is composed of despised individuals or couples—and this in a society in which the basic units of sociality are neither individuals nor couples, but families, age cohorts, clubs, and so on.

In the Samoan diaspora (primarily in New Zealand, Australia, Hawai'i, and the continental United States), when *tomboy* couples live together, their lives remain difficult. Parents and friends display little patience for them, refusing to visit or receive them. "What have I done to be thus punished by God?" asks a mother of her *tomboy* lesbian daughter. The *tomboy* may be blamed for her parents' illnesses, and decades into adulthood siblings continue to hate her for the shame that she has brought upon the family. Rarely do such strong feelings surround the presence of a *fa'ateine* in a family.

Fa'ateine who have migrated sometimes establish significant relationships with a partner—if the relationship is long-term, the partner is in all likelihood a Westerner. When the *fa'ateine* visits her family back in the islands or in other diasporic communities, she is unlikely to bring her partner along, choosing to travel alone or in the company of other *fa'ateine*. Her visit will be a delight to her mother, aunts, and sisters, who will have looked forward to spending lively and animated evenings gossiping and telling "women's stories" (often of a salacious nature). Most *fa'ateine* are consummate conversationalists, cultivating the art of being both brilliant and amusing, not unlike the specialists of the local traditional theatre or *fale aitu*, who in fact often appear on stage impersonating *fa'ateine* (Pearson, this volume).

But if a migrant lesbian *tomboy* visits her family with another woman, the situation is very different. Everyone immediately will assume that they are a couple, which is frequently the case, because lesbian *tomboy*s do not seek each other's company simply for the sake of sociability. In the situations that I have witnessed, everyone looks ill-at-ease. Such visits are brief and focus on sorting out family matters. They will not be punctuated by the animated conversations and gales of laughter throughout the evening that characterize the sociability of adults with *fa'ateine*.

Now to the issue of children. Few *fa'ateine* who remain so in adulthood have children in their charge. In contrast, few adult *tomboys* are without children (at least in the diaspora), but this fact is consistent with Samoan mainstream ideologies of gender: since *tomboys* remain women, a desire to have children is fundamental to their identity. How they acquire children varies: in one case, a *tomboy* was married heterosexually while she was still young and had children, whom she kept when she and her husband separated and she entered into a relationship with another woman; in another case, a *tomboy* had sex with a man with the explicit purpose of getting pregnant while she was between same-sex relationships. As she lives in the diaspora, the *tomboy* mother is considered to be a single mother with children (she does not officially declare her same-sex relationship) and thus qualifies for substantial government assistance. But problems emerge in the relationship between *tomboy* mothers or couples and their children, particularly boys, stemming from the attitude of the rest of the immediate and extended family—friends, fellow church members, and so on—who find every opportunity to express their pity for the children of a mother living in shame. As a result, it is not uncommon for young children of *tomboy* mothers to run away from home.

The title of this section of course evokes Margaret Mead's famous study of adolescence in Samoa (Mead 1928). Mead did not take into account transgender youth, but any discussion of Samoan past and present norms of sexuality must refer to her views of Samoan adolescent norms. Her understanding of Samoan sexuality was obviously shaped by stereotypes of Polynesian "free sexuality" that the Western world had nurtured since eighteenth-century contacts with Tahiti, which was not at all applicable to Samoa, whether in the 1920 or later. Though her published work presented a picture of "free love" during adolescence, her own field notes (partially published in Orans 1996) reveal that this was not the picture she actually witnessed. Ironically, these notes also reveal that, while claiming to present the perspective of adolescent girls, Mead was in fact strongly influenced by a Samoan male discourse that asserted, and continues to do so today, that boys have easy sexual access to girls (Tcherkézoff 2001). Indeed, Mead's notes bear witness to the depth of the contradiction between the norms imposed on female adolescents (preserving virginity until marriage) and those imposed on male adolescents (the ideal type of a strong "warrior" whose strength allows him to perform physically demanding work but also to "conquer" in sport and sex). This apparently was the normative context in the 1920s and certainly is the case today.

Normative Gender and Sexuality

But the contrast is not only between two gendered norms. Dynamics of gender in Samoan society are better understood in terms of a contrast between two systems of social relations than in terms of two genders (Tcherkézoff 1993, 2003). In one system, which I term the "realm of light" (in a cosmological, social, and everyday sense—i.e., the realm of the visible), the dominant social relation is the brother–sister relationship. In a traditional village, everyone is related to one another through this cross-sibling relationship, even though the village is made up of unrelated extended families or 'āiga, as the ceremonial groups of "sons" and "daughters of the village" are said to be in a brother–sister relationship. This is the world of the *aganu'u fa'a-Sāmoa* or "Samoan custom" (literally, the "essence of the community living in the Samoan way"). The other system of social relations that makes up gender is the realm where humans are just "living creatures" or *mea ola*. There, humans and animals are considered to be somewhat alike, particularly with respect to sexuality. This realm is situated outside of *aganu'u* and away from visible village life, and there one finds only "males" and "females" (as opposed to men and women). This is where the term "*fafine*" finds its meaning—that is, woman as defined in terms of the contrast between male and female, and thus in terms of potential or actual heterosexual union. Whatever form it takes, human sexuality is located in this realm of "living creatures," and thus outside of the family and village life in its visible form. A striking illustration is the fact that, according to Samoans of whatever age or gender, making love is something "that you do not do in the house, but outside"—the house, being a place where rank and genealogy are rooted, is not a "private" space but a "meeting" place, even if people sleep inside it at night.

In every situation in which men and women are defined as male and female, what emerges is *inequality* between a "stronger" and a "weaker" sex, categories that resemble those that operate in Western societies. Activities like flirting and premarital sex express male domination, and so do aspects of the wedding ceremony (Tcherkézoff 2003). The characteristics ascribed to either sex emerge from their respective essentialized "natures."

But in the realm of the socially visible, the "community" (*nu'u*) is peopled by three metaphorical categories of gendered humans: "chiefs," who can be men or women and are in a certain way outside of gender distinctions; their "daughters," that is, all girls and women belonging to the families of the village (excluding exogamous wives); and the latter's "brothers," that is, all untitled boys and men. Inequality also emerges here, but of an opposite kind: daughters, as "sacred sisters," embody the brother–sister relationship. Men are only defined as "brothers" in relation to women.

Practically speaking, this sharp distinction between sister–brother hierarchy and male–female inequality means that, in most matters relating to rank and titles, genealogy, and land, women as "sisters" have a very strong say and often can impose their views. They can do so because they are "sacred" (Schoeffel 1979; Tcherkézoff 2008b). Their superiority is based on "respect," or *fa'aaloalo,* ultimately backed by supernatural sanctions. But as soon as we revert to the realm of males and females, inequality is only backed by "strength"—that is, male strength.

This in turn informs the path of life-stages for boys and girls. These dynamics are encapsulated in a traditional song that accompanies men's ritual tattooing, which states that the destiny of males *(tane)* is to be tattooed, while the destiny of females *(fafine)* is to bear children (Tcherkézoff 2003: 408). Tattooing was the ritual transition to a life of strength: the boy became a member of the youth of the village, ceremonially called "the strength of the community," ready for hard work as well as courting girls—ideally with the end point of marriage, but also for the purpose of masculine competition over the number of conquests. The girls, of course, were expected to remain virgins until they were married.

Within this ideal binary world, there was and is no place for transgender. *Fa'ateine* can be "as if" sisters, but they will never marry. *Tomboys* do not follow boys' life path: they will never be tattooed with male designs and their physique and demeanor will never make them into any kind of "conquerors of virgin girls."

Fa'ateine, Tomboys, and Sexuality

This normative system has one major consequence for both *fa'ateine* and *tomboys*, at least as soon as they are viewed as potential or actual sexual partners. They are then both trapped within this realm, outside visible customary village life, locked into a world of sexuality under the sign of male domination. This ultimately explains many of the difficulties they encounter in their pursuit of sexual desires, as well as the asymmetry between them.

Heteronormative sisters and brothers know to leave sexuality outside the realm of visible village customary life, away from the household and the village, in order for it not to spoil the social categories "sister" and "brother." Thus, before marriage, sexual relations must remain hidden, and they continue to be so in certain ways even after marriage: in public, husband and wife comport themselves like brother and sister, avoiding physical contact and any allusion to sexuality.

What happens, then, to the *fa'ateine*? In the visible context of village life, her identity operates essentially without difficulty when she takes part in group activities with girls and contributes her labor as a girl in her house-hold, together with her sisters. Within the household, however, her father and brothers fail to consider her as a daughter and sister respectively, and this is where she becomes the object of affective, verbal, and sometimes physical violence. More serious problems emerge in regard to sex, because in the realm of "living creatures" to which sexuality must remain confined, only heterosexual relations are thinkable. If two men engage in sexual relations, the mainstream discourse holds that one of them (and only one) must be "in the way of a (sexual) woman"—a *fa'afafine;* they cannot be "homosexual." While many people today know what these terms mean overseas, they also state that there is no Samoan equivalent and that the practice "does not exist in Samoa." Sex between two male-bodied persons is heterosexual, in that one is "straight" and the other "in the way of a woman" (and pleasure is thought to be located only in the first party, for better or for worse). Heteronormativity is maintained, and perhaps even reinforced.

In actual practice, however, things are more nuanced. While the norm in sex (either oral or anal) is for the *fa'ateine* to take the insertee role and the "straight" man to take the inserter role, the reverse sometimes takes place (cf. Besnier 1997 for Tonga). Some *fa'ateine* explicitly reject the possibility of sex-reassignment surgery, arguing that they may lose sexual sensitivity as a result. Yet the affective dynamics of the relationship are circumscribed by a heteronormative order, in that, whatever actually takes place during sex, the *fa'ateine* lives as a *teine* and is thus trapped in the heteronormative order—indeed, she is only attracted to straight men, an attraction that is both sexual and affective. Her dreams of settling down with him as a couple remain in the realm of impossibility in Samoa itself, as straight men dream of finding the right woman (both the object of his affection and the proper choice for kinship politics). Relations between straight men and *fa'ateine* remain temporary, which for the *fa'ateine* spells out affective loneliness. While many in Samoa maintain that straight men have sex with *fa'ateine* only when nothing else is available, the situation is more complex in that they may develop an affective attachment to *fa'ateine;* but there is no room within the confines of Samoan society to permit this attachment in the form of a stable and open relationship (cf. Besnier 2004 for Tonga).

Heteronormative hegemony applies equally, although more severely, to women's same-sex relationships. The negativity with which parents respond to *tomboy* behavior in daughters is itself the consequence of that hegemony. If half-hidden sexual play between same-sex female adolescents is common currency in Samoa as in many other societies, this laissez-faire does not apply to adults. No group of women is defined by sexual nonconformity and there is no vocabulary with which to talk about it. The very idea of a sexual relationship between women is thus disallowed by hegemonic ideology, and the lack of terminology in the Samoan language to describe it is another sign of its repression. Finally, a lesbian *tomboy* who may have a *fa'ateine* brother will find no comfort there, as the latter strives to be assimilated with her heteronormative sisters; and together, the *fa'ateine* brother and her sisters will not welcome their sister *tomboy.*

A couple can only consist of a woman and a man. While in mainstream representations a man can conceivably "act like a woman" sexually, neither heteronormative nor *fa'ateine* Samoan discourse admits that a woman can really take on a male sexual role. While mainstream Samoans believe and state that some *tomboys* seek to have sex with "straight" girls, the possibility arouses great embarrassment in people of all ages and genderings. To seek a sexual relationship of whatever kind with a woman makes the *tomboy* appear as a *fafine,* a woman defined by her sexual activity.

Status Asymmetry, Gender, and Heteronormativity

In contrast to a male-bodied person who claims to be a girl and sexually "acts like a woman," a female-bodied person cannot claim to be "like a boy/ man" who seeks female sexual partners. When a woman is sexually active (through marriage or otherwise), she can only be a *fafine* and cannot claim to be "like" another category of sex or gender.

This asymmetry is already striking at the time of adolescence. A boy risks losing status by appearing not to be masculine enough and thus to be labeled *"fa'afafine,"* while a woman risks losing status by becoming the target of gossip to the effect that she has lost her virginity before marriage and thus be labeled *"fafine"* (Schoeffel 1979; Shore 1981; Schmidt 2010). For both genders, the negativity is located with the female and in sexuality. This in itself says a great deal about male domination in Samoan society.

Terms like *"fa'atamaloa"* cannot be made to imply a same-sex female sexuality because the word *"tamaloa"* (and others like it) denotes a male adult without any connotation of sexuality. Men's gendering can thus be defined without any reference to sexuality, while this is not the case with women's gendering. The resultant ideological asymmetry between the genders also generates an asymmetry between them as sexual categories and, above all, in the way in which women and men become sexually active beings: when they do so, boys are not confined in a category and thus can take on various personae; whereas girls encounter a restriction of who they are once they pass the point of no return—namely, the loss of their virginity.

A strong sign of this asymmetry is the fact that, in Samoa, there is no concept of "male virginity." In practice, the first time a boy has sex is a non-event. What concerns him is to convince his friends that he has already had sex with girls even if it is not the case. In the cultural representation of his body, the first time he has sex with a girl is no different from numerous other occasions on which the simulation of sex takes place—through masturbation, sexual games between male cousins, fondling a girl without penetration, or sex with a *fa'ateine.* In contrast, the representation of female virginity is marked by a rich vocabulary and, in former times, by a striking ritual—namely, the public manual defloration that was part of the marriage ceremony, performed on the village green when the girl was from a high-ranking family, otherwise inside the house.

In conclusion, the dominance of the heteronormative order in sexuality that reigns in Samoa leaves little room for the sexual paths that *fa'ateine* and *tomboys* sometimes seek to follow. Male dominance in all matters sexual generates a particular asymmetry between the two "transgender" categories, very much to the detriment of *tomboys*, which in turns generates inequality.

Notes

1. This chapter is a revised version of a paper presented at a conference organized in Canberra and Nouméa in October 2011, cosponsored by the Australian National University, the ANU center of the École des hautes études en sciences sociales, and the Centre des nouvelles études sur le Pacifique of the University of New Caledonia. I thank Niko and Kalissa for encouraging me to develop the materials on *tomboys* and for their tremendous work on editing my "Frenglish."
2. For a critique of this approach in a Samoan context, see Tcherkézoff (1993, 2003, 2008a, 2008b: 319–321). For a comparative perspective, see Tcherkézoff (2011), where I discuss recent critiques by French sociologist Irène Théry.
3. This situation, however, has changed since the creation, in the first decade of the new millennium, of identity-based associations such as The Samoa Faafafine Association and SOFIAS: Sosaiete o Faafafine i Amerika Samoa. As we shall see, the word "*fa'afafine*" was and still is seen as conveying morally negative meanings. Inverting its value and claiming it as a marker of pride is a recent phenomenon. It emerges in relation to earlier global networks, such as The United Territories of Polynesian Islanders Alliance (UTOPIA), "started in San Francisco in 1998 to support the Polynesian gay, lesbian, bisexual and transgender community" (http://www.utopiahawaii.com).
4. The English word "straight" has become part of the Samoan lexicon. It is applied to women and men whose gendered labor contribution and reputed sexual desires conform to what is expected of her/his sex assigned at birth.
5. Global commentaries about Samoa reflect this lack of visibility: while a Google search using the key words "Samoan fa'afafine," "Samoan transgender," or "Samoan effeminates" returns dozens of results, not a single one is obtainable for "Samoan *tomboys*" or "Samoan girls who act like boys."
6. Levy's (1971, 1973) famous analysis of *māhū* in Tahitian villages is a variant on the same theme (Elliston, Alexeyeff and Besnier, this volume).
7. The aesthetic valuation of fair complexion predates contact with the West and is thus not the result of the internalization of a colonial racism (see Tcherkézoff 2008a, 121–122 and many others).

References

Alexeyeff, Kalissa. 2008. Globalizing Drag in the Cook Islands: Friction, Repulsion, and Abjection. *The Contemporary Pacific* 20: 143–161.

———. 2009. *Dancing from the Heart: Gender, Movement and Cook Islands Globalisation.* Honolulu: University of Hawai'i Press.

Besnier, Niko. 1997. Sluts and Superwomen: The Politics of Gender Liminality in Urban Tonga. *Ethnos* 62: 5–31.

———. 2002. Transgenderism, Locality, and the Miss Galaxy Beauty Pageant in Tonga. *American Ethnologist* 29: 534–566.

———. 2004. The Social Production of Abjection: Desire and Silencing amongst Transgender Tongans. *Social Anthropology* 12: 301–323.

———. 2011. *On the Edge of the Global: Modern Anxieties in a Pacific Island Nation.* Stanford, CA: Stanford University Press.

Chodorow, Nancy. 1978. *The Reproduction of Mothering: Psychoanalysis and the Sociology of Gender.* Berkeley: University of California Press.

Grépin, Laure-Hina. 1995. Tikehau: Des paradoxes sociaux autour de l'adolescence masculine contemporaine dans un atoll de Polynésie française. Masters thesis, École des hautes études en sciences sociales.

———. 2001. L'adolescence masculine aux Tuamotu de l'Est aujourd'hui—Le Taure'are'a: Contradictions et transformations d'une catégorie sociale traditionnelle. PhD diss., École des hautes études en sciences sociales.

Kulick, Don. 1998. *Travestí: Sex, Gender and Culture among Brazilian Transgendered Prostitutes.* Chicago: University of Chicago Press.

Levy, Robert I. 1971. The Community Functions of Tahitian Male Transvestites. *Anthropological Quarterly* 44: 12–21.

———. 1973. *Tahitians: Mind and Experience in the Society Islands.* Chicago: University of Chicago Press.

Mead, Margaret. 1928. *Coming of Age in Samoa: A Psychological Study of Primitive Youth for Western Civilisation.* New York: William Morrow & Co.

National Geographic. 2007. Taboo: Sex Change. http://www.youtube.com/watch?v=EronVtKYroc (accessed March 2012).

Orans, Martin. 1996. *Not Even Wrong: Margaret Mead, Derek Freeman, and the Samoans.* Novato, CA: Chandler & Sharp.

Schmidt, Johanna. 2001. Redefining Fa'afafine: Western Discourses and the Construction of Transgenderism in Samoa. *Intersections* 6. http://wwwsshe.murdoch.edu.au/intersections/issue6/schmidt.html (accessed March 2012).

———. 2010. *Migrating Genders: Westernisation, Migration, and Samoan Fa'afafine.* Farnham, Surrey, UK: Ashgate.

Schoeffel, Penelope. 1979. Daughters of Sina: A Study of Gender, Status and Power in Western Samoa. PhD diss., Australian National University.

Shore, Bradd. 1981. Sexuality and Gender in Samoa: Conceptions and Missed Conceptions. In *Sexual Meanings: The Cultural Construction of Gender and Sexuality,* ed. Sherry Ortner and Harriet Whitehead, pp. 192–215. Cambridge: Cambridge University Press.

Tcherkézoff, Serge. 1993. The Illusion of Dualism in Samoa: "Brothers-and-Sisters" are not "Men-and-Women." In *Gendered Anthropology,* ed. Teresa del Valle, pp. 54–87. London: Routledge.

———. 2001. Is Anthropology about Individual Agency or Culture? Or Why "Old Derek" is Doubly Wrong. *Journal of the Polynesian Society* 110: 59–78.

———. 2003. *Fa'aSamoa, une identité polynésienne* (économie, *politique, sexualité*)*: L'anthropologie comme dialogue culturel.* Paris: L'Harmattan.

———. 2008a. *First Contacts in Polynesia, The Samoan Case* (1722–1848)*: Western Misunderstandings about Sexuality and Divinity.* Canberra: ANU E Press.

———. 2008b. Hierarchy Is Not Inequality, in Polynesia for Instance. In *Persistence and Transformation in Social Formations,* ed. Knut Rio and Olaf H. Smedal, pp. 299–329. Oxford: Berghahn.

———. 2011. La distinction de sexe, la sociologie holiste et les Îles Samoa: À propos du livre de Irène Théry, *La distinction de sexe, une nouvelle approche de l'égalité. L'Homme* 198–199: 333–354.

Chapter 7

Race and Ethnicity

DISCUSSION QUESTIONS

1. What was the prevalent understanding of race during the 19th century, as described by Baker? How did anthropology contribute to this understanding?
2. How was evolution used as a model for understanding race by Spencer and others? How did evolution and its social counterpart, Social Darwinism, promote a particular idea of racial inferiority? What does it do to these ideas to establish them as "scientific fact"? In contrast, in what ways are the racial categories Naber discusses "open-ended and arbitrary"?
3. Naber discusses the construction of Muslims within the United States as "other." How and by whom is this "otherness" constructed and signified? Is there a similar sense of othering present in the notions of race that Baker discusses?
4. In Naber's account, how does racism operate in conjunction with other forms of oppression based on social traits, such as class, gender, and sexuality?

KEY TERMS

Race
Social Darwinism
Cultural racism
Nation-based racism
Intersectionality

Baker, Lee D. 1998. "The Ascension of Anthropology as Social Darwinism." In *From Savage to Negro: Anthropology and the Construction of Race: 1896–1954*. Berkeley: University of California Press.

THE RISE OF ACADEMIC ANTHROPOLOGY IN the United States occurred in the late 1880s and was concurrent with the rise of American imperialism and the institutionalization of racial segregation and disfranchisement. And like the anthropology that bolstered proslavery forces during the antebellum period, professional anthropology bolstered Jim Crow and imperial conquests during the 1890s. Before the 1880s the study of anthropology—or ethnology, as it was also called—tended to be an ancillary interest of naturalists and a romantic pastime for physicians interested in the so-called races of mankind. As discussed in the previous chapter, Samuel Morton, Josiah Nott, and Louis Agassiz contributed to the first school of American anthropology during the mid-nineteenth century, but these so-called men of science were not professional anthropologists employed by museums or departments of anthropology.[1] Anthropology moved from the margins of natural history into the center of the academy when other areas of natural history emerged as specific disciplines.

Following the Civil War, universities and government agencies quickly established departments of geography, physics, and geology when the proliferation of industries like railroads, steel, and mining demanded new technology.[2] Capitalists began to extol the virtues of science because it was the backbone for the development of technology, so important to the material ends of industrial development.

Industrializing America also needed to explain the calamities created by unbridled westward, overseas, and industrial expansion. Although expansion created wealth and prosperity for some, it contributed to conditions that fostered rampant child labor, infectious disease, and desperate poverty. As well, this period saw a sharp increase in lynchings and the decimation of Native American lives and land.[3] The daily experience of squalid conditions and sheer terror made many Americans realize the contradictions between industrial capitalism and the democratic ideals of equality, freedom, and justice for all. Legislators, university boards, and magazine moguls found it useful to explain this ideological crisis in terms of a *natural* hierarchy of class and race caused by a struggle for existence wherein the fittest individuals or races advanced while the inferior became eclipsed.

Professional anthropology emerged in the midst of this crisis, and the people who used anthropology to justify racism, in turn, provided the institutional foundations for the field. By the last decade of the nineteenth century, college departments, professional organizations, and specialized journals were established for anthropology.[4] The study of "primitive races of mankind" became comparable to geology and physics.[5] These institutional apparatuses, along with powerful representatives in the American Association for the Advancement of Science (AAAS), prestigious universities, and the Smithsonian Institution, gave anthropology its academic credentials as a discipline in the United States. The budding discipline gained power and prestige because ethnologists articulated theory and research that resonated with the dominant discourse on race.

The Laws of Science and the Law of the Land

In January 1896 Daniel G. Brinton, the president of the AAAS and the first professor of anthropology in the United States, wrote in *Popular Science Monthly* that "the black, the brown and the red races differ anatomically so much from the white ... that even with equal cerebral capacity they never could rival its results by equal efforts."[6] In April of the same year John Wesley Powell, the first director of the Bureau of American Ethnology (BAE) at the Smithsonian Institution, concurred with Brinton when he lectured at the U.S. National Museum (USNM). Powell explained that "the laws of evolution do not produce kinds of men but grades of men; and human evolution is intellectual, not physical.... All men have pleasures, some more, some less; all men have welfare, some more, some less; all men have justice, some more, some less."[7]

Three weeks later, at the opposite end of the National Mall, Melville Fuller, the chancellor of the Smithsonian Institution and the chief justice of the U.S. Supreme Court, joined the Court's majority opinion in *Plessy v. Ferguson,* which stated that "if one race be inferior to the other socially, the Constitution of the United States cannot put them upon the same plane."[8] The Supreme Court constitutionalized segregation by grounding its rationale on notions of racial inferiority informed by Social Darwinism.[9]

Tenets of Social Darwinism emerged as important themes for the legal, scientific, and business communities—serving to glue one to the other.[10] Although ideas of racial inferiority and social evolution were not new to the United States, Social Darwinist ideas became increasingly dominant because they were viewed as scientific in an era when science reigned supreme. Early advocates of Social Darwinist (or, technically more accurate, Spencerist) thought retooled certain ideas of the Enlightenment for an industrializing society. Herbert Spencer, one of its chief proponents, grafted Thomas Hobbes's notion that the state of nature was a state of war—each individual taking what it could—onto Adam Smith's system of perfect liberty, later known as laissez-faire economics.[11] After Darwin's *Origin of Species* appeared, Social Darwinists blurred the idea of *natural* selection to scrutinize society and culture.[12]

Proponents of Social Darwinism believed that it was morally wrong for the government and charity organizations to provide public education, public health, or a minimum wage because these efforts only contributed to the artificial preservation of the weak.[13] A cross section of people, from politicians to world's fair organizers, White preachers to Black leaders, were influenced by this unique combination of social theory, and each used variations to explain inequalities in terms of the natural order of society. John D. Rockefeller even explained to a Sunday school class: "The American beauty rose can be produced ... only by sacrificing early buds which grow around it."[14]

Two trajectories or planks emerged within Social Darwinian rhetoric in the United States. One emphasized the personal or individual struggle for existence; the other, racial and cultural evolution. The racial plank demarcated a hierarchy of races beginning with the inferior savage and culminating with the civilized citizen. The class plank presumed that the poor were biologically unfit to struggle for existence. Turn-of-the-century ethnologists took on the racial plank as their particular charge and played an important role in extending it.[15] And it was the racial plank that emerged as a means of reconciling animosity between the North and the South.

During the 1890s, ideas of Social Darwinism and racial inferiority were explicitly incorporated into political efforts to reunify the nation.[16] By 1896 the old ideas about Manifest Destiny, industrial progress, and racial inferiority (enlivened by Social Darwinism) served as an ideological cement that was able to form capitalist development, imperialism, scientific progress, racism, and the law into a rock-solid edifice within U.S. society. Social Darwinian ideas helped explain inequality in America, but Herbert Spencer's voluminous writings gave it scientific authority.

Herbert Spencer, America's Social Darwinist (1820–1903)

Herbert Spencer hailed from England, where Henry Ward Beecher adeptly wrote to him, observing that "the peculiar condition of American society has made your writings far more fruitful and quickening here than in Europe."[17] Spencer sold more than 300,000 copies of his books in the United States alone—a number unprecedented for nonfiction literature.[18]

The principal tenet of Spencer's synthetic philosophy was the organic analogy, an analogy drawn between biological organisms and society. The principles of biology, he argued, could be applied to society. Even before Darwin's *Origin of Species*, Spencer had worked out the basic elements for evolution. It was Spencer, not Darwin, who furnished the two famous phrases that became associated with the notion of evolution: "survival of the fittest" and "the struggle for existence." Spencer not only applied a biological analogy to society but also incorporated laws of astronomy, physics, geology, and psychology into a comprehensive scheme governed by something he called "the persistence of force."

The universe, as Spencer envisioned it, evolved from a state of homogeneity to one of heterogeneity. He argued that different scientific fields only explored certain facets of the evolutionary process. For example, astronomy and geology are distinct sciences, "but Geology is nothing more than a chapter continuing in detail one part of a history that was once wholly astronomic."[19] Likewise, sociology and psychology are extensions of biology, which are extensions of geology, astronomy, and physics.

Spencer devoted much of his attention to the evolution of human faculties, linking and ranking intellectual, social, and biological attributes. Minds, bodies, and social institutions (such as families and governments) thus fit neatly into an evolutionary framework. As he suggested, "Intellectual evolution, as it goes on in the human race [goes] along with social evolution, of which it is at once a cause and a consequence."[20] Within this evolutionary hierarchy, the most inferior were the savages; the next up the ladder were the semi-civilized, and finally we reached the civilized men.

Spencer applied this line of thought in "The Comparative Psychology of Man" (1876), presented to the London Anthropological Institute and circulated in the United States by *Popular Science Monthly.* In it, Spencer confidently ranked and ordered racial-cultural groups while detailing his familiar argument about the natural progress of societies. The labels he assigned to different people were concoctions of religions, continents, races, or languages, and he argued that anthropologists should thus prove whether his hierarchy was consistently maintained throughout all orders of races, from the lowest to the highest, "whether, say, the Australian differs in this respect from the Hindoo, as much as the Hindoo does from the European."[21]

This address revealed three particularly racist themes that were reproduced and canonized within U.S. anthropology. First, Spencer identified the "orders of races" by language, religion, or continent. This is important because race, language, culture, nationality, ethnicity, and so forth were all viewed as one and the same in Spencer's racial and cultural scheme. Second, Spencer asserted, with the conviction of a scientific law, that racial-cultural inferiority and superiority exist. For example, he advised the London Anthropological Institute to prove just how much inferiority there was based on his evolutionary assumptions.[22]

Finally, Spencer took his place in the long line of philosophers and scholars to scientifically affirm the association of *black* with evil, savagery, and brutishness, thus recapitulating the widely held idea that the lighter races are superior to the darker ones. These themes were subsequently reproduced in the mass media as science, integrated into domestic and foreign policy, and appropriated by White supremacist demagogues. They were not successfully challenged until the United States entered World War II.

Anthropological Social Darwinists

As anthropology emerged in the United States as a discipline in the late nineteenth century, only a handful of ethnologists were influential in shaping it. The most influential were John

Wesley Powell the research leader, Frederic Ward Putnam the museum builder, and Daniel G. Brinton the academician.[23] Between 1889 and 1898 each held the presidency of the AAAS, then the most powerful scientific organization in the United States. Although none of these ethnologists was a strict Social Darwinist in the Spencerian tradition, each was an evolutionist advancing ideas of the superiority and inferiority of particular races when Social Darwinism was a dominant ideology in the United States.[24]

The discipline of anthropology in 1896 was being carved out of various sciences and studies. The scope of the new discipline varied. Powell envisioned it as encompassing just about everything including somatology, esthetology, sociology, philology, and sophiology. The most significant scholars in the development of the field called themselves ethnologists, but for some time no real consensus existed as to what constituted ethnology. Brinton perhaps best captured the aim of the new science. Ethnology was to "compare dispassionately all the acts and arts of man, his philosophies and religions, his social schemes and personal plans, weighing and analyzing them, separating the local and temporal in them from the permanent and general, explaining the former by the conditions of time and place and the latter to the category of qualities which make up the oneness of humanity."[25]

Daniel G. Brinton, Academician (1837–1899)

DANIEL G. BRINTON, A.M., M.D., PROFESSOR OF ETHNOLOGY AT THE ACADEMY OF NATURAL SCIENCES, PHILADELPHIA, AND OF AMERICAN ARCHAEOLOGY AND LINGUISTICS IN THE UNIVERSITY OF PENNSYLVANIA; PRESIDENT OF THE AMERICAN FOLK-LORE SOCIETY AND OF THE NUMISMATIC AND ANTIQUARIAN SOCIETY OF PHILADELPHIA; MEMBER OF THE ANTHROPOLOGICAL SOCIETIES OF BERLIN AND VIENNA AND THE ETHNOGRAPHICAL SOCIETIES OF PARIS AND FLORENCE, OF THE ROYAL SOCIETY OF ANTIQUARIES, COPENHAGEN, THE ROYAL ACADEMY OF HISTORY OF MADRID, THE AMERICAN PHILOSOPHICAL SOCIETY, THE AMERICAN ANTIQUARIAN SOCIETY, ETC., ETC.

This pillar of titles consumes the title page of Brinton's *Races and Peoples: Lectures on the Science of Ethnography* (1890) (Figure 7.1). The litany of titles framed the authority from which Brinton pioneered the discipline. The "etc." included being president of the AAAS and twice vice president and once president of the International Congress of Americanists.[26] Brinton only assumed these more powerful positions after the publication of *Races and Peoples*.

FIGURE 7.1 Daniel Garrison Brinton. (Courtesy of the American Philosophical Society)

Brinton was largely responsible for changing anthropology from a romantic pastime to an academic discipline. He had an undaunted commitment to developing ethnology into a full-fledged scientific discipline, and he wielded his academic prowess, credentials, and reputation to develop and legitimate the field. Brinton had a penchant for source citation, demanded rigor, and maintained that ethnological research must adhere to standards of academic excellence. He also saw the need for a national organization of professionals with a publishing arm that explored all the fields of anthropology. Brinton developed the field, however, by advancing claims of the racial superiority of Whites and the racial inferiority of people of color. He anchored anthropology to an evolutionary paradigm, and he, perhaps more than any other early ethnologist, assimilated the current sociopolitical ideas about race and gender and restated them as science.

Like most ethnologists in the United States, Brinton was initially interested in Native American languages, customs, and prehistory and had only ancillary interest in evolutionary theory and racial classification. Although he first became interested in Native Americans when he discovered Delaware artifacts while wandering near his home in Thornbury, Pennsylvania, his first professional interest was medicine.[27] He graduated from Yale

University in 1858 and pursued medicine at Jefferson Medical College in Philadelphia and postdoctoral research in Paris and Heidelberg. In 1862 he entered the Union Army and was soon commissioned as surgeon-in-chief of the Second Division, Eleventh Corps, of the Army of the Potomac.[28]

Even before the war Brinton was interested in Native American society and language. Although he never engaged in ethnographic fieldwork, he meticulously analyzed the mounds of the Mississippi Valley. He was one of the first scholars to ridicule the notion that previous races built the mounds, arguing that Native Americans from the Mississippi Valley engineered and built the structures.[29] Brinton became an expert on Native American linguistics and grammar, and his reputation, especially in Philadelphia, grew. He was elected to the American Philosophical Society in 1869, became professor of ethnology at the Academy of Natural Sciences of Philadelphia in 1884, and was named professor of American archaeology and linguistics at the University of Pennsylvania in 1886 (where he also sat on the board of what is now the University of Pennsylvania Museum of Archaeology and Anthropology). He was then elected president of the International Congress of Anthropology in 1893 and president of the AAAS in 1894. He published frequently in various journals and had a regular column in *Science* entitled "Current Notes on Anthropology."

The organs of the American Philosophical Society, the AAAS, and the Academy of Natural Sciences became regular outlets for Brinton's scholarship on racial inferiority, ethnology, and the grammar of Native Americans.[30] Regna Darnell, Brinton's biographer, explains that during the 1890s his career blossomed and he rose to power in the scientific community, which helped to validate and establish the scientific authority of ethnology.[31] During this period he shifted from Indian linguistics and grammar to evolutionary theory and ethnology. His writings on ethnology, published primarily in the 1880s and 1890s, explicitly articulated ideas of evolution by espousing racial inferiority. They were concurrent with, and congruent to, Social Darwinism, White supremacist demagoguery, increased lynchings, disfranchisement, and Jim Crow segregation. His shift from Indian linguistics to evolutionary theory correlated with his acquisition of unprecedented power for an ethnologist.[32]

By employing Darnell's distribution analysis of Brinton's publications, one can view the relationship between Brinton's rise to power and his scientific validation of racial inferiority. The total distribution of Brinton's ethnological writings included 13 articles in the 1860s, 10 in the 1870s, 78 in the 1880s, and 108 in the 1890s.[33]

The pivotal publication that solidified Brinton's national reputation seems to have been *Races and Peoples*. The book was a series of lectures on ethnography that consolidated the "latest and most accurate researches."[34] The first chapter, "Lectures on Ethnography," begins with a survey of craniology detailing a range of features used to classify and rank races. These characteristics included: cranial capacity, color, muscular structure, vital powers, and sexual preference. He summarized these under the subheading "Physical Criteria of Racial Superiority" and concluded: "We are accustomed familiarly to speak of 'higher' and 'lower' races, and we are justified in this even from merely physical considerations. These indeed bear intimate relations to mental capacity. ... Measured by these criteria, the European or white race stands at the head of the list, the African or negro at its foot."[35]

In the next chapter, Brinton linked "physical elements of ethnography" to so-called social and psychological elements of ethnography. He proposed that the only way to accurately order and classify the races was to consider both mental and physical characteristics, explaining: "The mental differences of races and nations are real and profound. Some of them are just as valuable for ethnic classification as any of the physical elements I referred to in the last lecture, although purely physical anthropologists are loath to admit this."[36]

The entire first section of the book amounted to a periodic table of the "elements of ethnography," with instructions for ranking, ordering, and classifying races—literally a how-to guide. In chapter 3, "The Beginnings and Subdivisions of Races," he launched into a discussion of evolution, and he tended to favor the Lamarckian view that acquired characteristics were transmitted from parent to offspring.[37] He provided a detailed description of each race, beginning with the White or "the leading race in all history." For the various stocks and groups of Black people he merely restated rancorous racial stereotypes as science.

The tradition of racist imagery in the United States is long, of course, and he wove together science and imagery found in widely circulated magazines, minstrel shows, and the Uncle Tom's Cabin shows that were crisscrossing the country. Old stereotypes became scientific fact. Some were blatant: Brinton suggested that "The true negroes are passionately fond of music, singing and dancing."[38] Other statements were subtle but caustic. Brinton reproduced the stock stereotypes the entertainment and advertising industries had found profitable, including the idea that African Americans resembled apes. Brinton reiterated this image in his scheme for measuring cranial capacities and facial angles by placing the "African negro midway between the Orang-utang and the European white."[39] In another text he unabashedly stated that "the African black ... presents many peculiarities which are termed 'pithecoid' or apelike."[40]

The familiar ideas that Brinton recast as science were routinized in American popular culture by the myriad degrading images of African Americans used for everything from selling toothpaste to entertaining children.[41] These stereotypes drove industries like minstrel shows, trading cards, and sheet music of "coon songs."

Serious political ramifications followed when scientists like Brinton legitimated popular images within authoritative texts. Because Negroes were placed on the bottom rung of an immutable ladder to civilization, they were absolved of the responsibilities (voting) and denied the privileges (social equality) of civilization. This notion of a virtually permanent inferiority resonated with the logic of the Supreme Court's *Plessy* decision.

The parallels are striking. Brinton stated that the "Hottentot is rather a hopeless case for civilization efforts. He hates profoundly work, either physical or mental, and is passionately fond of rum and tobacco"; social equality among the races is not possible because of the *natural* inequality between the races.[42] Such was the line of thought articulated by the Supreme Court when it interpreted the Fourteenth Amendment in *Plessy*. The Court decided that the amendment was intended to enforce equality between the two races before the law. The amendment was not intended to impose an unnatural or impossible social equality. Just as Brinton elicited the notion of evolutionary rungs, Justice Brown used the term *plane* to evoke a similar symbol of racial inequality.[43]

Brinton did not stop at perpetuating racist stereotypes to buttress the logic for racial segregation. He provided the "scientific" justification for the "lynch law." The number of lynchings was steadily increasing in 1890, when *Races and Peoples* was published.[44] The Republicans had just lost control of Congress, cotton prices were plummeting, and the acts to secure African American suffrage were on the chopping block. Terrorists of the Democratic Party effectively used the lynch law to ensure home-rule and White supremacy (Figure 7.2). In both popular and scientific literature African American men, in particular, were depicted as savages who harbored a bestial lust for White women. These depravities, many believed, could be curbed only by sadistic tortures and lynchings.[45] The routine violence perpetrated by lynch mobs was always portrayed as justice served in the name of chivalry and the "protection" of White southern women.[46] Brinton goaded White supremacists with one more justification:

> It cannot be too often repeated, too emphatically urged, that it is to the women alone of the highest race that we must look to preserve the purity of the type, and with it the claims of the race to be the highest. They have no holier duty, no more sacred mission, than that of transmitting in its integrity the heritage of ethnic endowment gained by the race throughout thousands of generations of struggle. ... That philanthropy is false, that religion is rotten, which would sanction a white woman enduring the embrace of a colored man.[47]

Brinton's call to preserve White womanhood must be viewed as White supremacist demagoguery knighted by scientific authority. Ethnology as a science gave to rich and poor southern Whites symbols of pure nationality while it helped to reinforce the cult of White womanhood.[48] Brinton's cloaked assertion that women need men and are inferior to men exemplifies Sandra Harding's assertion that science helps to interlock gender, race, and class hierarchies.[49]

FIGURE 7.2 Justice? A lynch mob preparing to burn a man alive in Paris, Texas, ca. 1890. (Courtesy of the Library of Congress)

After *Races and Peoples* was published, Brinton articulated these ideas from positions of national leadership. In his 1895 presidential address to the AAAS he espoused the same rhetoric that he had detailed in his 1890 book. However, this address had a much wider audience than the book because it was published by *Popular Science Monthly* (1896). Brinton employed the same evolutionary construct based on racial inferiority and insisted that anthropology "offers a positive basis for legislation, politics, and education as applied to a given ethnic group."[50]

The president of the AAAS issued a call for laws and educational reform which applied the scientific fact that Negroes were inferior. That same year the highest court in the land seemingly answered the call and ruled on *Plessy*, thereby codifying into constitutional law the idea of racial inferiority that forced African Americans into inferior schools, bathrooms, and the train cars of Jim Crow.

John Wesley Powell, Research Leader (1834–1902)

In the late nineteenth century the BAE and the Anthropological Society of Washington mobilized more men, women, and resources to pursue ethnology than did any other organization in the nation.[51] John Wesley Powell was the person directly responsible for generating interest, dollars for research, and the growing body of research (Figure 7.3). In 1888 he was elected president of the AAAS. Although Native American ethnology was his sideline interest, he leveraged prestige, political savvy, and healthy budgets to establish the new field.

FIGURE 7.3 John Wesley Powell at his desk at the Bureau of American Ethnology. (Courtesy of the National Anthropological Archives, Smithsonian Institution)

Powell was a powerful man in the elite circles of Washington, establishing almost single-handedly both the U.S. Geological Survey (USGS) and the BAE. The power he wielded in the House Appropriation Committee, the AAAS, the Smithsonian Institution, and the National Academy of Sciences was contingent on maintaining a strong alliance of support within these organizations. His base was made up of a coterie of Washington insiders, Harvard naturalists, government bureaucrats, BAE ethnologists, and members of Washington scientific societies. He had to continually shore up these alliances with favors, contracts, publications, and grants.[52]

Although Powell used ideas of evolution and racial hierarchies to produce his own theory and research, he did not espouse the rhetoric that was characteristic of Brinton and other scientists. Powell explicitly distanced himself from scientific racism. The distance was chimerical, because the people who supported him simply did not share his benign outlook toward people of color. In fact, Powell embraced some of the most ardent champions of racial inferiority to ensure his power and develop the research needed to legitimate the new field.

The Bureau's (Theoretical) Foundation

John Wesley Powell was born in 1834 and grew up in the Midwest. As a youth he wanted to make a career out of natural history, and in 1858 he went to Oberlin College to launch it. Oberlin had a long tradition of racial and gender integration, and it was a bastion of radical abolitionist thought and action when Powell attended. Although sympathetic to the radical students of Oberlin, Powell devoted himself fulltime to natural history.[53]

When the Civil War broke out, Powell was forced to decide between his commitment to natural history and his commitment to the Union. He decided to answer Abraham Lincoln's call for volunteers and joined the Twentieth Regiment of Illinois Volunteers. He was quickly promoted and served courageously, even after he lost his right arm in combat. He was also one of the few officers who trained and outfitted an African American regiment for the Union Army.[54]

After the war Powell continued to pursue his chosen field. He envisioned a museum of natural history for the state of Illinois and successfully lobbied the Illinois legislature for an appropriation. Powell wanted his museum to be the "best in the West," so he immediately orchestrated a specimen-collecting expedition to the Rocky Mountains. He understood that a scientific expedition on the scale he envisioned needed unprecedented financial support. He was able to parlay his access to President Ulysses S. Grant (which he gained from the war) into the underwriting of his expedition by the public and private sectors.[55] Before he unpacked from his first expedition, he undertook the preparations for his second one, a geological and ethnological survey of the Grand Canyon. Between 1867 and 1877 Powell made more than thirty federally funded expeditions, and he emerged as the expert on the geological and ethnological classification of the Rocky Mountains and the Great Basin.[56]

Powell began as a dispassionate scientist, but he developed into a crusader to save public land and Native American societies. In the late 1870s he began to lobby the scientific community and Congress to reform land-acquisition legislation. He worked to convince the National Academy of Sciences to draft legislation to reform the way the federal government disposed of land and to consolidate the various federal surveying agencies.[57]

Although the National Academy of Sciences sponsored the bill, the land-reform legislation was not passed because it was hotly contested by railroad and development interests.[58] When the bill was in committee, Powell submitted his *Report on the Methods of Surveying the Public Domain* (1878) to the Department of the Interior, and it was reviewed during the congressional hearings for the bill. In the report he justified establishing the USGS and the BAE. Although the land-reform bill died, his report formed the basis from which both the USGS and the BAE were established under the Sundry Civil Appropriation Bill of March 3, 1879.[59]

In the report, Powell made seemingly contradictory statements for the justification of the BAE. Above all, he looked to science to remedy the Indian problem.[60] The theoretical position he took fits squarely within an anthropological strand of Social Darwinism, even though it challenged some of the assumptions Brinton and Spencer put forth regarding people of color. Powell opposed the idea that members of Indian societies were inferior to members of civilized societies and explained that "Savagery is not inchoate civilization; it is a distinct status of society with its own institutions, customs, philosophy, and religion" (Figure 7.4). He immediately, however, anchored the crux of the BAE justification to notions of evolution. Federal agents, he explained, must study indigenous customs because they "must necessarily be overthrown before new institutions, customs, philosophy, and religion can be introduced."[61]

FIGURE 7.4 John Wesley Powell inquiring about water in the Southwest. (Courtesy of the National Anthropological Archives, Smithsonian Institution)

Although Powell may have been benevolent toward Native Americans, there was no doubt about what race he viewed as superior. In an 1888 article for the first issue of the *American Anthropologist*, entitled "From Barbarism to Civilization," he explained that "in setting forth the evolution of barbarism to civilization, it becomes necessary to confine the exposition ... to one great stock of people—the Aryan race."[62]

As director of the BAE Powell contracted and hired an array of scientists to conduct research on Native Americans under the rubric of what he called "anthropologic knowledge." The projects and studies sponsored by the BAE were compiled into large annual reports and distributed liberally throughout academic institutions around the world. Under Powell's direction the BAE published nineteen annual reports full of multicolored lithographs and scientific papers, forming the first comprehensive corpus of research for ethnology.

Ethnological research, under Powell, became field research and departed from Brinton's ethnography, which sought only to classify the races. Brinton could not compete with the sheer magnitude of research generated by the BAE and its collaborative approach. Actually, he did not attempt to compete with the bureau because he was philosophically opposed to the utilitarian approach of government science.[63]

Although Brinton was ostensibly not competing, he wrote the definitive text on Native American grammar. This effort culminated in *The American Race: A Linguistic Classification and Ethnographic Description of the Native Tribes of North and South America* (1891). While conducting research for the book, Brinton met resistance from the BAE and was denied access to unpublished manuscripts in its collections. Brinton exposed the rift between the two emerging axes of anthropology when he indicted Powell in his introduction. He lamented the fact that "access to this [material at the BAE] was denied me except under the condition that I should not use in any published work the information thus obtained, a proviso scarcely so liberal as had expected."[64]

Powell did not share Brinton's approach to ethnography, his disdain for applied research, or his view of people of color as perpetually inferior. The only thing Brinton and Powell shared were results presented at scientific meetings and in published papers. Powell believed that the federal government ought to shoulder the moral responsibility to uplift Native Americans to a status approaching civilized society. Unlike Brinton, Powell's later work did not attribute the state of savagery to racial inferiority.[65] For example, in "Sociology, or the Science of Institutions,"[66] he explicitly confronted the way savagery was viewed in the popular culture:

> To the ethnologist a savage is a forest dweller. In common conception the savage is a brutal person whose chief delight is in taking scalps. Sometimes the sylvan man is cruel,—but even civilized men are sometimes cruel. Savagery is a status of culture to the ethnologist, who recognizes four such states, of which savagery is the lowest. Some of the Amerindian tribes belong to this lowest stage; while others belong to a higher stage which is called barbarism.... [C]onsider the savage not as a man of cruelty, but as a man who takes part in a regularly organized government, with laws, that are obeyed and enforced.[67]

However paternal, this passage represents a departure from his views in 1888 and from Brinton's notion that culture and race were one and the same. It also was consistent with the views of Lewis Henry Morgan. Powell was largely self-taught in natural history and held no advanced degrees. Though not his formal teacher, Morgan influenced many of Powell's views, and most of the research at the BAE was shaped by Morgan's ideas about race and culture.[68]

Lewis Henry Morgan, Powell's Ally (1818–1881)

Lewis Henry Morgan also made a tremendous contribution to the foundation of U.S. ethnology, and in 1879 he was the first in a line of ethnologists to use the presidency of the AAAS as a bully pulpit to validate and legitimate ethnology in the United States (Figure 7.5). A long-time resident of upstate New York, he was trained in law, served in the state assembly and senate, and invested in railroads serving the Great Lakes region.

Morgan's contributions to ethnology were made somewhat earlier than were those of Brinton, Powell, and Putnam. And although he had an important theoretical impact, he did not play a major hands-on role in establishing the institutional foundations of the field. His accolades came late in his life. *Ancient Society, or Researches in the Lines of Human Progress from Savagery through Barbarism to Civilization,* his magnum opus, was published in 1877; he was elected to the presidency of the AAAS in 1879 but died a year after his term ended. He was interested in ideas of progress as well as Native American social organization and turned to ethnology to unite them.

He published widely on Native American kinship systems, but his most influential work was *Ancient Society,* in which he developed an elaborate evolutionary scheme to portray the development of human society. He argued that the road to civilization passed through a series of stages, each with its own distinctive culture and mode of subsistence. Morgan also seemingly observed that "with the production of inventions and discoveries, and with the growth of institutions, the human mind necessarily grew and expanded; and we are led to recognize a gradual enlargement of the brain itself."[69] He thus argued that there was a correlation between "cranial capacity" and social as well as technological development, asserting the belief that contemporary races were arranged hierarchically and reflected different stages in the evolution to civilization. Though similar to Spencer's ideas of the racial-cultural evolution, Morgan differed because he linked cultural evolution to materialist development. He claimed that the development of technology and modes of production led to civilization, which suggested that races of people were not necessarily shackled to a permanent status of inferiority.

FIGURE 7.5 Lewis Henry Morgan, ca. 1877. (Courtesy of the National Anthropological Archives, Smithsonian Institution)

Powell worked closely with Morgan, and he supplied Morgan with ethnographic information about the kinship organization of the Hopi and other Great Basin groups for *Ancient Society*.[70] Morgan, like Powell, was influential in government circles. Prior to the Civil War—before Powell and Brinton were national figures—Morgan was regarded as *the* authority on Native American affairs.[71] It appears that Morgan was looked to as an expert on African American affairs as well. When the Compromise of 1850 was being made in Congress, Morgan advised William Seward—an old friend and U.S. senator from New York—that

> it is time to fix some limits to the reproduction of this black race among us. It is limited in the north by the traits of the whites. The black population has no independent vitality among us. In the south, while the blacks are property, there can be no assignable limit to their reproduction. It is too thin a race intellectually to be fit to propagate and I am perfectly satisfied from reflection that the feeling toward this race is one of hostility in the north. We have no respect for them whatever.[72]

Although Morgan has been championed for his "materialist conception of history," this letter reveals the White supremacist perspective embedded in *Ancient Society* that later emerged as the theoretical underpinning of the BAE.[73] Powell distributed copies of the book to the members of his staff, who used it as an ethnographic handbook in the field and a guide for organizing museum exhibits.[74]

Morgan was not the only colleague in Powell's alliance who advanced the notion of racial inferiority: others had an even more devastating impact. One of the most outspoken scientists in the late nineteenth century on the inferiority of African Americans was Nathaniel Southgate Shaler.

Nathaniel Southgate Shaler, Powell's Ally (1841–1906)

Nathaniel Southgate Shaler was initially trained by Louis Agassiz and became a geographer, geologist, and dean of the Lawrence Scientific School at Harvard University. By the turn of the century he was one of the most respected scholars in the country.[75] Powell, who was always looking, found powerful support in Shaler. Powell secured Shaler's support by granting him research funding and an appointment as director of the Atlantic Coast Division of the USGS.[76] The funding and appointment paid off.

In 1884 both the BAE and the USGS were in jeopardy because Congress was investigating the necessity of all scientific agencies. Powell's integrity, the bureau, and the survey were each scrutinized. The joint commission, chaired by Senator William B. Allison, investigated

Powell's appointments and his fiscal responsibility. Simultaneously, the Treasury Department scrutinized every ledger under Powell's authority. The investigations lasted for a year, and Powell emerged victorious with the staunch support of Shaler.

From the beginning of the investigation Powell took the offensive by showcasing a myriad of statistics about aridity and settlement patterns and confirming them with an array of topographic maps. He challenged the commission on one point after another.[77] During the whole scandal Shaler aligned himself with Powell.[78] On Powell's behalf, Shaler admonished his Harvard colleague, Alexander Agassiz, who testified against Powell.[79] Their performance in the Allison Commission investigation propelled both of them into the national spotlight, and together they were regarded as national leaders in the applied sciences.[80] Although Shaler's reputation was fashioned in the academic community as an applied scientist, around the country middle-class Americans knew him as the Harvard professor who made science accessible to the general public. Shaler was recognized as the "purveyor of science to the nation" because of his widely circulated scientific exposes in magazines like the *Atlantic Monthly, Popular Science Monthly,* and the *North American Review.*[81] He did not limit his exposés to geology: he wrote widely on social issues and provided a scientific analysis of the so-called Negro problem for the American public.

For the 1890 volume of the *Atlantic Monthly,* Shaler wrote "Science and the African Problem." It appeared just months before the elections for the Fifty-second Congress (which repealed many of the federal election bills). It illustrates how popular versions of anthropology buoyed racist political projects. Shaler the geologist turned into Shaler the anthropologist to advocate "the study of the negroes by the methods of modern anthropology."[82] Like Brinton, Shaler entwined stereotypes with anthropology, but he did so in the mass media:

But it is not only as an experiment in practical anthropology that this transplantation of the negro in America will interest our successors. ... We can see how English, Irish, French, Germans, and Italians may, after time of trouble, mingle their blood and their motives in a common race, which may be as strong, or even stronger, for the blending to these diversities. We cannot hope for such a result with the negro, for an overwhelming body of experience shows that the third something which comes from the union of the European with the African is not as good material as either of the original stocks; that it has not the vital energy and the character required for the uses of the state. The African and European races must remain distinct in blood.[83]

Shaler also reproduced the image that the affairs of "darkies" inevitably degenerate into chaos:[84]

> But experience shows us that if we could insulate a single county in the South, and give it over to negroes alone, we should in a few decades find that his

> European clothing, woven by generations of education, had fallen away, and the race gone down to a much lower state of being than that it now occupies. In other words, the negro is not as yet intellectually so far up in the scale of development as he appears to be; in him the great virtues of the superior race, though implanted, have not yet taken firm root, and are in need of constant tillage, lest the old savage weeds overcome the tender shoots of the new and unnatural culture.[85]

Moreover, Shaler presented the stereotype of Negroes' mythic sense of rhythm as science:

> There are reasons for believing that the negroes can readily be cultivated in certain departments of thought in which the emotions lend aid to labor; as, for instance, in music. There is hardly any doubt that they have a keener sense of rhythm than whites of the same intellectual grade,—perhaps than any grade whatever. ... [T]hese considerations lead me to think that music may be one of the lines on which careful inquiry may develop great possibilities for the race.[86]

In "The Negro Problem" (1884), also published in the *Atlantic Monthly,* Shaler offered a scientific rationale to support disfranchisement and segregation. He based the article on a common premise that African Americans were inherently incapable of shouldering the responsibility of citizenship.[87] The dean of the Lawrence Scientific School reported to the American public that African Americans were "a folk, bred first in a savagery that had never been broken by the least effort towards a higher state, and then in a slavery that tended almost as little to fit them for a place in the structure of a self-controlling society. Surely, the effort to blend these two people by a proclamation and a constitutional amendment will sound strangely in the time to come. ... [R]esolutions cannot help this rooted nature of man."[88] Based on this framework, Shaler justified the many statutes declaring Negroes "unfit" to vote, sit on juries, and testify against White persons in a court of law, explaining, "I hold it to be clear that the inherited qualities of the negroes to a great degree unfit them to carry the burden of our own civilization."[89]

Shaler was the decipherer of science for the nation and the instructor of more than 7,000 Harvard graduates; he dispensed racial stereotypes in the classroom as science and saturated the most popular monthly publications with the same.[90] More than Brinton, Powell, and Putnam, it was Shaler who marshaled anthropological ideas to sway public opinion against Negro suffrage. Shaler was a self-proclaimed "practical anthropologist." By articulating the racial plank of Social Darwinism he helped foster the acquiescence of the North to southern ideas of racial inferiority and provided the scientific stamp of approval for McKinley's overtures to White supremacy, the Republican Party's abandonment of African American interests, widespread disfranchisement, and Jim Crow segregation.[91]

Powell's public association, support, and appreciation of Shaler must be scrutinized. Powell implicitly supported Shaler's agenda and did not explicitly reject Shaler's "practical anthropology." The ethnologist on whom Shaler relied for credibility was Powell, not Frederic Ward Putnam, who was also at Harvard as the curator of the Peabody Museum of American Archaeology and Ethnology. Similarly, Powell's connection with Harvard's powerful lobby in Washington was Shaler, not Putnam. Indicative of these relationships, Shaler was the Harvard faculty member who hosted Powell when he accepted an honorary degree at the university's 250th anniversary in November 1886.[92]

Powell's greatest contribution to the discipline of anthropology was a successful negotiation of Washington's political and bureaucratic terrain, which allowed him to lay an institutional and financial foundation to sustain the discipline. Although Powell challenged particular notions of racial inferiority, he never attacked the members of his elite circles who embraced Social Darwinian ideas of racial inferiority. Powell accommodated White supremacist ideology as he carried out the BAE's congressional mandate to study Native American institutions so they could be overthrown and replaced.

Frederic Ward Putnam, Museum Builder (1839–1915)

Frederic Ward Putnam anchored the New England axis of the institutional and curricular development of anthropology at the Peabody Museum of American Archaeology and Ethnology. He was also instrumental in the development of three later institutional foci for the discipline. These included the Department of Anthropology at the American Museum of Natural History (AMNH) in New York City, the Department of Anthropology at the Field Museum of Natural History in Chicago, and the Phoebe Apperson Hearst Museum of Anthropology at the University of California, Berkeley. Putnam's academic focus was American archaeology, which differed from Powell and Brinton's focus on ethnology and linguistics. Putnam forged Native American archaeology, linguistics, and ethnology together, insisting on the term *anthropology* to encompass all three.[93]

Like Brinton, Putnam "had to wrench the study of 'early man and his work' out of the hands of the amateur and of the dilettante and place scientific foundations under a structure which, at first, had only very vague oudines."[94] Following Morgan, Powell, and Brinton, Putnam also became the president of the AAAS in 1898.

Putnam was born in Salem, Massachusetts, in 1839. Both of his parents were descendants of the early New England elites. In his obituary the *Harvard Graduate's Magazine* boasted that "the father, grandfather, and great grandfather of Professor Putnam were all graduates of

Harvard College, and the associations of his mother's family had been close with the institution from its beginning."[95]

Putnam entered Harvard College in 1856 but never formally matriculated into a degree program. The following year he became an assistant to Louis Agassiz at the Museum of Comparative Zoology, where he founded the journal *American Naturalist* in 1867. Although he established the Salem Press to publish that journal, the press also started publishing the *Proceedings of the American Association for the Advancement of Science.*[96] Putnam was the permanent general secretary of the AAAS for twenty-five consecutive years beginning in 1875, and his editorial leadership—which came with owning the press—helped define the direction of science during the final quarter of the nineteenth century.[97]

Anchoring the New England Axis

Three distinct institutional axes formed as the discipline matured: Powell anchored government anthropology in Washington at the BAE; Brinton anchored linguistic and evolutionary anthropology in Philadelphia at the University of Pennsylvania; and Putnam anchored archaeological anthropology in New England at Harvard University. As we will see, a power struggle over the direction of anthropology developed when Franz Boas dropped an anchor for cultural anthropology in New York City at Columbia University.

George Foster Peabody, an American-born London financier, provided the impetus for the New England axis. He endowed three Peabody Museums, one at Harvard University, another at Yale University, and the third in Salem, Massachusetts. Putnam was the first director of the Peabody Museum in Salem and later became the director of the one at Harvard.[98] In 1866 Peabody endowed Harvard University for a museum and professorship of American archaeology and ethnology. Putnam became curator of the Peabody Museum in 1875 and was appointed professor in 1885.[99]

Once in a position of leadership, Putnam orchestrated massive expeditions all over the Western Hemisphere to collect artifacts and conduct research for the Peabody Museum. He organized archaeological research in Central America, Ohio, New Jersey, and the Plains States. To publish the findings, he established the *Papers of the Peabody Museum of American Archaeology* in 1876 and a series of *Memoirs* in 1896. Like Powell's annual reports for the BAE, Putnam's *Papers of the Peabody* formed the corpus of research from which Native American archaeology advanced.

Another significant contribution Putnam made was to expose the public to anthropology through museums and world's fair exhibits; this was also his most significant contribution to the social construction of race. The organizers of the 1893 World's Columbian Exposition selected Putnam as the chief of Department M (anthropology). He began in earnest to fashion an ethnographical exhibition of the past and present peoples so that each stage of evolution could be observed.[100] He successfully lobbied top administrators for an anthropological building dedicated to the three-field approach to the discipline. The structure was simply called the Anthropological Building, and it was the first time the term *anthropology* was introduced widely to the American public.[101]

Under the rubric of anthropology and under the roof of the Anthropological Building, the images of racial inferiority imposed on the "lesser races" were brought to life for millions of Americans by "living ethnological exhibits." Putnam hired agents to collect indigenous people from all over the world and then instructed the "native representatives" where to set up their "habitations." He deliberately positioned their encampments along the Midway Plaisance to reflect his idea of an evolutionary hierarchy. As Harlan I. Smith, one of Putnam's assistants, stated, "From first to last, the exhibits of this department will be arranged and grouped to teach a lesson; to show the advancement of evolution of man."[102] The images Putnam produced for popular consumption helped solidify the notion of racial and cultural inferiority imposed on African Americans, Native Americans, and other "savages" the world over.

Although the *Papers of the Peabody* and the world's fair were important, it was Putnam's organizational skills and institution building that created his important legacy, which includes initiating new regional centers of anthropology, in Chicago, New York, and Berkeley. He was important in Chicago because he helped to curate the first collections of the Department of Anthropology at the Field Museum of Natural History. The Field Museum's first acquisitions were the collections displayed at the 1893 Chicago world's fair. As chief of Department M, he was responsible for curating the fair's anthropological collections as well as overseeing the museum's adoption of them.

Putnam also helped institutionalize anthropology in New York City. In April 1894, immediately after the fair, the AMNH appointed him curator of the Department of Anthropology, where he served until 1903. He assembled a staff who developed a series of explorations and publications for the museum. One of the most influential staff members was Franz Boas, Putnam's assistant at the world's fair in Chicago. Under the joint leadership of Putnam and Boas, the Department of Anthropology conducted the Jesup North Pacific Expedition and the Hyde Expeditions to the Southwest, up to that point the most far-reaching anthropological investigations ever conducted.[103]

Putnam also helped institutionalize anthropology in California. In 1903 Phoebe Hearst endowed the University of California, Berkeley, to establish an anthropological museum and a chair of anthropology. Hearst invited Putnam to assemble the museum and assume the chair. From 1903 to 1909 he was professor of anthropology and director of the Phoebe Apperson Hearst Museum of Anthropology.[104]

Although Putnam extended his talent, skill, and commitment around the country, the Department of Anthropology and the Peabody Museum of American Archaeology and Ethnology at Harvard remained under his fastidious tutelage. Charles Peabody summarized Putnam's commitment to forging the foundations of anthropology: "He started movements, societies, methods, plans,—anything to help anthropology, anything to help our knowledge of man and his works."[105] Similarly, Franz Boas wrote that Putnam "took up anthropological studies with that enthusiastic worship of material data as the indispensable basis for inductive studies that has dominated his life and that, together with his skill as an organizer, have made him the most potent factor in the development of anthropological institutions all over the country."[106]

The Prevailing Construct of Race and Anthropology

No one can deny the formidable contributions Brinton, Powell, and Putnam made to developing anthropology from a romantic pastime into an academic discipline: they established anthropology in the United States. However, one cannot divorce the institutionalization of American anthropology from its historical context. Anthropology was legitimated as a rigorous and practical science in prestigious universities and national museums—the very loci where intellectuals produce and promote ideological hegemony. An examination of how Putnam, Powell, and Brinton established the academic foundations for U.S. anthropology in a way that resonated with prevailing views about race will help us better understand how anthropologists of the next generation used those same institutions to challenge those views.

The historical specifics of the three "founding fathers" of American anthropology make it clear that there was not an orchestrated effort to develop a unified approach to the study of race. Yet the texts, images, and exhibits produced by Brinton, Powell, and Putnam clearly worked in concert. The anthropology they produced complemented and reinforced other projects by intellectuals, artists, and journalists that contributed to a larger discourse on race which converged to bolster the late-nineteenth-century views held by a large swath of Americans about civilization, people of color, the Fourteenth and Fifteenth amendments, and Jim Crow statutes.

Each of these men articulated an evolutionary paradigm imbued with ideas of progress and racial inferiority. In turn, politicians and others within specific institutions used these or similar ideas to justify the oppression of people of color. During this process each of these early anthropologists was awarded the presidency of the AAAS, endowed chairs, directorships, and funds to conduct more research along these very lines. Each of them took advantage of their powerful positions, appointments, and networks to establish the institutional and theoretical foundations for the discipline—anthropology.

Notes

1. During the 1870s much of the institutional support for anthropology was provided by the Museum of Comparative Zoology at Harvard University and the USGS at the Department of the Interior.
2. Nancy Leys Stepan and Sander L. Gilman, "Appropriating the Idioms of Science: The Rejection of Scientific Racism," in *The Bounds of Race: Perspectives on Hegemony and Resistance,* ed. D. LaCapra (Ithaca, N.Y.: Cornell University Press), 77.
3. This period also witnessed the denial of women's rights, the destruction and assimilation of many Chicanos, violence against and exclusion of Chinese immigrants, and pogrom attacks on labor unions and Eastern European immigrants. Trade unions became battlegrounds between race and class because managers used various notions of racial inferiority to undermine working-class solidarity. These as well as many other examples contributed increasingly vivid contradictions between the pillars of democracy and the persistent articulation of sexism, racism, and nativism.
4. Stocking, *Race, Culture, and Evolution,* 22; John S. Flagg, "Anthropology: A University Study," *Popular Science Monthly* 51, no. 4 (1897): 510–513.
5. The relative authority that anthropology obtained by the mid-1890s can be gauged by the amount of money Congress appropriated for the BAE. For 1895 Congress approved $30,817.80 for BAE professional and support staff salaries, an amount equal to the salaries of the entire scientific staff at the USNM and three times the entire budget for the Astro-Physical Observatory. The Smithsonian Institution Board of Regents set these funding priorities. The chancellor was Chief Justice Melville Fuller, and other members of the board included Adlai E. Stevenson, vice president of the United States under Grover Cleveland, and William P. Breckinridge, an avowed Social Darwinist and congressman from Kentucky (J. B. Henderson, "Report of the Executive Committee of the Board of Regents of the Smithsonian Institution," in *Annual Report of the Board of Regents of the Smithsonian Institution, July 1895* [Washington, D.C.: Government Printing Office, 1896], xix–xl; Breckinridge, "Race Question," 45).
6. Daniel G. Brinton, "The Aims of Anthropology," *Popular Science Monthly* 48, no. 1 (1896): 68.
7. John Wesley Powell, "Relation of Primitive Peoples to Environment, Illustrated by American Examples," in *Smithsonian Institution Annual Report* [1895] (Washington, D.C.: Government Printing Office, 1896), 625, 631.
8. *Plessy v. Eerguson,* 163 US 552 (1896).
9. See Wilson, *Black Codes of the South,* 96–116; Bernstein, "Case Law in *Plessy v. ferguson,*" 198; Rosen, *Supreme Court,* 23–45; Freidel, "Sick Chicken Case," 192.
10. Hofstadter, *Social Darwinism.*
11. See Daniel G. Brinton, *Races and Peoples: Lectures on the Science of Ethnography* (New York: Hodges, 1890), 76; David *Knowledge and Social Imagery* (Chicago: University of Chicago

Press, 1991 [1976]), 70; Tucker, *Racial Research,* 26. Even before Charles Darwin introduced the theory of natural selection, scholars were incorporating ideas of social evolution into nascent fields like archeology, comparative law, and ethnology. Henry Sumner Maine, M. Boucher de Perthes, Lane Pitt-Rivers, Lewis Henry Morgan, John Lubbock, Edward B. Tylor, and Robert Dunn were among the scholars who advanced ideas of social evolution prior to the 1880s. See David N. Livingstone, *Nathaniel Southgate Shaler and the Culture of American Science* (Tuscaloosa: University of Alabama Press, 1987), 79; John W. Burrow, *Evolution and Society: A Study in Victorian Social Theory* (London: Cambridge University Press), 1966; John W. Burrow, "Evolution and Anthropology in the 1860's: The Anthropological Society of London, 1863–1871," *Victorian Studies* 7 (1963): 137–154; Stanton, *Leopard's Spots;* Haller, *Outcasts from Evolution.* In Europe, where ideas of progress and evolution were in vogue much earlier, scientists used ideas about the hierarchy of races to validate the conquest and exploitation of people of color in Europe's colonial empire (Stanley Diamond, *In Search of the Primitive: A Critique of Civilization* [New Brunswick, N.J.: Transaction Books, 1987], 24–33).

12. What Social Darwinism actually encompasses has been debated. For example, Roger Bannister limited his scope to science and concluded that "the early Darwinians were not social Darwinists; likewise, many so-called social Darwinists (such as Spencer) were not Darwinians" (Robert C. Bannister, *Social Darwinism: Science and Myth in Anglo American Social Thought* [Philadelphia: Temple University Press, 1979], 16). I have followed Richard Hofstadter's and Stephen Gould's more general view, however (Hofstadter, *Social Darwinism;* Stephen Jay Gould, "Curveball," in *The Bell Curve Wars: Race, Intelligence, and the Future of America,* ed. Steven Fraser [New York: Basic Books, 1995], 12). I too view the variety of ideas regarding social, cultural, and racial evolution under the broad ideological rubric of Social Darwinism.

    Jerry Watts proposed that "[t]he claim by Hofstadter and others that it was the prevailing public philosophy at the turn of the century may in fact be a significant overstatement" (Jerry Watts, "On Reconsidering Park, Johnson, Du Bois, Frazier and Reid: Reply to Benjamin Bowser's 'The Contribution of Blacks to Sociological Knowledge,'" *Phylon* 44, no. 4 [1983]: 273–291). However, Watts added that Spencer's "thought when simplified in America to the doctrine of 'the survival of the fittest' and used as an endorsement of the status quo must be considered merely an ideology" (p. 277). Although Watts depreciates the role of ideology in American society, he is correct that Social Darwinism was a bulwark for the status quo.

13. Tucker, *Racial Research,* 27.
14. Hofstadter, *Social Darwinism,* 45.
15. John S. Haller, "Race and the Concept of Progress in Nineteenth Century American Ethnology," *American Anthropologist* 73 (1971): 711.

16. Woodward, *Jim Crow*, 51; Haller, *Outcasts from Evolution*, 173–174; Du Bois, *Black Reconstruction in America*, 700; Charles H. Wesley, "The Concept of Negro Inferiority in American Thought," *Journal of Negro History* 25, no. 2 (1940): 541; Hofstadter, *Social Darwinism*, 172.
17. David Duncan, *The Life and Letters of Herbert Spencer* (New York: Appleton, 1908), 128.
18. Tucker, *Racial Research*, 27.
19. Herbert Spencer, *Principles of Psychology*, 3d ed. (New York: Appleton, 1880), 1: 136.
20. Ibid., 2: 535.
21. Herbert Spencer, "The Comparative Psychology of Man," *Popular Science Monthly* 8 (1896): 260.
22. Ibid.
23. Panchanan Mitra, *A History of American Anthropology* (Calcutta: University of Calcutta Press, 1933), 141.
24. Early ethnologists shared an understanding that all people shared a psychic unity or human nature. These ideas were influenced more by Adolph Bastion and Edward B. Tyler than by Spencer. See Adolf Bastian, *Der Mensch in Der Geschichte Zur Begrundung Einer Psychologischen Weltanschauung* (Leipzig: O. Wigand, 1860); Edward B. Tylor, *Primitive Culture: Researches into the Development of Mythology, Philosophy, Religion, Art, and Custom* (London: J. Murray, 1871).
25. Brinton, "Aims of Anthropology," 65.
26. Regna D. Darnell, "Daniel Garrison Brinton: An Intellectual Biography" (Ph.D. diss., University of Pennsylvania, 1967), 18.
27. Ibid., 3.
28. Albert Smyth, Memorial Address, in *Report of the Brinton Memorial Meeting*, ed. Albert Smyth (Philadelphia: American Philosophical Society, 1899), 18–19.
29. Daniel G. Brinton, *Notes on the Florida Peninsula, Its Literary History, Indian Tribes and Antiquities* (Philadelphia: Joseph Sabin, 1859), 172, 174, 197; Daniel G. Brinton, 'The Mound-Builders of the Mississippi Valley," *Historical Magazine* II (1866): 33–37.
30. Darnell, "Daniel Garrison Brinton: An Intellectual Biography," II.
31. Ibid., 9–21.
32. Ibid., 5.
33. Regna D. Darnell, *Readings in the History of Anthropology* (New York: Harper and Row, 1974), 5.
34. Brinton, *Races and Peoples*, 5.
35. Ibid., 47–48.
36. Ibid., 51.
37. Haller (*Outcasts from Evolution*, 153) and Stocking (*Race, Culture, and Evolution*, 254) have characterized Brinton's theoretical orientation as neo-Lamarckian in the tradition of Spencer. A good example of Brinton's neo-Lamarckian thought is demonstrated by his assertion that: 'The Fuegian savage is one of the worst specimens of the genus; but put him when young in an English school, and he will grow up an intelligent member of civilized society. However

low man is, he can be instructed, improved, redeemed; and it is this most cheering fact which should encourage us in incessant labour for the degraded and the despised of humanity" (Daniel Brinton, *The Basis of Social Relations* [New York: G. P. Putnam and Sons, 1901], 18).

38. Brinton, *Races and Peoples,* 192.
39. Ibid., 25.
40. Brinton, *Basis of Social Relations,* 133.
41. Karen C. Dalton, "Caricature in the Service of Racist Stereotypes: Evolution of Nineteenth-Century Caricatures of African Americans" (paper presented at the W. E. B. Du Bois Institute for Afro-American Studies Colloquia Series, Harvard University, March 31, 1993).
42. Brinton consistently conflated or collapsed the distinctions he made between specific African ethnolinguistic groups and African Americans. Although he is speaking of Africans on the African continent in this particular case, one can infer from all of the other examples in which he interchanges the "ethnic elements" of continental Africans and African Americans that he included African Americans in this stereotype. See Brinton, *Races and Peoples,* 180.
43. *Plessy v. Ferguson,* 163 US 552 (1896).
44. In *Mob Rule in New Orleans* ([New York: Arno Press, 1969 (1900)], 47) Ida B. Wells-Barnett reported these grim statistics created by lynch mobs:

    1888, Negroes murdered by mobs..........143
    1889, Negroes murdered by mobs..........127
    1890, Negroes murdered by mobs..........176
    1891, Negroes murdered by mobs..........192
    1892, Negroes murdered by mobs..........241
    1893, Negroes murdered by mobs..........200
    1894, Negroes murdered by mobs..........190
    1895, Negroes murdered by mobs..........171
    1896, Negroes murdered by mobs..........131

45. Wells-Barnett, *Southern Horrors,* 9–54.
46. See Gossett, *Race,* 270; James R. McGovern, *Anatomy of a Lynching: The Killing of Claude Neal* (Baton Rouge: Louisiana State University Press, 1982), 2.
47. Brinton, *Races and Peoples,* 287.
48. Haller, "Race and the Concept of Progress," 721; Daniel G. Brinton, "The Nation as an Element in Anthropology: From Proceedings of the International Congress of Anthropology at Chicago, 1893," in *Smithsonian Institution Annual Report* (Washington, D.C.: Government Printing Office, 1894), 589–600; Brinton, *Basis of Social Relations,* 153–157.
49. Harding, *"Racial" Economy of Science,* 12. Hall, in *Revolt against Chivalry,* explained that many White women resisted this ideology of White womanhood and documented how members of the Association of Southern Women for the Prevention of Lynching attacked the apologetics

of lynching by disassociating the image of the vulnerable southern lady and the mob violence. She also explained how members of the association attacked the paternalism of chivalry. The claim that lynching was necessary as a protection of White women, they argued, masked the racism out of which mob violence really sprang. The presumptive tie between lynching and rape cast White women in the position of sexual objects—ever threatened by black lust, ever in need of rescue by their White protectors (p. 194).

50. Brinton, "Aims of Anthropology," 69; Haller, "Race and the Concept of Progress," 722.
51. Darnell, "Daniel Garrison Brinton: An Intellectual Biography," 50. The Anthropological Society of Washington had several women in its membership. For example, in 1894 the membership roster included Miss Alice C. Fletcher, Miss Katherine Foote, Dr. Anita Newcombe McGee, Miss Sarah A. Scull, and Mrs. Matilda Coxe Stevenson. See Marcus Baker, comp. *Directory of Scientific Societies of Washington: Comprising the Anthropological, Biological, Chemical, Entomological, Geological, National Geographic, and Philosophical Societies* (Washington, D.C.: Joint Commission, 1894).
52. Livingstone, *Shaler*, 35–39; Curtis M. Hinsley, *Savages and Scientists: The Smithsonian Institution and the Development of American Anthropology, 1846–1910* (Washington, D.C.: Smithsonian Institution Press, 1981), 139, 147–157. Powell was the founder and first president of the Cosmos Club in 1878. It was then and still remains one of Washington's most elite men's clubs (Wilcomb E. Washburn, *The Cosmos Club of Washington: A Centennial History, 1878–1978* [Washington, D.C.: Cosmos Club, 1978], 18–21). This locates Powell right at the center of the Washington's power elite, where he could cut deals and shore up his power base.
53. Grove Karl Gilbert, "John Wesley Powell," in *Smithsonian Institution Annual Report, 1902* (Washington, D.C.: Government Printing Office, 1903), 633.
54. Gilbert, "John Wesley Powell," 633–634; William Culp Darrah, *Powell of the Colorado* (Princeton, N.J.: Princeton University Press, 1951), 68.
55. Powell was an occasional cartographic advisor to Grant, and he parlayed his clout with the president into federal support for the expedition. In addition to the federal government, Powell lobbied the railroad companies to assist in transportation; American Express and Wells Fargo to carry specimens back to the museum; General William T. Sherman (his former commander) to provide a military escort across the Badlands; and Joseph Henry of the Smithsonian Institution to provide equipment for collecting specimens (Darrah, *Powell of the Colorado*, 81–83).
56. John Wesley Powell, *Exploration of the Colorado River of the West and Its Tributaries: Explored in 1869, 1870, 1871, and 1872* (Washington, D.C.: Government Printing Office, 1875).
57. Powell's primary concern was the policies of the Department of the Interior. Deploring the way in which the agency parceled out all the land west of the Mississippi River in equal allotments, without regard to its geological and ecological disposition, he argued that the West

was not a monolithic, endless tract of land waiting for homesteaders, developers, railroads, and mines. He pointed out that the land was extremely diverse and that much of it could not support agriculture because of variations in precipitation and fertility.

58. On the House floor, the bill was debated along regional, not party, lines. Part of the bill was passed, and Powell was successful in consolidating the various surveying agencies under the Department of the Interior. However, he met resistance to the bill by Congress and by the various organizations that were to be centralized. For example, the consolidation was challenged by George M. Wheeler, Ferdinand Hayden, the War Department, and the Public Land Office. Powell literally orchestrated a hostile takeover of the various surveys with the aid of the National Academy of Sciences and sympathetic congressional members. The bill that Congress passed consolidated King's Geological Survey of the Fortieth Parallel, Hayden's Geological Survey of the Territories, Powell's own United States Geological and Geographical Survey of the Rocky Mountain Range, and Wheeler's Geological Surveys West of the One Hundredth Meridian (see Livingstone, *Shaler,* 35).
59. HR. 6140; 45th Cong., 3d sess., H2361.
60. Powell began his argument for the federal agency devoted to American ethnology by outlining the scientific value of studying disappearing societies: "The field of research is speedily narrowing because of the rapid change in the Indian population now in progress ... and in a very few years it will be impossible to study our North American Indians in their primitive conditions except from recorded history. For this reason ethnologic studies in America should be pushed with utmost vigor" (John Wesley Powell, *Report on the Methods of Surveying the Public Domain* [Washington, D.C.: Government Printing Office, 1878], 15). He went on to explain the cogent reasons by touting the practical purposes of ethnology: "[T]he rapid spread of civilization since 1849 had placed the white man and the Indian in direct conflict throughout the whole area, and the 'Indian Problem' is thus thrust upon us and it *must* be solved, wisely or unwisely. Many of the difficulties are inherent and cannot be avoided, but an equal number are unnecessary and are caused by the lack of our knowledge relating to the Indians themselves" (p. 15).
61. Ibid.
62. John Wesley Powell, "From Barbarism to Civilization," *American Anthropologist* 1 (1888): 109.
63. Regna D. Darnell, *Daniel Garrison Brinton: The "Fearless Critic" of Philadelphia* (Philadelphia: Department of Anthropology, University of Pennsylvania, 1988), 43–50.
64. Daniel G. Brinton, *The American Race: A Linguistic Classification and Ethnographic Description of the Native Tribes of North and South America* (New York: Hodges, 1891), vi.
65. See John Wesley Powell, "Esthetology, or the Science of Activities Designed to Give Pleasure," *American Anthropologist* 1 (1899): 1–40; John Wesley Powell, "Sociology, or the Science of

Institutions," *American Anthropologist* 1 (1899): 475–509, 695–745; John Wesley Powell, "Technology, or the Science of Industries," *American Anthropologist* 1 (1899): 319–349.

66. Powell, "Sociology."
67. Ibid., 695.
68. Darrah, *Powell of the Colorado*, 262–267; Stocking, *Race, Culture, and Evolution*, 116; Carl Resek, *Lewis Henry Morgan: American Scholar* (Chicago: University of Chicago Press, 1960), 150.
69. Lewis Henry Morgan, *Ancient Society, or Researches in the Lines of Human Progress from Savagery through Barbarism to Civilization* (New York: Henry Holt, 1877), 37.
70. Resek, *Lewis Henry Morgan*, 134.
71. Ibid., 79–81.
72. Morgan to Seward, February 2, 1850, William Henry Seward Papers, Rush Rhees Library, University of Rochester, Rochester, New York. In 1849 Seward was elected as a member of the Whig Party to serve in the U.S. Senate. During the turbulent 1850s he increasingly resisted the Whig attempt to compromise on the slavery issue, and when the party collapsed (1854–1855), Seward joined the newly organized Republican Party and made a firm stand against expansion of slavery into the territories.
73. Friedrich Engels, *Origin of the Family, Private Property and the State, in the Light of the Researches of Lewis H. Morgan* (New York: International Publishers, 1972 [1884]), Haller ("Race and the Concept of Progress," 712) has summarized their position: "John Wesley Powell and Lewis Henry Morgan, although they spoke optimistically of progress for all peoples, actually limited the full meaning of the term to only those peoples whose race history clearly evidenced a progression out of savagery and barbarism and into civilization. The American Indian, who had not yet developed an agricultural society, contained no 'progressive spirit' from which 'there was no hope of elevation.' "
74. Resek, *Lewis Henry Morgan*, 50.
75. Livingstone, *Shaler*, 6; Haller, *Outcasts from Evolution*, 152.
76. On March 8, 1884, Powell wrote to Shaler and asked him to direct the surveying of New England for the USGS. Shaler accepted the invitation and later became director of the Atlantic Coast Division of the USGS (Papers of Nathan Southgate Shaler [1872–1914], Harvard University Archives, HUG: 1784, Cambridge, Mass.).
77. John Wesley Powell, *On the Organization of Scientific Work of the General Government: Extracts from the Testimony Taken by the Joint Commission of the Senate and House of Representatives.* Washington, D.C.: Government Printing Office, 1885.
78. Livingstone, *Shaler*, 39.
79. Alexander Agassiz, the son of Louis Agassiz, detested Powell's practical approach to science. He also supported the opposition in the congressional investigation. The contention between Powell and Alexander Agassiz was perhaps deeper than a philosophical disagreement. Agassiz's

considerable fortune was tied to copper mining, and the federal land reform, which Powell advocated, would have jeopardized his wealth (John Murray, "Alexander Agassiz: His Life and Scientific Work," *Bulletin of the Museum of Comparative Zoology* 54, no. 3 [1911]: 140–141).

80. Livingstone, *Shaler,* 40; Nathaniel Southgate Shaler, "Aspects of the Earth," *Nation* 1282 (1890): 79.
81. Livingstone, *Shaler,* 40.
82. Nathaniel Southgate Shaler, "Science and the African Problem," *Atlantic Monthly* 66 (1890): 40.
83. Ibid., 37.
84. Dalton, "Caricature."
85. Shaler, "Science and the African Problem," 42.
86. Ibid., 43.
87. Lee D. Baker, "Savage Inequality: Anthropology in the Erosion of the Fifteenth Amendment," *Transforming Anthropology* 5, no. 1 (1994): 29–30.
88. Nathaniel Southgate Shaler, "The Negro Problem," *Atlantic Monthly* 54 (1884): 697.
89. Ibid., 703.
90. Haller, *Outcasts from Evolution,* 168; Shaler, "Negro Problem"; Shaler, "Science and the African Problem"; Nathaniel Southgate Shaler, "The Nature of the Negro," *Arena* 2 (1890): 660–673; Nathaniel Southgate Shaler, "Our Negro Types," *Current Literature* 29 (1900): 44–45; Nathaniel Southgate Shaler, "The Future of the Negro in the Southern States," *Popular Science Monthly* 57 (1900): 147–156; Nathaniel Southgate Shaler, "The Negro since the Civil War," *Popular Science Monthly* 57 (1900): 29–39; Nathaniel Southgate Shaler, "The Transplantation of a Race," *Popular Science Monthly* 56 (1900): 513–524.
91. Haller, *Outcasts from Evolution,* 173; Daniels, *In Freedom's Birthplace,* 114.
92. Darrah, *Powell of the Colorado,* 297.
93. A. M. Tozzer, *Frederic Ward Putnam, 1839–1915,* National Academy of Sciences Biographical Memoirs, 16 (Washington, D.C.: National Academy of Sciences, 1935), 129.
94. Ibid., 133.
95. R. B. Dixon, "Frederic W. Putnam 1839–1915," *Harvard Graduate's Magazine* 24 (1915): 305.
96. E. S. Morse, "Frederic W. Putnam, 1839–1915: An Appreciation," *Essex Institute Historical Collections* 52 (1916): 194.
97. Tozzer, *Frederic Ward Putnam,* 131. See also Franz Boas, *Anthropological Essays Presented to Frederic Ward Putnam in Honor of His Seventieth Birthday, April 16, 1909* (New York: G. E. Strechert, 1909).
98. Morse, "Frederic W. Putnam," 193.
99. Although the Harvard Corporation made the appointment in 1885, it was not confirmed by the Board of Overseers until 1887. Technically, Putnam was the second professor of an anthropological field in the United States because he followed Brinton, who had become

professor of American archeology and linguistics at the University of Pennsylvania in 1886. See Tozzer, *Frederic Ward Putnam*, 128.

100. Ralph Dexter, "Putnam's Problems Popularizing Anthropology," *American Scientist* 54 (1966): 316.

101. Tozzer, *Frederic Ward Putnam*, 132.

102. Harlan Ingersoll Smith, "Man and His *Works*," *American Antiquarian* 15 (1893): 117

103. Alfred Kroeber, "Frederic Ward Putnam," *American Anthropologist* 17 (1915): 716.

104. Tozzer, *Frederic Ward Putnam*, 132.

105. Charles Peabody, "Frederic W. Putnam," *Journal of American Folk-Lore* 28 (1915): 304.

106. Franz Boas, "Frederic Ward Putnam," *Science* 42 (1915): 330.

Bibliography

Baker, Lee D. "Savage Inequality: Anthropology in the Erosion of the Fifteenth Amendment." *Transforming Anthropology* 5, no. 1 (1994): 28–33.

Baker, Marcus, comp. *Directory of Scientific Societies of Washington: Comprising the Anthropological, Biological, Chemical, Entomological, Geological, National Geographic, and Philosophical Societies.* Washington, D.C.: Joint Commission, 1894.

Bannister, Robert C. *Social Darwinism: Science and Myth in Anglo American Social Thought.* Philadelphia: Temple University Press, 1979.

Bastian, Adolf. *Der Mensch in Der Geschichte Zur Begrundung Einer Psychologischen Weltanschauung.* Leipzig: O. Wigand, 1860.

Bernstein, Barton J. "Case Law in *Plessy v. Ferguson*" *Journal of Negro History* 47 (1962): 192–198.

Bloor, David. *Knowledge and Social Imagery.* Chicago: University of Chicago Press, 1991 [1976].

Boas, Franz. "Frederic Ward Putnam." *Science* 42 (1915): 330–332.

________, ed. *Anthropological Essays Presented to Frederic Ward Putnam in Honor of His Seventieth Birthday, April 16, 1909.* New York: G. E. Strechert, 1909.

Breckinridge, William C. P. "The Race Question." *Arena* 2 (1890): 39–56.

Brinton, Daniel G. "The Aims of Anthropology." *Popular Science Monthly* 48, no. 1 (1896): 59–72.

________. *The American Race: A Linguistic Classification and Ethnographic Description of the Native Tribes of North and South America.* New York: Hodges, 1891.

________. *The Basis of Social Relations.* New York: G. P. Putnam and Sons, 1901.

________. "The Mound-Builders of the Mississippi Valley." *Historical Magazine* II (1866): 33-37.

________. "The Nation as an Element in Anthropology: From Proceedings of the International Congress of Anthropology at Chicago, 1893." In *Smithsonian Institution Annual Report*, 589–600. Washington, D.C.: Government Printing Office, 1894.

———. *Notes on the Florida Peninsula, Its Literary History, Indian Tribes and Antiquities.* Philadelphia: Joseph Sabin, 1859.

———. *Races and Peoples: Lectures on the Science of Ethnography.* New York: Hodges, 1890.

Burrow, John W. "Evolution and Anthropology in the 1860's: The Anthropological Society of London, 1863–1871." *Victorian Studies* 7 (1963): 137–154.

———. *Evolution and Society: A Study in Victorian Social Theory.* London: Cambridge University Press, 1966.

Dalton, Karen C. "Caricature in the Service of Racist Stereotypes: Evolution of Nineteenth-Century Caricatures of African Americans." Paper presented at the W. E. B. Du Bois Institute for Afro-American Studies Colloquia Series, Harvard University, March 31, 1993.

Daniels, John. *In Freedom's Birthplace: A Study of the Boston Negroes.* Boston: Houghton Mifflin, 1914.

Darnell, Regna D. "Daniel Garrison Brinton: An Intellectual Biography." Ph.D. diss., University of Pennsylvania, 1967

———. *Daniel Garrison Brinton: The "Fearless Critic" of Philadelphia.* Philadelphia: Department of Anthropology, University of Pennsylvania, 1988.

———. *Readings in the History of Anthropology.* New York: Harper and Row, 1974.

Darrah, William Culp. *Powell of the Colorado.* Princeton, N. J.: Princeton University Press, 1951.

Dexter, Ralph. "Putnam's Problems Popularizing Anthropology." *American Scientist* 54 (1966): 315–332.

Diamond, Stanley. *In Search of the Primitive: A Critique of Civilization.* New Brunswick, N. J.: Transaction Books, 1987.

Dixon, R. B. "Frederic W. Putnam 1839–1915." *Harvard Graduate's Magazine* 24 (1915): 305–308.

Du Bois, W. E. B. *Black Reconstruction in America.* New York: World Publishing, 1952 [1935].

Duncan, David. *The Life and Letters of Herbert Spencer.* New York: Appleton, 1908.

Engels, Friedrich. *Origin of the Family, Private Property and the State, in Light of the Researches of Lewis Henry Morgan.* New York: International Publishers, 1972 [1884].

Flagg, John S. "Anthropology: A University Study." *Popular Science Monthly* 51, no. 4 (1897): 510–513.

Freidel, Frank. "The Sick Chicken Case." In *Quarrels That Have Shaped the Constitution,* edited by John A. Garraty, 191–209. New York: Harper and Row, 1964.

Gilbert, Grove Karl. "John Wesley Powell." In *Smithsonian Institution Annual Report, 1902,* 633–640. Washington, D.C.: Government Printing Office, 1903.

Gossett, Thomas. *Race: The History of an Idea.* 4th ed. New York: Schocken Books, 1970 [1963].

Gould, Stephen Jay. "Curveball." In *The Bell Curve Wars: Race, Intelligence, and the Future of America,* edited by Steven Fraser, 11–22. New York: Basic Books, 1995.

Hall, Jacquelyn Dowd. *Revolt against Chivalry: Jessie Daniel Ames and the Women's Campaign against Lynching.* New York: Columbia University Press, 1979.

Haller, John S. *Outcasts from Evolution: Scientific Attitudes of Racial Inferiority, 1859–1900*. Chicago: University of Illinois Press, 1971.

________. "Race and the Concept of Progress in Nineteenth Century American Ethnology." *American Anthropologist* 73 (1971): 710–722.

Harding, Sandra. *The "Racial" Economy of Science: Toward a Democratic Future.* Bloomington: Indiana University Press, 1993.

Henderson, J. B. "Report of the Executive Committee of the Board of Regents of the Smithsonian Institution." In *Annual Report of the Board of Regents of the Smithsonian Institution, July 1895*, xix-xl. Washington, D.C.: Government Printing Office, 1896.

Hinsley, Curtis M. *Savages and Scientists: The Smithsonian Institution and the Development of American Anthropology, 1846–1910*. Washington, D.C.: Smithsonian Institution Press, 1981.

Hofstadter, Richard. *Social Darwinism in American Thought.* Boston: Beacon Press, 1960 [1944].

Kroeber, Alfred. "Frederic Ward Putnam." *American Anthropologist* 17 (1915): 712–718.

Livingstone, David N. *Nathaniel Southgate Shaler and the Culture of American Science.* Tuscaloosa: University of Alabama Press, 1987.

McGovern, James R. *Anatomy of a Lynching: The Killing of Claude Neale.* Baton Rouge: Louisiana State University Press, 1982.

Mitra, Panchanan. *A History of American Anthropology.* Calcutta: University of Calcutta Press, 1933.

Morgan, Lewis Henry. *Ancient Society, or Researches in the Lines of Human Progress from Savagery through Barbarism to Civilization.* New York: Henry Holt, 1877.

Morse, E. S. "Frederic W. Putnam, 1839–1915: An Appreciation." *Essex Institute Historical Collections* 52 (1916): 193–196.

Murray, John. "Alexander Agassiz: His Life and Scientific Work." *Bulletin of the Museum of Comparative Zoology* 54, no. 3 (1911): 139–158.

Peabody, Charles. "Frederic W. Putnam." *Journal of American Folk-Lore* 28 (1915): 302–306.

Powell, John Wesley. "Esthetology, or the Science of Activities Designed to Give Pleasure." *American Anthropologist* 1 (1899): 1–40.

________. *Exploration of the Colorado River of the West and Its Tributaries: Explored in 1869, 1870, 1871, and 1872.* Washington, D.C.: Government Printing Office, 1875.

________. "From Barbarism to Civilization." *American Anthropologist* 1 (1888): 97–123.

________. *On the Organization of Scientific Work of the General Government: Extracts from the Testimony Taken by the Joint Commission of the Senate and House of Representatives.* Washington, D.C.: Government Printing Office, 1885.

________. "Relation of Primitive Peoples to Environment, Illustrated by American Examples." In *Smithsonian Institution Annual Report* [1895], 625–637. Washington, D.C.: Government Printing Office, 1896.

———. *Report on the Methods of Surveying the Public Domain.* Washington, D.C.: Government Printing Office, 1878.

———. "Sociology, or the Science of Institutions." *American Anthropologist* 1 (1899): 475–509, 695–745.

———. "Technology, or the Science of Industries." *American Anthropologist* 1 (1899): 319–349.

Resek, Carl. *Lewis Henry Morgan: American Scholar.* Chicago: University of Chicago Press, 1960.

Rosen, Paul L. *The Supreme Court and Social Science.* Urbana: University of Illinois Press, 1972.

Shaler, Nathaniel Southgate. "Aspects of the Earth." *Nation* 1282 (1890): 79.

———. "The Future of the Negro in the Southern States." *Popular Science Monthly* 57 (1900): 147–156.

———. "The Nature of the Negro." *Arena* 2 (1890): 660–673.

———. "The Negro Problem." *Atlantic Monthly* 54 (1884): 696–709.

———. "The Negro since the Civil War." *Popular Science Monthly* 57 (1900): 29–39.

———. "Our Negro Types." *Current Literature* 29 (1900): 44–45.

———. "Science and the African Problem." *Atlantic Monthly* 64 (1890): 36–45.

———. "The Transplantation of a Race." *Popular Science Monthly* 56 (1900): 513–524.

Smith, Harlan Ingersoll. "Man and His Works." *American Antiquarian* 15 (1893): 115–117.

Smyth, Albert. "Memorial Address." In *Report of the Brinton Memorial Meeting,* edited by Albert Smyth, 16–29. Philadelphia: American Philosophical Society, 1899.

Spencer, Herbert. "The Comparative Psychology of Man." *Popular Science Monthly* 8 (1896): 257–269.

———. *Principles of Psychology.* 2 vols. 3d ed. New York: Appleton, 1880.

Stanton, William Ragan. *The Leopard's Spots: Scientific Attitudes toward Race in America, 1815–1859.* Chicago: University of Chicago Press, 1960.

Stepan, Nancy Leys, and Sander L. Gilman. "Appropriating the Idioms of Science: The Rejection of Scientific Racism." In *The Bounds of Race: Perspectives on Hegemony and Resistance,* edited by D. LaCapra, 73–103. Ithaca, N.Y.: Cornell University Press, 1991.

Stocking, George W. *Race, Culture, and Evolution: Essays in the History of Anthropology.* New York: Free Press, 1968.

Tozzer, A. M. *Frederic Ward Putnam, 1839–1915.* National Academy of Sciences, Biographical Memoirs, 16, 1935. Washington, D.C.: National Academy of Sciences.

Tucker, William A. *The Science and Politics of Racial Research.* Urbana: University of Illinois Press, 1994.

Tylor, Edward B. *Primitive Culture: Researches into the Development of Mythology, Philosophy, Religion, Art, and Custom.* London: J. Murray, 1871.

Washburn, Wilcomb E. *The Cosmos Club of Washington: A Centennial History, 1878–1978.* Washington, D.C.: Cosmos Club, 1978.

Watts, Jerry. "On Reconsidering Park, Johnson, Du Bois, Frazier and Reid: Reply to Benjamin Bowser's 'The Contribution of Blacks to Sociological Knowledge.' " *Phylon* 44, no. 4 (1983): 273–291.

Wells-Barnett, Ida B. *Mob Rule in New Orleans.* New York: Arno Press, 1969 [1900].

________. *Southern Horrors: Lynch Law in All Its Phases.* New York: New York Age, 1892.

Wesley, Charles H. "The Concept of Negro Inferiority in American Thought." *Journal of Negro History* 25, no. 2 (1940): 540–560.

Wilson, Theodore B. *The Black Codes of the South.* Tuscaloosa: University of Alabama Press, 1965.

Woodward, C. Vann. *The Strange Career of Jim Crow.* New York: Oxford University Press, 1957 [1955].

Principal Cases Cited

Plessy v. Ferguson, 163 US 537 (1896).

Naber, Nadine. 2008. "'Look, Mohammed the Terrorist Is Coming!' Cultural Racism, Nation-Based Racism, and the Intersectionality of Oppressions After 9/11." In Jamal, Amaney & N. Naber, eds., *Race and Arab Americans Before and After 9/11: From Invisible Citizens to Visible Subjects*. Syracuse: Syracuse University Press.

In an October 2006 speech to the National Endowment for Democracy, George Bush used the phrase "Islamo-fascism" in defining "the enemy of the nation" in "the war on terror." He argued that "These extremists distort the idea of jihad into a call for terrorist murder against Christians and Jews and Hindus—and also against Muslims from other traditions, who they regard as heretics. The murderous ideology of the Islamic radicals is the great challenge of our new century. These militants are not just thé enemies of America, or the enemies of Iraq, they are the enemies of Islam and the enemies of humanity" (Bush 2005). Bush's spokesman, Tony Snow, explained that Bush uses the term "Islamo-fascists" in order to clarify that the war on terror does not apply to all or most Muslims, but to tiny factions (Nir 2006). Since the attacks of September 11, 2001, Bush has repeatedly claimed that "this is not a war against Islam" and that the "war on terror" is a confrontation with a particularly militant Islamic ideology. Yet federal government discourses coupled with the local and global implementation of the "war on terror" tell a different story—a story of an open-ended arbitrary war against a wide range of individuals and communities.

This chapter provides a historically situated, ethnographic account of the ways in which "the war on terror" took on local form within the particular "anthropological location" of Arab immigrant communities in the San Francisco Bay Area of California within the first two years following September 11, 2001.[1] In part 1, I will explore the ways in which dominant United States discourses on "terrorism" and "Islamic fundamentalism" were reproduced within 9/11-related immigration policies in California.[2]

I argue that official federal government policies such as special registration, detentions, and deportations have constituted particular subjects as potential enemies within the nation—specifically working-class nonresident Muslim immigrant men from Muslim majority countries. In this sense, a set of solid and fixed signifiers have come to demarcate the "Muslim Other/enemy within" (e.g., masculinity, foreignness, and Islam). Yet at the same time, a wide range of subject positions have been drawn into the "war on terror" through federal government policies, including Arab Christians, Iranian Jews, Latinos/as, and Filipinos/as, women, and queer people, among others, illustrating that dominant U.S. discourses on "Islam" and "Muslims" are not only malleable and fluid but are arbitrary, fictional, and imaginary at best.[3] Here I draw upon Althusser's (2003, 51; 1971, 121–73) definition of "the hailed individual." He argues that capitalism constitutes us as subjects by "interpellating" us—calling out to us in the way a policeman calls out to someone in the street. Althusser writes, "the hailed individual will turn around. By this mere one-hundred-and-eighty-degree physical conversation, he becomes a subject" (1971, 164). As Althusser's policeman creates a subject from the solitary walker in the street, one answerable to the law and to the state and system behind it, post-September 11 federal government and media discourses have created an arbitrary "potential terrorist" subject—intrinsically connected to "Islamic fundamentalism" and "terrorism."[4] I use the term "dominant U.S. discourses" to refer to systems of meaning about the "war on terror" produced among the federal government's policy makers, the defense industry, the corporate media, and neoconservative think tanks. In the demarcation of boundaries between good versus evil and between "those who are with us" and "those who are with the terrorists," dominant U.S. discourses on "terrorism" and "Islamic fundamentalism" have provided "definitions of patriotism, loyalty, boundaries and ... belonging" (Said 2002, 578). They have also sparked nationalist sentiments that articulate subjects associated with "us" as those who are to be protected and those associated with "them" as those who are to be disciplined and punished.

In part 2, I explore the ways in which dominant U.S. discourses on terrorism were reproduced within the context of the post-9/11 backlash in the public sphere or in cases of harassment and hate crimes at school, at work, on the bus, and in the streets. I argue that the arbitrary, open-ended scope of the domestic "war on terror" emerged through the association between a wide range of signifiers such as particular names (e.g., Mohammed), dark skin, particular forms of dress (e.g., a headscarf or a beard) and particular nations of origin (e.g., Iraq or Pakistan) as signifiers of an imagined "Arab/Middle Eastern/Muslim" enemy.

In this sense, the category "Arab/Middle Eastern/Muslim" operated as a constructed category that lumps together several incongruous subcategories (such as Arabs and Iranians, including Christians, Jews, and Muslims, and all Muslims from Muslim-majority countries, as well as persons who are perceived to be Arab, Middle Eastern, or Muslim, such as South Asians, including Sikhs and Hindus).[5] Persons perceived to be "Arab/Middle Eastern/Muslim" were targeted by harassment or violence based on the assumption "they" embody a potential for terrorism and are thus threats to U.S. national security and deserving of discipline and punishment. Although these markers (name, skin color, dress, and nation of origin) were not the only signifiers that hailed individuals into associations with "Islamic fundamentalism" or "terrorism," they were among those most prevalent within my research participants' encounters with the post-9/11 backlash. While these signifiers were not mutually exclusive and operated relationally, particular signifiers were more salient than others, depending on the person or the situation. For example, in some contexts, a name such as Mohammed coupled with a beard signified the "Arab/Middle Eastern/Muslim" identity and in other contexts, it was nation of origin coupled with dark skin and a form of dress that signified the "Arab/Middle Eastern/Muslim."

I further argue that the post-9/11 backlash has been constituted by an interplay between two racial logics, cultural racism and nation-based racism (see footnote 3). I refer to "cultural racism" as a process of othering that constructs perceived cultural (e.g., Arab), religious (e.g., Muslim), or civilizational (e.g., Arab and/or Muslim) differences as natural and insurmountable.[6] Here, I build upon Minoo Moallem's analysis of contexts in which religion may be considered "as a key determinant in the discourse of racial inferiority" (2005, 10) and Balibar's argument that "race," when coded as culture, can be constituted by a process that makes no reference to claims of biological superiority, but instead associates difference and inferiority with spiritual inheritance (1992, 25). In such instances, "culture can also function like a nature, and it can in particular function as a way of locking individuals and groups a priori into a genealogy, into a determination that is immutable and intangible in origin" (Balibar 1992, 22). As in European histories of anti-Semitism, histories of Islamophobia have deployed biological features in the racialization process. In this analysis, as in European histories of anti-Semitism, biological features are deployed, but "within the framework of cultural racism" (Balibar 1992, 22).[7] In other words, bodily stigmata become signifiers of a spiritual inheritance as opposed to a biological heredity (Balibar 1992, 22). In the context of my research, the term "cultural racism" refers to cases in which violence or harassment was justified on the basis that persons who were perceived to be "Arab/Middle Eastern/Muslim" were rendered as inherently connected to a backward, inferior, and potentially threatening Arab culture, Muslim religion, or Arab Muslim civilization.

I use the term "nation-based racism" to refer to the construction of particular immigrants as different than and inferior to whites based on the conception that "they" are foreign and therefore embody a potentiality for criminality and/ or immorality and must be "evicted, eliminated, or controlled."[8] In the context of the "war on terror," the interplay between culture-based racism and nation-based racism has articulated subjects perceived to be "Arab/Middle Eastern/Muslim" not only as a moral, cultural, and civilizational threat to the "American" nation, but also as a security threat. The mapping of cultural racism onto nation-based racism has been critical in generating support for the idea that going to war "over there" and enacting racism and immigrant exclusion "over here" are essential to the project of protecting national security. Under the guise of a "war on terror," cultural and nation-based racism have operated transnationally to justify U.S. imperialist ambitions and practices as well as the targeting and profiling of persons perceived to be "Arab/Middle Eastern/Muslim" in the diaspora.[9]

Throughout my field sites, "racism" did not operate as a separate, mutually exclusive, axis of power. Rather, it intersected with multiple axes of oppression, such as class, gender, and sexuality. According to Linda Burnham, the idea of a simultaneity of oppressions "emerged among women of color feminists in fierce contention with the notion that racial identity trumps all other identities and that the struggle against racism should take precedence over all other forms of resistance to inequity" (2001, 9). My research illustrates that intersections between race, class, gender, and sexuality produced a range of engagements with "racism" among my research participants, depending on their social positioning. For example, the reproduction of government policies and media discourses in day-to-day interactions at work, on the bus, or on the streets were more violent and life threatening in working class urban locations than in upper-middle-class locations (Naber 2006). Because of their class privilege and the longer duration in which they had been in the United States, middle-to upper-class research participants had access to social, cultural, and economic privileges that allowed them to distance themselves from proximity to the "potential terrorists" compared to their working-class counterparts. Alternately, working-class immigrants were often perceived to be in closer proximity to "geographies of terror" (i.e., Muslim-majority nations) and were therefore perceived to be in closer proximity to the "potential terrorists" than their middle-class counterparts.[10] Throughout my field site, socioeconomic class intersected with race and gender in that dominant discourses tended to construct working-class masculinities as agents of terrorism and working-class femininities as passive victims of "the terrorists."

Research Methods

This essay is based on ethnographic research among Arab immigrants and Arab Americans in the San Francisco Bay Area between September 2002 and September 2003. Most of the research took place among two Arab/Arab American community networks, one that includes recent Arab Muslim immigrants and refugees from Iraq, Yemen, Palestine, and North Africa living in poverty and the other, middle-and upper-class professionals who are predominantly first and second generation and include Muslims and Christians from the Levant. The research entailed intensive interviews and participant observation with thirty board members representing eight religious, civil rights, and community-based organizations that serve Arabs/Arab Americans among their constituencies.[11] I conducted intensive interviews with six lawyers whose work was vital to community-based efforts in response to the anti-Arab/South Asian/Muslim backlash in the San Francisco Bay Area in the aftermath of September 11.[12] I also conducted intensive interviews and participant observation among fifty community members from various class, generational, and religious backgrounds and various countries of origin in the Arab world.

Considering that the backlash had an impact not only on Arabs and Arab Americans, my research focused on the experiences of Arabs and Arab Americans as one among other entry points into interrogating the complex, nuanced ways in which the post–September 11 backlash operated. I thus conducted participant observation and open-ended interviews among diverse activists from various community-based organizations, multiracial coalitions, progressive organizations, and antiwar coalitions, including the American Arab Anti-Discrimination Committee, San Francisco Chapter; the Women of Color Resource Center; United Communities Against War and Racism; the National Lawyers Guild; Nosei; Asian Pacific Islanders for Community Empowerment; Asian Pacific Islanders Against War; La Raza Centro Legal; the Alliance of South Asians Taking Action; and the Committee for Human Rights in the Philippines.

Historical Context

On a global scale, the repeated framing of the aftermath of September 11 as an endless, fluid war has facilitated the Bush administration's conflation of diverse individuals, movements, and historical contexts such as bin Laden, Saddam Hussein, any and all forms of Palestinian resistance to Israeli occupation, Hizballah, Hamas, and al-Qaeda under the rubric "Islamic fundamentalists/Muslim terrorists."[13] It has also justified war on Afghanistan and Iraq, support for Israeli occupation, Israel's war on Lebanon, and the transfer to the Philippines of U.S. troops who have enacted human rights violations against local people under the guise of "saving innocent people from terrorism." Within the geographic borders of the United States, the "war on terror" took on local form in the expansion of anti-immigrant discourses and practices beyond the axes of "illegal criminal" to "evil terrorist enemy within." On April 6, 2002, former attorney general John Ashcroft succinctly captured the federal government's framing of the aftermath of September 11 as a war against terrorists who are everywhere and anywhere with the following statement: "In this new war our enemy's platoons infiltrate our borders, quietly blending in with visiting tourists, students and workers. They move unnoticed through our cities, neighborhoods and public spaces.... Their tactics rely on evading recognition at the border and escaping detection within the United States" (Ashcroft 2002).

September 11-related immigration policies have targeted immigrants who fit amorphous characterizations of a "terrorist profile" through FBI investigations and spying, INS police raids, detentions, deportations, and interrogations of community organizations and activists. The INS targeted noncitizens from Muslim-majority countries as well as some individuals from Muslim-majority countries who were naturalized. These tactics were part of the federal government's implementation of a "wide range of domestic, legislative, administrative, and judicial measures in the name of national security and the war on terrorism" (Cainkar

2003, l).[14] The "war on terror" also justified an intensification of anti-immigrant policies that affected a range of immigrant communities, particularly those historically racialized as non-white. For example, in the months following September 11 in San Francisco, the INS passed as local police in an effort to uphold Ashcroft's message that undocumented immigrants are the enemy, and members of local law enforcement are part of the solution. Reflecting on this period, Rosa Hernandez, a Latina community activist, reported in an interview that "the INS was engaging in random raids—at supermarkets, bus stops, and among unlicensed flower vendors." In February 2002, the federal government officially took over airport security. In the San Francisco Bay Area, this meant marking Filipino/a airport screeners as scapegoats in the attacks and laying them off en masse. Improving security meant replacing noncitizen workers with citizens who tended to be retired white military and police who received better pay, more benefits, and more respect. Several scholars and activists have added that the "war on terror" has legitimized an intensification of police brutality within working-class communities of color, exposed low-income students of color to unprecedented levels of military recruitment, and forced massive budget cuts that have disproportionately diminished social services and funding for schools in low-in come communities of color.[15]

1. Anti-Immigrant Legislation in California

Behtan Safeed,[16] a leading Iranian American immigrant-rights lawyer who represented more than six hundred clients in cases related to the post-9/11 backlash, summarized the impact of federal government policies on persons perceived to be Arab, Middle Eastern, South Asian, and/or Muslims as follows:

> They locked our men and our boys and our senior citizens away for the most ridiculous charges. A lot of them had valid visas. The edict that came from Attorney General Ashcroft, from the Department of Justice, was "guilty until proven innocent." No one who was held received a Notice to Appear. Even if they were served a bond for a Bond Hearing, it was going to be days—if not weeks—and in some cases months away, for no reason. It happened in stages: first came the PATRIOT Act; then came the first 5,000 men placed on a list; then came random FBI investigations; then came missing placed in lock down for 24 hours at a time while their families didn't know anything about them.

My research indicates that the FBI would either stop by a person's house without previous warning or arrange for a phone interview. In the Tenderloin, a low-income neighborhood where several thousand recent Arab Muslim immigrants reside, many people received consecutive phone calls from the FBI.[17] On several occasions, the FBI went from building to building and did not explain that the interviews were voluntary. While lawyers, social service providers, and community activists who worked closely with the individuals and communities disproportionately targeted by 9/11-related legislation articulated the *kinds* of anti-immigrant measures that the federal government implemented with ease, their explanations of exactly *whom* these measures targeted were less explicit. The range of explanations they provided about exactly *who* was targeted, and the inconsistencies in their narratives, epitomizes this point. Consider the following three quotes. As Lana Salam,[18] an immigrant-rights lawyer and community activists explained, "I'd have to say that they focused on people with student visas and nonimmigrant visas—although it was also more broad-based and included people with green cards and U.S. citizenship. It also focused on known Muslim thinkers, writers, and clerics. It seemed focused mostly on Muslims—people who went to Friday prayers. I think they were looking for people with Islamic affiliations. I specifically recall that they interviewed Hamzah Yousef."[19]

Community leader and activist Ahmad Masri, a university lecturer and the director of two Muslim American organizations, explained, "Definitely, the policies impacted immigrants more than indigenous Muslims. That doesn't mean that in the long run the indigenous Muslims aren't going to be dragged into it, willingly or unwillingly. Among immigrants, the impact on Arabs was higher than other immigrant communities, with the exception of Pakistanis, who were also included in this." According to immigrant rights lawyer Behtan Safeed, "It was mostly Muslims [who] were detained, but there were Christians among them. There was an Iranian Armenian family. There were Jews among them. The gamut. The ones that look darker were more targeted. There was a particular age group I saw—twenty-somethings and forty-somethings, but I also saw sixteen-year-olds and I saw sixty-four-year-olds." These quotes reflect a broader pattern emergent throughout the San Francisco Bay Area within the first two years following 9/11. While particular persons were disproportionately targeted by federal government policies (most were Arab or South Asian and most were Muslim), the Bush administration's "terrorist profile" had the potential to single out a wide range of individuals, including Arab and Pakistani Muslims, non-Arab/non-South Asian Muslims; Christians and Jews; aliens, permanent residents, and citizens; and young men in addition to teenagers and the elderly.

A closer exploration of the process of special registration, part of the National Security Entry-Exit Registration System, exemplifies the arbitrary scope of the federal government's "terrorist profile." Special registration required nonresident men, such as students, visitors, and those conducting business in the U.S. from North Korea and twenty-four Muslim majority countries, to be fingerprinted, photographed, and interviewed.[20] According to Ashcroft, those required to register were "individuals of elevated national security concern who stay in the country for more than thirty days" (Ashcroft 2002). According to activists who monitored the process of Special Registration, the interviews entailed questions about the immigrants' family members and their names and addresses, their e-mail address, the names and addresses of their contacts in the U.S., and a form of identification other than their passport and immigration documents. Interviewers tended to ask how the person arrived in the United States and when as well as whether they have any connection to any "terrorist organizations" (Revolutionary Worker Online 2002). They asked about the interviewees' religious and political affiliations and about the mosques they attended. Interviewees were digitally photographed and fingerprinted—and the photo and prints were processed against various criminal and immigration service databases. Special registration resulted in the deportation of more than thirteen thousand individuals. Not one terrorist suspect was found in the process.[21]

The Bush administration purported that special registration would assist the federal government in locating "militant Islamic fundamentalists." That Iranian Jews were detained along with Muslims from Iran, Iraq, Libya, Sudan, and Syria during the first phase of Special Registration in Los Angeles (Jan. 27, 2003 and Feb. 7, 2003) is but one example of the arbitrary identity of groups linked to "militant Islam." Sources from the Iranian Jewish community said that up to a dozen Iranian Jews had been detained or arrested, though one attorney in Los Angeles had stated that he was trying to raise bail of $1,500 per person for thirty-five Iranian Jews. Moreover, eight of the Jewish detainees had moved from Iran to Israel and later came to the United States, and many held Israeli citizenship. Zvi Vapni, the Israeli deputy consul general in Los Angeles, said he had received complaints that Iranian Jews faced "very hard conditions," perhaps because of overcrowding, and had conveyed the consulate's concern to the INS (Fitleberg 2002).

Referencing the 9/11 attacks, Attorney General Ashcroft determined that "certain non-immigrant aliens require closer monitoring." Thus, policy makers have named particular Muslims from particular countries of origin as those who fit this profile. Yet because the enforcement of such policies has been directed at such a broad range of identities, the question of exactly *who* these "immigrants" *are* remains unclear. On the one hand, the category "Muslim" is signified by fixed, solid referents (i.e., Muslim men from Muslim majority countries). On the other hand, it is open-ended and arbitrary in its potential to draw a wide range of subjects into association with "terrorism." Paralleling the Bush administration's "endless, fluid war," 9/11-related immigration policies have targeted persons who tend to "fit" the federal government's profile of a "potential terrorist" (i.e., Muslim immigrant men from Muslim majority countries), yet at the same time, they have rendered a range of subject positions as deserving of discipline and punishment under the guise of the "war on terror." This, in turn, facilitates any abuse or "defense" against them.

2. Emblems of Terrorism: The Open-Ended Terrorist on the Streets

Paralleling federal government policies, day-to-day forms of harassment, violence, and intimidation in the public sphere also operated to hail a range of subject positions into discourses of "Islamic fundamentalism" and "terrorism." Consider the series of murders that took place within weeks after 9/11. On September 15, 2001, a Sikh man, Balbir Singh Sodhi, was gunned down in Mesa, Arizona, outside his gas station. According to Anya Cordell, who launched the *Campaign for Collateral Compassion* in February 2002 to bring attention to murders associated with September 11, Sodhi's killer spent the hours before the murder in a bar, bragging of his intention to "kill the ragheads responsible for September 11" (Hanania 2004). On September 15, 2001, a forty-six-year-old Pakistani, Waqar Hasan of Dallas, Texas, was shot to death in his convenience store. The man convicted of murdering him was also convicted of murdering Vasudev Patel days later in Mesquite, Texas. Anya Cordell explained that he admitted to authorities to blinding a third victim, a Bangladeshi, in between the murders of Hasan and Patel and that after his arrest he stated, "I did what every American wanted to do after September 11th but didn't have the nerve." On September 15, 2001, Adel Karas, a Coptic Christian grocer, was killed in his store in San Gabriel, California. On September 21, 2001, Ali Almansoop, a Yemeni American citizen and father of four, was murdered in his Detroit, Michigan, home (Hanania 2004). These murders took place within a broader context of a 1,600 percent increase in hate-based incidents against persons perceived to be Arab, Muslim, or South Asian in the United States (between 2000 to 2001).[22] These incidents illustrate how racialization within the context of the post-9/11 backlash operated throughout the United States to constitute South Asians from diverse religious backgrounds, Arab Christians, and Muslim immigrants from Muslim-majority countries as somehow intrinsically connected to Islamic fundamentalism and terrorism.

Among Arab immigrants and Arab Americans in the San Francisco Bay Area, September 11-related hate crimes and other forms of harassment in the public sphere disproportionately targeted persons who displayed what dominant government and corporate media discourses often constructed as emblems of a constructed "Arab/Middle Eastern/Muslim" identity, including particular kinds of names, appearances, or nations of origin that signified an association with the enemy of the nation. Such identity markers hailed multiple subject positions into the "war on terror" through hate crimes and various forms of violence, harassment, and intimidation in the public sphere—at school, on the bus, at work, at home, and on the streets.

Names and Naming: "Look, Mohammed the Terrorist Is Coming!"

Repeatedly throughout my research, participants' narratives on harassment in the public sphere were stories in which particular names operated as signifiers of an "Arab/Middle Eastern/Muslim" identity. Teachers and youth group leaders agreed that boys with names such as Mohammed or Osama were disproportionately harassed at school. Consider the following stories. Nayla, a Muslim American youth group leader, recalled an incident where school kids would frequently shout, "Look, Mohammed the terrorist is coming!" when a young boy named Mohammed would enter the playground. Amira, a college student, recalled reading the words, "I hate Mohammed. All Mohammeds should die," on a wall outside the Recreation and Sports Facilities Building at the University of California, Berkeley. Reflecting on difficulties that he and his wife faced in deciding whether or not to name their son Mohammed, Saleh, a small business owner, explained: "After September 11 no one would have thought about naming their son Mohammed in this country if they wanted him to be treated like a normal person. We thought about what would happen to our son in school, and how he would be discriminated against growing up. But we felt that this is our religion and our culture, and long before September 11 we decided that if we had a second son, we would name him Mohammed. We decided not to change what we stood for, but imagine what happens when your neighbor says, 'what is that cute little boy's name?' You say 'Mohammed' and they say, 'Oh ...' This is how September 11 impacted even the relationship between you and your neighbor."

Several Christian Arabs and Arab Americans with whom I interacted were similarly targeted based on associations between their name and the notion of a "potential enemy of the nation." In such cases, Christians were perceived to be Muslim because they had Arabic names, illustrating the ways that federal government and corporate media discourses that conflate the categories "Arab" and "Muslim" take on local form in the public sphere. A youth group leader at a Roman Catholic Arab American church reported that after their son Osama was repeatedly called "Muslim terrorist," his parents changed his name to "Sam." Recurring throughout the period of my research were similar stories of individuals who changed their Arabic names to anglicized names, including an Arab American Christian who changed his name from Fouad to Freddy after facing 9/11-related harassment. Misidentifications of Arab Christians as Muslims reify the absurd generalizations and misconceptions underlying hegemonic constructions of the category "Arab" or "Muslim." They also reify that encounters with racism are informed by fiction and comprise a wide variety of complexities and contradictions. As Amitava Kumar puts it, "In those dark chambers, what is revealed always hides something else" (2000, 74). In the cases of misidentified Arab Christians, the simple reality that not all Arabs are Muslim and not all Muslims are Arabs is hidden and erased from history.

Like federal government legislation, harassment against "potential terrorist men" in the public sphere operated within the logic of nation-based racism that considers discipline and punishment the "proper mechanism to set the tide of criminality intrinsic to them" (Ono and Sloop 2002, 33). Nation-based racism is not specific to the post-9/11 environment, but it has been critical to the justification of many cases of immigrant exclusion by the idea that citizens should be protected against "others" who are "potentially or already criminal" (33), or in this case, terrorists. Ono and Sloop argue that the post–Cold War period has witnessed a proliferation of the notion of the enemy of the nation and that discourse is constituted by the idea that "enemies threaten the moral, cultural, and political fabric of the nation state and must be evicted, eliminated, or controlled.... The production and proliferation of new enemies to blame, to oppose, and to conquer is part of a distinct contemporary culture" (35). Referring to histories of Asian immigrant exclusion, Lisa Lowe (1994, 55) writes that nation-based racism has operated through the construction of a binary opposition between patriot and enemy. After 9/11, in the process of legitimizing imperialist ambitions through appeals to nationalist narratives about protecting national security, dominant U.S. discourses have refashioned post-Cold War binaries from patriot versus enemy to those who are with us versus those who are with the terrorists.[23] Names signifying an "Arab/Middle Eastern/Muslim" identity rendered particular men and boys at once foreign, or alien, to the nation, but at the same time connected, in the most familial and instinctive terms, to "the terrorists." In this sense, nation-based racism conflates "Arab/Middle Eastern/Muslim" masculinities with an inherent potential for violence and terrorism and legitimizes the discipline and punishment of "Arab/Middle Eastern/Muslim" masculinities "over there" (in the countries the United States is invading) and "over here" (within the geographic borders of the U.S.). Moreover, that Saleh, in the narrative above, reconsidered whether to name his son Mohammed indicates that he came to understand that he was required to engage with the hegemonic conflation of names such as Mohammed with Muslim masculinity and terrorism. In this sense, the interpellation of subjects through hegemonic discourses produced disciplinary effects in them. While the conflation of the "Arab/ Middle Eastern/Muslim" and "terrorism" brought into play dualistic mechanisms of exclusion (patriot vs. enemy/with us or against us), it simultaneously induced within individuals a state of consciousness that I refer to as "internment of the psyche" (Naber 2006). I use this term to refer to the ways in which engagements with racialization produced a sense of internal incarceration among my research participants that was emotive and manifested in the fear that at any moment one could be harassed, beaten up, picked up, locked up, or disappeared.

Although gender permeated nation-based racism through the conflation of particular names with Muslim masculinity and terrorism, a mapping of nation-based racism onto cultural racism also operated to articulate "Arab/Middle Eastern/Muslim" masculinity as inherently violent toward women. One cab driver told a story of his passengers' reaction to him after they read that his name was Mohammed: "Once, a woman got in my car. She looked at me, then read my name, then asked me if I was Muslim. When I said 'yes' she replied, 'how many girls have you killed today?'" In this case, a form of cultural racism that essentializes Muslimness as if the association between violence against women and Muslim masculinity is natural and insurmountable constitutes the articulation of Muslim masculinity as intrinsically connected to misogynist savagery. The woman's reaction to the cab driver reifies what Moallem refers to as "representations of Islamic fundamentalism in the West" that are "deeply influenced by the general racialization of Muslims in a neo-racist idiom which has its roots in cultural essentialism and a conventional Eurocentric notion of people without history."

Here, "religion" functions like a nature (Balibar 1999, 22) as "Mohammed," like the Osama and Fouad references above, becomes monstrously subversive, a metonymic source of sedition and danger within the nation, as well as to U.S. "interests" and to "American" bodies, white and nonwhite.

Appearances: Unveiling the Terrorist's Daughter

The intersection of race and gender was also apparent in the harassment of women who wore a headscarf. A general consensus among community leaders was that federal government policies disproportionately targeted men while hate crimes and incidents of harassment in the public sphere disproportionately targeted women. As Farah, a Muslim American woman community activist put it, "Women who wear *hijab* were more of a target because they're more visible than Muslim men in public. The awareness that they were in more danger and were more impacted than men could be seen by all of the events that were organized in solidarity with veiled women in response to the backlash. There were days of solidarity organized across the nation." Several cases in which employers fired women from their jobs for wearing headscarves instilled a sense of apprehension about the acceptability of discrimination against Muslim women in the public sphere among several of my research participants. As Manal, a university student explained, "We felt supported, but at the same time, there was a concern for our safety. I had never carried pepper spray. I started carrying pepper spray after 9/11 and was really being mindful of my surroundings. I remember the Muslim Student Association meetings—afterwards everyone would make sure that no one was walking alone to their cars." Several Muslim American community leaders recalled cases in which women debated whether they should remove their scarves. As Amal, another university student put it, "I knew I had to prepare for at least some kind of backlash because I was visually identifiable. My mother, who doesn't cover, specifically told me 'Don't go outside for a month or two. Wait till things die down.' I was like, 'I shouldn't hide. I shouldn't be scared or restrain my lifestyle because of ignorance.'" In this sense, considerations of whether and to what extent one should wear or remove a headscarf or go out in public generated an "internment of the psyche" or the awareness that one must become habitually concerned about hegemonic misinterpretations and mistranslations.

While "Arab Muslim" masculinities were produced as the subjects of discourses that construct their primary and stable identity as violent agents of terrorism and/or misogyny, or the "true" enemy of the nation, "Arab Muslim" femininities, signified by the headscarf, were articulated as extensions of those practices.[24] In several cases, that headscarves signified an identification that transformed particular women into daughters or sisters of terrorists in general, or Osama or Saddam in particular, exemplifies one of the ways in which gender permeated nation-based racism in the context of the "war on terror." Lamia, a community activist summarized what she witnessed through her work among Arab Muslim youth in the Tenderloin, "After September 11, girls who wear *hijab* received lots of harassment on the bus, at school and on the street. People would try and pull their *hijab* off." The following excerpt from a group interview with Iraqi youth elucidates Lamia's point:

> *Maha:* "My sister was coming home from school one day and people were calling her, 'Osama's daughter.'"
>
> *Salma:* "At school, kids take off their shirts and put them on their heads and say, 'We look like Osama's daughter now. We look like you now.' Some kids would come up to us and say, 'Why don't you take it off? Are you still representing Osama?'"

In this narrative, young Arab Muslim girls are constructed as though patriarchal kinship ties are the sole determinants of their identities. Reduced to "daughters of Osama," they are transformed into the "property," "the harmonious extension" (Shohat and Stam 1994) of the enemy of the nation within, or symbols that connect others to the "real actors" or "terrorists" but who do not stand on their own (and lack agency). The "daughter of a terrorist" metaphor also articulates a condemnation of Muslim women for veiling.[25] Reifying the logic of nation-based racism that constructs a binary between us versus them and good, or moral Americans versus bad immoral potential criminal terrorists, Salma's peer not only asks her to "unveil" but also reduces her realm of possibilities to either "taking off her veil" or "representing Osama." For Salma's peer, either she is unveiled/with us, or she is with terrorism. In this sense, the "veil" serves as a boundary marker between "us" and "them," and as long as women remain "veiled" they remain intrinsically connected to "potential terrorists."

Dark-Skinned, Bearded Terrorists, and the "Queery-ing" of "Muslim Masculinities"

Several research participants reported incidents in which beards, coupled with dark skin and in some cases a particular form of religious dress, emerged as signifiers of "Islamic fundamentalism" or "terrorism." Salah Masri, director of one of the largest mosques in San Francisco, explained,

> I know this man who is a peaceful Tunisian Muslim that dresses in white robe with a long beard. He is extremely quiet and polite. He is a good engineer. He is an internet web designer. After September 11, we didn't see him at the *masjid* for a long time. When we asked about him, it turned out he didn't feel comfortable changing his clothes or shaving his beard so he decided to stay home. Some people didn't want to look Muslim. I know people who dyed their hair blond. One of them was a Turkish guy who dyed his hair blond because he thought he looked Arab or Middle Eastern. We had many cases of people shaving their beards or people who stopped attending the mosque. But why dye your hair?! He still looked Middle Eastern with it!

That Salah conflates "looking Muslim" with "looking Arab or Middle Eastern" epitomizes a consensus among many of my research participants that dominant U.S. discourses do not distinguish between "Arabs," "Middle Easterners," or "Muslims" and construct an image of an "Arab/Middle Eastern/Muslim look." Persons who closely resembled the corporate media's "Arab/Middle Eastern/Muslim look" were particularly vulnerable to federal government policies and harassment on the streets.[26] One immigrant-rights lawyer explained that the federal government went after "the CNN version of what a terrorist looks like. He was dark, Middle Eastern, and had a full beard. He was the typical terrorist looking guy—or at least the guy who CNN portrays as the terrorist. Timothy McVeigh is a terrorist, but he is not associated with terrorism because he does not look like the typical terrorist-looking guy." My research indicated that men who had beards, coupled with dark skin, were among those most severely concerned for their safety—particularly if they wore religious forms of dress perceived to be associated with Islam. That non-Muslim South Asian men such as Sikhs who wear turbans were repeatedly misidentified as Muslims (and in some cases killed) points to the ways that a range of signifiers can stand in as symbols of an "Arab/Middle Eastern/ Muslim look." Cases such as these reify dominant U.S. distinctions between those who are with us and those who are with the terrorists by rendering particular kinds of bodies not only as unassimilable or "fundamentally foreign and antipathetic to modern American society and cultures" (Lowe 1996, 5), but also as threatening to national security and therefore legitimate targets of violence and harassment. Moreover, cases in which men considered shaving their beards or avoiding attendance at their mosque illustrate that while dominant discourses on "potential terrorists" often pulled particular bodies into associations with a violent "crazy" Muslim masculinity, they simultaneously produced an "internment of the psyche" that they themselves come to resist, transform, or reproduce.

On the streets, perpetrators of incidents of harassment often deployed sexualized tropes in targeting men whose appearances "fit" the "terrorist profile," reifying what Eman Desouky (2000) refers to as the "queery-ing" of Arab-Muslim subjectivities. Dominant U.S. discourses have often depicted the United States as feminist and gay-safe through comparisons between U.S. and Afghan views on gender and sexuality. Yet, as Puar and Rai explain, "the U.S. state, having experienced a castration and penetration of its capitalist masculinity, offers up narratives of emasculation as appropriate punishment for bin Laden, brown-skinned folks, and men in turbans" (2002, 10). A highly patriarchal and homophobic discourse has been central to the racialization of persons associated with "Islamic fundamentalism" and justifications for violence against them. In one case I learned of, hegemonic conflations between queerness, sexual deviancy, and the monstrous figure of "the terrorist" (2002, 126) underpinned the subjection of particular masculinities to physical or epistemic violence because they "appeared" to be Muslim. Consider the following community activist's narrative:

> A guy from Afghanistan called into the hate-crime hot-line. He had gone to help his friend whose car had broken down when he was doing some off-roading a couple of miles away from his house—which is also near a military base in Dublin. By the time his friend got out there to help him, there were two tow trucks out there. The tow truck drivers called the police because the men had beards so the drivers thought they were terrorists. They were near a reservoir and the tow truck drivers were saying things like, "Oh, okay... they're tapping the water." So they took them to the military base to interrogate them. Fifteen to twenty cops came. They all thought they were trying to contaminate the water. One of the guys had prayer beads with him and officers said quotes like, "your faggot beads. We're going to f____you up; we're going to [give you oral sex]." The officers were intimidating them.

In this narrative, the tow-truck drivers transform the Afghan men into terrorists vis-à-vis assumptions that conflate "the beard" with "Muslim masculinity" and "terrorism." Inscribing hegemonic discourses that "they" are trying to kill/penetrate "us" on the Afghan men's bodies, the tow-truck drivers transform them into terrorist threats/enemies within. Here, patriarchal, homophobic discourses of emasculation mark Islam—represented by the prayer beads—as "faggot," or not quite the right/straight kind of masculinity. The police's speech implicitly positions heterosexuality on the side of good and queerness on the side of evil. Moreover, as the police punish Muslim masculinities (read terrorists) with the threat of sodomy, a logic of militarized patriotism intensifies the normativity of heterosexuality. In this incident, as in the Abu Ghraib prison scandal, homophobia and racism intersect in the conceptualization that sexual degradation and the transformation of Muslim masculinities into "faggots" is an appropriate form of punishment.

Underlying this conceptualization is the heteronormative conflation of shame, humiliation, and homosexuality. Several LGBTST activists of color have produced alternative frameworks for understanding this conflation. Trishala Deb of the Audre Lorde Project argues that we need to ask ourselves what this latest chapter (Abu Ghraib) teaches us about the inevitable homophobia and racism in military culture as well as cultures of militarization (Deb and Mutis 2004, 7). She adds "that there are more than two genders and the subjugation of people who are any of those genders is not closer to femininity [or emasculization] but to dehumanization" (6).[27]

Nation of Origin and the Silencing of Political Dissent

My research indicated that emblems signifying particular nations of origin also placed persons into associations with the "potential terrorist" enemy of the nation. This process was based upon a logic that conflated particular nations with "Arabness," "Islam," and a potentiality for "terrorism." The signifier "nation of origin" often intersected with other emblems signifying the "Arab/Middle Eastern/Muslim" (such as name, skin color, facial hair, or headscarf). In particular, emblems representing "geographies of terror," or the nations that the Bush administration has referred to as terrorist-harboring countries or terrorist training grounds (e.g., Palestine or Iraq), tended to operate as signifiers of the enemy of the nation. Moreover, the potential for encountering harassment was often exacerbated when one was perceived to be an "Arab/Middle Eastern/Muslim" *and* simultaneously expressed solidarity with one or more of these nations. For example, Zainab, a Palestinian woman who wore a *kuffiyah* (a scarf representing Palestinian resistance) on a daily basis and posted a sticker of a Palestinian flag on a window near the front door of her home encountered some of the most severe forms of harassment I learned of throughout the period of my research. Zainab lived in the Mission District of San Francisco. She described her experience as follows: "I walked out [our door] and saw all this graffiti. I didn't know.... Should I be afraid? angry? Then I looked at the sidewalk and saw 'Kill Arabs' in big blocks right in front of our house. The graffiti was all done in black spray paint. On top of the door, it said 'Die pig' in big block letters over where the Palestinian flag is. On the side wall were the words, 'Die pig.'" Afterwards, the perpetrator returned to her home five times. In one incident he threw feces and garbage all over her front door. "Whatever it is that he hits us with," she explained, "you can't leave. You can't open the door and get out, because it's just shit and garbage all over the place."[28]

For Zainab, the "war on terror" took on local form in that her public expression of Palestinian identity and political solidarity with Palestinian people put her in close proximity with the "terrorists." The perpetrator's articulation of violence against Zainab paralleled the Bush administration's rhetoric that violence is essential to patriotism, Americanness, and the protection of national security in the context of the "war on terror." In the ongoing hate crimes that took place in the two-year period following 9/11, vandalism and death threats emerged as critical venues for the articulation of nation-based racism against persons who were perceived to be intrinsically associated with "Islamic fundamentalism" and "terrorism" in the public sphere. Perpetrators deployed tactics "officially" banned by the state that simultaneously supported government discourses on militarized patriotism and war against the enemies of the nation—in this case, Palestinian Arabs.

Acts of harassment and intimidation against Arab and Arab American activists who participated in antiwar and/or Palestine solidarity movements exemplify the ways in which the targeting of activists who were perceived to be Arab/Middle Eastern/Muslim was influenced by an interplay between cultural and nation-based racism. This interplay set the stage for incidents of anti-Arab/Muslim racism coupled with political repression. On one university campus, for example, a series of peaceful demonstrations organized by an active Palestinian students' organization sparked an official university reaction that rendered members of the student group potentially "dangerous." Nadeem, a university student, recalling one of these demonstrations, explained,

> The police set up a barricade around us in the shape of a horseshoe so people would have to walk an extra 150 meters to get into the demonstration and so that they could protect people from us. The cops came, locked all the barricades together with plastic handcuffs and then his group of students stood outside the barricades shouting things like, "Sand nigger, camel jockey, f_____ ing terrorists, get the f_____out of here." Students from our group got upset and were shouting back things like, "F_____you, you know, blah, blah, blah." Later, the university president came out with a letter completely blasting the Palestinian students saying that in his fourteen years at this university, this was the most severe case of "lack of civility" that he has ever seen. A month later, the university imposed sanctions on our group and we were put under probation. We did not receive funding after that for a year.

Similar attacks targeted Arab and Arab American activists on other university campuses in the San Francisco Bay Area. Tamara, recalling an event on another university campus explained, "We were having a memorial for victims of the Israeli massacre of the refugee camp Jenin. Two people came over to disrupt the event. They were saying, 'Go blow yourself up' to a group of Arab American students who were there." This quote further illustrates the ways in which the silencing of political dissent, when directed against Arab student activists, took on specific form that connected them intrinsically to "the terrorists."

The difference between how official public discourses in the local media, among civil rights organizations, and among university officials represented white American and Arab American student involvement in the Palestine solidarity movement illustrates the racial logic underpinning the silencing of political dissent in the context of the "war on terror." In spring 2002, during a period of intense Israeli aggression against Palestinian civilians, two student groups on two different college campuses in the San Francisco Bay Area organized similar demonstrations in support of Palestinian people. The first group was composed of predominantly white students, and the second group was composed primarily of Arab students. The university tried to impose harsh punishments on the first group, including administrative detention and suspension. In this case, various civil rights groups quickly came to the student activists' support and framed the problem as an attack on political dissent on that campus. On the other campus, where the students were predominantly Arab, the same civil rights groups did not lend their support when the university imposed similar restrictions on the student organization. This response reflected a broader official discourse in that both universities and local media reports framed the tensions on the first campus as a free-speech issue while referring to the incidents on the second campus in terms of potentially dangerous Palestinian students. An immigrant-rights lawyer and community activists who worked with the Palestinian student group explained, "It was really easy to see the anti-Arab anti-Muslim sentiment in the university's assumptions that they were fighting the war on terrorism and that Palestinian students were dangerous supporters of terrorism."

In the cases above, nation-based racism was exacerbated in contexts where persons perceived to be "potential terrorists" by virtue of their name, appearance, or nation of origin engaged in public expressions of dissent, particularly against U.S. and/or Israeli policies in Arab homelands. As Tadiar argues, "from the dominant cultural logic of the U.S. state, terrorism embodies an other relation to death, and it is on this basis that racism operates against other peoples who are deemed close to this other relation to death (epitomized by the would be suicide bomber) " (2005). By framing Palestinian students as potentially dangerous and therefore deserving of disciplinary measures, dominant local discourses reified dominant corporate media and government discourses that position Palestinians in close proximity to "real terrorists" and thus legitimize statements such as "get out of here" and "go blow yourselves up." In referring to Palestinian students as "dangerous" and "lacking in civility," the university president reifies racialized representations that construct Palestinians as not only inherently violent, full of hate, and threatening to Israeli and U.S. national security, but also as backward and uncivilized. By justifying the targeting of students in terms of a civilizational discourse (i.e., their "lack of civility"), the university president deploys the logic of cultural racism that defines difference in terms of an "incompatibility of lifestyles and traditions" that are insurmountable. In this sense, a liberal politics of progress, legitimated by cultural racism, naturalizes the distinctions between self and Other, tradition and modernity, barbarism and civilization. Cultural racism and nation-based racism become critical to the structures of power through which the exclusion of particular Arabs and Arab Americans has functioned in a post-9/11 environment.

Conclusion

In the aftermath of September 11, 2001, in response to the backlash, the category "Arab, Muslim, South Asian" has been incorporated into liberal U.S. multicultural discourses. Consider, for example, diversity initiatives that have operated to single out Arabs, Muslims, and South Asians as the *only* "targeted communities" in the post-9/11 moment (Lee 2002). In such instances, terms such as "targeted communities" have reinforced a multicultural rainbow where specific marginalized groups are associated with specific historical moments while occluding the long-term historical circumstances that produce oppression, marginality, and institutionalized racism, and overshadowing links between groups that have shared similar histories of immigrant exclusion and racism. That many liberal immigrant-rights organizations referred to anti-immigrant policies underlying the PATRIOT Act of 2001 as an "Arab, Muslim, and South Asian" issue and the "Border Protection" Bill HR4437 of 2006 as a Latino/a issue—even though both pieces of legislation affected Arabs, Muslims, South Asians, Latinos/as (and other immigrants as well as citizens) and even though the intensified anti-immigrant sentiment sparked by the aftermath of September 11 facilitated support for the HR4437—exemplifies this pattern.

Transgressing liberal multicultural approaches, many racial justice activists and scholars have agreed that while survivors of 9/11-related federal government policies and incidents of harassment in the public sphere tended to be Arab, Muslim, and South Asian, this is not an isolated case of group marginalization.[29] A new racial justice discourse thus emerged that called attention to anti-Arab/Muslim/South Asian racism; insisted that racial justice movements take the link between U.S.-led war in Muslim majority countries and the marginalization of Arabs, Muslims, and South Asians in the United States seriously; and linked the targeting of Arabs, Muslims, and South Asians to experiences of other communities with shared histories of oppression, including, but not limited to, Japanese Americans, Filipinos, Latinos/as, and African Americans. Despite these efforts, prevailing articulations of "race" within U.S. racial and ethnic studies tend to preclude comparative research and teaching on the links between the racialization of Arabs, Muslims, Middle Easterners, and South Asians and other communities that have been historically targeted by racism and state violence.

In the late 1960s, San Francisco State University was the site of the longest campus strike in the nation's history, spearheaded by the Black Students Union and the Third World Liberation Front (a coalition of the Black Students Union, the Latin American Students Organization, the Filipino-American Students Organization, and El Renacimiento, a Mexican American student organization). This movement demanded the expansion of the college's new Black Studies Department (the nation's first), the creation of a School of Ethnic Studies, and increased recruiting and admissions of minority students. On March 21, 1969, this strike officially came to an end with the establishment of the School of Ethnic Studies, which included a focus on Asian Americans, Latinos/as and Native Americans, and an expanded Black Studies Department (San Francisco State Univ. 2003). This movement, based on the strategic deployment of the terms "Third World people" and "people of color," legitimized the establishment and expansion of ethnic studies programs that place communities that have shared histories of oppression by the United States government at the center of study, analysis, activism, and empowerment. Yet this paradigm, which operates according to a 1960s understanding of what constitutes racism, limits our categories of analysis to those established during the height of student movements for ethnic studies in the 1960s. Contemporary articulations of this paradigm foreclose discussions on how the meaning of "race" has continued to shift and preclude analyses of how "racism" is constantly being remade. At the same time, many recent conversations within U.S. racial and ethnic studies have explored how research on emergent forms of racialization in relationship to both previous as well as new and current historical processes might contribute to conceptualizations of race and racism in a post-9/11 environment.[30]

In this chapter I sought to bring new questions to bear on the study of race and racism within U.S. racial and ethnic studies: What are the implications of continually reevaluating our understanding of racialized-gendered identities in light of new and changing historical moments? What are the possibilities for envisioning U.S. racial and ethnic studies in ways that remain connected to the 1960s student and civil rights struggles through which they were produced while becoming more attentive to current gendered racialization processes? How might becoming attentive to the gendered racialization of Arabs, South Asians, and/or Muslims contribute to explorations of the relationship between race, gender, sexuality, and empire or the structures of racism, sexism, and homophobia that operate against immigrants with whose homelands the United States is at war?

This chapter has reinforced existing theoretical approaches that tend to define U.S. race and ethnic studies that contend that "race" is malleable and shifting, that racial categories are socially and historically constructed, and that the construction of racial categories is a continuous process that takes on new and different form within different historical moments. It has also affirmed existing women of color feminist approaches that have called attention to differences within racialized groups (such as those of class, gender, sexuality, and religion) and contended that experiences of oppression that are shaped by both racism and sexism simultaneously cannot be subsumed within either a feminist framework that critiques sexism or an antiracist framework that is only critical of racism (Crenshaw 1991).[31] It has also illustrated that research on the gendered racialization of the "Middle Eastern/ Muslim" or the "Arab/Muslim/South Asian" "enemy within" can generate important new questions, such as: To what extent does the rhetoric of an endless, fluid "war or terror" that "knows no boundaries" produce new forms of gendered racialization that are similarly arbitrary, open-ended, and transgress borders and particular geographic places?

Notes

Parts of this chapter originally appeared in *Cultural Dynamics* 18:235–67. Reproduced with permission from Nadine Naber, "The Rules of Forced Engagement: Race, Gender and the Culture of Fear among Arab Immigrants in San Francisco Post-9/11, Copyright (© Sage Publications, 2006), by permission of Sage Publications Ltd. This research was funded by the Russell Sage Foundation. I am grateful to each and every person who participated in this project. I am indebted to my research assistant Eman Desouky and to the following people for their invaluable feedback and support: Sarita See, Matt Stiffler, Jessi Gan, Lee Ann Wang, Maylei Blackwell, Frances Hasso, and Paola Bachetta.

1. Here I use Akhil Gupta and James Ferguson's term "anthropological locations." They define such "location work" as "an attentiveness to social, cultural, and political *location* and a willingness to work self-consciously at shifting or realigning our own location while building epistemological and political links with other locations" (1997).
2. Here I build upon Andrea Smith's notion of "racial logics." She argues against the assumption that all communities have been impacted by white supremacy in the same way. Instead, white supremacy operates through separate yet still related racial logics. Multiple logics operate depending on the context: "This framework does not assume that racism and white supremacy is enacted in a singular fashion; rather, white supremacy is constituted by separate and distinct, but still interrelated, logics" (2006, 67).
3. See Moallem (2002) for further analysis of discourses on "Islamic fundamentalism." She argues, for example, that discourses on "Islamic fundamentalism ... [reduce] all Muslims to

fundamentalists, and all fundamentalists to fanatical anti-modern traditionalists and terrorists, even as it attributes a culturally aggressive and oppressive nature to all fundamentalist men, and a passive, ignorant, and submissive nature to all fundamentalist women.

4. Here I use Kent Ono's term, "potential terrorists." Ono argues that "potential terrorists" serves as a useful concept to begin to address political and media discourses that produce a creative, if fictional, 'network' or interconnection along racial, gender, national, sexual, political, and ideological lines. Hate crimes, surveillance by the repressive apparatus of the state, and surveillance and disciplining technologies have erected a powerful discursive barrier to full participation in society by those marked as 'potential terrorist'" (2005, 443).
5. The category "Arab/Middle Eastern/Muslim" as a signifier of the "enemy of the nation" was not produced after 9/11 but has permeated government and corporate media discourses for decades. After the attacks of September 11, 2001, the subcategory "South Asian" has been encompassed within dominant U.S. discourses on the "Arab/Middle Eastern/Muslim" enemy (Rana and Rosas 2006; Maira and Shihade 2006). Federal government policies, for example, tended particularly to target Arabs and South Asians, and hate crime incidents following 9/11 throughout the U.S. disproportionately targeted Arabs and South Asians, illustrating that Arabs and South Asians have been similarly associated with "Islamic fundamentalism," "terrorism," and the "enemy of the nation" in the context of the "war on terror." Because my research did not include a focus on South Asian communities, I will focus specifically on how Arab and Arab American research participants were perceived to be associated with the notion of an "Arab/Middle Eastern/Muslim" enemy, even though this term has taken on different form in other contexts.
6. See Moallem (2005), Balibar (1991), and Goldberg (1993).
7. See Stockton (1994), Rana and Rosas (2006), and Moallem (2005) for further analysis of cultural racism and the relationship between anti-Semitism and Islamophobia. Moallem, for example, argues that "this imputation of an intrinsic nature to a cultural or religious system has roots in European race theory, in particular, in the discourse of anti-Semitism" (10).
8. Although the construction of an Arab Muslim Other has permeated dominant U.S. national discourses for decades, it became increasingly pronounced—and expanded in scope—in the aftermath of September 11 (Ono and Sloop 2002, 35). See Abraham (1989), Joseph (1999), Saliba (1999), and Suleiman (1989) for analyses of the history of Arab American marginalization.
9. See Robert Young for further analysis of the concept of "imperialism" (2001, 25–44). Also see Harvey (2003), who maintains that the New Imperialism represents U.S. efforts to resort to military power in the process of controlling the world's oil resources and to ensure continued U.S. dominance in the global arena. Also see Rashid Khalidi, *Resurrecting Empire* for a historical analysis of Western intervention and empire in the Middle East (2004).

10. Here I build upon Tadiar's theorization of racism in the context of the "war on terror." She argues, "from the dominant cultural logic of the U.S. state, terrorism embodies an other relation to death, and it is on this basis that racism operates against other peoples who are deemed close to this other relation to death epitomized by the would be suicide bomber" (2005).
11. I selected organizations that have played key roles in responding to the post–September 11 backlash, attracted the most members, and have the greatest membership size. I also selected organizations that were diverse, focusing on a range of issues that were educational, religious, cultural, and political and serving persons from various generations, socioeconomic class backgrounds, and countries or origin within the Arab world.
12. The lawyers who participated in this research worked on a wide range of issues and projects in solidarity with Arab and Muslim immigrant communities on a day-to-day basis. One lawyer, for example, was the co-chair of the Bay Area Arab American Attorneys Association and served via mayoral appointment on the San Francisco Human Rights Commission. The program director at the San Francisco Bay Area chapter of the National Lawyers Guild also participated in this research and helped to develop a "Know Your Rights" campaign. Several lawyers worked closely with special registration cases. Another lawyer helped organize a project that documented and monitored INS abuses in the city of San Francisco. A lawyer who was appointed as the Human Rights Commissioner of the city of San Francisco and participated in this research also organized a series of hearings where individuals targeted by the post-9/11 backlash narrated and recorded their stories.
13. The differences between Hizballah and al-Qaeda affirm this point. Hizballah is "a political party" and "a powerful actor in Lebanese politics" and "a provider of important social services" (Deeb 2006). According to Deeb, Hizballah's militia arose to battle Israel's occupation of southern Lebanon in 1982–2000 and to advocate for Lebanon's disenfranchised Shi'i Muslim community. Hizballah represents approximately 40 percent of the Lebanese population and has seats in the Lebanese government and a radio and a satellite TV station, as well as various social development programs. There is no international consensus that Hizballah is a terrorist organization, and the European Union does not list Hizballah as a terrorist organization. Al-Qaeda is an international alliance of militant Islamist organizations, a fringe group and, a diffuse movement, comprising individual nonstate actors or small cells operating independently.
14. Cainkar argues: "These measures have included mass arrests, secret and indefinite detentions, prolonged detention of 'material witnesses,' closed hearing and use of secret evidence.... FBI home and work visits, seizures of property, removals of aliens with technical visa violations and mandatory special registration" (2003, 1).
15. Rania Masri argues that "People of color communities comprise 60 percent of the U.S. military's front line: African Americans, Latinos, and, let us not forget, Native American" (2003).

16. I use pseudonyms to protect the confidentiality of research participants.
17. The Tenderloin, where over 70 percent of the residents live in low-income households, is one of San Francisco's most impoverished neighborhoods. It is an urban inner city, densely inhabited, low-income neighborhood with many homeless people and single-resident-occupancy (SRO) hotels. Within San Francisco, the Tenderloin is where the greatest incidents of homicides, aggravated assaults, and drug use take place. Despite these statistics, over 25,000 people live in the Tenderloin. Most Arab Muslims living in the Tenderloin came to the United States from Iraq, Egypt, Tunis, Morocco, and Yemen. While no research exists on the number of Arab Muslims in the Tenderloin neighborhood, community activists agree that there are approximately 100 Yemeni families and over 1,500 Yemeni men who have citizenship or green cards and are in the country supporting their parents, siblings, wives, and/or children who live in Yemen. The majority of Arab Muslims in the Tenderloin are single men who share studio apartments with two to four other single men. In addition to working within the Tenderloin, I also conducted interviews and participant observation among a group of Iraqi refugees who had recently moved out of this neighborhood to Santa Clara, California, where they were granted better housing conditions through the Section 8 Certificate and Housing Program.
18. Lana Salam was the director of legal education and outreach for the American Arab Anti-Discrimination Committee directly after September 11 and played a key role in community education on legal topics relevant to a post-9/11 political landscape. She also organized a legal workshop on FBI questioning among local Arab American communities when the FBI starting questioning thousands of Arab men.
19. Hamza Yusuf is a white American convert to Islam. In some cases, he is referred to as the "Great White Sheikh." See http://www.islamonline.net/english/views/2001/11/article8.shtml.
20. Under Special Registration, the U.S. Immigration and Customs Enforcement established mechanisms to track nonimmigrants who enter the United States each year by interviewing immigrants in person and restricting entry and departure to specially designated ports (see U.S. Immigration and Customs Enforcement 2006).
21. See Rana and Rosas's argument that "'Muslim' has come to represent an ambiguous racial community that encompasses persons perceived to belong to the homogenous, fictional category, 'Arab-Middle Eastern-Muslim;' South Asians (including Christians, Hindus, Muslims and Sikhs), and possibly Latinas/os, and African Americans" (2006).
22. A press release posted on the American Arab Anti-Discrimination Committee website from Congresswoman's Marcy Kaptur's office states: "The FBI reports that the number of anti-Muslim incidents rose 1600% from 2000 to 2001, largely due to post-9/11 backlash" (Kaptur 2003).
23. See Howell and Shryock (2003) for further analysis on the implications of the binary "those who are with us and those who are with terrorists" on Arab American identities and experiences.

24. For further analysis on representations of femininity as extensions of masculinity, "abject beings," or the construction of the feminine as objects that supply the site through which the phallus penetrates, see Butler (1993, 56–60). Also see Tadiar (2002, 5) for a discussion of the ways that women within a colonialist, patriarchal society are not only imprisoned within particular ideals about gender, but also function as useful objects that serve patriarchal, national, and international structures and processes.
25. See Shohat and Stam for an analysis of colonialist discourses on "veiling." Ella Shohat and Robert Stam, in their critique of colonialist Hollywood films write, "The orient is... sexualized through the recurrent figure of the veiled woman, whose mysterious inaccessibility, mirroring that of the orient itself, requires Western unveiling to be understood" (1994, 149).
26. See Shaheen (1984) and Shohat and Stam (1994) for further analysis on the corporate media's representation of an Arab or Muslim "look."
27. Trishala Deb argues that the military police and interrogation officials who oversaw these acts [of torture] might have intended to inflict what they perceived to be worst form of sexual degradation possible—which included what looks like gay sex (Deb and Mutis 2004, 5).
28. With very little assistance from the local police, Zainab and her friend discovered who the perpetrator was by tape recording him in action. She discovered he lived a block away from her home. She continued to face resistance from the local police to put a restraining order on him or assist her with the case.
29. Among the widespread responses to the backlash among civil rights advocates, The New York City Commission of Human Rights published the report "Discrimination Against Muslims, Arabs, and South Asians in New York City since 9/11" (2003). In San Francisco, the organization Grantmakers concerned with Immigrants and Refugees published a report entitled, "Arab, Middle Eastern, Muslim, and South Asian Communities in the San Francisco Bay Area" to "inform the Bay Area foundation community about the most salient issues facing these communities and encourage foundations to support programs and strategies that respond to these issues" (Ahuja, Gupta, and Petsod 2004, 4). The U.S. Equal Employment Opportunity Commission issued a report entitled, "Questions and Answers about Workplace Rights of Muslims, Arabs, South Asians, and Sikhs" (2002). The national antiwar organization Not in Our Name, produced a documentary entitled, "'Under Attack:' Arab, Muslim and South Asian Communities Since 9/11" (2004) and a coalition of over two hundred individuals and organizations supported the first national day of solidarity with Muslim, Arab, and South Asian Immigrants (2002). The aftermath of September 11 also sparked new alliances between Arab American, Muslim American, and South Asian American organizations that joined forces in resisting the post–September 11 backlash against their communities and the expanding U.S.-led war in their homelands (Naber 2002).
30. See Ono (2005), Volpp (2003), and Maira and Shihade (2006).

31. I draw from Kimberlé Crenshaw's work on intersectionality. She argues that women of color often have to choose between participation in an antiracist movement or a feminist movement, yet the experiences of women of color mark intersections that cannot be captured *only* by a gender or race analysis that stand separate from each other. Crenshaw's work on the intersectionality transgresses this limitation by opening up a space for intersectional organizing/resistance (1991).

Works Cited

Abraham, Nabeel. 1989. "Arab-American Marginality: Mythos and Praxis." In *Arab Americans: Continuity and Change,* edited by Baha Abu-Laban and Michael Suleiman, 17–44. Belmont, Mass.: Assoc. of Arab-American Univ. Graduates Press.

Ahuja, Sarita, Pronita Gupta, and Daranee Petsod. 2004. *Arab, Middle Eastern, Muslim and South Asian Communities in the San Francisco Bay Area: An Introduction to Grantmakers.* San Francisco: Asian American/Pacific Islanders in Philanthropy with Grantmakers Concerned with Immigrants and Refugees.

Althusser, Louis. 1971. "Ideology and Ideological State Apparatuses." In *Lenin and Philosophy, and Other Essays,* translated by Ben Brewster, 127–86. New York: Monthly Review Press.

American Arab Anti-Discrimination Committee (ADC). 2003. *Report on Hate Crimes and Discrimination Against Arab Americans: The Post–September 11 Backlash.* Washington, D.C.: ADC.

Ashcroft, John. 2002. *Attorney General Prepared Remarks on the National Security Entry-Exit System.* Washington, D.C., June 6. http://www.usdoj.gov/archive/ag/speeches/2002/060502agprepare-dremarks.htm (Feb. 8, 2007).

Balibar, Etienne. 1991. "Is There a 'Neo-Racism'?" In *Race, Nation, Class: Ambiguous Identities,* edited by Etienne Balibar and Immanuel Wallerstein, 17–28. London: Verso.

Burnham, Linda. 2001. "Introduction." In *Time to Rise,* edited by Linda Burnham, Maylei Blackwell, and Jung Hee Choi, 7–16. Berkeley: Women of Color Resource Center.

Bush, George W. 2005. "The President Discusses War on Terror," Norfolk, Va. Oct. 28. http://www.whitehouse.-gov/news/releases/2005/10/20051028-l.html (Feb. 6, 2007).

Butler, Judith. 1993. *Bodies Matter: On the Discursive Limits of "Sex."* New York: Routledge.

Cainkar, Louise. 2003. "Targeting Muslims, at Ashcroft's Discretion," *Middle East Report Online.* Mar. 14. http://www.merip.org/mero/mero031403.html.

Crenshaw, Kimberlé. 1991. "Mapping the Margins: Intersectionality, Identity Politics, and Violence Against Women of Color." *Stanford Law Review* 43:1241–99.

Deb, Trishala, and Rafael Mutis. 2004. "Smoke and Mirrors: Abu Ghraib and the Myth of Liberation." *Colorlife! Magazine* (Summer). http://www.alp.org/colorlife/index.php (Feb. 6, 2006).

Deeb, Lara. 2006. "Hizballah: A Primer." *Middle East Report Online,* July 31. http://merip.org/mero/mero073106.html.

Desouky, Eman. 2000. *Re-que(e)rying the Queer: Imagining Queer Arab Women Through the Politics of Marginality and the Nation.* Master's thesis, Univ. of California, Santa Cruz.

Fitleberg, Gary. 2002. "Iranian Jews and Muslims Detained in Los Angeles." *The Iranian,* Dec. 20. http://www.iranian.com/Features/2002/December/LA2/index.html (Feb. 6, 2006).

Goldberg, David Theo. 1993. *Racist Culture.* Oxford and Cambridge: Blackwell.

Gupta, Akhil, and James Ferguson. 1997. "Discipline and Practice: 'The Field' as Site, Method, and Location in Anthropology." In *Anthropological Locations: Boundaries and Grounds of a Field Science,* edited by Akhil Gupta and James Ferguson, 1–46. Berkeley: Univ. of California Press.

Hanania, Ray. 2004. *Fighting for the Last Victims of September 11.* http://www.hanania.com/hatevictims.html (Feb. 6, 2006).

Harvey, David. 2003. *The New Imperialism.* Clarendon Lectures in Geography and Environmental Studies. Oxford: Oxford Univ. Press.

Howell, Sally, and Andrew Shryock. 2003. "Cracking Down on Diaspora: Arab Detroit and America's 'War on Terror.'" *Anthropological Quarterly* 76, no. 3:443–62.

Kaptur, Marcy. 2003. "Kaptur Bill Safeguards Civil Liberties for All: H. Res. 234 Seeks to Protect Against Religious, Ethnic Persecution." Press release by Congresswoman Marcy Kaptur (D-Ohio), May 15. http://www.adc.org/index.php?id=1803 (Feb. 8, 2007).

Khalidi, Rashid. 2004. *Resurrecting Empire: Western Footprints and America's Perilous Path in the Middle East.* Boston: Beacon.

Kumar, Amitava. 2000. *Passport Photos.* Berkeley: Univ. of California Press.

Lee, Kien S. 2002. "Building Intergroup Relations after September 11." *Analyses of Social Issues and Public Policy* 2, no. 1:131–41.

Lowe, Lisa. 1996. *Immigrant Acts: On Asian American Cultural Politics.* Durham, N.C.: Duke Univ. Press.

Maira, Sunaina, and Magid Shihade. 2006. "Meeting Asian/Arab American Studies: Thinking Race, Empire, and Zionism in the U.S." *Journal of Asian American Studies* 9, no. 2:117–40.

Masri, Rania. 2003. "Fog of War, Speech Given on April 5, 2003, at the 20th Annual Black Workers for Justice Banquet; Raleigh, N.C." Apr. 5. http://www.zmag.org/content/showarticle.cfm?ItemID=3433 (Feb. 6, 2006).

Moallem, Minoo. 2002. "Whose Fundamentalism?" *Meridians: Feminisms, Race, Transnationalism* 2, no. 2:298–301.

———. 2005. *Between Warrior Brother and Veiled Sister: Islamic Fundamentalism and the Politics of Patriarchy in Iran.* Berkeley: Univ. of California Press.

Naber, Nadine. 2002. "So Our History Doesn't Become Your Future: The Local and Global Politics of Coalition Building Post September 11th." *Journal of Asian American Studies* 5, no. 3:217–42.

———. 2006. "The Rules of Forced Engagement." *Cultural Dynamics* 18, no. 3:235–68.

New York City Commission on Human Rights. 2003. *Discrimination Against Muslims, Arabs, and South Asians in New York City since 9/11*. New York: New York City Commission on Human Rights.

Nir, Ori. 2006. "Bush Riles Muslims With 'Islamic Fascist' Remark." *Jewish Daily Forward,* Aug 18.

Ono, Kent. 2005. "Asian American Studies after 9/11." In *Race, Identity and Representation in Education,* 2d ed., edited by Cameron McCarthy, Warren C. Richlow, Greg Dimitriadis, and Nadine Dolby, 439–51. New York: Routledge.

Ono, Kent A., and John M. Sloop. 2002. *Shifting Borders: Rhetoric, Immigration, and California's Proposition 187*. Philadelphia: Temple Univ. Press.

Puar, Jasbir K., and Amit Rai. 2002. "Monster, Terrorist, Fag: The War on Terrorism and the Production of Docile Patriots." *Social Text* 20, no. 3:117–48.

Rana, Junaid, and Gilberto Rosas. 2006. "Managing Crisis." *Cultural Dynamics* 18, no. 3:219–34.

Revolutionary Worker Online. 2002. *Profiled and Persecuted: How the U.S. Government Is Terrorizing Immigrants from 20 Arab and Muslim Countries.* http://rwor.org/a/v24/1181-1190/1182/immigrants.htm (Feb. 6, 2006).

Said, Edward. 2002. *Reflections on Exile and Other Essays.* Boston: Harvard Univ. Press.

Saliba, Therese. 1999. "Resisting Invisibility: Arab Americans in Academia and Activism." In *Arabs in America: Building a New Future,* edited by Michael Suleiman, 304–19. Philadelphia: Temple Univ. Press.

San Francisco State Univ. 2003. *A History of SF State.* San Francisco: San Francisco State Univ. http://www.sfsu.edu/~100years/history/long.htm (Feb. 8, 2007).

Shaheen, Jack. 1984. *The TV Arab.* Madison: Univ. of Wisconsin Press, Popular Press.

Shohat, Ella, and Robert Siam. 1994. *Unthinking Eurocentrism: Multiculturalism and the Media.* New York: Routledge.

Smith, Andrea. 2006. "Heteropatriarchy and the Three Pillars of White Supremacy: Rethinking Women of Color Organizing." In *Color of Violence: The Incite! Anthology,* 66–73. Cambridge, Mass.: South End Press.

Stockton, Ronald. 1994. "Ethnic Archetype and the Arab Image." In *The Development of Arab American Identity,* edited by Ernest McCarus, 119–53. Ann Arbor: Univ. of Michigan Press.

Suleiman, Michael. 1989. "America and the Arabs: Negative Images and the Feasibility of Dialogue." In *Arab Americans Continuity and Change,* edited by Baha Abu-Laban and Michael Suleiman, 251–72. Washington, D.C.: Arab American Univ. Graduates.

Tadiar, Neferti. 2002. "Filipinas 'Living in a Time of War.'" In *Body Politics: Essays on Cultural Representations of Women's Bodies,* edited by Maria Josephine Barrios and Odine De Guzman, 2–18. Quezon City: Univ. of the Philippines Center for Women's Studies.

———. 2005. Comments made as part of the panel discussion "Race, Geopolitics, and Feminisms." Center for Cultural Studies, Univ. of California, Santa Cruz, May 13.

U.S. Equal Employment Opportunity Commission. 2002. *Questions and Answers about Workplace Rights of Muslims, Arabs, South Asians, and Sikhs.* Washington D.C.: Equal Employment Opportunity Commission.

U.S. Immigration and Customs Enforcement. 2006. "What Is Special Registration?" http://www.ice.gov/pi/specialregistration/archive.htm (Feb. 8, 2007).

Volpp, Leti. 2003. "The Citizen and the Terrorist." In *September 11 in History: A Watershed Moment?* edited by Mary L. Dudziak, 147–62. Durham, N.C.: Duke Univ. Press.

Young, Robert. 2001. *Postcolonialism: An Historical Introduction.* Oxford: Blackwell.

Unit III

Systems of Thought, Practice, and Conflict

Chapter 8

Economies, Class, and Inequality

DISCUSSION QUESTIONS

1. Mauss describes a system of reciprocal exchange in Polynesia. How does this exchange system differ from that described in Enloe's reading? What drives and regulates exchange in Polynesian gift giving? What about in the global sneaker market?
2. In Mauss's account of Polynesian exchange, property retains a spirit of the original owner as it is passed from person to person, and thus, a gift is thought to contain a soul. Do you think the goods described in Enloe's discussion of the global sneaker market have a spirit? If so, how, and how does it affect their exchange? How might the global market operate differently if consumers considered the lives of the original makers of the goods they buy?
3. Can you think of exchange practices in your own cultural context that are similar to the gift exchange described by Mauss? How are they similar? How do they differ?
4. What does the story of Korean women factory workers reveal about the global manufacturing industry and its operation within the global market? What role, if any, do nation-states play in global economic processes?

KEY TERMS

Tonga
Oloa
Hau
Potlatch
Trade agreements
Labor unions

Mauss, Marcel. 2001 [1950]. "The Exchange of Gifts and the Obligation to Reciprocate." In *The Gift*. London: Routledge.

I

'Total Services', 'Maternal[1] Goods' Against 'Masculine Goods'[2] (Samoa)

During this research into the extension of contractual gifts, it seemed for a long time as if potlatch proper did not exist in Polynesia. Polynesian societies in which institutions were most comparable did not appear to go beyond the system of 'total services', permanent contracts between clans pooling their women, men, and children, and their rituals, etc. We then studied in Samoa the remarkable custom of exchanging emblazoned matting between chiefs on the occasion of a marriage, which did not appear to us to go beyond this level.[3] The elements of rivalry, destruction, and combat appeared to be lacking, whereas this was not so in Melanesia. Finally, there were too few facts available. Now we would be less critical about the facts.

First, this system of contractual gifts in Samoa extends far beyond marriage. Such gifts accompany the following events: the birth of a child,[4] circumcision,[5] sickness,[6] a daughter's arrival at puberty,[7] funeral rites,[8] trade.[9]

Next, two essential elements in potlatch proper can be clearly distinguished here: the honour, prestige, and *mana* conferred by wealth;[10] and the absolute obligation to reciprocate these gifts under pain of losing that *mana*, that authority–the talisman and source of wealth that is authority itself.[11]

On the one hand, as Turner tells us:

> After the festivities at a birth, after having received and reciprocated the *oloa* and the *tonga*–in other words, masculine and feminine goods—husband and wife did not emerge any richer than before. But they had the satisfaction of having witnessed what they considered to be a great honour: the masses of property that had been assembled on the occasion of the birth of their son.[12]

On the other hand, these gifts can be obligatory and permanent, with no total counter-service in return except the legal status that entails them. Thus the child whom the sister, and consequently the brother-in-law, who is the maternal uncle, receive from their brother and brother-in-law to bring up, is himself termed a *tonga*, a possession on the mother's side.[13] Now, he is:

> the channel along which possessions that are internal in kind,[14] the *tonga*, continue to flow from the family of the child to that family. Furthermore, the child is the means whereby his parents can obtain possessions of a foreign kind (*oloa*) from the parents who have adopted him, and this occurs throughout the child's lifetime.
>
> This sacrifice [of the natural bonds] facilitates an easy system of exchange of property internal and external to the two kinship sides.

In short, the child, belonging to the mother's side, is the channel through which the goods of the maternal kin are exchanged against those of the paternal kin. It suffices to note that, living with his maternal uncle, the child has plainly the right to live there, and consequently possesses a general right over the latter's possessions. This system of 'fosterage' appears very close to that of the generally acknowledged right of the maternal nephew in Melanesian areas over the possessions of his uncle.[15] Only the theme of rivalry, combat, and destruction is lacking, for there to be potlatch.

Let us, however, note these two terms, *oloa*, and *tonga*, and let us consider particularly the tonga. This designates the permanent paraphernalia, particularly the mats given at marriage,[16] inherited by the daughters of that marriage, and the decorations and talismans that through the wife come into the newly founded family, with an obligation to return them.[17] In short, they are kinds of fixed property—immovable because of their destination. The *oloa*[18]—designate objects, mainly tools, that belong specifically to the husband. These are essentially movable goods. Thus nowadays this term is applied to things passed on by Whites.[19] This is clearly a recent extension of the meaning. We can leave on one side Turner's translation: *oloa* = foreign; *tonga* = native. It is incorrect and insufficient, but not without interest, since it demonstrates that certain goods that are termed *tonga* are more closely linked to the soil,[20] the clan, the family, and the person than certain others that are termed *oloa*.

Yet, if we extend the field of our observation, the notion of *tonga* immediately takes on another dimension. In Maori, Tahitian, Tongan, and Mangarevan (Gambier), it connotes everything that may properly be termed possessions, everything that makes one rich, powerful, and influential, and everything that can be exchanged, and used as an object for compensating others.[21] These are exclusively the precious articles, talismans, emblems, mats, and sacred idols, sometimes even the traditions, cults, and magic rituals. Here we link up with that notion of property-as-talisman, which we are sure is general throughout the Malaysian and Polynesian world, and even throughout the Pacific as a whole.[22]

II

The Spirit of the Thing Given (Maori)

This observation leads us to a very important realization: the *taonga* [sic] are strongly linked to the person, the clan, and the earth, at least in the theory of Maori law and religion. They are the vehicle for its *mana*, its magical, religious, and spiritual force. In a proverb that happily has been recorded by Sir George Grey[23] and C.O. Davis[24] the *taonga* are implored to destroy the individual who has accepted them. Thus they contain within them that force, in cases where the law, particularly the obligation to reciprocate, may fail to be observed.

Our much regretted friend Hertz had perceived the importance of these facts. With his touching disinterestedness he had noted down 'for Davy and Mauss', on the card recording the following fact. Colenso says:[25] 'They had a kind of exchange system, or rather one of giving presents that must ultimately either be reciprocated or given back.' For example, dried fish is exchanged for jellied birds or matting.[26] All these are exchanged between tribes or 'friendly families without any kind of stipulation'.

But Hertz had also noted—and I have found it among his records—a text whose importance had escaped the notice of both of us, for I was equally aware of it.

Concerning the *hau*, the spirit of things, and especially that of the forest and wild fowl it contains, Tamati Ranaipiri, one of the best Maori informants of Elsdon Best, gives us, completely by chance, and entirely without prejudice, the key to the problem.[27]

> I will speak to you about the *hau* ... The *hau* is not the wind that blows—not at all. Let us suppose that you possess a certain article (*taonga*) and that you give me this article. You give it me without setting a price on it.[28] We strike no bargain about it. Now, I give this article to a third person who, after a certain lapse of time, decides to give me something as payment in return (utu).[29] He makes a present to me of something (*taonga*). Now, this *taonga* that he gives me is the spirit (*hau*) of the *taonga* that I had received from you and that I had given to *him*. The *taonga* that I received for these *taonga* (which came from you) must be returned to you. It would not be fair (*tika*) on my part to keep these *taonga* for myself, whether they were desirable (*rawe*) or undesirable (*kino*). I must give them to you because they are a *hau*[30] of the *taonga* that you gave me. If I kept this other *taonga* for myself, serious harm might befall me, even death. This is the nature of the *hau*, the *hau* of personal property, the *hau* of the *taonga*, the *hau* of the forest. *Kati ena* (But enough on this subject).

This text, of capital importance, deserves a few comments. It is purely Maori, permeated by that, as yet, vague theological and juridical spirit of doctrines within the 'house of secrets', but at times astonishingly clear, and presenting only one obscure feature: the intervention of a third person. Yet, in order to understand fully this Maori juridical expert, one need only say:

> The *taonga* and all goods termed strictly personal possess a *hau*, a spiritual power. You give me one of them, and I pass it on to a third party; he gives another to me in turn, because he is impelled to do so by the *hau* my present possesses. I, for my part, am obliged to give you that thing because I must return to you what is in reality the effect of the *hau* of your *taonga*.

When interpreted in this way the idea not only becomes clear, but emerges as one of the key ideas of Maori law. What imposes obligation in the present received and exchanged, is the fact that the thing received is not inactive. Even when it has been abandoned by the giver, it still possesses something of him. Through it the giver has a hold over the beneficiary just as, being its owner, through it he has a hold over the thief.[31] This is because the *taonga* is animated by the *hau* of its forest, its native heath and soil. It is truly 'native':[32] the *hau* follows after anyone possessing the thing.

It not only follows after the first recipient, and even, if the occasion arises, a third person, but after any individual to whom the *taonga* is merely passed on.[33] In reality, it is the *hau* that wishes to return to its birthplace, to the sanctuary of the forest and the clan, and to the owner. The *taonga* or its *hau*—which itself moreover possesses a kind of individuality[34]—is attached to this chain of users until these give back from their own property, their *taonga*, their goods, or from their labour or trading, by way of feasts, festivals and presents, the equivalent or something of even greater value. This in turn will give the donors authority and power over the first donor, who has become the last recipient. This is the key idea that in Samoa and New Zealand seems to dominate the obligatory circulation of wealth, tribute, and gifts.

Such a fact throws light upon two important systems of social phenomena in Polynesia and even outside that area. First, we can grasp the nature of the legal tie that arises through the passing on of a thing. We shall come back presently to this point, when we show how these facts can contribute to a general theory of obligation. For the time being, however, it is clear that in Maori law, the legal tie, a tie occurring through things, is one between souls, because the thing itself possesses a soul, is of the soul. Hence it follows that to make a gift of something to someone is to make a present of some part of oneself. Next, in this way we can better account for the very nature of exchange through gifts, of everything that we call 'total services', and among these, potlatch. In this system of ideas one clearly and logically realizes that one must give back to another person what is really part and parcel of his nature and substance, because to accept something from somebody is to accept some part of his spiritual essence, of his soul. To retain that thing would be dangerous and mortal, not only because it would be against law and morality, but also because that thing coming from the person not only morally, but physically and spiritually, that essence, that food,[35] those goods, whether movable or immovable, those women or those descendants, those rituals or those acts of communion—all exert a magical or religious hold over you. Finally, the thing given is not inactive. Invested with life, often possessing individuality, it seeks to return to what Hertz called its 'place of origin' or to produce, on behalf of the clan and the native soil from which it sprang, an equivalent to replace it.

III

Other Themes: The Obligation to Give, The Obligation to Receive

To understand completely the institution of 'total services' and of potlatch, one has still to discover the explanation of the two other elements that are complementary to the former. The institution of 'total services' does not merely carry with it the obligation to reciprocate presents received. It also supposes two other obligations just as important: the obligation, on the one hand, to give presents, and on the other, to receive them. The complete theory of these three obligations, of these three themes relating to the same complex, would yield a satisfactory basic explanation for this form of contract among Polynesian clans. For the time being we can only sketch out how the subject might be treated.

It is easy to find many facts concerning the obligation to receive. For a clan, a household, a group of people, a guest, have no option but to ask for hospitality,[36] to receive presents, to enter into trading,[37] to contract alliances, through wives or blood kinship. The Dayaks have even developed a whole system of law and morality based upon the duty one has not to fail to share in the meal at which one is present or that one has seen in preparation.[38]

The obligation to give is no less important; a study of it might enable us to understand how people have become exchangers of goods and services. We can only point out a few facts. To refuse to give,[39] to fail to invite, just as to refuse to accept,[40] is tantamount to declaring war; it is to reject the bond of alliance and commonality.[41] Also, one gives because one is compelled to do so, because the recipient possesses some kind of right of property over anything that belongs to the donor.[42] This ownership is expressed and conceived of as a spiritual bond. Thus in Australia the son-in-law who owes all the spoils of the hunt to his parents-in-law may not eat anything in their presence for fear that their mere breath will poison what he consumes.[43] We have seen earlier the rights of this kind that the *taonga* nephew on the female side possesses in Samoa, which are exactly comparable to those of the nephew on the female side (*vasu*) in Fiji.[44]

In all this there is a succession of rights and duties to consume and reciprocate, corresponding to rights and duties to offer and accept. Yet this intricate mingling of symmetrical and contrary rights and duties ceases to appear contradictory if, above all, one grasps that mixture of spiritual ties between things that to some degree appertain to the soul, and individuals, and groups that to some extent treat one another as things.

All these institutions express one fact alone, one social system, one precise state of mind: everything—food, women, children, property, talismans, land, labour services, priestly functions, and ranks—is there for passing on, and for balancing accounts. Everything passes to and fro as if there were a constant exchange of a spiritual matter, including things and men, between clans and individuals, distributed between social ranks, the sexes, and the generations.

IV

Note: The Present Made to Humans, and The Present Made to The Cods

A fourth theme plays a part in this system and moral code relating to presents: it is that of the gift made to men in the sight of the gods and nature. We have not undertaken the general study that would be necessary to bring out its importance. Moreover, the facts we have available do not all relate to those geographical areas to which we have confined ourselves. Finally, the mythological element that we scarcely yet understand is too strong for us to leave it out of account. We shall therefore confine ourselves to a few remarks.

In all societies in Northeast Siberia[45] and among the Eskimos of West Alaska,[46] as with those on the Asian side of the Behring Straits, potlatch[47] produces an effect not only upon men, who vie with one another in generosity, not only upon the things they pass on to one another or consume at it, not only upon the souls of the dead who are present and take part in it, and whose names have been assumed by men, but even upon nature. The exchange of presents between men, the 'namesakes'—the homonyms of the spirits, incite the spirits of the dead, the gods, things, animals, and nature to be 'generous towards them'.[48] The explanation is given that the exchange of gifts produces an abundance of riches. Nelson[49] and Porter[50] have provided us with a good description of these festivals and of their effect on the dead, on wild life, and on the whales and fish that are hunted and caught by the Eskimos. In the kind of language employed by the British trappers they have the expressive titles of 'Asking Festival',[51] or 'Inviting-in Festival'. They normally extend beyond the bounds of the winter villages. This effect upon nature is clearly brought out in one of the recent studies of these Eskimos.[52]

The Asian Eskimos have even invented a kind of contraption, a wheel bedecked with all kinds of provisions borne on a sort of festive mast, itself surmounted by a walrus head. This portion of the mast projects out of the ceremonial tent whose support it forms. Using another wheel, it is manipulated inside the tent and turned in the direction of the sun's movement. The conjunction of all these themes could not be better demonstrated.[53]

It is also evident among the Chukchee[54] and the Koryaka of the far northeast of Siberia. Both carry out the potlatch. But it is the Chukchee of the coast, just like their neighbours, the Yuit, the Asian Eskimos we have just mentioned, who most practise these obligatory and voluntary exchanges of gifts and presents during long drawn-out 'Thanksgiving Ceremonies',[55] thanksgiving rites that occur frequently in winter and that follow one after another in each of the houses. The remains of the banqueting sacrifice are cast into the sea or scattered to the winds; they return to their land of origin, taking with them the wild animals killed during the year, who will return the next year. Jochelson mentions festivals of the same kind among the Koryak, but he has not been present at them, except for the whale festival.[56] Among the latter, the system of sacrifice seems to be very well developed.[57]

Bogoras[58] rightly compares these customs with those of the Russian *Koliada:* children wearing masks go from house to house demanding eggs and flour that one does not dare refuse to give them. We know that this custom is a European one.[59]

The relationships that exist between these contracts and exchanges among humans and those between men and the gods throw light on a whole aspect of the theory of sacrifice. First, they are perfectly understood, particularly in those societies in which, although contractual and economic rituals are practised between men, these men are the masked incarnations, often Shaman priest-sorcerers, possessed by the spirit whose name they bear. In reality, they merely act as representatives of the spirits,[60] because these exchanges and contracts not only bear people and things along in their wake, but also the sacred beings that, to a greater or lesser extent, are associated with them.[61] This is very clearly the case in the Tlingit potlatch, in one of the two kinds of Halda potlatch, and in the Eskimo potlatch.

This evolution was a natural one. One of the first groups of beings with which men had to enter into contract, and who, by definition, were there to make a contract with them, were above all the spirits of both the dead and of the gods. Indeed, it is they who are the true owners of the things and possessions of this world.[62] With them it was most necessary to exchange, and with them it was most dangerous not to exchange. Yet, conversely, it was with them it was easiest and safest to exchange. The purpose of destruction by sacrifice is precisely that it is an act of giving that is necessarily reciprocated. All the forms of potlatch in the American Northwest and in Northeast Asia know this theme of destruction.[63] It is not only in order to display power, wealth, and lack of self-interest that slaves are put to death, precious oils burnt, copper objects cast into the sea, and even the houses of princes set on fire. It is also in order to sacrifice to the spirits and the gods, indistinguishable from their living embodiments, who bear their titles and are their initiates and allies.

Yet already another theme appears that no longer needs this human underpinning, one that may be as ancient as the potlatch itself: it is believed that purchases must be made from the gods, who can set the price of things. Perhaps nowhere is this idea more characteristically expressed than among the Toradja of Celebes Island. Kruyt[64] tells us 'that there the owner must "purchase" from the spirits the right to carry out certain actions on "his" property', which is really theirs. Before cutting "his" wood, before even tilling "his" soil or planting the upright post of "his" house, the gods must be paid. Whereas the idea of purchase even seems very little developed in the civil and commercial usage of the Toradja,[65] on the contrary this idea of purchase from the spirits and the gods is utterly constant.

Malinowski, reporting on forms of exchange that we shall describe shortly, points to acts of the same kind in the Trobriand Islands. An evil spirit, a *tauvau* whose corpse has been found (that of a snake or land crab) may be exorcised by presenting to it one of the *vaygu'a*, a precious object that is both an ornament or talisman and an object of wealth used in the exchanges of the *kula*. This gift has an immediate effect upon the mind of this spirit.[66] Moreover, at the festival of the *mila-mila*,[67] a potlatch to honour the dead, the two kinds of *vaygu'a*, those of the *kula* and those that Malinowski for the first time[68] calls 'permanent' *vaygu'a*, are displayed and offered to the spirits on a platform identical to that of the chief. This makes their spirits benevolent. They carry off to the land of the dead[69] the shades of these precious objects, where they vie with one another in their wealth just as living men do upon returning from a solemn *kula*.[70]

Van Ossenbruggen, who is not only a theorist but also a distinguished observer living on the spot, has noticed another characteristic of these institutions.[71] Gifts to humans and to the gods also serve the purpose of buying peace between them both. In this way evil spirits and, more generally, bad influences, even not personalized, are got rid of. A man's curse allows jealous spirits to enter into you and kill you, and evil influences to act.

Wrongs done to men make a guilty person weak when faced with sinister spirits and things. Van Ossenbruggen particularly interprets in this way the strewing of money along the path of the wedding procession in China, and even the bride-price. This is an interesting suggestion from which a whole series of facts needs to be unravelled.[72]

It is evident that here a start can be made on formulating a theory and history of contract sacrifice. Contract sacrifice supposes institutions of the kind we have described and, conversely, contract sacrifice realizes them to the full, because those gods who give and return gifts are there to give a considerable thing in the place of a small one.

It is perhaps not a result of pure chance that the two solemn formulas of the contract—in Latin, *do ut des*, in Sanskrit, *dadāmi se, dehi me*[73]–also have been preserved in religious texts.

Note on Alms

Later, however, in the evolution of laws and religions, men appear once more, having become again the representatives of the gods and the dead, if they have ever ceased to be. For example, among the Hausa in the Sudan, when the Guinea corn is ripe, fevers may spread. The only way to avoid this fever is to make presents of this grain to the poor.[74] Also among the Hausa (but this time in Tripoli), at the time of the Great Prayer (*Baban Salla*), the children (these customs are Mediterranean and European) visit houses: 'Should I enter?' The reply is: 'O long-eared hare, for a bone, one gets services.' (A poor person is happy to work for the rich.) These gifts to children and the poor are pleasing to the dead.[75] Among the Hausa these customs may be of Moslem origin,[76] both Negro and European at the same time, and Berber also.

In any case here one can see how a theory of alms can develop. Alms are the fruits of a moral notion of the gift and of fortune[77] on the one hand, and of a notion of sacrifice, on the other. Generosity is an obligation, because Nemesis avenges the poor and the gods for the superabundance of happiness and wealth of certain people who should rid themselves of it. This is the ancient morality of the gift, which has become a principle of justice. The gods and the spirits accept that the share of wealth and happiness that has been offered to them and had been hitherto destroyed in useless sacrifices should serve the poor and children.[78] In recounting this we are recounting the history of the moral ideas of the Semites. The Arab *sadaka* originally meant exclusively justice, as did the Hebrew *zedaqa*:[79] it has come to mean alms. We can even date from the Mischnaic era, from the victory of the 'Poor' in Jerusalem, the time when the doctrine of charity and alms was born, which, with Christianity and Islam, spread around the world. It was at this time that the word *zedaqa* changed in meaning, because in the Bible it did not mean alms.

However, let us return to our main subject: the gift, and the obligation to reciprocate. These documents and comments have not merely local ethnographic interest. A comparison can broaden the scope of these facts, deepening their meaning.

The basic elements of the potlatch[80] can therefore be found in Polynesia, even if the institution in its entirety is not to be found there.[81] In any case 'exchange-through-gift' is the rule there. Yet, it would be merely pure scholasticism to dwell on this theme of the law if it were only Maori, or at the most, Polynesian. Let us shift the emphasis of the subject. We can show, at least as regards the *obligation to reciprocate*, that it has a completely different sphere of application. We shall likewise point out the extension of other obligations and prove that this interpretation is valid for several other groups of societies.

Notes

1. The French utérin, strictly speaking, relates to children of the same mother, but not necessarily of the same father. It is translated as 'maternal' and relates to the goods that are passed on to such children, i.e. 'maternal goods'.
2. 'Masculine goods' [biens masculins] relates to goods passed on to children through the father's side.
3. G. Davy (1922) 'Foi jurée', p. 140, has studied these exchanges in connection with marriage, and its relationship to contract. As we shall see, they have a different dimension.
4. Turner, *Nineteen Years in Polynesia*, p. 178; *Samoa*, p. 82 ff; Stair, *Old Samoa*, p. 175.
5. Krämer, *Samoa-Inseln*, vol. 2, pp. 52–63.
6. Stair, *Old Samoa*, p. 180; Turner, *Nineteen Years in Polynesia*, p. 225; *Samoa*, p. 142.
7. Turner, *Nineteen Years in Polynesia*, p. 184; *Samoa*, p. 91.
8. Krämer *Samoa-Inseln*, vol. 2, p. 105; Turner, *Samoa*, p. 142.
9. Krämer, *Samoa-Inseln*, vol. 2, pp. 96, 363. The commercial expedition, the *malaga* (cf. *walaga* in New Guinea) corresponds in fact very closely to the potlatch, which itself is characteristic of the expeditions carried out in the neighbouring Melanesian archipelago. Krämer uses the word *Cegenschenk* ['reciprocating present'] for the exchange of the *oloa* against the *tonga*, which we shall discuss. Moreover, although we must not fall into the exaggerations of British ethnographers of the Rivers and Elliot Smith school, nor into those of American ethnographers who, following Boas, see the whole of the American system of potlatch as a series of borrowings, we should, however, lay much weight on the fact that institutions, so to speak, travel around. This is especially true in this case, where a considerable amount of trade, from island to island and port to port, and over very great distances, from very early times must have served not only the passage of goods, but also the ways in which they were exchanged. Malinowski, in studies that we shall cite later, had a judicious appreciation of this fact. Cf. a study devoted to some of these institutions (Northwest Melanesia), in R. Lenoir (1924) 'Expéditions maritimes en Mélanesie', *Anthropologie*, September.
10. In any case rivalry between Maori clans is mentioned fairly often, particularly in connection with festivities. Cf. S.P. Smith, *Journal of the Polynesian Society* (henceforth, *JPS*), vol. 15, p. 87. (See also pp. 1, 59, n.4).
11. The reason why, in this case, we do not assert that potlatch proper exists, is because the element of usury in the reciprocal service rendered is lacking. However, as we shall see in considering Maori law, the fact that nothing is given in return entails the loss of *mana*, of 'face', as the Chinese say. In Samoa also, in order not to incur the same disadvantage, 'give and give in return' must be observed.

12. Turner, *Nineteen Years in Polynesia,* p. 178; *Samoa,* p. 52. This theme of ruin and honour is a basic one in the potlatch of the American Northwest. Cf. examples in Porter, 'Report...', *Eleventh Census,* p. 334.
13. Turner, *Nineteen Years in Polynesia,* p. 178; *Samoa,* p. 83, calls the young man 'adopted'. He is wrong. The custom is exactly that of 'fosterage', of education being given outside the family of birth; more precisely, this fosterage is a kind of return to the maternal family, since the child is brought up in the family of his father's sister–in reality in the home of his uncle on the mother's side, the sister's husband. It must not be forgotten that Polynesia is a region where there is a dual classification of kinship: maternal and masculine. Cf. our review of Elsdon Best's work, *Maori Nomenclature,* in *Année Sociologique* 7: 420, and Durkheim's observations in 5: 37.
14. Turner, *Nineteen Years in Polynesia,* p. 179; *Samoa,* p. 83.
15. Cf. our observations on *vasu* in Fiji, in 'Procès-verbaux de l'I.F.A', *Anthropologie,* 1921.
16. Krämer, *Samoa-Inseln,* see under: *toga,* vol. 1, p. 482; vol. 2, p. 90.
17. Ibid, vol. 2, p. 296; cf. p. 90 (*toga = Mitgift* ['dowry']); p. 94, exchange of the *oloa* against *toga.*
18. Ibid, vol. 1, p. 477. Violette, *Dictionnaire Samoan-Français,* under *toga,* expresses it well: 'riches of the region consisting of finely woven matting and *oloa,* riches such as houses, boats, cloth, and guns' (p. 194, col. 2); and he refers us back to *oa,* 'riches, possessions', which includes all foreign articles.
19. Turner, *Nineteen Years in Polynesia,* p. 179; cf. p. 186. Tregear, *Maori Comparative Dictionary,* p. 468 (at the word *toga,* given under the heading *taonga*), muddles up the goods that bear this name and those that bear the name *oloa.* This is clearly a slip.

    Rev. Ella, 'Polynesian Native Clothing', *JPS,* vol. 9, p. 165 describes the *ie tonga* ('mats') as follows:

    > They were the main wealth of the natives; formerly they were used as a form of money in exchanges of property, at marriages and on occasions demanding special courtesy. They are often kept in the families as heirlooms (substitute goods), and many of the old *ie* are known and valued very highly as having belonged to some famous family.

    Cf. Turner, *Samoa,* p. 120. All these expressions have their equivalent in Melanesia and North America, and in our own folklore, as we shall see.
20. Kramer, *Samoa-Inseln,* vol. 2, pp. 90, 93.
21. See Tregear, *Maori Comparative Dictionary,* under *taonga:* Tahitian, *tatoa,* 'to give property', *faataoa,* 'to compensate, to give property'; Marquises Islands, see Lesson, *Polynésiens,* vol. 2, p. 232, *taetae;* cf. Radiguet, *Derniers Sauvages, tiau tae-tae,* 'presents given, gifts and goods of their country given in order to obtain foreign goods'. The root of the word is *tahu,* etc.

22. See M. Mauss (1914), 'Origines de la notion de monnaie', *Anthropologie,* ('Procès-verbaux de l'I.F.A.'), in which almost all the facts cited, except those concerning Central Africa and America, relate to this area.
23. G. Gray, *Proverbs,* p. 103 (translation, p. 103).
24. C.O. Davis, *Maori Mementos,* p. 21.
25. In *Transactions of the New Zealand Institute,* vol. 1, p. 354.
26. Theoretically the tribes of New Zealand are divided, by Maori tradition itself, into fishermen, cultivators, and hunters, and are deemed to exchange their products with one another constantly. Cf. Elsdon Best, 'Forest Lore', *Transactions of the New Zealand Institute,* 42: 435.
27. Ibid, Maori text, p. 431, transi, p. 439.
28. The word *hau* designates, as does the Latin *spiritus,* both the wind and the soul–more precisely, at least in certain cases, the soul and the power in inanimate and vegetal things, the word *mana* being reserved for men and spirits. It is applied less frequently to things than in Melanesian.
29. The word *utu* is used for the satisfaction experienced by blood-avengers, for compensations, repayments, responsibility, etc. It also designates the price. It is a complicated notion relating to morality, law, religion, and economics.
30. *He hau.* The whole translation of these two sentences has been shortened by Elsdon Best, whom I am nevertheless following.
31. A large number of facts to illustrate this last point had been gathered by R. Hertz for one of the paragraphs of his translation of *Sin and Expiation.* They demonstrate that the punishment for theft is merely the magical and religious effect of *mana,* the power that the owner retains over the good that has been stolen. Moreover, the good itself, hedged in by taboos and marked with the signs of ownership, is completely charged by these with *hau,* spiritual power. It is this *hau* that avenges the person suffering the theft, which takes possession of the thief, casts a spell upon him, and leads him to death or obliges him to make restitution. These facts are to be found in the book by Hertz, which we shall be publishing, under the paragraphs relating to *hau.*
32. In R. Hertz's work are to be found the documents relating to the *maori* to which we refer here. These *maori* are at the same time talismans, palladiums, and sanctuaries in which dwells the spirit of the clan, *hapu,* its *mana,* and the *hau* of its soil.

    The documents of Elsdon Best concerning this point require comment and discussion, in particular those that relate to the remarkable expressions of *hau whitia* and of *kai hau.* The main passages are in 'Spiritual Concepts', *Journal of the Polynesian Society* 10: 10 (Maori text); and 9: 198. We cannot deal with them as we should, but what follows is our interpretation: '*hau whitia,* averted *hau*', states Elsdon Best, and his translation seems exact. For the sin of theft or that of nonpayment or nonrendering of total counter-services is indeed a perverting of the soul, of *hau*, such as in cases (where it is confused with theft) of the refusal to enter into an exchange or give a present. On the contrary, *kai hau* is badly translated when it is considered as the mere equivalent of *hau whitia*. It does indeed designate 'the act of eating the soul' and is certainly the synonym of *whangai hau:* cf. Tregear, *Maori Comparative Dictionary* (*MCD.*), under the headings of *kai* and *whangai;* but this equivalence is not a simple one. For the typical present is that of food, *kai*, and the word refers to that system of food communion, and to the wrong that persists by remaining unredressed. There is something more: the word *hau* itself comes into the same order *of* ideas: Williams, *Maori Dictionary*, p. 23, under the heading *hau*, states, 'present given as a form of thanks for a present received'.

33. We draw attention also to the remarkable expression *kai-hau-tai*, Tregear, *MCD*, p. 116: 'to give a present of food offered by one tribe to another; "festivity" (South Island)'. The expression means that this present and the festivity returned are really the soul of the first 'service' returning to its point of departure: 'food that is the *hau* of the food'. In these institutions and these ideas are intermingled all sorts of principles between which our European vocabularies, on the contrary, take the greatest care to distinguish.
34. Indeed the *taonga* seem to be endowed with individuality, even beyond the *hau* that is conferred upon them through their relationship with their owner. They bear names. According to the best enumeration (that of Tregear, loc. cit., p. 360, under the heading *pounamu*, extracted from the Colenso manuscripts), they specifically include only the following categories: the *pounamu*, the famous jades, the sacred property of the chiefs and the clans, usually the *tiki*, very rare, very personal, and very well carved; then there are various sorts of mats, one of which, doubtless emblazoned as in Samoa, bears the name *korowai*. (This is the sole Maori word that evokes for us the Samoan word *oloa*, the Maori equivalent of which we have failed to discover.)

    A Maori document gives the name of *taonga* to the *karakia*, the individually named magic formulas that are considered to be personal talismans capable of being passed on: *JPS* 9:126 (transl. p. 133).
35. Elsdon Best, 'Forest Lore', p. 449.
36. Here might be placed the study of the system of facts that the Maoris class under the expressive term of 'scorn of *Tahu*'. The main document relating to this is to be found in Elsdon Best, 'Maori Mythology', in *JPS* 9:113. *Tahu* is the 'emblematic' name for food generally; it is its personification. The expression *Kaua e tokahi ia Tahu*—'do not scorn Tahu' is used for a person who has refused the food that has been put before him. But the study of these beliefs concerning food in Maori areas would carry us far. Suffice it to say that this god, this hypostasis of food, is identical with Rongo, the god of plants and peace. Thus we shall understand better the association of ideas between hospitality, food, communion, peace, exchange, and law.
37. See Elsdon Best, 'Spiritual Concepts', *JPS* 9:198.

38. See Hardeland, *Dayak Wörterbuch*, vol. 1, pp. 190, 397a, under the headings *indjok, irak, pahuni*. The comparative study of these institutions may be extended over the whole area of Malaysian, Indonesian, and Polynesian civilization. The sole difficulty consists in recognizing the institution. Let us give an example. It is under the heading of 'forced trade' that Spenser St John describes how, in the State of Brunei (Borneo), the nobles exacted tribute from the Bisayas by first making them gifts of cloth that were afterwards paid for at an usurious rate over a number of years (*Life in the Forests of the Far East*, vol. 2, p. 42). The error already arose among the civilized Malaysians themselves, who exploited a custom of their less civilized brothers, and no longer understood them. We shall not list all the Indonesian facts of this kind (see elsewhere the review of the study by M. Kruyt, *Koopen in Midden Celebes*).

39. To omit to invite someone to a war dance is a sin, a wrong that in the South Island bears the name of *puha*. See H.T. de Croisilles, 'Short Traditions of the South Island', *JPS* 10: 76 (note: *tahua*, 'gift of food').

    The ritual of Maori hospitality includes: an obligatory invitation that the new arrival cannot refuse, but which he must not request either. He must make his way to the house of his host (who differs according to his caste) without looking about him. His host must have a meal prepared expressly for him, and must be humbly present. Upon leaving, the stranger receives a parting present (Tregear, *Maori Race*, p. 29). Cf. p. 1, the *identical* rites of Hindu hospitality.

40. In reality the two rules blend inextricably together, as do the antithetical and symmetrical services that they prescribe. A proverb expresses this intermingling: Taylor (*Te ika a maui*, p. 132, proverb no. 60) translates it roughly, 'When raw it is seen, when cooked, it is taken'. 'It is better to eat half-cooked food than to wait until the strangers have arrived', when it is cooked and one has to share it with them.

41. Chief Hekemaru (mistake for Maru), according to the legend, refused to accept 'the food' unless he had been seen and greeted by the village to which he was a stranger. If his retinue had passed by unnoticed and messengers had then been sent to request that he and his companions should retrace their steps and share in the eating of food, he would reply that 'the food should not follow after his back'. By this he meant that the food offered to 'the sacred back of his head' (namely, when he had gone beyond the village) would be dangerous for those who gave it to him. Hence the proverb, 'the food will not follow Hekemaru's back' (Tregear, *Maori Race*, p. 79).

42. The Tuhoe tribe commented upon these principles of mythology and law to Elsdon Best ('Maori Mythology', *JPS* 8: 113). 'When a famous chief is to visit the locality, his *mana* precedes him.' The people in the area set out to hunt and fish in order to procure good food. They catch nothing: 'it is because our *mana* who has gone ahead' has made all the animals and fish invisible; 'our *mana* has banished them ... ' etc. (There follows an explanation of the ice and snow, of the *Whai riri* [the sin against water], which keeps the food away from men).

In reality this somewhat obscure commentary describes the state of a territory of a *hapu* of hunters whose members had not done what was necessary in order to receive the chief of another clan. They would have committed a '*kaipapa*, a sin against the food', and thus have destroyed their harvests, their game and fisheries, their own food.

43. Examples: the Arunta, the Unmatjera, and the Kaitish (cf. Spencer and Gillen, *Northern Tribes of Central Australia*, p. 610).
44. On the *vasu* see in particular the old treatise of Williams (1858) *Fiji and the Fijians*, vol. 1, p. 34. See also Steinmetz, *Entwicklung der Strafe*, vol. 2, p. 241 ff. This right of the nephew on the mother's side merely corresponds to the family communism system. But it allows one to gain some idea of other rights, for example, those of relations by marriage and what is generally called 'legal theft'.
45. See Bogoras, *The Chukchee* (Jesup North Pacific Expedition, Memorandum of the American Museum of Natural History), vol. 7, New York. The obligations to be carried out for receiving and reciprocating presents, and for hospitality, are more marked among the Chukchee of the maritime areas than among those living in reindeer country. Cf. *Social Organization* . ..., pp. 634, 637, Cf. the rule for the sacrifice and the slaughter of reindeer. Cf. *Religion* ... , vol. 2, p. 375: the duty to invite, the right of the guest to ask for whatever he wants, and the obligation laid upon him to give a present.
46. The theme of the obligation to give is a profoundly Eskimo one. Cf. our study of the 'Variations saisonnières dans les sociétés eskimo' *Année Sociologique* 9: 121. One of the recent collections of stories of Eskimos published contains stories of this kind that preach generosity. Cf. Hawkes, *The Labrador Eskimos* (Canadian Geological Survey, Anthropological Series), p. 159.
47. We have (in 'Variations saisonnières dans les sociétés eskimo', *Année Sociologique* 9: 121) considered the festivities of the Alaskan Eskimos as a combination of Eskimo elements and of borrowings made from the Indian potlatch proper. But since writing about this, the potlatch, as well as the custom of presents, has been identified as existing among the Chukchee and the Koryak of Siberia, as we shall see. Consequently the borrowing could just as well have been made from these as from the American Indians. Moreover, we must take into account the fine, and plausible hypotheses of Sauvageot (1924) (*Journal des Américanistes*) relating to the Asiatic origin of the Eskimo languages. These hypotheses are confirmed by the very strong ideas of archeologists and anthropologists about the origins of the Eskimos and their civilization. Finally, everything demonstrates that the Eskimos of the west, instead of being rather degenerate as compared with those of the east and the centre, are closer, linguistically and ethnologically, to the source. This seems now to have been proved by Thalbitzer.

    In these conditions one must be more definite and say that potlatch exists among the eastern Eskimos and that it was established among them a very long time ago. However, there remain the totems and masks, which are somewhat peculiar to such festivals in the west, and a certain number of which are of Indian origin. Finally, the explanation is fairly unsatisfactory as accounting for the disappearance of the Eskimo potlatch from the east and centre of the American Arctic, unless it is explicable through the diminution in eastern Eskimo societies.

48. Hall, *Life with the Esquimaux,* vol. 2, p. 320. It is extremely remarkable that this expression has been given to us, not through observations made of the Alaskan potlatch, but as relating to the Eskimos of the centre, who only hold winter festivals for communistic activities and the exchange of presents. This demonstrates that the idea goes beyond the bounds of the institution of potlatch proper.
49. Nelson, 'Eskimos about Behring Straits', *Seventeenth Annual Report,* Bureau of American Ethnology, p. 303 ff.
50. Porter, *Alaskan Eleventh Census,* pp. 138, 141; and, especially, Wrangell, *Statische Ergebnisse* ..., p. 132.
51. Nelson. Cf. 'asking stick' [sic] in Hawkes, *The Inviting-in Feast of the Alaskan Eskimos,* Geological Survey: Memoir 45, Anthropological Series 2, p. 7.
52. Hawkes, loc. cit, pp. 3, 7, 9 gives a description of one of these festivals, that of Unalaklit versus Malemiut. One of the most characteristic features of this collection is the comic series of 'total services' on the first day and the presents that they entail. The tribe that succeeds in making the other one laugh can ask from it what it likes. The best dancers receive valuable presents (pp. 12–14). It is a very clear and extremely rare example of ritual representations (I know of no other examples save in Australia and America) of a theme which, on the contrary, is very frequent in mythology: that of the jealous spirit who, when he laughs, lets go of the thing that he is holding.

    The rite of the 'Inviting-in festival' ends, moreover, by a visit from the *angekok (shamane)* to the inua, the spirit-men whose mask he wears, and who indicate to him that they have enjoyed the dances and will send him some game. Cf. the present made to the seals. Jennes (1922) 'Life of the Copper Eskimos', *Report of the Canadian Arctic Expedition,* vol. 12, p. 178, n. 2.

    The other themes of the law of gifts are also very well developed. For example, the *näsnuk* chief has not the right to refuse any present, or dish presented, however rare it may be, under pain of being disgraced for ever. Hawkes, ibid, p. 9.

    Hawkes is perfectly correct in considering (p. 19) that the festival of the Dene (Anvik) described by Chapman (1907) (*Congrès des Américanisles de Québec,* vol. 2) is a borrowing by the Indians from the Eskimos.
53. See figure in Bogoras, *The Chukchee,* vol. 7 (2): 403.
54. Bogoras, ibid, pp. 399–401.
55. Jochelson, 'The Koryak', Jesup North Pacific Expedition, vol. 6, p. 64.
56. Ibid, p. 90.
57. See p. 38, 'This for Thee'.

58. Bogoras, *The Chukchee*, p. 400.
59. On customs of this kind, see Frazer, *Golden Bough*, 8th edn, vol. 3, pp. 78–85, 91 ff.; vol. 10, p. 169 ff; vol. 5, pp. 1, 161.
60. On the Tlingit potlatch, see, pp. 38 and 41. This characteristic is basic to all the potlatches in the American Northwest. It is, however, hardly apparent because the ritual is too totem-like for its effect upon nature to be very marked, on top of its effect upon the spirits. In the Behring Straits area, particularly in the potlatch between the Chukchee and the Eskimos on St Lawrence Island, it is much more apparent.
61. See Bogoras, *Chuckchee Mythology*, p. 14, line 2 ff. for a potlatch myth. A dialogue is begun between two Shamans: 'What will you answer?' namely 'give as return present'. This dialogue finishes in a wrestling match. Then the two Shamans make a contract with each other. They exchange with each other their magic knife and their magic necklace, and their spirit (these attend upon magic), and finally their body (p. 15, line 2). But they are not perfectly successful in making their flights and landings. This is because they have forgotten to exchange their bracelets and their tassels, 'my guide in motion' (p. 16, line 10). In the end they succeed in performing their tricks. It can be seen that all these things have the same spiritual value as the spirit itself, and are spirits.
62. See Jochelson, 'Koryak Religion', Jesup North Pacific Expedition, vol. 6, p. 30, A Kwakiutl chant of the dance of the spirits (the Shamanism of the winter ceremonies) comments upon the theme:

    You send us everything from the other world, O spirits, you who take away from men their senses.
    You have heard that we were hungry, O spirits . . .
    We shall receive much from you, etc . . .

    See: Boas, *Secret Societies and Social Organization of the Kwakiutl Indians*, p. 483.
63. Davy, 'Foi jurée', p. 224, ff. See also p. 37.
64. *Koopen in midden Celebes*, Mededelingen der Koninglijke Akademie van Wetenschaapen, Afdeeling Letterkunde, 56; series B, no. 5, pp. 158, 159, 163–8.
65. Ibid, pp. 3, 5 of the extract.
66. Malinowski, *Argonauts of the Western Pacific*, p. 511.
67. Ibid, pp. 72, 184.
68. P. 512 (those who are not the objects of obligatory exchange). See Baloma (1917) 'Spirits of the *Dead'*, *Journal of the Royal Anthropological Institute*.
69. A Maori myth, that of Te Kanava. Grey, *Polyn. Myth*, p. 213, tells how the spirits, the fairies, took on the shade of the *pounamu* (jades, etc.), alias *taonga*, laid out in their honour. Wyatt

Gill, *Myths and Songs from the South Pacific*, p. 257 recounts an exactly identical myth from Mangaia, which tells the same story about necklaces made of discs of red mother-of-pearl, and how they won favour with the beautiful Manapa.

70. P. 513. Malinowski (*Argonauts of the Western Pacific*, p. 510 ff.) somewhat exaggerates the novelty of these facts, which are exactly identical to those of the Tlingit and Haïda potlatches.
71. 'Het primitieve denken, voorn. in Pokkengebruiken', *Bijdr. tot de Taal-, Land–en Volksdenken v. Nederl, Indië*, vol. 71, pp. 245, 246.
72. Crawley, *Mystic Rose*, p. 386, has already launched a hypothesis of this kind and Westermarck has taken up the question and is beginning to prove it. See especially, *History of Human Marriage*, 2nd edn, vol. 1, p. 394 ff. But he did not see clearly its purport through not having identified the system of total services and the more developed system of potlatch in which all the exchanges, and particularly the exchange of women and marriage, are only one of the parts. Concerning the fertility in marriage ensured by gifts made to the two spouses, see Ch. 3, n. 112, p. 152.
73. Vâjasaneyisamhita. See Hubert and Mauss, 'Essai sur le sacrifice', *Année Sociologique* 2: 105.
74. Tremearne (1913) *Haussa Superstitions and Customs*, p. 55.
75. Tremearne (1915) *The Ban of the Bori*, p. 239.
76. Robertson Smith, *Religion of the Semites*, p. 283. 'The poor are the guests of God.'
77. The Betsimisaraka of Madagascar tell of two chiefs, one of whom gave away everything that he possessed, while the other gave away nothing and kept everything for himself. God gave good fortune to the one who was generous, and ruined the miser (Grandidier, *Ethnographie de Madagascar*, vol. 2, p. 67.
78. On notions concerning alms, generosity, and liberality, see the collection of facts gathered by Westermarck, *Origin and Development of Moral Ideas*, vol. 1, chapter 23.
79. Concerning the value still attached at the present day to the magic of the *sadqâa*, see below.
80. We have not been able to carry out the task of re-reading an entire literature. There are questions that can only be posed after the research is over. Yet we do not doubt that by reconstituting the systems made up of unconnected facts given us by ethnographers, we would still find other important vestiges of the potlatch in Polynesia. For example, the festivals concerning the exhibiting of food, *hakari*, in Polynesia (see Tregear, *Maori Race*, p. 113) consist of exactly the same displays, the same heaps of food piled up one on another, the same distribution of food, as the *hakarai*, the same festivals with identical names among the Koita Melanesians. See Seligmann, *The Melanesians*, pp. 141–5, and *passim*. On the *hakari*, see also Taylor, *Te ika a Maoui*, p. 13; Yeats (1835) *An Account of New Zealand*, p. 139; Tregear, *Maori Comparative Dictionary*, under *hakari*. A myth in Grey, *Polyn. Myth*, p. 213 (1855 edn), and p. 189 (Routledge's popular edn), which describes the *hakari* of Maru, the god of war, in which the solemn designation of the recipients is absolutely identical to that in the festivals of New

Caledonia, Fiji, and New Guinea. Below is also a speech constituting an *uma taonga (taonga* 'oven'), for a *hikairo* (food distribution), preserved in a song (given in Sir E. Grey (1835) *Ko nga Moteata: Mythology and Traditions in New Zealand,* p. 132), in so far as I am able to translate it (second verse):

> Give me on this side my *taonga,*
> Give me my *taonga,* so that I may heap them up,
> That I may place them in a heap pointing towards land,
> And in a heap pointing towards the sea,
> Etc.... towards the east...
> Give me my *taonga.*

The first verse doubtless refers to stone *taonga. We* can see just how much the very notion of the *taonga* is inherent in the ritual of the festival of food. See Percy Smith, 'Wars of the Northern against the Southern Tribes', *JPS* 8:156 (the *hakari* of Te Toko).

81. Even assuming that the institution is not found in present-day Polynesian societies, it may well have existed in civilizations and societies that the immigration by Polynesians has absorbed or replaced, and it may well also be that the Polynesians had it before their migration. Indeed there is a reason for its having disappeared from part of this area. It is because the clans have definitively become hierarchized in almost all the islands and have even been concentrated around a monarchy. Thus there is missing one of the main conditions for the potlatch, namely the instability of a hierarchy that rivalry between chiefs has precisely the aim of temporarily stabilizing. Likewise, if we find more traces (perhaps of secondary origin) among the Maori than in any other island, it is precisely because chieftainship had been reconstituted there, and isolated clans had become rivals.

    For the destruction of wealth on Melanesian or American lines in Samoa, see Krämer, *Samoa-Inseln,* vol. l, p. 375. (See Index, under *ifoga.*) The Maori *muru,* the destructions of goods because of misdoing, may also be studied from this viewpoint. In Madagascar, the relations between the *Lohateny,* who should trade with one another, who may insult one another, and wreak havoc among themselves, are likewise vestiges of the ancient potlatches. See Grandidier, *Ethnographie de Madagascar,* vol. 2, p. 131 and n.; pp. 132–3. See also p. 155.

Enloe, Cynthia. 2004. "The Globetrotting Sneaker." In *The Curious Feminist: Searching for Women in a New Age of Empire*. Berkeley: University of California Press.

FOUR YEARS AFTER THE FALL OF the Berlin Wall marked the end of the Cold War, Reebok, one of the fastest-growing companies in recent United States history, decided that the time had come to make its mark in Russia. Thus it was with considerable fanfare that Reebok's executives opened their first store in downtown Moscow in July 1993. A week after the grand opening, store managers described sales as well above expectations.

Reebok's opening in Moscow was the perfect post–Cold War scenario: commercial rivalry replacing military posturing, consumerist tastes homogenizing heretofore hostile peoples, capital and managerial expertise flowing freely across newly porous state borders. Russians suddenly had the freedom to spend money on U.S. cultural icons like athletic footwear, items priced above and beyond daily subsistence: at the end of 1993 the average Russian earned the equivalent of $40 a month. Shoes on display were in the $100 range. Almost 60 percent of Russia's single parents, most of whom were women, were living in poverty. Yet in Moscow and Kiev, shoe promoters had begun targeting children, persuading them to pressure their mothers to spend money on stylish Western sneakers. And as far as strategy goes, athletic shoe giants have, you might say, a good track record. In the United States many inner-city boys who see basketball as a "ticket out of the ghetto" have become convinced that certain brand-name shoes will give them an edge.

But no matter where sneakers are bought or sold, the potency of their advertising imagery has made it easy to ignore this mundane fact: Shaquille O'Neal's Reeboks are stitched by someone; Michael Jordan's Nikes are stitched by someone—so are your roommate's, so are your grandmother's. Those someones are women, mostly Asian women who are supposed to believe that their "opportunity" to make sneakers for U.S. companies is a sign of their country's progress— just as a Russian woman's chance to spend two months' salary on a pair of shoes for her child allegedly symbolizes the new Russia.

As the global economy expands, sneaker executives are looking to pay women workers less and less, even though the shoes that they produce are capturing an ever-growing share of the footwear market. By the end of 1993 sales in the United States alone had reached $11.6 billion. Nike, the largest supplier of athletic footwear in the world, posted a record $298 million profit for 1993—earnings that had nearly tripled in five years. And still today sneaker companies continue to refine their strategies for "global competitiveness"—hiring supposedly docile women to make their shoes, changing designs as quickly as we fickle customers change our tastes, and shifting factories from country to country as trade barriers rise and fall.

The logic of it all is really quite simple; yet trade agreements such as the North American Free Trade Agreement (NAFTA) and the World Trade Organization (WTO) are often talked about in a jargon that alienates us, as if they were technical matters fit only for economists and diplomats. The bottom line is that all companies operating overseas depend on trade agreements made between their own governments and the regimes ruling the countries in which they want to make or sell their products. Korean, Indonesian, and other women workers around the world know this better than anyone. They are tackling trade politics because they have learned from hard experience that the trade deals their governments sign do little to improve the lives of workers. Guarantees of fair, healthy labor practices, of the rights to speak freely and to organize independently, will usually be left out of trade pacts—and women will suffer. The 1990s passage of both NAFTA and WTO ensured that a growing number of private companies would now be competing across borders without restriction. The result? Big business would step up efforts to pit working women in industrialized countries against much lower-paid working women in "developing" countries, perpetuating the misleading notion that they are inevitable rivals with each other in the global job market.

All the "New World Order" really means to corporate giants like athletic shoemakers is that they now have the green light to accelerate long-standing industry practices. In the early 1980s the field marshals commanding Reebok and Nike, which are both now U.S.-based, decided to manufacture most of their sneakers in South Korea and Taiwan, hiring local women. L.A. Gear, Adidas, Fila, and Asics quickly followed their lead. In a short time, the coastal city of Pusan, South Korea, became the "sneaker capital of the world." Between 1982 and 1989 the United States lost 58,500 footwear manufacturing jobs to cities like Pusan, which attracted sneaker executives because its location facilitated international transport. More to the point, in the 1960s to mid-1980s South Korea's government was a military government, and, as such, it had an interest in suppressing labor organizing. This same military government also had a comfortable military alliance with the United States government. Korean women at the time seemed accepting of Confucian philosophy, which measured a woman's morality by her willingness to work hard for her family's well-being and to acquiesce to her father's and husband's dictates. Their acceptance of Confucian values, when combined with their sense of patriotic duty, seemed to make South Korean women the ideal labor force for modern export-oriented factories.

U.S. and European sneaker company executives were also attracted by the ready supply of eager Korean male entrepreneurs with whom they could make profitable arrangements. This fact was central to Nike's strategy in particular. When they moved their production sites to Asia to lower labor costs, the executives of the Oregon-based company decided to reduce their corporate responsibilities further. Instead of owning factories outright, a more efficient strategy, Nike executives decided, would be to subcontract the manufacturing to wholly foreign-owned—in this case, South Korean—companies. The new American managerial attitude was: Let Korean male managers be responsible for workers' health and safety. Let them negotiate with newly emergent unions. Nike officials, safely ensconced in their Oregon offices, would retain control over those parts of sneaker production that gave them the greatest professional satisfaction and the ultimate word on the product: design and marketing. Although Nike was following in the historic footsteps of garment and textile manufacturers, it set the trend for the rest of the athletic footwear industry.

At the same time, nevertheless, women workers were developing their own strategies. As the South Korean pro-democracy movement grew throughout the 1980s, increasing numbers of women rejected traditional notions of feminine duty. Women began organizing in response to the dangerous working conditions, daily humiliations, and low pay built into their work. Such resistance was profoundly threatening to the government, since South Korea's emergence as an industrialized "tiger" had depended on women accepting their feminized role in growing industries like sneaker manufacture. If women reimagined their lives as daughters, as wives, as workers, as citizens, it wouldn't just rattle their Korean employers and those men's foreign corporate clients; it would shake the very foundations of the whole political system. At the first sign of trouble, factory managers called in government riot police to break up employees' meetings. Troops sexually assaulted women workers, stripping, fondling, and raping them "as a control mechanism for suppressing women's engagement in the labor movement," reported Jeong-Lim Nam of Hyosung Women's University in Taegu.[1] The heavy-handed coercion didn't work. It didn't work because the feminist activists in groups like the Korean Women Workers Association (KWWA) helped women factory workers understand and deal with the assaults. The KWWA held consciousness-raising sessions in which notions of feminine duty and respectability were tackled along with wages and benefits. They organized independently of Korea's male-led labor unions to ensure that women's issues would be taken seriously, both in labor negotiations and in the pro-democracy movement as a whole.

The result was that women were at meetings with management, making sure that in addition to issues such as long hours and low pay, sexual assault at the hands of managers and women workers' health care were on the table. Their activism paid off: not only did they win the right to organize women's unions, but their earnings grew. In 1980 South Korean women in manufacturing jobs earned 45 percent of the wages of their male counterparts; by 1990 they were earning more than 50 percent. Modest though it was, the pay increase represented concrete progress, given that the gap between women's and men's manufacturing wages in Japan, Singapore, and Sri Lanka actually widened during the 1980s. Last but certainly not least, women's organizing was credited with playing a major role in toppling South Korea's military regime and forcing open elections in 1987.

Having lost that special kind of workplace control that only an authoritarian government could offer, American and European sneaker executives knew that it was time to move. In Nike's case, its famous advertising slogan—"Just Do It"—proved truer to its corporate philosophy than its women's "empowerment" ad campaign, designed to rally women's athletic (and consumer) spirit. In response to South Korean women workers' newfound activist self-confidence, the sneaker company and its subcontractors began shutting down a number of their South Korean factories in the late 1980s and early 1990s. After bargaining with government officials in nearby China and Indonesia, many Nike subcontractors set up new sneaker factories in those countries, while some went to Thailand. In the 1990s China's government remained only nominally communist; in Indonesia the country's ruling generals were only toppled in the late 1990s. The regimes were authoritarian regimes. Both shared the belief that if women can be kept hard at work, low-paid, and unorganized they can serve as a magnet for foreign investors. Each of these regime attributes proved very appealing to American and European sneaker company executives as they weighed where next to set up their factories.

Where does all this leave South Korean women—or any woman who is threatened with a factory closure if she demands the right to organize, decent working conditions, and a fair wage? They face the dilemma confronted by thousands of women from dozens of countries. The risk of job loss is especially acute for women working in relatively mobile industries; it is easier for a sneaker, garment, or electronics manufacturer to pick up and move the factory than it is for an automaker or a steel producer. In the case of South Korea, poor women had moved from rural villages into the cities in the 1960s searching for jobs to support not only themselves, but parents and siblings. The late 1980s exodus of sneaker-manufacturing jobs forced more women into the growing "entertainment" industry. The kinds of bars and massage parlors offering sexual services that mushroomed around U.S. military bases during the Cold War now opened up across the country.

Yet despite facing this dilemma, many women throughout Asia are organizing, knowing full well the risks involved. Theirs is a long-term view; they are taking direct aim at companies' nomadic advantage by building links among workers in countries targeted for "development" by multinational corporations. Through sustained grassroots efforts, women are developing the skills and confidence that will make it increasingly difficult to keep their labor cheap. Many looked to the United Nations conference on women in Beijing, China, in September 1995, as a rare opportunity to expand their cross-border strategizing.

The UN's Beijing conference also provided an important opportunity to call world attention to the hypocrisy of the governments and corporations doing business in China. Numerous athletic shoe companies had followed Nike in setting up factories in China, factories in which workers' independent organizing is suppressed. They included Reebok—a company claiming its share of responsibility for ridding the world of "injustice, poverty, and other ills that gnaw away at the social fabric," according to a statement of corporate principles.

Since 1988, Reebok has been giving out annual human rights awards to pro-democracy dissidents from around the world. But it was not until 1992 that the company adopted its own "human rights production standards"—after labor advocates made it known that the quality of life in factories run by its Korean, Taiwanese, and Hong Kong Chinese male subcontractors was just as dismal as that at most other athletic shoe suppliers in Asia. Reebok's code of conduct, for example, includes a pledge to "seek" those subcontractors who respect workers' rights to organize. The only problem is that independent trade unions are banned in China. Reebok has chosen to ignore that fact, even though Chinese dissidents have been the recipients of the company's own human rights award. As for working conditions, Reebok says it sends its own inspectors to production sites a couple of times a year. But they have easily "missed" what subcontractors are trying to hide—like 400 young women workers locked at night into an overcrowded dormitory near a Reebok-contracted factory in the town of Zhuhai, as reported in August 1994 in the *Asian Wall Street Journal Weekly.*

. . .

Nike's cofounder and CEO Philip Knight has said that he would like the world to think of Nike as "a company with a soul that recognizes the value of human beings." Nike, like Reebok, says it sends in inspectors from time to time to check up on work conditions at its factories; in Indonesia, those factories are run largely by South Korean subcontractors. But according to Donald Katz in a recent book on the company, Nike spokesman Dave Taylor told an in-house newsletter that the factories are "[the subcontractors'] business to run."[2] For the most part, the company relies on regular reports from subcontractors regarding its "Memorandum of Understanding," which managers must sign, promising to impose "local government standards" for wages, working conditions, treatment of workers, and benefits.

By April 1995 the minimum wage in the Indonesian capital of Jakarta was expected to be $1.89 *a day*— among the highest in a country where the minimum wage still varies by region. And managers were required to pay only 75 percent of the wage directly; the remainder could be withheld for "benefits." Nike has a well-honed response to growing criticism of its low-cost labor strategy. Such wages should not be seen as exploitative, says Nike, but rather as the first rung on the ladder of economic opportunity that Nike has extended to workers with few options. Otherwise, they would be out "harvesting coconut meat in the tropical sun," wrote Nike spokesman Dusty Kidd in a 1994 letter to the *Utne Reader.* The corporate executives' "all-is-relative" response craftily shifts attention away from a grittier political reality: Nike didn't move to Indonesia in the 1980s to help Indonesians; it moved to ensure that, despite some Asian women workers' success in organizing, its profit margin would continue to grow. And that is more likely to happen in a country where "local standards" for wages rarely take a worker over the poverty line. A 1991 survey by the International Labor Organization (ILO) found that 88 percent of women working at the Jakarta minimum wage at the time— slightly less than a dollar a day—were malnourished.

A woman named Riyanti might have been among the workers surveyed by the ILO. Interviewed by the *Boston Globe* in 1991, she told the reporter who had asked about her long hours and low pay: "I'm happy working here. ... I can make money and I can make friends."[3] But in fact, the reporter discovered that Riyanti had already joined her coworkers in two strikes, the first to force one of Nike's Korean subcontractors to accept a new women's union and the second to compel managers to pay at least the government's legal minimum wage. That Riyanti appeared less than forthcoming in talking to the American reporter about her activities isn't surprising. During the early 1990s, when Indonesia's government was dominated by military officers, many Indonesian factories had military men posted in their front offices, men who found no fault with managers who taped women's mouths shut to keep them from talking among themselves. They and their superiors had a political reach that extended far beyond the barracks. By 1998 Indonesia had all the makings for a political explosion, especially since the gap between rich and poor was widening into a chasm. It was in this setting that the government tried to crack down on any independent labor organizing—a policy that Nike profited from and indirectly helped to implement. Referring to an employees' strike in a Nike-contracted factory, Tony Nava, Nike representative in Indonesia, told the *Chicago Tribune* in November 1994 that the "troublemakers" had been fired. When asked by the same reporter about Nike policy on the issue, spokesman Keith Peters struck a conciliatory note: "If the government were to allow and encourage independent labor organizing, we would be happy to support it."[4]

Indonesian workers' efforts to create unions independent of governmental control were a surprise to shoe companies. Although their moves from South Korea were immensely profitable (see chart, page 54), the corporate executives do not have the sort of immunity from activism that they had expected. In May 1993 the murder of a female labor activist outside Surabaya set off a storm of local and international protest. Even the U.S. State Department was forced to take note in its 1993 worldwide human rights report, describing an Indonesian system of labor repression under then-military rule similar to that which generated South Korea's boom twenty years earlier: severely restricted union organizing, security forces used to break up strikes, low wages for men, lower wages for women—complete with government rhetoric celebrating women's contribution to national development.

Yet when President Bill Clinton visited Indonesia in November 1994, he made only a token effort to address the country's human rights problem. Instead, he touted the benefits of free trade, sounding indeed more enlightened, more in tune with the spirit of the post—Cold War era than do those defenders of protectionist trading policies who coat their rhetoric with "America first" chauvinism. But "free trade" as it is actually being practiced today is hardly *free* for any workers—in the United States or abroad—who have to accept the American corporate-fostered Indonesian, Chinese, or Korean workplace model as the price of keeping their jobs.

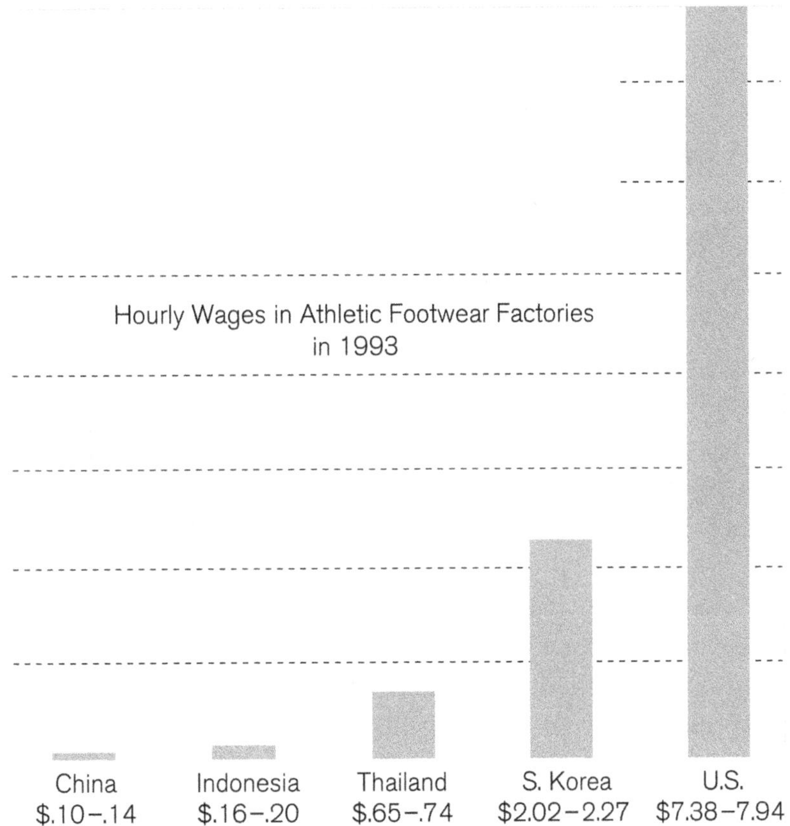

Figures are estimates based on 1993 data from the International Textile, Garment, and Leather Workers Federation; International Labor Organization; and the U.S. Bureau of Labor Statistics.

The not-so-new plot of the international trade story has been "divide and rule." If women workers and their government in one country can see that a sneaker company will pick up and leave if their labor demands prove more costly than those in a neighboring country, then women workers will tend to see their neighbors not as regional sisters, but as competitors who can "steal" their precarious livelihoods. Playing women off against each other is, of course, old hat. Yet the promotion of women-versus-women distrust remains as essential to international trade policies as the fine print in WTO agreements.

What do these young Chinese women factory workers think about "the politics of daughterhood"? Reacting in part to Indonesia's late 1990s pro-democracy movement, which mobilized thousands of Indonesian women factory workers, sneaker companies started moving their factories from Indonesia to China. Executives of Nike, Reebok, Adidas, and New Balance and their male factory-owning contractors were still pursuing in China what they had sought earlier in Korea and Indonesia: young women's labor that could be made cheap. (Photo by Erik Eckholm, © *The New York Times*, reprinted with permission)

Women workers allied through networks like the Hong Kong–based Committee for Asian Women, however, sought to craft their own post—Cold War foreign policy, one that could address women's own needs: for instance, their need to convince fathers and husbands that a woman going out to organizing meetings at night is not sexually promiscuous; their need to develop workplace agendas that respond to family needs; their need to work with male unionists who trivialize women's demands; their need to build a global movement of women workers based on mutual trust; their need to convince women consumers in the United States, Europe, Japan, and Russia that when they see an expensive row of Reeboks or Nikes on the store shelves, there is more to weigh than merely the price listed on the tag.

Notes

Cynthia Enloe's "The Globetrotting Sneaker" was originally published in *Ms.*, March–April 1995, 11–15. Reprinted by permission of *Ms.* Magazine, © 1995.

This essay draws from the work of South Korean scholars Hyun Sook Kim, Seung-kyung Kim, Katharine Moon, Seungsook Moon, and Jeong-Lim Nam.

1. Jeong-Lim Nam, "Reforming Economic Allocations in the Family: The Women's Movement and the Role of the State in South Korea," *Women's Studies International Forum* 18, no. 2 (1995): 113–23.
2. Donald Katz, *Just Do It: The Nike Spirit in the Corporate World* (New York: Random House, 1994): 191.
3. Vernon Loeb, "$75 Nikes, 15 Cents an Hour," *Boston Globe*, December 30, 1991.
4. M. Goozner, "Nike Manager Knows Abuses Do Happen," *Chicago Tribune*, November 7, 1994. For more on Nike's operations, see Miguel Korzeniewicz, "Commodity Chains and Marketing Strategies: Nike and the Global Athletic Footwear Industry," in Gary Gereffi and Miguel Korzeniewicz, eds., *Commodity Chains and Global Capitalism* (Westport, Conn.: Greenwood Press, 1993); Katz, *Just Do It*; Verité, "Workers Win Independent Union in Mexico," *Monitor: Exploring the Dynamics of the Global Assembly Line*, no. 6 (Fall 2002): 12–13.

Chapter 9

Law, Politics, and Global Conflict

DISCUSSION QUESTIONS

1. How do the readings by both Malinowski and Brehm, et al. make you think differently about what constitutes "law"? Would you consider the processes described in both readings "legal"? Why or why not?
2. What is the relationship between the legal processes described in these readings and formal institutions, such as governments? Does law require a government in which to operate?
3. How does the notion of expertise fit into how we think about law? Based on the accounts of law-like practices in both readings, do you think legal actions require professional or expert actors? If not, what other actors are involved, and how does their involvement compare to those of professional legal actors?
4. Can you think of activities in your own cultural context comparable to those described in the readings that have both law-like and non-legal features (or formal and informal legal features)?

KEY TERMS

Expertise
Transitional justice
Gacaca courts
Civil law

Malinowski, Bronislaw. 1985 [1926]. *Crime and Custom*. New York: Rowman & Littlefield.

XI

An Anthropological Definition Of Law

The rules of law stand out from the rest in that they are felt and regarded as the obligations of one person and the rightful claims of another. They are sanctioned not by a mere psychological motive, but by a definite social machinery of binding force, based, as we know, upon mutual dependence, and realized in the equivalent arrangement of reciprocal services, as well as in the combination of such claims into strands of multiple relationship. The ceremonial manner in which most transactions are carried out, which entails public control and criticism, adds still more to their binding force.

We may therefore finally dismiss the view that 'group-sentiment' or 'collective responsibility' is the only or even the main force which ensures adhesion to custom and which makes it binding or legal. *Esprit de corps,* solidarity, pride in one's community and clan exist undoubtedly among the Melanesians—no social order could be maintained without them in any culture high or low. I only want to enter a caution against such exaggerated views as those of Rivers, Sidney Hartland, Durkheim, and others, which would make this unselfish, impersonal, unlimited grouployalty the corner-stone of all social order in primitive cultures. The savage is neither an extreme 'collectivist' nor an intransigent* individualist '—he is, like man in general, a mixture of both.

It results also from the account here given that primitive law does not consist exclusively or even chiefly of negative injunctions, nor is all savage law criminal law. And yet it is generally held that with the description of crime and punishment the subject of jurisprudence is exhausted as far as a savage community is concerned. As a matter of fact the dogma of automatic obedience, i.e. the absolute rigidity of the rules of custom implies an over-emphasis of criminal law in primitive communities and a corresponding denial of the possibility of civil law. Absolutely rigid rules cannot be stretched or adapted to life, they need not be enforced—but they can be broken. So much even the believers in a primitive super-legality must admit. Hence crime is the only legal problem to be studied in primitive communities, there is no civil law among savages, nor any civil jurisprudence for anthropology to work out. This view has dominated comparative studies of law from Sir Henry Maine to the most recent authorities, such as Prof. Hobhouse, Dr. Lowie, and Mr. Sidney Hartland. Thus we read in Mr. Hartland's book that in primitive societies "the core of legislation is a series of taboos", and that "almost all early codes consist of prohibitions" (*Primitive Law*, p. 214). And again, "the general belief in the certainty of supernatural punishment and the alienation of the sympathy of one's fellows generate an *atmosphere of terror* which is quite sufficient to prevent a breach of tribal customs . . ." (p. 8—the italics are mine). There is no such "atmosphere of terror " unless perhaps in the case of a few very exceptional and sacred rules of ritual and religion, and on the other hand the breach of tribal customs is prevented by a special machinery, the study of which is the real field of primitive jurisprudence.

In all this again Mr. Hartland is not alone. Steinmetz in his learned and competent analysis of primitive punishment insists on the criminal character of early jurisprudence, on the mechanical, rigid, almost undirected and unintentional nature of the penalties inflicted and on their religious basis. His views are fully endorsed by the great French sociologists Durkheim and Mauss, who add besides one more clause: that responsibility, revenge, in fact all legal reactions are founded in the psychology of the group and not of the individual.[1] Even such acute and well-informed sociologists as Prof. Hobhouse and Dr. Lowie, the latter acquainted at first hand with savages, seem to follow the trend of the general bias in their otherwise excellent chapters on justice in primitive societies.

In our own province we have so far met with positive commandments only, the breach of which is penalized but not punished, and the machinery of which can by no procrustean methods be stretched beyond the line which separates *civil* from *criminal* law. If we have to provide the rules described in these articles with some modern, hence necessarily inappropriate label, —they must be called the body of 'civil law' of the Trobriand Islanders.

'Civil law,' the positive law governing all the phases of tribal life, consists then of a body of binding obligations, regarded as a right by one party and acknowledged as a duty by the other, kept in force by a specific mechanism of reciprocity and publicity inherent in the structure of their society. These rules of civil law are elastic and possess a certain latitude. They offer not only penalties for failure, but also premiums for an overdose of fulfilment. Their stringency is ensured through the rational appreciation of cause and effect by the natives, combined with a number of social and personal sentiments such as ambition, vanity, pride, desire of self-enhancement by display, and also attachment, friendship, devotion and loyalty to the kin.

It scarcely needs to be added that 'law' and 'legal phenomena', as we have discovered, described and defined them in a part of Melanesia, do not consist in any independent institutions. Law represents rather an aspect of their tribal life, one side of their structure, than any independent, self-contained social arrangements. Law dwells not in a special system of decrees, which foresee and define possible forms of non-fulfilment and provide appropriate barriers and remedies. Law is the specific result of the configuration of obligations, which makes it impossible for the native to shirk his responsibility without suffering for it in the future.

Ceremonial Offering of Yams, carried in specially made wooden measures. (*See* page 29)

XII

Specific Legal Arrangements

The rare quarrels which occur at times take the form of an exchange of public expostulation (*yakala*) in which the two parties assisted by friends and relatives meet, harangue one another, hurl and hurl back recriminations. Such litigation allows people to give vent to their feelings and shows the trend of public opinion, and thus it may be of assistance in settling disputes. Sometimes it seems, however, only to harden the litigants. In no case is there any definite sentence pronounced by a third party, and agreement is but seldom reached then and there. The *yakala* therefore is a special legal arrangement, but of small importance and not really touching the heart of legal constraint.

Some other specific legal mechanisms may also be mentioned here. One of them is the *kaytapaku*, the magical protection of property by means of conditional curses. When a man owns coco or areca palms in distant spots, where it is impossible to keep watch over them, he attaches a palm leaf to the trunk of the tree, an indication that a formula has been uttered, which automatically would bring down ailment on the thief.

Another institution which has a legal side is the *kaytu-butabu*, a form of magic performed over all the coco-nut trees of a community to bring about their fertility, as a rule in view of an approaching feast. Such magic entails a strict prohibition to gather the nuts or to partake of coco-nut, even when imported. A similar institution is the *gwara*.[2] A pole is planted on the reef, and this places a taboo on any export of certain valuable objects, exchanged ceremonially in the *kula,* while their importation on the contrary is encouraged. This is a sort of moratorium, stopping all payments, without any interference with the receipts, which also aims at an accumulation of valuable objects before a big ceremonial distribution. Another important legal feature is a sort of ceremonial contract, called *kayasa.*[3] Here the leader of an expedition, the master of a feast, or the *entrepreneur* in an industrial venture gives a big ceremonial distribution. Those who participate in it and benefit by the bounty are under an obligation to assist the leader throughout the enterprise.

All these institutions, *kayasa, kaytapaku,* and *kaytu-butabu,* entail special binding ties. But even they are not exclusively *legal.* It would be a great mistake to deal with the subject of law by a simple enumeration of these few arrangements, each of which subserves a special end and fulfils a very partial function. The main province of law is in the social mechanism, which is to be found at the bottom of all the real obligations and covers a very vast portion of their custom, though by no means all of it, as we know.

Notes

1. Steinmetz, *Ethnologische Studien zur ersten Entwickelung der Strafe,* 1894; Durkheim in *L'Année Sociologique,* i. pp. 353 sqq.; Mauss in *Revue de l'Histoire des Religions,* 1897.
2. Comp, the account of this institution in *Argonauts of the Western Pacific* (references in Index s.v. *Gwara*). Also descriptions in Prof. Seligman's "Melanesians", and in the present writer's" The Natives of Mailu" (*Trans. R. Soc. of S. Australia,* vol. 39), of the *gola* or *gora* among the Western Papuo-Melanesians.
3. *Argonauts.* See in Index s.v. *Kayasa.*

Brehm, Hollie Nyseth, Christi Smith, and Evelyn Gertz. 2019. "Producing Expertise in a Transitional Justice Setting: Judges at Rwanda's Gacaca Courts." *Law & Social Inquiry* 44(1):78-101.

In the aftermath of the 1994 Genocide Against the Tutsi, the Government of Rwanda created courts to hold hundreds of thousands of suspected génocidaires accountable. Faced with an unprecedented volume of cases, each community elected lay judges known as inyangamugayo to preside over the court proceedings. With no prior legal training, these individuals held trials for a decade, levying sentences ranging from minor fines to life in prison. This article draws from forty-six interviews with former inyangamugayo to make two primary contributions. First, we examine how professional boundaries shifted during a period of upheaval such that laypeople performed tasks typically undertaken by professionals. Second, we highlight the centrality of social capital—and, more specifically, reputations—in the inyangamugayo's election and tasks. In doing so, we illustrate how the inyangamugayo leveraged their reputations to secure the cooperation of fellow community members in adjudicating crimes of genocide.

Introduction

The 1994 Genocide Against the Tutsi left Rwanda and its institutions in shambles. In the aftermath, the new government sought to hold hundreds of thousands of Rwandan civilians accountable for the violence. As the existing justice system was not capable of processing this immense caseload, the government created local courts that were staffed by lay members of the community known as *inyanga-mugayo* ("people of integrity"). Although these individuals had no prior legal training and were not paid, they carried out tasks previously assigned to professionals to accomplish the urgent need of adjudicating crimes of genocide for their crimes. The majority of the inyangamugayo worked numerous hours every week for a decade, collectively presiding over 1.96 million trials across Rwanda (Nyseth Brehm, Uggen, and Gasanabo 2014).

This article relies on interviews with forty-six inyangamugayo to make two primary contributions. First, we highlight how the familiar processes that determine who performs professional work—such as the acquisition of formal credentials—were upended during a period of transitional justice. Instead, laymen and women presided over trials for genocide and completed tasks that are typically performed by those with some formal training. Our case study consequently accords with Eyal's (2013, 871) call for an expanded consideration of the social processes through which various actors, both credentialed and non-credentialed, contribute to the "speedy and superior execution of a task." Second, we illuminate some of the mechanisms that enabled laypeople to undertake their work in these courts, illustrating that social capital served as the requisite credential for their election and subsequent work. A primary component of the inyangamugayo's social capital was their reputation as upstanding members of their communities, and they accordingly sought to protect their reputations through public demonstrations of integrity, including policing potential corruption on their benches. The inyangamugayo likewise relied heavily on broader social networks to accomplish their tasks, further illustrating the importance of social capital in this context.

We begin with an overview of professions and the work of professionals in transitional justice settings, examining how a critical juncture can shift the bound-aries around who performs professional tasks. Next, we briefly discuss the case of Rwanda's post-genocide *gacaca* courts, followed by a summary of our interviews with forty-six inyangamugayo. We then demonstrate how laypeople presided over their fellow citizens' cases of genocide and thereby performed vital work in the aftermath of mass violence. Finally, we conclude by suggesting that reputations and social networks may take on an increased salience in the absence of formal credentialing processes.

Professions and Transitional Justice

Judgeships are professions, which sociologists have conceptualized as distinct from other occupations due to their autonomy over a field of work, the strong associations that protect entrée to and status of membership, and the authority to regulate and discipline professional members (Larson 1977; Abbott 1988; Bourdieu 1996). A robust body of scholarship has accordingly theorized professions as bounded categories whereby credentialed actors control their jurisdiction through boundary-making processes. To date, however, this work has overwhelmingly focused on professions in the United States and Western Europe (Faulconbridge and Muzio 2012; Kuhlmann 2013; Liu 2017). Scholarship on legal professions has likewise suffered from a Western bias, and scholars have recently suggested that jurisdictional studies of judges and related legal professions should transcend their limited focus on Western case studies (Michelson 2006, 2007; Liu 2013).

This article heeds these calls by examining the performance of legal work during a transitional justice process,[1] or the process by which a country transitions from mass violence or widespread human rights violations to a time of relative peace (Osiel 1997; Teitel 2000). The term "transitional justice" initially referred to the legal strategies that national and international actors implemented to aid countries as they transitioned to democracy (Kritz 1995). In recent decades, transitional justice has come to include the judicial and non-judicial mechanisms employed to respond to violent or repressive pasts (Kritz 1995; Roht-Arriaza and Mariezcurrena 2006; Sikkink 2011).[2] These transitional justice efforts are expansive and often involve numerous pursuits, such as truth and reconciliation commissions, memorials, reparations, and—most pertinent to our case—trials.

As transitional justice efforts have proliferated, international organizations have often orchestrated the proceedings (Teitel 2003). Scholars have accordingly examined the role of professionals in international tribunals and other international endeavors (Lefranc and Vairel 2014). These professionals include the lawyers, judges, and other legal personnel who staff international tribunals (e.g., Hagan 2003; Garbett 2012) as well as the international actors who have become transitional justice experts and entrepreneurs, such as representatives of international governmental organizations and human rights activists (e.g., Madlingozi 2010).

Transitional justice endeavors have also been localized[3] in the sense that local actors and organizations have been instrumental in creating, orchestrating, and assessing courts, truth commissions, and related mechanisms. In fact, many scholars lament the international legalization of transitional justice and have suggested that individuals residing where the violence or repression occurred should play a more prominent role (McEvoy 2007; Shaw, Waldorf, and Hazan 2010). However, the precise local actors who play this role tend to vary. In many cases, credentialed and licensed professionals spearhead local transitional justice efforts. Bosnia and Herzegovina's hybrid war crimes chamber, for instance, employed numerous licensed Bosnian judges and prosecutors (Ivanisevic 2008), while local Iraqi judges participated in post-2003 transitional justice efforts (Stover, Megally, and Mufti 2005). In other settings, nonprofessionals play key roles in the transitional justice process. For example, community elders led Uganda's *mato oput* rituals in the wake of violence committed by the Lord's Resistance Army (Baines 2007), meaning that individuals with no formal conflict resolution training or legal credentials were responsible for determining compensation paid to victims and/or their families.[4] In much the same way, members of civil society played core roles in shaping and implementing transitional justice mechanisms in East Timor, Peru, Sierra Leone, and Ghana (Gready and Robins 2010).

This article examines another case in which lay members of the community were prominently involved in a transitional justice process. Judges in Rwanda's gacaca courts had little legal training to guide them as they adjudicated difficult, legally binding cases of genocide. The gacaca courts consequently offer an important opportunity to analyze laypeople's roles in transitional justice efforts and, specifically, the factors that enabled laypeople to take on these roles and carry out the associated tasks. Before addressing this, however, we examine why laypeople came to adjudicate crimes of genocide and suggest that the sociology of expertise provides an appropriate lens through which to theorize their efforts.

Critical Junctures and Expertise

Although it may seem surprising that laypeople stepped into roles as judges in the aftermath of a genocide, the phenomenon of shifting institutional arrangements post-violence is not new. Rather, the shift stems (at least in part) from the transformative potential of mass violence. Often referred to as a "critical juncture," mass violence is period of significant change that reflects a discontinuation of the status quo and the possibility for new social processes and institutional arrangements (Mahoney 2000; Pierson 2004; Mann 2013). Perhaps most broadly, Tilly (1985, 170) argued that "wars make states," while Weber ([1922] 1978) suggested that the development of bureaucratic rationality within militaries significantly affected modern state institutions. Mass violence has likewise influenced the emergence of revolutions (e.g., Moore 1966; Tilly 1978; Skocpol 1979), welfare state and civic organization formation (e.g., Skocpol 1992), citizenship rights (e.g., Markoff 1996; Kestnbaum 2002), and women's political participation (e.g., Hughes and Tripp 2015; Berry 2018).

In the case of Rwanda, a critical juncture influenced an urgent need to try those suspected of participating in the genocide, which in turn took precedence over the desire to entrust only credentialed professionals with the duties of the judiciary. Specifically, due to the widespread death and displacement caused by the genocide, there were only twelve prosecutors and 244 judges in Rwanda, compared to the seventy prosecutors and 758 judges in the country before 1994 (Gacaca Report Summary 2012). The boundaries around certain professional tasks necessarily shifted to allow for laypeople to perform essential tasks.

To be certain, lay individuals perform legal work in other contexts. England's lay magistrates (Diamond 1990), for instance, have wielded substantial sentencing power, and some argue that such participatory practices offer an important intervention to the increasingly harsh criminalization of many capitalist states (Bond and Lemon 1981; Johnstone 2000). Likewise, US-focused scholarship suggests that noncredentialed actors can play meaningful roles representing clients during civil trials. For instance, Carpenter, Mark, and Shanahan (2016) found that experienced nonlawyer advocates can help parties with common court procedures.[5] Further, police in many societies make discretionary decisions every day as to whether to invoke the law, substantially impacting the administration of criminal justice and thus the judicial profession (Green 1997).

Before the genocide in Rwanda, however, individuals who had been trained and licensed presided over serious crimes (like homicide) in formal court systems. Although the gacaca courts were partially rooted in past practices, as we further describe below, they nonetheless represented a large departure from how Rwanda had previously handled serious crime. In this case, the social processes and shifting institutional arrangements that often stem from mass violence also extended to legal work. Although the gacaca court judges were clearly not professionals, they were tasked with prosecuting crimes of genocide and facilitating the reconciliation of a devastated nation, due in large part to the lack of trained legal professionals.

In line with this, Eyal (2013) articulates how many people—both skilled and unskilled—contribute to identifying problems and implementing solutions, which he calls constructing "expertise." Through his demonstration of how therapists, psychologists, and parents of children with autism influenced the rise of autism diagnoses in the United States, Eyal argues that laypeople can play an important role in addressing issues that often fall under the jurisdiction of professionals. He thus suggests that the sociology of professions needs to expand such that it includes individuals who are not credentialed professionals, but who nonetheless respond to pressing tasks and problems, regardless of the actual knowledge or skills they bring to such tasks.

Indeed, contributing to expertise does not make one an "expert." Rather, Eyal (2013, 869) highlights an important analytical distinction "between, on the one hand, the *actors* who make claims to jurisdiction over a task by 'professing' their disinterest, skill, and credibility and, on the other hand, the sheer *capacity* to accomplish this task better and faster." Rather than viewing expertise as a quality of professionals, this approach emphasizes the broader symbolic and material resources, concepts, and social arrangements necessary to accomplish tasks, conceptualizing expertise as networks that "link together objects, actors, techniques, devices, and institutional and spatial arrangements" (864; see also Cambrosio, Limoges, and Hoffman 1992; Epstein 1995, 408–37; 1996; Collins and Evans 2007). These networks produce, reproduce, and disseminate knowledge and/or performances, and Eyal argues that scholars must examine the mechanisms that influence links to and cooperation with such networks.

Though we certainly do not suggest that lay judges in Rwanda were able to accomplish tasks *better* than credentialed judges, the case of Rwanda presents a situation in which the need for speedy execution of tasks (in this case, criminal trials) trumped other considerations. In line with scholarship on the transformative power of mass violence, the genocide precipitated the need for gacaca court judges, thus shifting institutional arrangements and boundaries such that laypeople worked in tandem with their communities to perform the work of the judiciary. Guided by the sociology of expertise, our question, then, is what arrangements had to be in place for the tasks of the gacaca courts to be accomplished?

Rwanda's Gacaca Courts and The Inyangamugayo

The 1994 Genocide Against the Tutsi left between eight hundred thousand and one million two-hundred thousand people dead and millions displaced (Lemarchand 2013).[6] In the aftermath of the violence, the UN Security Council swiftly created the International Criminal Tribunal for Rwanda (ICTR). This tribunal was in Arusha, Tanzania, and had jurisdiction over war crimes, crimes against humanity, and genocide committed in Rwanda or by Rwandans in 1994 (ICTR Statute 1994).

The ICTR was meant to try those deemed most responsible for the violence, and it indicted ninety[7] individuals prior to closing in 2015. Consequently, the hundreds of thousands of Rwandan civilians who had participated in the genocide did not fall under the ICTR's jurisdiction, and the new Rwandan government began searching for people suspected of participating in the genocide and transporting them to Rwandan prisons in 1995 (Clark 2010; Bornkamm 2012). An estimated 120,000 people were brought to facilities that were built to hold forty-five thousand people (International Center for Prison Studies 2013), and the government began trying these individuals through the existing court system. However, it soon became clear that this was not a viable option due to the large caseload and the lack of trained legal professionals.

The Rwandan government consequently decided to modify a mechanism of dispute resolution—known as gacaca courts—to try suspected *génocidaires*. Gacaca loosely translates to "grass," and pre-colonial gacaca court hearings took place in schoolyards, empty marketplaces, and other public spaces as a response to petty crimes and disagreements. Community elders presided over these trials, though they became an officially sanctioned court system for petty crimes during the 1940s, illustrating that gacaca evolved into an institution associated with state power (Ingelaere 2016). The conciliatory and informal nature of gacaca remained core to the courts' endeavors after colonialism (Reyntjens 1990), however, and grave crimes generally remained under the jurisdiction of Rwanda's existing court system, where judges and lawyers who had typically received at least some credentials had professional jurisdiction (Prinsloo 1993).[8]

The government greatly modified the gacaca courts in the aftermath of the violence, creating a system that blended informal and formal legal practices (for detailed information, see Waldorf 2006; Clark 2010; Bornkamm 2012; Nyseth Brehm, Uggen, and Gasanabo 2014; Chakravarty 2015; Palmer 2015; Ingelaere 2016).[9] The post-genocide courts—known as *inkiko gacaca* but shortened here to gacaca—had close ties to the state, which mandated their creation through a series of decrees known as Organic Laws. Also unlike the previous gacaca courts, the new courts had jurisdiction over more serious crimes, as the government decided to shift all but the most serious genocide-related cases to the gacaca courts.[10] These courts were operational at the cell (*akagari*) and sector (*umurenge*) levels of geographic administration, which were small geographic areas akin to villages and counties. Cases were tried in the geographic regions where the crimes had occurred, with courts at the cell level trying less serious crimes (such as looting) and courts at the sector level trying comparatively more serious ones (such as genocidal murder). Adult members of communities were expected to attend and be actively involved in the trials.

Per newly instituted Organic Laws, Rwandans elected lay members of communities to preside over the post-genocide gacaca courts as judges, or inyangamugayo.[11] Inyangamugayo generally translates to "trustworthy person" or "person of integrity," and the position was, notably, unpaid. Unlike judges in the existing Rwandan justice system, legal training and credentials were not required to serve as inyangamugayo. Thus, although judges in pre-genocide gacaca trials did not have legal training—as they were community elders presiding over small disputes—laypeople adjudicating *grave* crimes represented a significant departure from Rwandan legal practice. Rather, inyangamugayo needed to fulfill the following criteria stipulated in Article 7 of Presidential Order Number 12/01:

1. To be of Rwandan nationality;
2. To have his or her residence in the cell where he or she needs to present his or her candidature;
3. To be at least twenty-one years old;
4. To be a person of good morals and conduct;
5. To be truthful and characterized by a spirit of sharing;
6. Not to have been sentenced to a penalty of at least six months of imprisonment;[12]
7. Not to have participated in genocide or other crimes against humanity;
8. To be free from sectarianism; and
9. To have no history of indiscipline.

The government instructed adult members of cells to gather in 2001 to elect the inyangamugayo. During the election process, community members could propose candidates before the General Assembly, which was comprised of the voting-age Rwandans (eighteen years and older) who resided in each cell. Those present could then express opinions about the candidates, which involved supporting the values of those who they thought acted with integrity and denouncing the candidates they considered unqualified. Candidates who were denounced were typically rejected, and criteria for rejection often included alcoholism, adultery, dishonesty, failure to pay debts, and committing violence, among other attributes or actions (CCM 2012).

After agreeing on the candidates, residents voted for a bench of judges, and those who received the most votes were officially elected. While there are no data (to our knowledge) on the number of people who refused to accept the position, much evidence suggests that the vast majority of people accepted their nominations (Clark 2010). Each individual then repeated the following statement as he or she was sworn in: "I, ___, in the name of God Almighty, solemnly swear to the Nation to honestly fulfill the mission entrusted to me by complying with the law; to always be guided by the spirit of impartiality and search for the truth; and to make justice triumph."

In total, more than 250,000 men and women were chosen through community elections to staff over 12,000 courts.[13] Most did not have any prior legal training, and some were illiterate (Honeyman et al. 2004; Clark 2010). While time did not allow for years of training, all inyangamugayo underwent several weeks of preparation. To facilitate this training, government officials first trained advanced law students and magistrates on the new laws governing the gacaca courts (Gacaca Report Summary 2012). In turn, these individuals taught groups of inyangamugayo about how gacaca courts were to function and the punishments they were to give (Bornkamm 2012). Specifically, panels of judges were responsible for reaching a verdict and for assigning the punishment, and they were given sentencing guidelines that instructed them to base punishments on the category of crime, confession, and, if applicable, time to confession. As such, the judges had the power to assign prison sentences up to a life sentence without possibility of release, though punishments for less serious crimes (such as property crimes) typically involved fines that convicted individuals were supposed to pay to victims or their families.

Judges also received training on how to gather information—a critical component of their duties because there were no lawyers in the gacaca court system. Preparation likewise included discussions of ethics as well as the judges' place within the broader justice system. Brief subsequent trainings[14] also covered security at the trials, conflict resolution, human rights, how to work with traumatized witnesses, and how to assist those victimized by sexual violence, among other topics (Gacaca Report Summary 2012; see Bornkamm 2012 for more on training).

While we emphasize the tasks and problems that the inyangamugayo and their communities addressed, it is important to note that the majority of existing scholarship on the gacaca courts has critically examined the laws and processes governing the trials. Early critiques highlighted the lack of due process, pretrial detention, the absence of lawyers, and the courts' emphasis on confessions, among other procedural legal issues (Sarkin 2001; Corey and Joireman 2004; Fierens 2005; Schabas 2005; Waldorf 2006; Apuuli 2009). Others have argued that the gacaca courts were too tightly tied to the state and have thus suggested that they functioned as a form of state power, emphasizing some crimes at the expense of others (Burnet 2008; Rettig 2008; Thomson 2011; Chakravarty 2015).[15]

Here, we do not examine the quality of the inyangamugayo's work or how legal practices were enacted within the courts. We likewise do not assess the role of the state, though the state likely vested the inyangamugayo with at least some authority when it dictated that community members should elect inyangamugayo and set the parameters for their election. Rather, we assess what facilitated these laypeople in carrying out tasks typically undertaken by credentialed professionals. Put another way, what mechanisms and arrangements enabled the inyangamugayo to undertake their duties once they had stepped into the new roles?

Methodology

We rely on forty-six interviews we conducted with former inyangamugayo in Rwanda in June and July 2015. Interviews were an appropriate methodology because they enabled us to learn about how the inyangamugayo approached their tasks and problems, which could not be understood from secondhand sources or even court ethnographies. Additionally, interviews shed light on community members' links to and cooperation with the inyangamugayo as they undertook their work, highlighting the networks of actors and arrangements that supported the gacaca court processes.

Participants were selected through a stratified random sampling procedure. Specifically, we chose three sectors near the capital city of Kigali: Gikondo, Gahanga, and Masaka. Although proximity to a central location partially guided this choice, these sectors were also chosen due to their comparatively urban (Gikondo) and semirural (Gahanga, Masaka) compositions, as we further address below.

Using a list of all gacaca court trials, we randomly selected twenty trials from each of the three sectors using a random number generator. Then, working in the gacaca court archives in Kigali, we identified all inyangamugayo involved in the randomly selected trials. This involved judges who served in cell, sector, and appeals courts (which also functioned at the sector level). We then obtained phone numbers or addresses through local contacts, contacted these individuals by phone or at their homes, and asked them to participate in the study. Participation was voluntary, though no judges who still resided within the sectors declined participation. We were, however, unable to interview some judges who had since relocated.

The first author administered the interviews with a small research team.[16] Respondents were able to conduct the interview in English, French, or Kinyarwanda. All chose Kinyarwanda, and the interviews were thus conducted with translators, with the exception of those conducted by one member of the research team whose first language was Kinyarwanda. All interviews took place in or around respondents' homes and lasted between one and two hours. Interviews followed a semi-structured interview guide that had been translated and back-translated into Kinyarwanda. Generally, each interview addressed participants' lives before and during 1994 and their subsequent involvement in the gacaca courts. Interviews also included discussions of their duties as inyangamugayo, their decision-making processes, and their opinions of court procedures and outcomes.

Twenty-five of the respondents were men; twenty-one were women. Although it is difficult to discuss ethnicity in Rwanda today,[17] the participants often explained that they were Hutu or Tutsi or noted that they were (or were not) part of the targeted group during the violence. Twenty-six of the interviewees were Tutsi; seventeen were Hutu individuals. Hutu judges typically had risked their lives to save Tutsis during the genocide or had refused to participate in the violence. Additionally, three participants were not born in Rwanda but had lived in the country from a young age. Participants' ages ranged from thirty-three to seventy-one at the time of the interviews in 2015. Most had completed at least some years of primary school and provided for their family through farming, though a minority had completed secondary school and held formal employment.[18] None had any legal training prior to their election.

Numerous scholars have noted the difficulties of conducting research in post-genocide Rwanda (Purdeková 2011; Straus and Waldorf 2011; Thomson 2013). For instance, many suggest that the state tightly regulates narratives related to the genocide. Some may thus worry that respondents would be reluctant to discuss the gacaca courts—which were created by the government. To mitigate this, we stressed that the results would be confidential and that no names or personally identifiable information would be included in any publications resulting from the study. We also spent time talking with participants prior to the interviews to develop rapport (Loyle 2016).

Of course, as with any study employing interviews, our positionality as Western scholars likely influenced the interviews. Yet, it is important to note that the vast majority of respondents were not reluctant to discuss their role in the gacaca courts. While some were noticeably hesitant (and even unwilling) to criticize the courts, many others openly discussed weaknesses and challenges, negative effects on their lives (e.g., grudges held by neighbors), and desires for compensation. This assured us that we had at least developed some rapport with participants. Additionally, as this article examines the tasks of the inyangamugayo rather than their opinions of the courts or how well they performed their duties, the content we rely on is less sensitive than other aspects of the interviews.

Upon completion of fieldwork, all interviews were transcribed. We then repeatedly read and analyzed interviews for key themes, which we present below. We modify the grammar in some quotes for clarity, but do not change anything that would alter the meaning of the statements.

Finally, as the forty-six individuals were randomly selected from three sectors (Gikondo, Masaka, and Gahanga), our results arguably generalize to the other inyangamugayo who served in these sectors. That said, the sectors are also comparable to many other sectors across the country. Gikondo has 17,146 residents (Census 2012), and all these individuals live in an urban area, since the sector is within Kigali province. Gahanga and Masaka are each larger sectors in terms of population (27,808 and 39,548 residents, respectively) and geographic size, leading to comparatively lower population densities. These sectors are also more rural, as 42 percent of Gahanga's residents and 49 of Masaka's residents reside in an urban area. Countrywide, the average population of the 416 sectors is 26,134, and the average percentage of urban residents in a sector is 12 percent. The sectors are thus relatively similar in population, though they are clearly more urban than the average sector.

It is unclear how the relative urbanicity of our three sectors influenced the results, though it is likely that judges in these and other more urban areas knew comparatively fewer of the defendants given the tight-knit nature of rural communities. It is also likely that the judges we interviewed are better educated than judges in comparatively more rural sectors and that there were more women judges. As there is no comprehensive (public) list of all inyangamugayo, these possibilities should be kept in mind, but unfortunately, they cannot be confirmed.

Results: Producing Expertise at Gacaca

Our interviews revealed that the inyangamugayo believed their ability to approach tasks and problems—and thus the production of expertise—stemmed from three interconnected factors that were all tied to their social capital. First, the inyangamugayo consistently explained that they were elected because of their reputations as people of integrity. Although the state set integrity as a qualification for their election, our interviews illustrate how the inyangamugayo *understood* integrity and suggest that the belief that their neighbors viewed them as people of integrity influenced their willingness to become judges. Second, once the inyangamugayo stepped into their roles, they relied on a broader network of actors to undertake their tasks. Most prominently, their fellow community members assisted in numerous aspects of gacaca court work, though state and international actors also played a part. Finally, the inyangamugayo stressed the importance of ensuring their reputations throughout the court process. Specifically, they continually sought to protect their reputations by appearing trustworthy, avoiding corruption, and policing the behavior of their fellow judges. This impression management seemingly was undertaken to ensure that their communities continued to view them as qualified and to sustain cooperation from fellow community members.

Election Based on Reputation

As noted above, the Rwandan government instructed adults to gather in their cells to elect the inyangamugayo. During the election process, any adult community member could propose a candidate, and those present could then express opinions about each candidate prior to electing the inyangamugayo through popular vote. There were no campaigns beforehand; rather, those who were elected were often surprised that they were chosen.

As such, many vividly remembered their election day and expressed their initial hesitation. For instance, Julienne, a thirty-seven-year-old resident of Gikondo, recounted how her community had gathered when government officials asked for nominations. She recalled, "I did not want ... to be chosen. The public chose me to be one of the selected people. I stood, and people made a line behind me. If you had a big line behind you, of course you became a judge." Noël, a sixty-five-year-old farmer in Gikondo, similarly explained: "At the beginning, I was surprised. I said, 'I never went to school. I never even completed high school. How am I going to manage being a judge?'"

Julienne, Noël, and the other inyangamugayo with whom we spoke nonetheless accepted the position despite the fact that none of them had formal legal training and that many had not even completed primary school. Reflecting on this, the inyangamugayo explained that they were not elected because of their credentials; rather, they believed they were elected because of their positive reputations and the trust they had earned from fellow citizens, and it was this belief that pushed them toward accepting the position. Indeed, when asked why they stepped into their roles, many participants explained that they agreed to serve as judges because their communities thought they would perform the tasks well. For instance, Noël later noted that his peers had encouraged him: "I knew very well that those people who elected me knew who I was. They told me, 'You will do it.'"

As they discussed the perceived trust from their communities, many inyangamugayo highlighted the particular importance of integrity. As Innocent, a forty-seven-year-old businessman in Gikondo, noted, "I think people selected me as a person of integrity. They trusted me." Félicité, a fifty-nine-year-old farmer, further remarked: "Even before the genocide, we were seen as people of integrity." Élina concurred, explaining: "The neighbors know you, your background; you have to have integrity to be chosen." As the government instructed citizens to take integrity into consideration (and as the term inyangamugayo is often translated to "a person of integrity"), this illustrates that the inyangamugayo believed their fellow citizens heeded this call.

Our conversations also shed light on how the inyangamugayo *understood* integrity. For some, their integrity was based in not having participated in crimes of genocide. Liberatha, a forty-six-year-old farmer, explained:

> Of course, you had to be a person of integrity. A person who never killed during [the] genocide. A person who had no accusations. Of course, you had to be a person of integrity. It is on that, that community members [elected me] as a

> judge ... [at first] I was reluctant. I was not willing to participate ... after considering the trust from the community members, of course I decided to join. As I saw that many people of integrity were elected, then I participated.

Mélanie, a forty-two-year-old farmer from Gahanga, likewise noted that "[t]hat day of my election, I was maybe chosen because first I did not participate [in] any killings," while Phenias shared, "I was elected because my neighbors knew I did not participate in killings, even looting others' property." Innocence was thus perceived as a cornerstone of integrity, though Hutu judges were notably more likely than Tutsi judges to mention their innocence as a reason for their election.

For others, being a person of integrity meant being honest and trustworthy. Odette, a fifty-four-year-old farmer from Gahanga, felt strongly that she was elected for her enduring honesty: "[I was elected] because people thought I was an honest person—a person of integrity—and of course I was." In a similar vein, Jean Bosco declared: "We were elected because people judge[d] [us] as always telling the truth." Isaac, a thirty-five-year-old farmer from Gikondo, also highlighted trust when he told us, "[p]eople trusted me because I was not supporting any lie"; while Marceline explained elections by noting that "the people of the same village sat together and tried to choose the *honest* people" (emphasis added).

Reputations—like those invoked in these statements—are a form of social capital (Fine 2001, 2–3). Reputations are consequently embedded within social relationships, and in this case, participants believed that their reputations as trustworthy, upstanding individuals proved more meaningful than formal credentials. This belief was one of the major reasons that the individuals with whom we spoke decided to accept their new roles.

Of course, we cannot prove the objective morality of the individual inyangamugayo, as reputations are socially constructed and as individuals tend to present themselves in a positive light. Nevertheless, as part of the larger research project, the first author and a research team interviewed eighty-two people who were defendants in the gacaca court system and thirty-six people who testified during the trials as witnesses. While these conversations did not address the reputations of the specific inyangamugayo who were interviewed for this project, each participant was asked about the factors they took into account when they were electing judges.

These interviews confirm the emphasis on reputation as a primary qualification for election, supporting the general perceptions of the inyangamugayo. For instance, a witness from Masaka described what he took into account on election day, noting: "We based [it] on one's behavior, especially on honesty and the importance that they can have in the community." Another witness shared the inyangamugayo's general understanding of integrity, explaining: "First of all, they have to [be] based on the fact that you did not get involved in any killings or any violence. Second, whether you are [an] innocent person; you are an honest person. For those two factors, you could be elected as a judge." A witness from a different sector likewise shared: "They actually had to be respected people with good ideas, and mature opinions ... those who actually fought against genocide, who never committed crimes during [the] genocide."

Some defendants also participated in the elections, and their sentiments were similar. A defendant from Masaka told us: "Judges were not elected because they had gone to school. They were elected only because they were people of integrity and people who could actually have good ideas and skills in deciding cases." Another defendant explained, "[w]e could propose names of those that we knew [had] never participated in the genocide," highlighting a common understanding of integrity as linked to innocence and honesty.[19] These and other interviews with community members thus support the judges' perceptions that it was their reputations—specifically that they had not participated in the genocide and that they were honest and trustworthy—that made them suitable in the eyes of their communities to sit in judgment over complex and painful proceedings.

Forging Networks of Expertise

As the inyangamugayo began their work, other actors and institutions were critical for the completion of their duties. This aligns with Eyal's (2013) conception of expertise, which again suggests that expertise involves a network that links actors, institutional arrangements, objects, and other social phenomena. In the case of Rwanda's inyangamugayo, their work was completed with the assistance of many others—most prominently their fellow community members, but also state and international actors—at every stage of the transitional justice process.

Although these individuals were generally elected based on their reputations, formal training was not disregarded, and the inyangamugayo underwent several brief training sessions after their election. These trainings were created and implemented through a collaboration of Rwandan government officials, legal professionals, and many individuals from other countries (Bornkamm 2012; Kaitesi 2014), demonstrating the network of individuals who came together to aid the inyangamugayo as they began their important work.

After training was complete, the first step was to gather details regarding who had committed crimes and who had been victimized to generate a list of suspected perpetrators and to prepare witnesses and evidence for trial. As Phenias, a fifty-two-year-old farmer from Gahanga, described: "The period of information collection was the core of gacaca activities." Importantly, this work relied heavily on community members, illustrating the networks that were forged to accomplish the judges' tasks. Épiphanie, a sixty-year-old farmer from Gikondo, explained: "The [population] would come together, they would give us information on what they saw during the genocide, or even what they had heard. [We] would write everything that people told us, and [that is how] we based files."[20] Community members were thus vital to the inyangamugayo as they began their tasks.

Upon gathering information, the inyangamugayo were primarily occupied with holding trials. These trials occurred publicly, and members of the community were expected to be present and participate in their proceedings. Specifically, after summoning the defendant—a task that sometimes required collaboration across communities, as individuals had often moved, died, or were in hiding—the trial would unfold in a public setting, and community members once again provided testimony about what they had witnessed during the genocide.

These tasks, accomplished with assistance from their communities, enabled the inyangamugayo to assess whether people were guilty of genocide and to hand down punishments accordingly. In property cases, the punishment was mostly restitution, and those found guilty were expected to pay back the value of what was stolen. In such cases, community members were likewise essential in determining the fines that were allocated. In Esther's words:

> We could base on a list given by the victim. We could go together with the community members through the list. Then we actualize the price of the items destroyed in collaboration with community members. Community members could help us determine the price of products mentioned within the list. Because, for example, a bed which was destroyed in 1994, its value changed, and we had to actualize the price according to the market price.

Pascal, a forty-one-year-old farmer, likewise explained that when his bench needed to ascertain the price of stolen property, such as a cow, they would convene a community meeting to debate and set the price.

Similarly, Jean Damascène informed us that while it was the judges who would sit together, deliberate over evidence, and eventually sign off on a sentence, disagreement on the bench sometimes required further consultation with members of the community. As he explained, in such an instance, the judges would "adjourn, and then reconvene the next day and gather more information from community members." Olive, a fifty-six-year-old tailor, further attests to such an occurrence, explaining that judges rigorously collected evidence and testimony (both for and against the defendant) with the aid of the community. In her words:

> We based on witnesses, the witnesses on both sides—those ones witnessing against and those ones who were witnessing in favor of the defendant. We could gather information from both, but again, in our court we started going

> to the field to gather more information after getting it from these two sources of information to make sure that we go by the right information.

In line with this, Phenias explained that his court relied on the community heavily during particularly difficult trials. He shared that if his bench of judges failed to reach consensus on a trial decision, they would postpone and "invite the defendants and the witnesses or the public to discuss the matter and try to make a decision together."

These narratives highlight the importance of the community in aiding the judges as they went about their tasks. From gathering information to holding trials and reaching verdicts, members of each community worked with the inyangamugayo at each step of the court process. International and state actors were likewise consequential, especially in training the inyangamugayo, but also in other ways we have not mentioned here, such as providing police when judges were worried about their safety or responding to legal questions about particularly tough cases. This network of actors and arrangements thus proved critical to the inyangamugayo throughout the ten years of their service.

Ensuring Reputations

Throughout these years, the inyangamugayo continued to rely heavily on the reputations that brought them to their position in the first place. During our conversations, the judges consistently stressed the importance of guarding their reputations by appearing trustworthy, steering clear of corruption, and policing the behavior of their fellow judges. This, in turn, would enable them to sustain their qualification to serve as a judge and to continue to rely on their community members for assistance.

For many judges, ensuring that members of their communities continued to view them as people of integrity—and thus maintaining their social capital—was linked to ensuring that people continued to view them as trustworthy. Paul, a sixty-one-year-old who works in construction, explained that this meant constantly being aware of confidentiality: "You could not go around mentioning somebody's name ... you were not allowed to do that. It required [you] to be careful and again to be a person of integrity."

Other judges similarly highlighted their critical ability to refrain from discussing sensitive information in front of others, thus maintaining their trustworthy status. For example, sixty-two-year-old Jacques noted that all decisions had "to be confidential from the beginning," while Hope likewise emphasized the importance of enduring confidentiality, elaborating that judges "were supposed to keep what we discussed in deliberation confidential." Again, the trials occurred publicly, and as we discussed above, the judges often relied on their fellow community members for assistance with certain aspects of their decisions. Judges with whom we spoke nonetheless stressed that confidentiality was key, especially when it came to their private deliberations as a bench and to particularly sensitive trials, such as those involving sexualized violence.

Apart from continuing to appear trustworthy, myriad judges likewise discussed the importance of remaining free from corruption and thus maintaining their image as honest community members. To them, this involved stepping down from the bench when necessary and refraining from taking bribes. Pertaining to the former, many judges explained it was their duty to remove themselves from the bench if they were concerned about conflicts of interest. Liberatha shared: "Of course, you were allowed to decree a conflict of interest in any case you had ... 'I do not want to participate in this case, because this is my friend, this is my relative.'"

Though not all inyangamugayo followed this rule,[21] several participants shared instances in which they did. Épiphanie told us that she stepped down anytime she felt that her preconceived notions about a defendant's behavior were too strong. She explained: "When it came to a person that I knew [had] participated in genocide, I never served on the judge's bench. I could join the witnesses and tell the judges what the person did during the genocide." Philippe, a thirty-seven-year-old farmer, similarly shared a story about recusing himself when his own father appeared for trial to avoid the appearance of corruption. He explained: "We were not allowed to judge a case of a relative. [My dad] was tried in the same court, but I had to step down. I had to go from the judge's bench and sit in the audience. I was not even allowed to sit with the judges to deliberate."

Another core aspect of avoiding corruption and maintaining an image as an honest person involved refusing bribes. Jean, a fifty-three-year-old farmer from Gahanga, explained: "There is a person who wanted to give me a bribe of one hundred thousand. This person was claiming that he/she was innocent. I did not take that bribe." Mélanie also noted that she did not take any money, noting that: "When we are judges, we have as a duty not to accept bribes or corruption."

Others explained that the bribe did not have to be monetary, as members of their communities tried to exploit friendships to receive more favorable sentences. Olive shared: "Many could want to befriend you to show you that they are innocent, to be your friend to make sure that you sympathized with them." Olive later emphasized the importance of remaining impartial, however, again emphasizing the importance of her reputation. Numerous others likewise explained that they needed to treat everyone equally rather than providing favors for their friends, again stressing the need to protect their reputations.

Finally, while the inyangamugayo strove to present themselves as people of integrity and avoid corruption, they also paid attention to the behavior and reputations of their fellow judges. Typically, this involved holding their fellow judges to the same standards to which they were holding themselves. More broadly, this involved safeguarding the general reputations of their courts, which would in turn influence their personal reputations. Likewise, it also invoked a degree of boundary policing similar to efforts to control the behavior of professionals in other contexts.

Mélanie relayed: "Before we start trial, we first of all invite the defendant. When he is present, *we make sure that there is no relative of the defendant among the judges. If we find that there is any relative among the judges, we set him aside*" (emphasis added). Olive likewise explained that resisting bribes and guarding against exploitation was often a group endeavor, as the inyangamugayo could reinforce one another's commitment to ethical behavior. In her words:

> I remember our court was never involved in corruption cases. It was never involved because we could listen to the only person who was willing to give us information but for those who could come wanting to give us bribes, we never accepted that.

In cases where their collective resistance of bribes failed, and someone did take a bribe or engage in otherwise corrupt behavior, the judges often sought to remove him or her from their bench. Épiphanie recalled that a judge was expelled from her court. She explained: "In our court, there was a person ... . [who] wanted to ... introduce corrupt tendencies to our court. He wanted to make us corrupt ... But our president had to expel him from the court." Hope, a forty-seven-year-old farmer from Gahanga, shared a similar story. She remembered: "In our court, there was a woman ... whose father was a defendant. She could always say that her father's trial was not fair. We then decided to expel her from the court."

Espérance, a seventy-one-year-old from Gikondo, likewise reports an experience in which judges were expelled from the judges' bench. In her case, she contacted several government officials after observing corruption, which resulted in the forcible removal of the individuals. In her words:

> But there is one time when I was with gacaca that I wanted to withdraw because I could see some people vacating into corruption ... and I was not happy with that. I was not happy with that, I even contacted top officials in the government, telling them that I am going to resign from gacaca. Then they asked me, "Why? Why? Why do you have to resign?" I told them that gacaca is not doing what it is supposed to do. "If you do not intervene, I am going to get out of gacaca." Fortunately, those people were forced to get out of gacaca.

Thus, in these instances and in many others, judges who failed to uphold their reputations and to live up to the meaning of inyangamugayo were removed from their benches by their fellow judges. More broadly, this further underscores the importance of the inyangamugayo's reputations, from the time they were elected to the time that the courts closed in 2012.

Discussion and Conclusion

This article illustrates how the processes that typically determine who undertakes professional tasks can be upended in a transitional justice setting. In the case of Rwanda's gacaca courts, laypeople completed tasks that were previously performed by those with credentials and formal training. More than two-hundred-fifty thousand "nonprofessionals" were elected to oversee prosecutions for genocide, hand down prison sentences, and preside over conversations meant to reconcile the nation.

We suggest that the critical juncture of mass violence influenced Rwanda'sjustice system such that new conceptions arose regarding the necessary qualities and credentials of a judge.[22] To make sense of these shifting institutional arrangements, we draw on the sociology of expertise. This approach highlights the importance of analyzing the execution of tasks and suggests that many actors—not just licensed and credentialed professionals—can carry out important tasks in a "superior and speedy" manner (Eyal 2013, 871). In the case of Rwanda, mass violence altered the existing institutional arrangements and precipitated the need for people to preside over hundreds of thousands of genocide-related trials. Although we certainly do not claim that the inyangamugayo were superior to licensed judges in their implementation of the law, they were essential to the speedy execution of trials that were beyond the capacity of the national justice system.

In the absence of a formal licensing process, we find that social capital and, in particular, reputations became vital to the election and subsequent work of the inyangamugayo. The Rwandan government instructed citizens to select people of "integrity" to staff the gacaca courts, and although the government thus played a role in constructing this criterion, the forty-six judges we interviewed considered integrity to be of utmost importance. We illustrate that these judges perceived integrity as rooted in innocence, honesty, and trustworthiness and likewise show that their perceptions of how their fellow community members viewed them influenced their decision to accept their nomination as a judge.

Reputation remained important throughout the execution of the judges' tasks, and the inyangamugayo engaged in impression management (Goffman 1959) to uphold their reputations by presenting themselves as people of integrity. This involved steering clear of corruption, such as removing themselves from the bench when there was a conflict of interest and refusing to take bribes. As some inyangamugayo did engage in corrupt behavior, impression management likewise involved policing the behavior of the other inyangamugayo. Such actions were likely undertaken, at least in part, to ensure that the inyangamugayo continued to be seen as qualified to undertake their tasks and that they could rely on assistance from their communities.

The election of judges based largely on reputation differs from the selection of judges for other Rwandan courts. As in the United States, pre-genocide judges in Rwanda often needed to acquire at least some educational credentials that helped grant them entry to the profession. Reputations nonetheless likely played a role in their selection, and judges in all contexts arguably safeguard their reputations throughout their tenure. Indeed, professional associations typically regulate their members by asking them to adhere to codes of ethics (Abbott 1983), and professionals have accordingly made claims of morality to ensure their status (Lamont 1992). Scholars have thus documented that judges try to present themselves in a positive light and that they engage in reputation management (e.g., Baum 2009).

Nevertheless, our study suggests that in absence of formal licensing and credentialing, reputations may take on an increased salience. Put another way, when laypeople had to undertake tasks typically pursued by professionals, the importance of reputation became amplified due to the lack of other qualifying characteristics. In the case of Rwanda, the inyangamugayo believe that their reputations for honesty and trustworthiness were the cornerstone of their elections and their subsequent abilities to execute tasks.

We likewise find that the inyangamugayo relied on a network of support to carry out their duties, falling in line with previous scholarship on expertise (Eyal 2013) and further underscoring the importance of social capital in this context. Specifically, the inyangamugayo relied on state and international actors for training, which was instrumental as they stepped into their new positions. Community members were particularly critical, as they collected information about crimes, participated in trials, and sometimes even aided in aspects of decision making. Much like reputation, this suggests that the importance of a strong network of support may be amplified in situations where laypeople take on duties previously enacted by professionals.

Again, this article does not take a moral or legal stance regarding the judges' reliance on community members[23] or the many other elements of the gacaca courts, but instead illustrates the network that was forged to accomplish important tasks. In line with this, our article does not address the quality of the inyangamugayo's work. For instance, an examination of their accuracy in decision making would require in-depth information about specific cases, evidence, and legal procedures, which is beyond the scope of this study. We also cannot speak to whether the individuals we interviewed were actually ethical in their decision-making processes; in fact, some inyangamugayo were quick to share stories of others' corrupt actions but would rarely point a finger at themselves. This falls in line with social desirability bias, as it is likely that these individuals overemphasized positive traits and behavior and underemphasized (or did not report) less desirable traits or behavior. Although this must be kept in mind, it also points to their continual efforts to fulfill the image of a "person of integrity." All people engage in identity negotiation and impression management, and these judges likewise appeared eager to maintain their image as inyangamugayo during our interviews.

As we have relied heavily on the inyangamugayo's perceptions, future research should examine community members' perceptions of the inyangamugayo. Scholars should likewise examine how reputations may have influenced gacaca court sentencing decisions, as previous work has suggested that judges make decisions based on institutional constraints, preferences, and incentives—including how they wish to be perceived by the public—rather than via a strictly orthodox interpretation of the law (Epstein, Williams, and Posner 2013; Klement and Neeman 2013). Additionally, studies should examine whether reputation becomes more salient in other settings where laypeople (or at least people without formal credentials) undertake the work of professionals and whether and how networks of support aid these individuals in their work.

This case study has demonstrated the importance of social capital in a situation where laypeople were tasked with the duties of professionals. As we noted above, laypeople have taken on the duties of professionals in other transitional justice settings, such as in the case of South Africa's Truth and Reconciliation Commission or Uganda's *mato oput*. Critical junctures likely shift institutional arrangements that affect other forms of expertise as well. For instance, Syria's White Helmets constitute a contemporary example of laypeople providing muchneeded medical assistance in crisis situations. Yet, while boundaries around tasks and other elements of expertise may shift following critical junctures, the new institutional arrangements are likely impermanent. The inyangamugayo, for instance, did not become judges after the gacaca courts closed in 2012. Many did become mediators in their communities, however, suggesting that boundaries do not simply shift "back" to where they were prior to the critical juncture and further underscoring the transformative effect of mass violence.

Notes

1. Other scholarship has examined the daily work of lawyers or judges during periods of upheaval (McEvoy 2011; see also Ellman 1995; Cheh 2005).
2. The 1990s saw a sharp increase in prosecutions for human rights violations (Sikkink 2011), while countries that had been mired in Cold War proxy wars struggled to address their pasts in the pursuit of stability (Kritz 1995; Teitel 2000).
3. See Nyseth Brehm and Golden (2017) for more on "local" transitional justice.
4. *Mato oput* was arguably a community reconciliation tool rather than a legal one, though elders wielded power over the process, including compensation outcomes.

5. Notably, networks of other court actors played a crucial role helping these non-experts develop legal expertise (Carpenter, Mark, and Shanahan 2016).
6. An estimated two-hundred-fifty thousand people were raped (United Nations 1996), and many were victimized in other ways (Mullins 2009), though see Lemarchand (2013) on victimization estimates. For more history, see Lemarchand (1970), Newbury (1988), Prunier (1995), Des Forges (1999), Mamdani (2001), Straus (2006), and Fujii (2011).
7. The ICTR website cites ninety-three individuals, though this counts one individual twice and includes two others who were indicted for contempt of court.
8. As Jones (2009, 81) discusses, the Rwandan legal system prior to the genocide was rife with issues and often facilitated impunity, due in part to lack of independence from the state. While some of those who were appointed to positions within the national court system did not have legal training, many others had completed schooling and relevant training for their professions.
9. As Ingelaere (2016) explains, the UN High Commissioner for Human Rights suggested as early as 1996 that gacaca could play a role in responding to genocide-related crimes.
10. The courts had jurisdiction over crimes committed in Rwanda between October 1, 1990, and December 31, 1994. Suspects were divided into three categories (Organic Law 13/2008). Category 1 was reserved for organizers of the genocide, officials and leaders who participated or incited participation, and those who committed rape and sexual torture. Category 2 included those who tortured others or defiled their bodies, killed or intended to kill, or served as accomplices in such acts. Finally, Category 3 was comprised of property offenders. Some of the Category 1 offenders were tried in the national courts.
11. The bench originally consisted of nineteen and was later reduced to fourteen and nine, with varying numbers needed to obtain a quorum and reach sentencing decisions. The precise number on the bench also varied slightly across communities.
12. A 2007 law added the obligation that judges should also be free from genocide ideology.
13. While more men were elected than women, the proportion of women judges rose as (mostly men) judges were replaced when it came to light that they had participated in the genocide. Exact statistics are not available, however, though fewer than 200,000 judges staffed the courts at their outset.
14. The pilot phase resulted in several changes to the laws governing the gacaca courts, influencing the need for additional training for inyangamugayo in 2004.
15. We unfortunately cannot address each of these important critiques within one article, though we refer the reader to the aforementioned works for additional information.
16. Permission from the National Commission for the Fight Against Genocide (CNLG), as well as from the presidents of the respective sectors, was granted for this study. The Director General of Research of CNLG assisted the first author in accessing information on gacaca court trials.

17. National laws passed in 2008 and 2013 deem the ethnic categories that existed before the genocide as part of a broader "genocide ideology." The national census likewise no longer includes questions about ethnicity. Thus, while it is possible to discuss previous ethnic categories, we did not directly ask about ethnicity.
18. Most participants served as judges throughout the time that the gacaca courts were operational, though a handful left their positions prior to the courts' closure in 2012. Some attributed their departure to family and work considerations, although several judges we interviewed had been accused of corruption.
19. As noted above, not having participated in the genocide was one of the official criteria. Nevertheless, there were many official criteria (such as being twenty-one), and this was the only one that consistently surfaced during interviews.
20. While many judges were not able to read or write, each court elected a secretary. This individual kept detailed records on trial events. The secretary also was responsible for completing court paperwork, such as forms that explained the outcome of each case.
21. Some inyangamugayo instead allowed their family and friends to benefit from their positions (Chakravarty 2015)
22. We do not suggest that the mass violence is the only reason that these conceptions arose. For instance, the previous gacaca system's reliance on community elders (rather than trained officials) may have likewise influenced this shift and may have influenced people's willingness to accept the gacaca courts.
23. Such reliance may have broken confidentiality, and power structures within communities likely influenced *which* members of the community were able to provide input during the proceedings.

References

Abbott, Andrew. "Professional Ethics." *American Journal of Sociology* 88 (1983): 855–85.

———. *The System of Professions: An Essay on the Division of Expert Labor.* Chicago: University of Chicago Press, 1988.

Apuuli, Kasaija Phillip. "Procedural Due Process and the Prosecution of Genocide Suspects in Rwanda." *Journal of Genocide Research* 11 (2009): 11–30.

Baines, Erin K. "The Haunting of Alice: Local Approaches to Justice and Reconciliation in Northern Uganda." *International Journal of Transitional Justice* 1, no. 1 (2007): 91–114.

Baum, Lawrence. *Judges and Their Audiences: A Perspective on Judicial Behavior.* Princeton, NJ: Princeton University Press, 2009.

Berry, Marie E. *Women, War, and Power in Rwanda and Bosnia-Herzegovina.* New York: Cambridge University Press, 2018.

Bond, Rod, and Nigel Lemon. "Training, Experience, and Magistrates' Sentencing Philosophies: A Longitudinal Study." *Law and Human Behavior* 5, no. 2–3 (1981): 123–39.

Bornkamm, Paul Christoph. *Rwanda's Gacaca Courts: Between Retribution and Reparation*. New York: Oxford University Press, 2012.

Bourdieu, Pierre. *The State Nobility: Elite Schools in the Field of Power*. Stanford, CA: Stanford University Press, 1996.

Burnet, Jennie. "The Injustice of Local Justice: Truth, Reconciliation and Revenge in Rwanda." *Journal of Genocide Studies and Prevention* 3, no. 2 (2008): 173–93.

Cambrosio, Alberto, Camille Limoges, and Eric Hoffman. "Expertise as a Network: A Case Study of the Controversies Over the Environmental Release of Genetically Modified Organisms." In *The Culture and Power of Knowledge*, edited by Nico Stehr and Richard V. Ericson, 341–61. Berlin: Walter de Gruyter, 1992.

Carpenter, Anna E., Alyx Mark, and Colleen F. Shanahan. "Trial and Error: Lawyers and Nonlawyer Advocates." *Law and Social Inquiry* 42 (2016): 1023–1057. doi:10.1111/lsi.12252.

Census. "Thematic Report: Population Size, Structure, and Distribution." *Fourth Population and Housing Census*. Rwanda. Kigali: National Institute of Statistics, 2012.

Chakravarty, Anuradha. *Investing in Authoritarian Rule: Punishment and Patronage in Rwanda's Gacaca Courts for Genocide Crimes*. New York: Cambridge University Press, 2015.

Cheh, Mary M. "Should Lawyers Participate in Rigged Systems: The Case of the Military Commissions." *Journal of National Security Law and Policy* 375 (2005): 1–53.

Clark, Phil. *The Gacaca Courts, Post Genocide-Justice and Reconciliation in Rwanda: Justice Without Lawyers*. Oxford: Oxford University Press, 2010.

Collins, Harry, and Robert Evans. *Rethinking Expertise*. Chicago: University of Chicago Press, 2007.

Conflict Management of the National University of Rwanda (CCM). "Gacaca Courts in Rwanda." Report published by the CCM. Kigali: CCM, 2012.

Corey, Allison, and Sandra F. Joireman. "Retributive Justice: The Gacaca Courts in Rwanda." *African Affairs* 103, no. 410 (2004): 73–89.

Des Forges, Alison. *Leave None to Tell the Story: Genocide in Rwanda*. New York: Human Rights Watch, 1999.

Diamond, Shari Seidman. "Revising Images of Public Punitiveness: Sentencing by Lay and Professional English Magistrates." *Law and Social Inquiry* 15, no. 2 (1990): 191–221.

Ellman, Stephen. "Struggle and Legitimation." *Law and Social Inquiry* 20, no. 2 (1995): 339–48.

Epstein, Lee, William M. Landes, and Richard A. Posner. *The Behavior of Federal Judges: A Theoretical and Empirical Study of Rational Choice*. Cambridge, MA: Harvard University Press, 2013.

Epstein, Steven. "The Construction of Lay Expertise: Aids Activism and the Forging of Credibility in the Reform of Clinical Trials." *Science, Technology, and Human Values* 20, no. 4 (1995): 408–37.

———. *Impure Science: Aids, Activism, and the Politics of Knowledge*. Berkeley, CA: University of California Press, 1996.

Eyal, Gil. "For a Sociology of Expertise: The Social Origins of the Autism Epidemic." *American Journal of Sociology* 118, no. 4 (2013): 863–907.

Faulconbridge, James, and Daniel Muzio. "Professions in a Globalizing World: Toward a Transnational Sociology of the Professions." *International Sociology* 27, no. 1 (2012): 136–52.

Fierens, Jacques. "Gacaca Courts: Between Fantasy and Reality." *Journal of International Criminal Justice* 3 (2005): 896–919.

Fine, Gary. *Difficult Reputations: Collective Memories of the Evil, Inept, and Controversial*. Chicago: University of Chicago Press, 2001.

Fujii, Lee Ann. *Killing Neighbors: Webs of Violence in Rwanda*. Ithaca, NY: Cornell University Press, 2011.

Gacaca Report Summary. "Summary of the Report Presented at the Closing of Gacaca Court Activities." National Service of Gacaca Jurisdictions. Kigali, Rwanda. June 18, 2012. On file with the first author.

Garbett, Claire. "Transitional Justice and 'National Ownership': An Assessment of the Institutional Development of the War Crimes Chamber of Bosnia and Herzegovina." *Human Rights Review* 13, no. 1 (2012): 65–84.

Goffman, Erving. *The Presentation of Self in Everyday Life*. New York: Doubleday Anchor, 1959.

Gready, Paul, and Simon Robins. "Rethinking Civil Society and Transitional Justice: Lessons from Social Movements and 'New' Civil Society." *International Journal of Human Rights* 21, no.7 (2010): 956–75.

Green, Thomas M. "Police as Frontline Mental Health Workers: The Decision to Arrest or Refer to Mental Health Agencies." *International Journal of Law and Psychiatry* 20, no. 4 (1997): 469–86.

Hagan, John. *Justice in the Balkans: Prosecuting War Crimes in the Hague Tribunal*. Chicago: Chicago University Press, 2003.

Honeyman, Catherine, Shakirah Hudani, Alfa Tiruneh, Justina Hierta, Leila Chirayath, Andrew Iliff, and Jens Meierhenrich. "Establishing Collective Norms: Potentials for Participatory Justice in Rwanda." *Peace and Conflict: Journal of Peace Psychology* 10, no. 1 (2004): 1–24.

Hughes, Mélanie M., and Aili Mari Tripp. "Civil War and Trajectories of Change in Women's Political Representation in Africa, 1985–2010." *Social Forces* 93, no. 4 (2015): 1513–40.

Ingelaere, Bert. *Inside Rwanda's Gacaca Courts: Seeking Justice After Genocide*. Madison: University of Wisconsin Press, 2016.

International Center for Prison Studies. 2013. http://www.prisonstudies.org.

Ivanisevic, Bogdan. "The War Crimes Chamber in Bosnia and Herzegovina: From Hybrid to Domestic Court." International Center for Transitional Justice, 2008. https://www.ictj.org/ sites/default/files/ICTJ-FormerYugoslavia-Domestic-Court-2008-English.pdf.

Johnstone, Gerry. "Penal Policy Making: Elitist, Populist or Participatory?" *Punishment and Society* 2, no. 2 (2000): 161–80.

Jones, Nicholas. *The Courts of Genocide: Politics and the Rule of Law in Rwanda and Arusha*. New York: Routledge, 2009.

Kaitesi, Usta. *Genocidal Gender and Sexual Violence: The Legacy of the ICTR, Rwanda's Ordinary Courts and the Gacaca Courts*. Cambridge: Intersentia, 2014.

Kestnbaum, Meyer. "Citizen-Soldiers, National Service and the Mass Army: The Birth of Conscription in Revolutionary Europe and North America." *Comparative Social Research* 20 (2002): 117–44.

Klement, Alon, and Zvika Neeman. "Does Information About Arbitrators' Win/Loss Ratios Improve Their Accuracy?" *Journal of Legal Studies* 42, no. 2 (2013): 369–97.

Kritz, Neil J. *Transitional Justice: How Emerging Democracies Reckon with Former Regimes*. Washington, DC: US Institute of Peace, 1995.

Kuhlmann, Ellen. "Sociology of Professions: Towards International Context-Sensitive Approaches." *South African Review of Sociology* 44, no. 2 (2013): 7–17.

Lamont, Michèle. *Money, Morals, and Manners: The Culture of the French and the American Upper-Middle Class*. Chicago: University of Chicago Press, 1992.

Larson, Magali S. *The Rise of Professionalism: A Sociological Analysis*. Berkeley: University of California Press, 1977.

Lefranc, Sandrine, and Frédéric Vairel. "The Emergence of Transitional Justice as a Professional International Practice." In *Dealing with Wars and Dictatorships*, edited by Liora Israel and Guillaume Mouralis, 235–52. The Hague: TMC Asser Press, 2014.

Lemarchand, René. *Rwanda and Burundi*. New York: Praeger, 1970.

________. "Rwanda: The State of Research." *Online Encyclopedia of Mass Violence*, 2013. http://citeseerx.ist.psu.edu/viewdoc/download?doi=10.1.1.692.7703&rep=rep1&type=pdf.

Liu, Sida. "The Legal Profession as a Social Process: A Theory on Lawyers and Globalization." *Law and Social Inquiry* 38, no. 3 (2013): 670–93.

________. "Overlapping Ecologies: Professions and Development in the Rise of Legal Services in China." *Sociology of Development* 3, no. 3 (2017): 212–231.

Loyle, Cyanne E. "Overcoming Research Obstacles in Hybrid Regimes: Lessons from Rwanda." *Social Science Quarterly* 97, no. 4 (2016): 923–35.

Madlingozi, Tshepo. "On Transitional Justice Entrepreneurs and the Production of Victims." *Journal of Human Rights Practice* 2, no. 2 (2010): 208–28.

Mahoney, James. "Path Dependence in Historical Sociology." *Theory and Society* 29, no. 4 (2000): 507–48.

Mamdani, Mahmood. *When Victims Become Killers: Colonialism, Nativism, and Genocide in Rwanda*. Princeton, NJ: Princeton University Press, 2001.

Mann, Michael. *The Sources of Social Power Volume 4: Globalizations, 1945–2011*. New York: Cambridge University Press, 2013.

Markoff, John. *Waves of Democracy: Social Movements and Political Change* (Vol. 10). New York: Sage, 1996.

McEvoy, Kieran. "Beyond Legalism: Towards a Thicker Understanding of Transitional Justice." *Journal of Law and Society* 34, no. 4 (2007): 411–40.

________. "What Did the Lawyers Do During the 'War'? Neutrality, Conflict and the Culture of Quietism." *Modern Law Review* 74, no. 3 (2011): 350–84.

Michelson, Ethan. "The Practice of Law as an Obstacle to Justice: Chinese Lawyers at Work." *Law and Society Review* 40, no. 1 (2006): 1–38.

________. "Lawyers, Political Embeddedness, and Institutional Continuity in China's Transition from Socialism." *American Journal of Sociology* 113, no. 2 (2007): 352–414.

Moore, Barrington. *Social Origins of Dictatorship and Democracy; Lord and Peasant in the Making of the Modern World*. Boston: Beacon Press, 1966.

Mullins, Christopher W. "'He Would Kill Me with His Penis': Genocidal Rape in Rwanda as a State Crime." *Critical Criminology* 17, no. 1 (2009): 15–33.

Newbury, Catharine. *The Cohesion of Oppression: Clientship and Ethnicity in Rwanda, 1860–1960*. New York: Columbia University Press, 1988.

Nyseth Brehm, Hollie, and Shannon Golden. "Centering Survivors in Local Transitional Justice." *Annual Review of Law and Social Science* 13(2017): 102–21.

Nyseth Brehm, Hollie, Christopher Uggen, and Jean-Damascène Gasanabo. "Genocide, Justice, and Rwanda's Gacaca Courts." *Journal of Contemporary Criminal Justice* 33, no. 3 (2014): 333–52.

Osiel, Mark. *Mass Atrocity, Collective Memory, and the Law*. New Brunswick, NJ: Transaction, 1997.

Palmer, Nicola. *Courts in Conflict: Interpreting the Layers of Justice in Post-Genocide Rwanda*. New York: Oxford University Press, 2015.

Pierson, Paul. *Politics in Time: History, Institutions, and Social Analysis*. Princeton, NJ: Princeton University Press, 2004.

Prinsloo, M. W. "Recognition and Application of Indigenous Law in Zaire, Rwanda, Burundi and Lusophone Africa." *Journal of South African Law* (1993): 541–51.

Prunier, Gérard. *The Rwanda Crisis: History of a Genocide*. New York: Columbia University Press, 1995.

Purdeková, Andrea. "'Even if I Am Not Here, There Are So Many Eyes': Surveillance and State Reach in Rwanda." *Journal of Modern African Studies* 49, no. 3 (2011): 475–97.

Rettig, Max. "*Gacaca*: Truth, Justice, and Reconciliation in Postconflict Rwanda?" *African Studies Review* 51, no. 3 (2008): 25–50.

Reyntjens, Filip. "Le Gacaca ou la Justice du Gazon au Rwanda." *Politique Africaine* 40 (1990): 31–41.

Roht-Arriaza, Naomi, and Javier Mariezcurrena. *Transitional Justice in the 21st Century: Beyond Truth Versus Justice*. Cambridge: Cambridge University Press, 2006.

Sarkin, Jeremy. "The Tension Between Justice and Reconciliation in Rwanda: Politics, Human Rights, Due Process and the Role of the *Gacaca* Courts in Dealing with the Genocide." *Journal of African Law* 45, no. 2 (2001): 143–72.

Schabas, William A. "Genocide Trials and *Gacaca* Courts." *Journal of International Criminal Justice* 3 (2005): 879–95.

Shaw, Rosalind, Lars Waldorf, and Pierre Hazan. *Localizing Transitional Justice: Interventions and Priorities After Mass Violence*. Stanford, CA: Stanford University Press, 2010.

Sikkink, Kathryn. *The Justice Cascade: How Human Rights Prosecutions Are Changing the World*. New York: W.W. Norton, 2011.

Skocpol, Theda. *States and Social Revolutions: A Comparative Analysis of France, Russia, and China*. New York: Cambridge University Press, 1979.

———. *Protecting Soldiers and Mothers: The Political Origins of Social Policy in the United States*. Cambridge, MA: Harvard University Press, 1992.

Straus, Scott. *The Order of Genocide: Race, Power, and War in Rwanda*. Ithaca, NY: Cornell University Press, 2006.

Straus, Scott, and Lars Waldorf. *Remaking Rwanda: State Building and Human Rights After Mass Violence*. Madison: University of Wisconsin Press, 2011.

Stover, Eric, Hanny Megally, and Hania Mufti. "Bremer's 'Gordian Knot': Transitional Justice and the US Occupation of Iraq." *Human Rights Quarterly* 27, no. 3 (2005): 830–57.

Teitel, Ruti G. *Transitional Justice*. Oxford: Oxford University Press, 2000.

———. "Transitional Justice Genealogy." *Harvard Human Rights Journal* 16 (2003): 69–94.

Thomson, Susan. "The Darker Side of Transitional Justice: The Power Dynamics Behind Rwanda's Gacaca Courts." *Africa* 81, no. 3 (2011): 373–90.

———. *Whispering Truth to Power: Everyday Resistance to Reconciliation in Postgenocide Rwanda*. Madison: University of Wisconsin Press, 2013.

Tilly, Charles. *From Mobilization to Revolution*. New York: McGraw-Hill, 1978.

———. "War Making and State Making as Organized Crime." In *Bringing the State Back In*, edited by Peter B. Evans, Dietrich Rueschemeyer, and Theda Skocpol, 169–91. Cambridge: Cambridge University Press, 1985.

United Nations. "Report on the Situation of Human Rights in Rwanda." E/CN.4/1996/68. New York: United Nations, 1996.

Waldorf, Lars. "Rwanda's Failing Experiment in Restorative Justice." In *Handbook of Restorative Justice: A Global Perspective*, edited by Dennis Sullivan and Larry Tifft, 422–34. New York: Routledge, 2006.

Weber, Max. *Economy and Society: An Outline of Interpretive Sociology*. Berkeley: University of California Press, [1922] 1978.

Statutes Cited

ICTR Statute. 1994. http://www.ohchr.org/EN/ProfessionalInterest/Pages/StatuteInternationalCriminalTribunalForRwanda.aspx.
Organic Law n° 13/2008 of May 19, 2008, Rwanda.

Chapter 10

Religious Systems and Practices

DISCUSSION QUESTIONS

1. How were religious symbols and texts shared among a variety of people and communities in both readings? How did the media through which these symbols and texts were shared contribute to how they were consumed and interpreted?
2. In what ways are "new" and "old" orders reflected in the production and consumption of religious artifacts in both readings?
3. Explain how the circulation of religious symbols and texts in both readings constitutes an example of syncretism, defined as an amalgamation of often disparate beliefs and practices, usually coming from two or more cultural traditions. How might all religions contain some form of syncretism? Can you think of some specific examples?
4. How does the sharing of religious symbols in both readings help constitute new kinds of communities?

KEY TERMS

Master Symbol
Diaspora
Sufism
Origin myth

Wolf, Eric R. 1958. "The Virgin of Guadalupe: A Mexican National Symbol." *The Journal of American Folklore* 71(279):34–39.

OCCASIONALLY, WE ENCOUNTER A SYMBOL WHICH seems to enshrine the major hopes and aspirations of an entire society.[1] Such a master symbol is represented by the Virgin of Guadalupe, Mexico's patron saint. During the Mexican War of Independence against Spain, her image preceded the insurgents into battle.[2] Emiliano Zapata and his agrarian rebels fought under her emblem in the Great Revolution of 1910.[3] Today, her image adorns house fronts and interiors, churches and home altars, bull rings and gambling dens, taxis and buses, restaurants and houses of ill repute. She is celebrated in popular song and verse. Her shrine at Tepeyac, immediately north of Mexico City, is visited each year by hundreds of thousands of pilgrims, ranging from the inhabitants of far-off Indian villages to the members of socialist trade union locals. "Nothing to be seen in Canada or Europe," says F. S. C. Northrop, "equals it in the volume or the vitality of its moving quality or in the depth of its spirit of religious devotion."[4]

In this paper, I should like to discuss this Mexican master symbol, and the ideology which surrounds it. In making use of the term "master symbol," I do not wish to imply that belief in the symbol is common to all Mexicans. We are not dealing here with an element of a putative national character, defined as a common denominator of all Mexican nationals. It is no longer legitimate to assume "that any member of the [national] group will exhibit certain regularities of behavior which are common in high degree among the other members of the society."[5] Nations, like other complex societies, must, however, "possess cultural forms or mechanisms which groups involved in the same over-all web of relationships can use in their formal and informal dealings with each other."[6] Such forms develop historically, hand in hand with other processes which lead to the formation of nations, and social groups which are caught up in these processes must become "acculturated" to their usage.[7] Only where such forms exist, can communication and coördinated behavior be established among the constituent groups of such a society. They provide the cultural idiom of behavior and ideal representations through which different groups of the same society can pursue and manipulate their different fates within a coördinated framework. This paper, then, deals with one such cultural form, operating on the symbolic level. The study of this symbol seems particularly rewarding, since it is not restricted to one set of social ties, but refers to a very wide range of social relationships.

The image of the Guadalupe and her shrine at Tepeyac are surrounded by an origin myth.[8] According to this myth, the Virgin Mary appeared to Juan Diego, a Christianized Indian of commoner status, and addressed him in Nahuatl. The encounter took place on the Hill of Tepeyac in the year 1531, ten years after the Spanish Conquest of Tenochtitlan. The Virgin commanded Juan Diego to seek out the archbishop of Mexico and to inform him of her desire to see a church built in her honor on Tepeyac Hill. After Juan Diego was twice unsuccessful in his efforts to carry out her order, the Virgin wrought a miracle. She bade Juan Diego pick roses in a sterile spot where normally only desert plants could grow, gathered the roses into the Indian's cloak, and told him to present cloak and roses to the incredulous archbishop. When Juan Diego unfolded his cloak before the bishop, the image of the Virgin was miraculously stamped upon it. The bishop acknowledged the miracle, and ordered a shrine built where Mary had appeared to her humble servant.

The shrine, rebuilt several times in centuries to follow, is today a basilica, the third highest kind of church in Western Christendom. Above the central altar hangs Juan Diego's cloak with the miraculous image. It shows a young woman without child, her head lowered demurely in her shawl. She wears an open crown and flowing gown, and stands upon a half moon symbolizing the Immaculate Conception.

The shrine of Guadalupe was, however, not the first religious structure built on Tepeyac; nor was Guadalupe the first female supernatural associated with the hill. In pre-Hispanic times, Tepeyac had housed a temple to the earth and fertility goddess Tonantzin, Our Lady Mother, who—like the Guadalupe—was associated with the moon. Temple, like basilica, was the center of large scale pilgrimages. That the veneration accorded the Guadalupe drew inspiration from the earlier worship of Tonantzin is attested by several Spanish friars. F. Bernardino de Sahagún, writing fifty years after the Conquest, says: "Now that the Church of Our Lady of Guadalupe has been built there, they call her Tonantzin too. . . . The term refers ... to that ancient Tonantzin and this state of affairs should be remedied, because the proper name of the Mother of God is not Tonantzin, but Dios and Nantzin. It seems to be a satanic device to mask idolatry . . . and they come from far away to visit that Tonantzin, as much as before; a devotion which is also suspect because there are many churches of Our Lady everywhere and they do not go to them; and they come from faraway lands to this Tonantzin as of old."[9] F. Martín de León wrote in a similar vein: "On the hill where Our Lady of Guadalupe is they adored the idol of a goddess they called Tonantzin, which means Our Mother, and this is also the name they give Our Lady and they always say they are going to Tonantzin or they are celebrating Tonantzin and many of them understand this in the old way and not in the modern way. . . ."[10] The syncretism was still alive in the seventeenth century. F. Jacinto de la Serna, in discussing the pilgrimages to the Guadalupe at Tepeyac, noted: ". . . it is the purpose of the wicked to [worship] the goddess and not the Most Holy Virgin, or both together."[11]

Increasingly popular during the sixteenth century, the Guadalupe cult gathered emotional impetus during the seventeenth. During this century appear the first known pictorial representations of the Guadalupe, apart from the miraculous original; the first poems are written in her honor; and the first sermons announce the transcendental implications of her supernatural appearance in Mexico and among Mexicans.[12] Historians have long tended to neglect the seventeenth century which seemed "a kind of Dark Age in Mexico." Yet "this quiet time was of the utmost importance in the development of Mexican Society."[13] During this century, the institution of the hacienda comes to dominate Mexican life.[14] During this century, also, "New Spain is ceasing to be 'new' and to be 'Spain.'"[15] These new experiences require a new cultural idiom, and in the Guadalupe cult, the component segments of Mexican colonial society encountered cultural forms in which they could express their parallel interests and longings.

The primary purpose of this paper is not, however, to trace the history of the Guadalupe symbol. It is concerned rather with its functional aspects, its roots and reference to the major social relationships of Mexican society.

The first set of relationships which I would like to single out for consideration are the ties of kinship, and the emotions generated in the play of relationships within families. I want to suggest that some of the meanings of the Virgin symbol in general, and of the Guadalupe symbol in particular, derive from these emotions. I say "some meanings" and I use the term "derive" rather than "originate," because the form and function of the family in any given society are themselves determined by other social factors: technology, economy, residence, political power. The family is but one relay in the circuit within which symbols are generated in complex societies. Also, I used the plural "families" rather than "family," because there are demonstrably more than one kind of family in Mexico.[16] I shall simplify the available information on Mexican family life, and discuss the material in terms of two major types of families.[17] The first kind of family is congruent with the closed and static life of the Indian village. It may be called the Indian family. In this kind of family, the husband is ideally dominant, but in reality labor and authority are shared equally among, both marriage partners. Exploitation of one sex by the other is atypical; sexual feats do not add to a person's status in the eyes of others. Physical punishment and authoritarian treatment of children are rare. The second kind of family is congruent with the much more open, mobile, manipulative life in communities which are actively geared to the life of the nation, a life in which power relationships between individuals and groups are of great moment. This kind of family may be called the Mexican family. Here, the father's authority is unquestioned on both the real and the ideal plane. Double sex standards prevail, and male sexuality is charged with a desire to exercise domination. Children are ruled with a heavy hand; physical punishment is frequent.

The Indian family pattern is consistent with the behavior towards the Guadalupe noted by John Bushnell in the Matlazinca speaking community of San Juan Atzingo in the Valley of Toluca.[18] There, the image of the Virgin is addressed in passionate terms as a source of warmth and love, and the *pulque* or century plant beer drunk on ceremonial occasions is identified with her milk. Bushnell postulates that here the Guadalupe is identified with the mother as a source of early satisfactions, never again experienced after separation from the mother and emergence into social adulthood. As such, the Guadalupe embodies a longing to return to the pristine state in which hunger and unsatisfactory social relations are minimized. The second family pattern is also consistent with a symbolic identification of Virgin and mother, yet this time within a context of adult male dominance and sexual assertion, discharged against submissive females and children. In this second context, the Guadalupe symbol is charged with the energy of rebellion against the father. Her image is the embodiment of hope in a victorious outcome of the struggle between generations.

This struggle leads to a further extension of the symbolism. Successful rebellion against power figures is equated with the promise of life; defeat with the promise of death. As John A. Mackay has suggested, there thus takes place a further symbolic identification of the Virgin with life; of defeat and death with the crucified Christ. In Mexican artistic tradition, as in Hispanic artistic tradition in general,[19] Christ is never depicted as an adult man, but always either as a helpless child, or more often as a figure beaten, tortured, defeated and killed. In this symbolic equation we are touching upon some of the roots both of the passionate affirmation of faith in the Virgin, and of the fascination with death which characterizes Baroque Christianity in general, and Mexican Catholicism in particular. The Guadalupe stands for life, for hope, for health; Christ on the cross, for despair and for death.

Supernatural mother and natural mother are thus equated symbolically, as are earthly and otherworldly hopes and desires. These hopes center on the provision of food and emotional warmth in the first case, in the successful waging of the Oedipal struggle in the other.

Family relations are, however, only one element in the formation of the Guadalupe symbol. Their analysis does little to explain the Guadalupe as such. They merely illuminate the female and maternal attributes of the more widespread Virgin symbol. The Guadalupe is important to Mexicans not only because she is a supernatural mother, but also because she embodies their major political and religious aspirations.

To the Indian groups, the symbol is more than an embodiment of life and hope; it restores to them the hopes of salvation. We must not forget that the Spanish Conquest signified not only military defeat, but the defeat also of the old gods and the decline of the old ritual. The apparition of the Guadalupe to an Indian commoner thus represents on one level the return of Tonantzin. As Tannenbaum has well said, "The Church . . . gave the Indian an opportunity not merely to save his life, but also to save his faith in his own gods."[20] On another level, the myth of the apparition served as a symbolic testimony that the Indian, as much as the Spaniard, was capable of being saved, capable of receiving Christianity. This must be understood against the background of the bitter theological and political argument which followed the Conquest and divided churchmen, officials, and conquerors into those who held that the Indian was incapable of conversion, thus inhuman, and therefore a fit subject of political and economic exploitation; and those who held that the Indian was human, capable of conversion and that this exploitation had to be tempered by the demands of the Catholic faith and of orderly civil processes of government.[21] The myth of the Guadalupe thus validates the Indian's right to legal defense, orderly government, to citizenship; to supernatural salvation, but also to salvation from random oppression.

But if the Guadalupe guaranteed a rightful place to the Indians in the new social system of New Spain, the myth also held appeal to the large group of disinherited who arose in New Spain as illegitimate offspring of Spanish fathers and Indian mothers, or through impoverishment, acculturation or loss of status within the Indian or Spanish group.[22] For such people, there was for a long time no proper place in the social order. Their very right to exist was questioned in their inability to command the full rights of citizenship and legal protection. Where Spaniard and Indian stood squarely within the law, they inhabited the interstices and margins of constituted society. These groups acquired influence and wealth in the seventeenth and eighteenth centuries, but were yet barred from social recognition and power by the prevailing economic, social and political order.[23] To them, the Guadalupe myth came to represent not merely the guarantee of their assured place in heaven, but the guarantee of their place in society here and how. On the political plane, the wish for a return to a paradise of early satisfactions of food and warmth, a life without defeat, sickness or death, gave rise to a political wish for a Mexican paradise, in which the illegitimate sons would possess the country, and the irresponsible Spanish overlords, who never acknowledged the social responsibilities of their paternity, would be driven from the land.

In the writings of seventeenth century ecclesiastics, the Guadalupe becomes the harbinger of this new order. In the book by Miguel Sánchez, published in 1648, the Spanish Conquest of New Spain is justified solely on the grounds that it allowed the Virgin to become manifest in her chosen country, and to found in Mexico a new paradise. Just as Israel had been chosen to produce Christ, so Mexico had been chosen to produce Guadalupe. Sánchez equates her with the apocalyptic woman of the Revelation of John (12: 1), "arrayed with the sun, and the moon under her feet, and upon her head a crown of twelve stars" who is to realize the prophecy of Deuteronomy 8: 7–10 and lead the Mexicans into the Promised Land. Colonial Mexico thus becomes the desert of Sinai; Independent Mexico the land of milk and honey. F. Francisco de Florencia, writing in 1688, coined the slogan which made Mexico not merely another chosen nation, but the Chosen Nation: *non fecit taliter omni nationi,*[24] words which still adorn the portals of the basilica, and shine forth in electric light bulbs at night. And on the eve of Mexican independence, Servando Teresa de Mier elaborates still further the Guadalupan myth by claiming that Mexico had been converted to Christianity long before the Spanish Conquest. The apostle Saint Thomas had brought the image of Guadalupe-Tonantzin to the New World as a symbol of his mission, just as Saint James had converted Spain with the image of the Virgin of the Pillar. The Spanish Conquest was therefore historically unnecessary, and should be erased from the annals of history.[25] In this perspective, the Mexican War of Independence marks the final realization of the apocalyptic promise. The banner of the Guadalupe leads the insurgents; and their cause is referred to as "her law."[26] In this ultimate extension of the symbol, the promise of life held out by the supernatural mother has become the promise of an independent Mexico, liberated from the irrational authority of the Spanish father-oppressors and restored to the Chosen Nation whose election had been manifest in the apparition of the Virgin on Tepeyac. The land of the supernatural mother is finally possessed by her rightful heirs. The symbolic circuit is closed. Mother; food, hope, health, life; supernatural salvation and salvation from oppression; Chosen People and national independence—all find expression in a single master symbol.

The Guadalupe symbol thus links together family, politics and religion; colonial past and independent present; Indian and Mexican. It reflects the salient social relationships of Mexican life, and embodies the emotions which they generate. It provides a cultural idiom through which the tenor and emotions of these relationships can be expressed. It is, ultimately, a way of talking about Mexico: a "collective representation" of Mexican society.

Notes

1. Parts of this paper were presented to the Symposium on Ethnic and National Ideologies, Annual Spring Meeting of the American Ethnological Society in conjunction with the Philadelphia Anthropological Society, on 12 May 1956.
2. Niceto de Zamacois, *Historia de México* (Barcelona-Mexico, 1878–82), VI, 253.
3. Antonio Pompa y Pompa, *Album del IV centenario guadalupano* (Mexico, 1938), p. 173.
4. F. S. C. Northrop, *The Meeting of East and West* (New York, 1946), p. 25.
5. David G. Mandelbaum, "On the Study of National Character," *American Anthropologist,* LV (1953) p. 185
6. Eric R. Wolf, "Aspects of Group Relations in a Complex Society: Mexico," *American Anthropologist,* LVII (1956), 1065–1078.
7. Eric R. Wolf, "La formación de la nación," *Ciencias Sociales,* IV, 50–51.
8. Ernest Gruening, *Mexico and Its Heritage* (New York, 1928), p. 235.
9. Bernardino de Sahagún, *Historia general de las cosas de nueva españa* (Mexico, 1938), I, lib. 6.
10. Quoted in Carlos A. Echánove Trujillo, *Sociología mexicana* (Mexico, 1948), p. 105.
11. Quoted in Jesús Amaya, *La madre de Dios: genesis e historia de nuestra señora de Guadalupe* (Mexico, 1931), p. 230.

12. Francisco de la Maza, *El guadalupismo mexicano* (Mexico, 1953), pp. 12–14, 143, 30, 33, 82.
13. Lesley B. Simpson, "Mexico's Forgotten Century," *Pacific Historical Review,* XXII (1953), 115, 114.
14. François Chevalier, *La formation des grands domaines au Mexique* (Paris, 1952), p. xii.
15. de la Maza, p. 41.
16. María Elvira Bermúdez, *La vida familiar del mexicano* (Mexico, 1955), chapters 2 and 3.
17. For relevant material, see: Bermúdez; John Gillin, "Ethos and Cultural Aspects of Personality," and Robert Redfield and Sol Tax, "General Characteristics of Present-Day Mesoamerican Indian Society," in Sol Tax, ed., *Heritage of Conquest* (Glencoe, 1952), pp. 193–212, 31–39; Gordon W. Hewes, "Mexicans in Search of the 'Mexican'," *American Journal of Economics and Sociology,* XIII (1954), 209–223; Octavio Paz, *El laberinto de la soledad* (Mexico, 1947), pp. 71–89.
18. John Bushnell, "La Virgen de Guadalupe as Surrogate Mother in San Juan Atzingo," paper read before the 54th Annual Meeting of the American Anthropological Association, 18 November 1955.
19. John A. Mackay, *The Other Spanish Christ* (New York, 1933), pp. 110–117.
20. Frank Tannenbaum, *Peace by Revolution* (New York, 1933), p. 39.
21. Silvio Zavala, *La filosofía en la conquista de America* (Mexico, 1947).
22. Nicolas León, *Las castas del México colonial o Nueva España* (Mexico, 1924); C. E. Marshall, "The Birth of the Mestizo in New Spain," *Hispanic American Historical Review,* XIX (1939), 161–184; Wolf, "La formación de la nación," pp. 103–106.
23. Gregorio Torres Quintero, *México hacía el fin del virreinato español* (Mexico, 1921); Eric R. Wolf, "The Mexican Bajío in the Eighteenth Century," *Middle American Research Institute Publication* XVII (1955), 180–199; Wolf, "Aspects of Group Relations in a Complex Society: Mexico."
24. de la Maza, pp. 39–40, 43–49, 64.
25. Luis Villoro, *Los grandes momentos del indigenismo en México* (Mexico, 1950), pp. 131–138.
26. Luis González y González, "El optimismo nacionalista como factor en la independencia de México," *Estudios de historiografía americana* (Mexico, 1948), p. 194.

University of Virginia
Charlottesville, Virginia

Anderson, Jon W. 2014. "Internet Islam: New Media of the Islamic Reformation." In D. L Bowen and E. A. Early, eds., *Everyday Life in the Muslim Middle East*. Bloomington: Indiana University Press.

With the advent of the Internet, a Muslim can find numerous Web sites with information about ritual, discussions of the many dimensions of ritual practice, and even religious edicts (fatwa, *pl.* fatawa). *Such sites may invite chat groups to discuss the pros and cons of interpretations of ritual and belief. Indeed, a modern-day Muslim can find and choose religious guidance electronically. This aspect of globalization, turning many religious discussions over to lay Muslims and making the pronouncements of national religious figures available to Muslims worldwide, may have repercussions on the future development of Islam. Programs on the UAE's al-Jazira television network have already countered other Middle Eastern nations' attempts to control religious discourse. —Eds.*

THE INTERNET HAS BECOME A SIGNIFICANT venue of Islamic expression and its contemporary reformation. Both traditional Muslim texts and contemporary Muslim conversation have found their way to the information superhighway's current leading edge. The venerable Al-Azhar University in Cairo, the establishment voice of Sunni Islam, and Shi'i counterparts in Iran, make use of the Internet to disseminate texts for religious education; conservative preachers such as Egypt's Shaykh Qaradawi post sermons and fatawa on the Web. Internet surfers find not only traditional models of Muslim witness but also tech-savvy students' and activists' contemporary versions of Muslim piety and advice. Many Islamic schools (*madrasas*) and training institutes, from the Tablighi-Jama'at Islami in Pakistan to an International Islamic University established by the international Organization of the Islamic Conference and the government of Malaysia and a modern-form School of Islamic and Social Sciences in northern Virginia, have Web sites; traditionally international organizations such as the Naqshbandiyya Sufi order have also come on-line. Muslim student associations provide guides to these burgeoning on-line resources, as do Web sites maintained by Arab press groups and information services, to which the faithful are directed by advertisements and notices in print and broadcast media from Morocco to Indonesia.

Muslims worldwide have taken to the Internet, and taken their religion to the Internet, in the context of a media expansion which began with print in the nineteenth century and a rise in mass education over the past three decades. Today, the Muslim world is awash in religious media, from cassette tapes of sermons to Islamic novels to multimedia instructional material, from new journals for the discussion of legal codification to banners announcing new preachers and organizations, in megacities like Cairo and small towns throughout the Muslim world—indeed, wherever Muslims are in the world (Eickelman and Anderson 1999).

The Internet absorbs these trends in its own social dynamics. Whereas the mass media depend on expensive presses and studios, publishing organizations, and licenses to utilize public airwaves, it takes little more skill or investment to produce content for the Internet than to use it. Nearly all the initial uses come from ordinary Muslims bringing the texts of Islam and its propagation on-line.

Among the first to bring Islam to the Internet were students who went or were sent abroad in the early 1980s for study in technical fields where the Internet was developed out of interactive, multi-user, networked computing. In these high-tech precincts, students and researchers in non-Muslim societies of the West followed the example of their colleagues, who also used this medium, developed for scientific communication, to bring other interests on-line and to establish "virtual communities" of like-minded individuals everywhere the Internet reached. As pious acts of witness for Islam in cyberspace, they scanned and posted translations of the Holy Qur'an and collections of *hadith* that together are principal sources of the *sharīʿa,* the practical guides to correct belief and practice, and created a series of on-line discussion forums. They utilized each new format of the Internet, from file archives to discussion groups to electronic bulletin boards and now the World Wide Web, both to establish contact and to bear witness to their religious interests.

These activities were combined with pious acts and networking with others, particularly with other members of the contemporary diasporas of Middle Eastern and South Asian Muslims. Other academics and, around them, other professionals gained access to the Internet throughout the 1980s, and more Muslims became adept in the new medium. To the common texts, they often added personal "spin" in selection and emphasis on practices and views. Their outreach was typically, but not exclusively, to other Muslims with access to this on-line information space. A notable early example was "Selim, the Cybermuslim," the virtual alter ego of the diaspora, creator of a "*Masjid* [mosque] of the Ether," with brief accounts of Muslim beliefs and practices updated to the life, times, and vernacular of the World Wide Web.

Individual efforts to foster on-line communities and services were followed by the early 1990s by organizations, again largely among the contemporary Muslim diaspora, particularly in the West. Early examples, such as Muslim student associations on North American campuses, were followed by national Muslim associations in the United Kingdom, the U.S., Europe, and Australia that posted practical information relevant to leading a Muslim life, particularly in non-Muslim societies, from where to find mosques and *halal* butchers to prayer timers, matrimonials, and cheap flights home. Links to religious bookstores and providers of materials for children's religious instruction also attest to the diaspora character of organizations trying to meet the individual, familial, and community needs of Muslims living in modern societies of both Muslim-majority countries and in countries where Muslims find themselves minorities.

These Web pages expanded early on to include intense discussion of issues in home countries, particularly Islamic politics but also strictly religious matters, notably of interpretation (Anderson 1997). In the absence of the conventional guidance of *'ulama* (scholars) and without madrasas or other forums where seekers could meet the learned, these diaspora pioneers developed a contemporary creolized discourse (Anderson 1995). Pioneers of on-line Islam drew on the intellectual techniques of their modern educations to address religious issues, problems, and, above all, interpretations. Such interpretations are often scorned or dismissed by those with more traditional religious training; or they are tolerated as intermediate steps. But the characteristic feature of these efforts is that they return to religious matters from perspectives of adulthood and alternative schooling (Eickelman 1992). An example might be the Web site created by a Muslim student to offer fatawa to others like himself in situations like his own.

From these efforts emerges a contemporary continuum of Islamic discourse and networking between communities otherwise separated by styles and channels of communication. This is not new in Muslim history: intermediate communities have frequently arisen between the spiritually minded and the scripturalist, between the often detached Islam of the madrasa and more engaged, more socially embedded, vernacular expressions of religiosity. Islam on-line is part of such a continuum, with the difference that cyberspace transcends distance and limitation to physical places, substituting for them a more purely social "space."

This Islamization of cyberspace has deepened with each new technology of the Internet, beginning with simple file archives and electronic mailing lists and culminating in the World Wide Web, which has become a major medium of publication (Anderson 1998). It is a medium, moreover, in which any number can participate as message creators nearly as easily as they participate as message receivers, and its techniques spread as fast as the Web itself. So diaspora pioneers have been followed on-line by more conventional Islamic organizations dedicated to witnessing, outreach, and proselytization, and finally by educational institutions, which all grasped the potentials of the new technology. The Internet can not only spread messages far and wide, in the way that since the Iranian revolution audiocassette tapes have carried the sermons of prominent and obscure preachers alike. It can also reach a modern vanguard, the technical intelligentsia in the engineering professions that created and first made use of the Internet—in other words, an up-market audience, transnational in habits, training, and other social resources.

Organizations that rose to the challenge that the medium poses to more orthodox voices included both activists and traditional *da'wa* organizations, which offer justifications of the faith for non-Muslims and instructional material for the faithful, particularly for the dispersed faithful who need it for their children's education as well as their own growth as Muslims. Access to technology intersects what Dale Eickelman has called the contemporary Islamic Reformation, which is marked by wider participation in public discussion of Islam's requirements in the modern world and how to lead a Muslim life where practices and beliefs cannot be taken for granted to the extent customary in traditional Muslim societies (see chapter 22, this volume). This is already a worldwide phenomenon, having begun before the Internet with newer and more accessible forms of print (Eickelman and Anderson 1997), and it has been well underway throughout the past century in mixed traditional and modern organizations (Gilsenan 1973; Hefner 1993; Bowen 1998). The Internet is a useful medium as new interpreters and new interpretations form a widening public sphere of debate and discussion, in which new views are measured against old and against new situations, above all those situations in which the growing professional middle classes find themselves.

This new meeting ground not only enforces its distinctive leveling on those who enter it. It also rebalances the expressive ecology of Islam that traditionally channeled impulses of spiritual renewal into Sufism, the organized expression of Islam's more spiritual side, sometimes contradicting and sometimes complementing the scripturalism of the ᶜulama. Sufism has served as a conduit for new persons and practices, new accommodations of Islam, and new ways of integrating religion with contemporary experience. Contemporary professional middle-class people, who often already use the Internet for other purposes, already know its techniques, already accept its logic as a new public space with open access and participation, often find that it is peculiarly fitted to their expressions and participation in interpretation. Indeed, it is too much so in the view of some officials and scholars, who find their authority in this medium discounted and who have to master a new one. In this, the Internet joins existing trends toward wider participation and more diversity of techniques and views, trends already set in motion by the print media that also spread Islam's more institutionalized forms. The Internet encourages the diversification both of Islam and of authority, religious and secular, and provides a space for grassroots interpretations of religious beliefs and practice and their integration into organizational and everyday life.

Although ᶜulama were initially suspicious of new *ijtihad* (reasoning about religion) and disdainful of the qualifications of its practitioners, they rarely express this disdain in their own on-line efforts. Instead, they create a sense of meeting Muslims as such, of invigorating traditional views of the equality of all believers, if not quite of all beliefs; this last is still widely adjudged part of Western "individualism" (Sardar 1993). Islamic expression extends from sermons and fatwas by Shaykh Qaradawi and others to movements and parties with

Islamicizing political programs; on-line, it easily includes everything from political-religious movements like Hizbullah to new apologetics, particularly among the middle classes and the growing professional classes that increasingly dominate the contemporary Muslim as well as wider world.

The registers of this participation are the willingness to state and to take responsibility for interpretations accessible to everyone, the advantage earned by Internet skills, and a new internationalism that marks its scope and reach. These extend the range of interpretation and communication, which are, in practice, part of Islamic tradition and the right and responsibility of believers (Rahman 1982). In the long run, perhaps the more profound effect of the Internet and its predecessor technologies, from print to cassette recordings to satellite television, is the elevation of these principles from the background to the foreground of Islam.

References

Anderson, Jon W. 1995. "Cybarites, Knowledge Workérs, and New Creoles of the Information Superhighway." *Anthropology Today* 11, no. 4 (August): 13–15.

———. 1997. "Globalizing Politics and Religion in the Muslim World." *Journal of Electronic Publishing* 3, no. 1 (September). At http://www.press.umich.edu/ jep/archive/Anderson.html, April 2001.

———. 1998. *Arabizing the Internet.* Occasional Paper no. 30. Abu Dhabi: Emirates Center for Strategic Studies and Research.

Bowen, John. 1998. "*Qur'an,* Justice, Gender: Internal Debates in Indonesian Islamic Jurisprudence." *History of Religions* 38, no. 1 (August): 52–78.

Eickelman, Dale F. 1992. "Mass Higher Education and the Religious Imagination in Contemporary Arab Societies." *American Ethnologist* 19, no. 4 (November): 643–55.

Eickelman, Dale F., and Jon W. Anderson. 1997. "Print, Islam, and the Prospects for Civic Pluralism: New Religious Writings and Their Audiences." *Journal of Islamic Studies* 8, no. 1: 43–62.

———, eds. 1999. *New Media in the Muslim World: The Emerging Public Sphere.* Bloomington: Indiana University Press.

Gilsenan, Michael. 1973. *Saint and Sufi in Modern Egypt: An Essay in the Sociology of Religion.* Oxford: Clarendon Press.

Hefner, Robert. 1993. "Islam, State, and Civil Society: ICMI and the Struggle for the Indonesian Middle Class." *Indonesia* 56 (October): 1–35.

Rahman, Fazlur. 1982. *Islam and Modernity: Transformation of an Intellectual Tradition.* Chicago: University of Chicago Press.

Sardar, Ziauddin. 1993. "Paper, Printing, and Compact Disks: The Making and Unmaking of Islamic Culture." *Media, Culture, and Society* 15, no. 1 (January): 43–60.

CPSIA information can be obtained
at www.ICGtesting.com
Printed in the USA
LVHW100741060121
675689LV00005B/32